Taiwan in the Global Economy

From an Agrarian Economy to an Exporter of High-Tech Products

Edited by Peter C. Y. Chow

Foreword by Robert E. Lipsey

Westport, Connecticut
London

Library of Congress Cataloging-in-Publication Data

Taiwan in the global economy : from an agrarian economy to an exporter of high-tech products / edited by Peter C. Y. Chow; foreword by Robert E. Lipsey.
    p. cm.
  Includes bibliographical references and index.
  ISBN 0-275-97079-5 (alk. paper)
    1. Taiwan—Economic conditions—1975– 2. Taiwan—Foreign economic relations. 3. Globalization I. Chow, Peter C. Y.

HC430.5 .T296 2002
337.5124'9—dc21   2001036679

British Library Cataloguing in Publication Data is available.

Library of Congress Catalog Card Number: 2001036679
ISBN: 0-275-97079-5

First published in 2002

Praeger Publishers, 88 Post Road West, Westport, CT 06881
An imprint of Greenwood Publishing Group, Inc.
www.praeger.com

Printed in the United States of America

The paper used in this book complies with the Permanent Paper Standard issued by the National Information Standards Organization (Z39.48-1984).

10 9 8 7 6 5 4 3 2 1

Contents

Foreword

Taiwan is one of the legendary stories of rapid economic development. In the early 1950s, the real per capita income (measured in 1990 prices) of an average Taiwanese was about 10 per cent of that of an average American. It was lower than the level of an average American in the early 1800s, if one can believe these historical calculations. But by the early 1990s, average real income in Taiwan was about half the U.S. level. Thus, in forty years, average income in Taiwan grew as much as that in the United States had grown in almost a century and a half. Countries that had far higher living standards than Taiwan in the early 1950s, such as Argentina, Brazil, and Chile, fell far behind Taiwan in the next forty years. By the 1990s, average incomes in these countries were one-third to a half lower than average income in Taiwan. Taiwan did not reach Western European levels, but was at about the same income level as the Southern European countries that eventually joined the European Union.

   Much of that history of growth is connected to Taiwan's extensive involvement in international trade and investment. That connection is one of the main themes of this valuable conference organized by Prof. Peter Chow, drawing on scholars from Taiwan, The United States, and Japan. This outward orientation, or active participation in the world economy, was a common feature of the development of the successful

East Asian economies, although their specific policies toward trade and investment differed substantially.

Taiwan's openness to trade, as measured by ratios of exports and imports to gross domestic product (GDP), started out at Latin American levels in the early 1950s. It moved above them by the early 1960s, and became far greater by the 1980s. The two East Asian entrepôt countries, Hong Kong and Singapore, were much more open to trade. Taiwan has always been more open to trade than Korea, although part of that difference is related to the greater size of the Korean economy. In both Taiwan and Korea, the level of openness increased greatly between the 1960s and the 1980s.

The two former Japanese colonies, Taiwan and Korea, probably influenced by Japan's example, were less open to inward foreign direct investment (FDI) than Hong Kong, and especially Singapore. Inflows of FDI relative to GDP in Taiwan were close to those of Hong Kong through the middle 1980s, but then fell behind as Hong Kong became a channel for FDI flows to China. However, Taiwan received much more FDI, relative to its size, than Korea. If one tries to estimate the expected inflows of FDI to the four countries from their respective GDP, per capita GDP, growth rates, schooling levels, and trade openness, Korea would have been expected to receive about the same level as Taiwan. However, Taiwan's inflow was much closer to that expected, indicating a more liberal policy toward inward investment. Of the four countries, only Singapore received more inward investment than would be predicted from these variables, showing it to have been the most FDI-friendly of the four. Korea's inflow and accumulated stock were far below the predicted levels, indicating the least open policy toward FDI, although that changed considerably after 1997.

The ten papers in this volume deal with all of these issues. Three discuss aspects of Taiwan's growth and its progress toward catching up to the world's leading countries. Three papers deal with policy toward direct investment and its role in Taiwan's development. And four papers involve discussions of trade and Taiwan's role in the world trading system. Thus, the three major international aspects of Taiwan's economic advance are covered in these informative papers.

ROBERT E. LIPSEY

Professor of Economics, Emeritus, Queens College and the Graduate
Center, City University of New York
Research Associate, National Bureau of Economic Research

Preface

Many social scientists I know have long been thinking about compiling a book on Taiwan's modernization. As modernization is a long-term development process, many of them considered that half a century might be a sufficient length of time to objectively review or reassess Taiwan's postwar developments. From 1998 to 1999, several initiatives were undertaken to convene a conference on "Taiwan's Modernization in the Global Perspective" in conjunction with the fiftieth anniversary of Taiwan's rule by the Nationalist party (Kuomintang [KMT]). Unfortunately, an unprecedented earthquake devastated Taiwan on September 21, 1999, preventing many participants from attending. The rescheduled conference date of April 1, 2000, signified not only a turning point in Taiwan's history in the new millennium, but also the historic peaceful governmental transition from an incumbent KMT to its opposition party, the Democratic Progressive Party (DPP), as a result of the presidential election on March 18. This historically poignant event fueled the significance of the conference and the publication of this book.

Modernization is a long-term, dynamic, multidimensional development process in socioeconomic and political transformation. However, modernization theory is a disparate field of study given that scholars usually concentrate in specific areas in spite of interdisciplinary phenomena. Hence, from the very beginning, I was puzzled over the exact nature of the conference because a scope either too broad or overly narrow would be inappropriate. Fortunately, many of my colleagues in different disciplines generously offered their assistance and invaluable guidance. Among them, I would like to thank Thomas Bellows, George Chen, Cal Clark, Jau-Yuan Hwang, Wen-hui Tsai, Henry Wan, Jr., and Jiunn-Rong Yeh. Through their efforts and the strength of their academic reputations, distinguished scholars in various fields of modernization were willing to contribute papers to the conference. All in all, more than fifty prominent academic calibers attended the conference, exchanged scholarly ideas, and engaged in intellectual dialogue.

The Academic Foundation for Asia Pacific Culture and Economy in Taipei and the Economics Department at the City College of the City University of New York sponsored the conference with generous financial contributions. I would like to thank Dr. Stanley Friedlander, Dr. Shui-Teh Hsu, Dr. Ching-Fu Hsu, and Dr. Anthony Kuang-Sheng Liao for their enthusiastic support in various capacities to make the conference possible. Thanks are due to all conference participants for the contributions of their expertise and research outputs, which culminated in productive discussions during all sessions and which made it an extremely successful and stimulating conference. In editing the volume, I received invaluable advice and constructive opinions from Thomas Bellows, Cal Clark, Frank S. T. Hsiao, Steven Lin, Wen-hui Tsai, and Henry Wan. Two of my energetic and capable student assistants, Mr. Iwao Tanaka and Mr. Mickey Ting Ying Wei, offered their excellent service to me in various capacities at each stage. All their contributions are acknowledged and greatly appreciated, but I am solely responsible for its eventual outcome and the final product. Needless to say, views expressed during the conference and published in the volumes are those of each author and do not reflect the sponsoring institutions.

Gratitude is due to Ms. Cynthia Harris, senior editor at Greenwood Publishing Group. Ms. Harris's strong interest in my proposal at an early stage of negotiation was a great encouragement to me. She offered her rightful suggestion to publish two companion books: *Taiwan's Modernization in Global Perspective* includes papers on constitutional reform, democratic transition and consolidation, Taiwan's globalization and international status, and societal developments; *Taiwan in the Global Economy* more specifically deals with economic development and globalization. Given the normal length of a book, Cynthia's suggestion was perfect. However, because economic development could not occur in a perfect vacuum of institutional setups, and democracy and societal development require economic affluence, these two books strive to serve as complementary reading for all readers interested in Taiwan's modernization.

Finally, I would like to thank my family: my wife Alice, my daughter Isabella, and my son Philbert for their tolerance of my neglect of family responsibilities while I worked for the conference and edited these two books.

Introduction

Taiwan in the Global Economy analyzes Taiwan's economic development in the context of the global economy. Though literature on Taiwan's success story is voluminous, this book focuses more on the mutual interactions between Taiwan's economic development and the world economy from the global perspective. The main objective is not just to argue that in spite of the country's small size, Taiwan's economic development is very successful, but also to highlight its importance on the global scale and its significance in the world economy. The book addresses three major topics pertinent to development economics. The first is to recapture some lessons of Taiwan's experiences, which may be less visible yet are very relevant to development economics. In the first three chapters, Taiwan's lessons are assessed from different perspectives. Ranis (chapter 1) argues that Taiwan as a role model of development is "neither miracle nor crisis," but favorable initial conditions coped with sound governance of flexible policies. Amsden and Chu recasted (chapter 2) the old theories of firm-level institutions to suit the latecomers of industrialization by presenting the leading firms of the "second movers." Chen and Hsu (chapter 3) provided some less visible aspects of structural transformation from labor-intensive to capital and technology-intensive industries by a case study of the manmade fiber industry, which significantly contributed to the studies for late industrialization.

The second objective is to address the role of foreign investment on structural transformation and globalization. Both inward and outward foreign direct investments (FDI, chapter 4 by Lin), offshore sourcing by multinational corporations (MNCs, chapter 5 by Chen and Ku), and the boomerang effect of FDI on the source country (chapter 6 by Tien) are analyzed in Part II of this book.

The third objective is to examine Taiwan's economy in the global perspective. Wan (chapter 7) evaluates its role on the world market. Hsiao and Hsiao (chapter 8) examine its global role from the past to the future. Twu (chapter 9) explains its evolutionary role from a colony to a newly industrialized country (NIC) by blending with Japan's globalization. Finally, in chapter 10 Chow illustrates how a small country like Taiwan can make significant impacts on the world economy by becoming more and more interdependent with the Organization for Economic Cooperation and Development (OECD).

The significance of studying a small country like Taiwan in understanding the world economy is usually ignored. Because Taiwan has actively penetrated into the world market by exporting its manufactured goods and has increasingly interacted with major industrial powers as a strategic partner for many OECD countries, to better understand the world economy, one could not automatically ignore Taiwan because of its small size and population. Many small, low-income countries in the world should be encouraged by looking at Taiwan's economic development paths and performances to realize that it is not impossible for a small, backward agrarian economy like Taiwan to pursue economic development and to transform itself into one of the largest producers and exporters of high-tech products in the world market within decades. Taiwan's economic performances may be unique and not totally or easily reproducible, but much of its lessons can be very useful for many developing countries.

The world economy consists of nearly 200 national economies with different characteristics: small and large, rich and poor, technologically advanced and backward. The growth of the world economy depends not only on the collective growth of all national economies but also on their mutual interactions. In fact, economic growth in any nation is reciprocally associated with its interactions with outsiders and mutually interdependent with the world economy. Economic interactions among nations were further aggravated by the drive for globalization of the world economy after the completion of the Uruguay Round of trade liberalization in the 1990s. With the increasing trade and investment flows as well as deepening financial integration among the industrialized and developing countries, all economies in the world, industrialized or not, have become more integrated as a "global village." The "new world economy" has become further globalized by the drive of segmentation and compartmentalization of global production networks spread around the world. Consequently, globalization of production networks has undercut the significance of factor endowment and transportation cost in international trade and has also generated more and more interdependency among nations. As of the 1990s, Taiwan has become a "hub of global production network" in many high-tech industries.[1] Therefore, to better understand the world economy, it is important to know Taiwan's economy and its paths of development.

Moreover, it is no longer valid to dichotomize the world by developed and developing countries, distinguished by income disparities and/or levels of technological advancement. A group of emerging newly industrialized countries (NICs) in the world have served as the intermediary functions for technological flows and economic transactions between developed and developing countries. Hence, to study economic development of the NICs as a group or as an individual entity such as Taiwan from a global perspective is of crucial importance to understand the new world economy.

Certainly, the emergence of the NICs in the past decades has provided us with a handful of role models for country studies. Given their adoption of the "export promotion" and/or "outward looking" developments at an earlier stage than Latin American countries, East Asian NICs—that is, Hong Kong, Korea, Singapore, and Taiwan—became the natural candidates for country studies. Among East Asian NICs, Hong Kong and Singapore are the city-states with their unique entrepot positions and have had more significant interactions with the world economy in financial services than in manufactures. Therefore, Korea and Taiwan, probably due to their differences rather than similarities, become an ideal pair of countries for comparative studies on economic development. This is why Taiwan is singled out as a role model of economic development in this book, and why many authors in this book and elsewhere popularly make comparisons on economic developments between Korea and Taiwan.

LESSONS FROM TAIWAN'S DEVELOPMENT PATH

In chapter 1, Ranis argues that Taiwan's lessons of performances are "neither miracle, nor crisis." Having traced more than fifty years of Taiwan's development in the postwar period, Ranis identifies Taiwan's enviable record as one with "consistent high growth without pronounced fluctuations." But, Taiwan's remarkable performances were not a miracle like the manna from the heaven. According to Ranis, Taiwan took great advantage by shaping its initial conditions for taking off: colonial legacies in basic and institutional infrastructures; land reform in the 1950s; emphasis on education to nurture the necessary human capital, which compensates for the paucity of natural resources, for development; and aid from the United States. Moreover, economic policies could not be undertaken in a vacuum of superstructures. Institutional setups such as secularism, egalitarianism, and nationalism in Taiwan were conducive for pursuing policy choices that were favorable for economic development. The combination of initial conditions and sound policy actions undertaken by its government enabled Taiwan to avoid the financial crisis that occurred in other Asian countries.

Ranis illustrates Taiwan's flexible policy responses, which Chow (chapter 10) labels as an "eclectic approach," to changing factor endowments, technological capabilities, and external demand. Taiwanese policymakers were "more accommodating rather than obstructive" to the underlying economic conditions faced by Taiwan. Especially, its trade and exchange rates policies were much more flexible than most other Asian countries—most of these troubled countries had pegged their currencies with the U.S. dollar and had an extended period of trade protection. Taiwan's gradualism in liberalizing its capital account, its conservative attitude of holding foreign exchange reserves and foreign borrowings had avoided the pro-cyclical "stampede" of inward and outward capital flows that aggravated the oscillations of capital movements and exchange rates fluctuations that occurred in Indonesia, Korea, and Thailand in the pre-1997 financial crisis.[2] Ranis concludes that the double blessing of economic development and democratization in Taiwan was made possible by a spillover effect from the decentralized market mechanism at an early stage, which nurtured the rising of the "middle class" amidst the small and medium enterprises, to the political democracy that emerged in the late 1980s.[3]

Because development economics deals with economies in the late industrializing countries, so the study of latecomers' advantages in their pursuit of industrialization is one of its core subjects. In chapter 2, Amsden and Chu analyze how a latecomer in industrialization like Taiwan could climb to the top of the ladder of "comparative advantage"(Meier, 1995, p. 458). Different from conventional literature, which addresses the shift of "comparative advantage" from the national level, Amsden and Chu study the upscaling of industry by focusing on the firm-level institutional theories. They argue that the trends of division of labor between advanced economies and latecomers, and those within each latecomer, may not necessarily converge.

Characteristics of latecomers in industrialization include the engagement in mature rather than newly innovated products, the new scale in information and signalism, the limitations to domestic subcontracting, and the lack of cutting-edge skills by comparison with the "first mover" in the industrialized countries. The principal agents of industrialization for the latecomers are the dominant firms aided by the "visible hand" of government on the domestic network. In general, the dominant firms, though not in the Schumpeterian sense in terms of innovation, were initially characterized by oligopolistic market power domestically and then globally after they successfully penetrated into the world market. The survival and growth for the "second mover" firms in the late industrialized countries depends crucially on the government provision of skilled labor and government protection of domestic production of parts and components. Based on the assumptions of developing "mature product" and reliance on "national ownership," Amsden and Chu conclude that some leading firms in Taiwanese electronics and the entrants of newly liberalized sectors such as telecommunication could become more like those from the "first mover" countries by exploiting the scale economies. They point out that in the late industrializing countries, the "second mover" firms, aided by the visible hand from their government, need to engage in "an intense upscaling process" so as to "achieve minimum efficient scale and related managerial and technological skills" in a shorter "shake-out" period than what was experienced in advanced economies. As these "second movers" become encircled by the challenges of rising real wages at home and the competition for lower profit margins from OECD, they could enjoy some comparative advantages in the world market only through the upscaling process and offshore production.

Being a latecomer of industrialization, Taiwan has to identify its "comparative advantage" in some mature products with available domestic capital, both physical and human, and provide government support for those "second movers." Moreover, as a latecomer in industrialization, Taiwan relies on its adaptation of the "first mover model" by restructuring its industrial organization. The survival of small and medium enterprises (SMEs), which are the backbone of Taiwan's economy, depends on their capabilities to exploit scale economies in the mature industries, which have comparative advantage in the world market, and their ability to acquire domestic capital and production skills. Hence, there is a very significant tendency of industrial concentration in those rapid development industries, which is different from those of the traditional style of SMEs and are characterized by gigantic oligopolistic firms by the world standard (Taiwan Semi-Conductor Manufacturing Co., Ltd. [TSMC], United Microelectronics Corp. [UMC], Acer, etc.).

Government provisions of educated elites, skilled labor, research and development (R & D), as well as policies supporting the development of import-substitutes on key parts and components in those industries are crucial for Taiwanese firms to move up the ladder of comparative advantage. Different from firms in a competitive market, the "second movers" in Taiwan have to rely on government supports to achieve the minimum efficient scale and overcome the challenges from industrial leaders and followers in the world. Hence, the lesson from Taiwan's rapid growth in electronics industries and other high-tech sectors (to be addressed by Chow in chapter 10) in the 1980s and 1990s is its success in the exploitation of the second mover advantage. The role of government in development, rather than a passive one like classical laissez-faire, is to actively intervene at the right direction (Rodrik, 1995). According to Amsden and Chu, "the effectiveness of government intervention depends on the discipline."

In recapping Taiwan's success story, Chen and Hsu (chapter 3) focus on the less visible transition mechanism in the development process from labor-intensive to capital and technology-intensive by a case study of development in the man-made fiber (MF) industry. Industrialization in many countries was accompanied by the development of the textile/apparel industry, but few countries had benefited so much from the development of their textile/apparel industry by its "backward linkage" effect on other industries as did Taiwan. Chen and Hsu found that, in terms of "catching up" in production technology in the MF industry, Taiwan shifted from an importer of foreign technology in the 1960s and 1970s, to a self-reliant provider of technology based on its indigenous R & D in the 1980s, and to an exporter of technology in the 1990s.

In general, the initiation and development of appropriate industry consistent with the nation's comparative advantage are crucial to success at the early stage of economic development. Chen and Hsu also hold a positive view on the role of government during the initial stages of industrialization, as Amsden and Chu did for the later stage of "catching up." Given the inadequate supply of qualified entrepreneurs in most developing countries at the early stage, government interventions, though not successful all the time, seems to be necessary to coordinate investors' behaviors so as to entice myopic entrepreneurs to adopt the more risky but more modern technology for successful development. Comparing Taiwan and Korea, Chen and Hsu argue that government interventions were successful in correcting the "coordination failure" of investment behavior in developing the MF industry in these two countries. However, Taiwanese government intervened in the MF industry in a unique way, which was different from what happened in Korea. The Taiwanese government initiated a new industry by first building "public or semi-public enterprises," then via its "indicative planning" it provided private firms with market signals as well as "moderate protection." Hence, the investment risks were reduced by the demonstration effect offered by the government. A higher level of equilibrium on industrial development with more technological and capital-intensive production techniques was reached than would have been otherwise.

However, government intervention for industrialization in Korea was quite different. The Korean government nurtured the establishment of industry by providing preferential interest rates and or "concessionary loans" to the private sector through state banks, undervalued currency, tax incentives, and other benefits. Moreover, entry barriers were established to protect existing firms in Korea. For the sources of technology in the MF industry, in spite of the common experience of being former Japanese colonies, Korea adopted its MF technology mainly from Japan whereas Taiwan diversified its technology sources due to the migration of Chinese entrepreneurs after 1949. On the format of technology adoption, licensing agreement with foreign firms was the most popular method in Taiwan whereas joint ventures played an equally important role as licensing agreements in Korea. For R & D and technological advancement, the methods in Korea and Taiwan were also different from each other. Due to the differences of industrial organization between these two countries, the SMEs in Taiwan relied much on government support for R & D for technological and product development whereas Korean firms usually took the initiative to engage in R & D by themselves to fulfill the conditions for government supports.

Adoption of appropriate technology is a crucial issue in development. Taiwan picked up the right winner of textile/apparel industry for its development of labor-intensive exports in the 1960s and 1970s. Moreover, the development of the MF industry in Taiwan provided an important "turning point" from labor-intensive to capital and technology-intensive industries and offered some learnable lessons for many labor-surplus developing countries in their struggles for development. Realizing China's rapid penetration into the world textile/apparel markets within two decades after its adoption of an "open door" policy, and its threatening challenge after its accession to the World Trade Organization (WTO), Chen and Hsu offer two recommendations for the future survival of the Taiwanese MF industry: a horizontal innovation of developing "newer and finer fiber," and a vertical innovation of upgrading the quality of currently existing products. Lessons derived from Chen and Hsu are not limited to the MF industry only, but could be generalized to overall industrial development strategy or to many latecomers, too.

FOREIGN INVESTMENT, OFFSHORE SOURCING, AND BOOMERANG EFFECTS

Taiwan's economy had not only become more globalized, it had also shifted from a recipient to a provider of foreign direct investments (FDI) within two decades between the 1960s and the late 1980s. After the late 1980s, there was a simultaneous flow of both outward FDI from and inward FDI to Taiwan, which was a fascinating phenomenon of globalization in the late-industrialized country. In chapter 4, Lin first analyzes Taiwan's trade structures and inward FDI, then deals with the shifts of its status from a recipient to a source country of FDI, which was accompanied by its structural transformation. Starting with the 1960s, Japanese multinational corporations (MNCs) engaged their FDI in Taiwan (as well as other Asian newly industrialized countries [NICs]) first in the labor-intensive manufactures and then the lower end of high-tech industries. Lin considers that the selective inducement of inward FDI could partially contribute to transfer of technology, managerial skills, and marketing network. Hence, Taiwan's "export-led" growth was boosted by the inflows of FDI in the 1960s and 1970s.

Nevertheless, the "wild geese flying" pattern of trade expansion was recaptured in the foreign investment flows (Ozawa, 1992, 49). Faced with rising labor and land costs, and currency appreciation after the Plaza Accord in the mid-1980s, Taiwanese enterprises sought cost advantages by engaging in offshore productions overseas through outward FDI. Hence, within two decades, Taiwan transformed itself from a recipient to a provider of outward FDI.

With some qualifications, the ASEAN-4 (Indonesia, Malaysia, the Philippines, and Thailand) are usually referred to as the second tier of NICs in Asia (Bradford, 1987) for their following in the footsteps of the NICs. The ASEAN-4 and China are the major recipient/host countries for Taiwan's outward FDI since the 1980s, and Taiwan became one of the largest investors in many South East Asian countries. The increasing trade and investment flows between Taiwan and the second tier of developing Asian countries has not only boosted trade growth and industrialization in those host countries, but they also have promoted the economic integration in the Asia-Pacific region. Hence, the drive of globalization in Taiwan has substantially contributed to regional economic integration and development.

Due to political disputes on Taiwan's independent sovereignty between China and Taiwan, Lin expresses his concern about Taiwan's dependency on China's market and the "hollowing out" effect of outward FDI on indigenous industries, including those labor-intensive and higher-technology sectors. Lin argues that outward FDI needs to be expanded "in terms of functions and locations" in order to further stimulate Taiwan's trade and economic growth as well as structural transformation. In addition to cost advantage, Taiwanese firms need to assess other functions of outward FDI such as market penetration and accession to specialized capabilities to complement their core competencies. Lin's view is shared by Chow (1999), who argues that Taiwanese

entrepreneurs need to be more cosmopolitan in their foreign investments, and need to be more aggressive in their investment strategies,
and not just defensively seek low-cost labor when they engage in
offshore productions overseas. Hence, Lin advocates diversification of
Taiwan's outward FDI so as to maximize the long-term rates of returns
and to reduce investment risks, including political risks on a global
basis. Moreover, diversification in high-tech industries is also advocated when Taiwan upgrades its indigenous industries. Lin proposes
that Taiwan leapfrog into additional high-tech industries beyond the
semiconductor to mitigate the adverse effects of business fluctuations
in the world market as well as to further its economic growth. On the
challenge of globalization, Lin also advocates acquisitions and mergers
of existing firms to make those state-owned enterprises (SOEs) more
globally competitive, and privatization of the SOEs to upgrade
Taiwan's industries. Lin counts on Taiwan's accession to the World
Trade Organization (WTO) as an opportunity to further its globalization, its expansion in trade, investment, and technological and marketing alliances.[4]

Globalization of the world economy is accompanied by the fragmentation of production processes and outsourcing of parts and components. In fact, offshore sourcing by MNCs from the OECD has become
a major source of international trade, especially in some high-tech
sectors. In chapter 5, Chen and Ku analyze Taiwan's role in "global
logistics" from a different angle of offshore sourcing by MNCs. Taiwan
has become "one stop" shopping for many world-class firms in the
information technology (IT) industry. Purchasing orders of IT products
from the international procurement office (IPO) of MNCs in Taiwan
accounted for 40 percent of Taiwan's exports in that industry. Through
that capacity, Taiwan became an important player in the world market
by teaming up with many MNCs from the OECD and others.

Chen and Ku separate two kinds of offshore sourcing: both cost and
noncost advantages for MNCs. Noncost advantages include flexibility
in serving markets, marketing strategy, performance in product quali-
ties and varieties. Many Taiwanese firms became globalized by selling
products without their own brand names and by providing components
and parts for many final products in the high-tech industry. By using
ninety-six cases of IPOs from MNCs in Taiwan, Chen and Ku empirically tested the significance of the characteristics of the firms—whether
they are merchandise or manufactured companies, manufactured firms
with or without production plants, length of stay in Taiwan, and the
degree of globalization of parent company and country of origin.

Among other findings, manufactured firms are more concerned with
cost advantages, whereas merchandise firms are more concerned with
flexibility on serving markets. In that regard, distance played a more

important factor for the MNCs in choosing the suppliers. Using four different scales to measure product maturity, Chen and Ku present some interesting findings on the product cycle theory. Foreign buyers tend to maintain a technology gap between internal production and outsourcing. Therefore, it is consistent with the "technology gap" hypothesis for those technologically leading firms to purchase more modern products than others. Moreover, for the control of technology diffusion, both the nationality and characteristics of firms matter. It was found that when an MNC subsidiary engages in local production, its control on suppliers' choice of technology is much more stringent, whereas the degree of globalization of the firm and whether parent companies are manufacturing or not, are not significantly different from others in the control of their offshore suppliers.

For those buyers aiming to improve product quality, to supplement production capacity at the home base, and to maintain supply flexibility, they intend to order "advanced products" more often than those who are merely looking for cost advantages. European firms tended to purchase more modern products than their counterparts from Japan. European firms also maintained the most durable relationship with a single supplier in Taiwan and provided more autonomy in terms of suppliers' choice of technology as well.

With the increase of Japan's procurement of components and subassemblies in the IT industry from Taiwan, there was a dramatic shift in the division of labor between these two countries. The role of Taiwan in the global economy has upgraded from "an offshore assembly platform" for Japanese MNCs in the past to become a licensed producer and provider of indigenous components and subassemblies to Japan. Furthermore, to avoid the "branch plant" syndrome,[5] many Taiwanese contract manufacturers have become a full supply chain system in the world market by delivering the products to end users in a timely and flexible manner. Therefore, they conclude that Taiwan has become the "ideal hub for offshore sourcing" for MNCs in the world. Recently, much of Taiwan's effort to enhance its infrastructure is intended to build up a "quick and flexible response" network system so as to integrate Taiwan into global production chains.

After rapid structural transformation, agriculture has almost become a "residual sector" in Taiwan's economy. However, in spite of its decreasing significance in total Gross Domestic Product (GDP), which dropped from 32.2 percent in 1952 to less than 4 percent in the 1990s,[6] the agricultural sector is still an important ingredient in production, ecology, and peoples' livelihood.[7] In its drive for globalization, Taiwan faced two major challenges in its agricultural sector since the 1990s. First is overall trade liberalization in the aftermath of the Uruguay

Round. Second is its trade with and investment in China, which has gigantic agricultural resources relative to those of Taiwan.

Similar to many other developed countries, such as the European Union and Japan, Taiwan faced a severe challenge from global trade liberalization in agricultural commodities, which had been more protected than any other sectors. Moreover, Taiwan is close to China not only geographically, but also culturally and/or ethnically.[8] Liberalization of agricultural trade with and investment in China has significant impacts on the domestic sector in Taiwan. In chapter 6, Tien analyzes the boomerang effect of Taiwan's agricultural investment in Mainland China on its domestic economy—an important topic that was generally ignored in the existing literature on outward FDI.

From the perspective of a source country, outward FDI could be either a complement to or a substitute for the export from indigenous industries in the source country.[9] However, outward FDI in the agricultural sector is different from that of manufactured by its using resources locally in the host country while providing capital and technology from the source to the host country. Initially, outward FDI could generate an induced effect on export of intermediate goods, such as seeds, seedlings, and stud animals, from the source country. But the positive effect of outward FDI on export of intermediate goods eclipses after outward foreign investors integrate with indigenous industries in the host country.

By using the empirical data from the input-out table, Tien concludes that the impacts of Taiwan's agricultural investment in China on the source country included (1) the reduction of investment funds for its domestic economy, (2) the resale of agricultural commodities from China back to Taiwan, and (3) the increase of international competition from China in the Japanese market—the largest market for agricultural commodities for both Taiwan and China. Because Taiwan's agricultural investment in China generated more negative than positive payoffs to Taiwan, Tien offers her policy recommendation for Taiwan to upgrade its agricultural productivity through a shift into more capital-intensive and technology-intensive areas. More policy adjustments in the agricultural sector are needed, once trade liberalization in agricultural commodities accelerates after Taiwan and China access to the WTO. Hence, Taiwan's outward agricultural investment in China needs to be scrutinized.

TAIWAN'S ECONOMY IN GLOBAL PERSPECTIVE

In chapter 7, Wan discusses Taiwan's role in the world market in five major areas: Taiwan as a trusted supplier of key parts and components in the Information Technology (IT) age; as a key link in the North–South technology diffusion; as a strategic partner in high-tech industries; as a source country for FDI; and as a role model of "team player," rather than a *prima donna*, in world trade. Even though Taiwan could not and will not be another industrial giant like Japan, its development lessons are worthwhile for the study of development economics. Taiwan's conservative path of growth—that is, its noninflationary finance and less heavy foreign borrowing, and its reliance on myriads of SMEs rather than on industrial conglomerates—enabled it to be less vulnerable to external shocks such as the energy crisis of 1974–1982 and the Asian financial crisis of 1997, in spite of its high degree of openness.

Using the development of the electronics industry in the downstream and the semiconductor in the upper stream as an example, Wan argues that government policymaking in Taiwan was "adaptable within a rapidly evolving environment," which differed substantially from the "bold initiatives with ready reversals" in Korea. Taiwanese firms such as TSMC and UMC, just to mention a couple, have become major producers and suppliers of personal computers and related products in the world market. However, many Korean chaebols (industrial conglomerates) were just about to be taken over by foreign firms after the 1997 financial crisis. The significance of Taiwan in the world economy is far beyond its size. Even though both Korea and Taiwan are showcases of development, Wan argues that "in the trading world, Taiwan is the more practical role model."

In chapter 9, Hsiao and Hsiao look at Taiwan's role in the global economy from a very long-term historical perspective from the past to the future. Given that Taiwan's (total) GDP level surpassed many developing countries like Mexico and any ASEAN countries, exceeded many developed countries such as Portugal, Sweden, and Denmark, and its per capita income was comparable with some OECD countries like Portugal and Spain, Hsiao and Hsiao argue that Taiwan is not a small potato in the world economy. Moreover, located at the center of East Asia and the western Pacific, Taiwan has been providing its neighborhood countries with a pivotal role in transshipment and international trade since the seventeenth century.

Hsiao and Hsiao divide Taiwan's globalization process into different periods during which it had had different degrees of economic significance in the world. Taiwan's trade with the world started as early as the seventeenth century when the Dutch and the Spanish used the island as an entrepôt between China and Japan. When Taiwan was colonized by the Dutch (1624–1662), the Dutch generated the second largest profits in Asia from its trade with Taiwan. After the retreat of the Dutch, except for the period of autarkic trade restrictions imposed by the Imperial Ch'ing (1683–1732), Taiwan's linkage with the world continued by trading with China, but significant volumes of trade across

Taiwan Strait occurred only after 1760. Though there was a sign of development of commercial capitalism in Taiwan, however, a full-blown Taiwanese capitalism took place only after the Japanese colonized Taiwan from 1895 to 1945. During the colonial period, Taiwan's trade with Japan dominated its overall trade with the rest of the world. Both agricultural and industrial sectors in Taiwan underwent rapid developments. They pointed out that the Taiwanese economy, the agricultural sector in particular, in fact, was quite advanced from the global perspective by the end of the fifty years of Japanese colonization. Taiwanese industries developed rapidly, especially as the Japanese empire was pushing for its drive of the "Great East Asia Co-Prosperity Sphere" (in the 1940s) during World War II.

The unique historic incident of being a Japanese colony created very favorable initial conditions for Taiwan's postwar developments. This thesis is similar to what was argued by Ranis in chapter 1 and Twu in chapter 9. Hsiao and Hsiao, however, go even one step further to assert that Taiwan's "institutional reform" for postwar rapid growth was already completed during the prewar period. They reiterate Taiwan's role in the Pacific triangle among Taiwan, Japan, and the United States in the postwar period; at the same time, they warn against the simplistic argument that the postwar export expansion policy promoted Taiwanese growth. They provide readers with a vivid scenario of Taiwan's active role in the world economy by analyzing its inward and outward FDI flows, its global ranking in international competitiveness by the International Institute for Management Development (IMD) as well as the World Economic Forum (WEF), and its trade and investment with the emerging market in China. Taiwan's major trading partners could be switched from the United States and Japan in the past to the emerging market of China in the future once China is admitted to the WTO.

Yet, there is a dilemma for Taiwan's trade with China, whose government has never renounced its use of forces to take over Taiwan. In fact, it was not only outsiders who could not fully understand why Taiwan had invested so heavily in a politically hostile host country like China—which accounted for more than 40 percent of Taiwan's total outward FDI—intellectuals and policymakers in Taipei had continually debated Taipei's policies on trade with and investment in China too.[10] Looking to the future, Hsiao and Hsiao conclude that Taiwan's drive for globalization could not avoid the "China" factor, in both politics and economics, and that the win–win situation would be that China returns to its prewar policy of recognizing Taiwan as a separate entity like Korea. This is a political problem, which is dealt with in our companion book *Taiwan's Modernization in Global Perspective*. Taiwan's dilemma on trade with and investment in China is also critically examined by Chow in chapter 10 of this book. Chow argues that if trade expansion across the Taiwan Strait after trade liberalization in the post–WTO era could be conducted on an intra-industry basis, then the risks of Taiwan's trade dependency on China would be reduced.

From colonization to NIEs'lization, Taiwan's economy was blended with Japan's globalization under different functions at different time periods, as argued by Twu (Muraoka) in chapter 9. Twu argues that Taiwan was the initial colony of the last imperialist in the world, Japan. Through that capacity, which was different from Korea on creating trade surplus for its master country Japan, Taiwan developed its axis function in the triangular economies through Japan and then to Korea. Colonial legacies, which were generated under the "direct rule" of the Japanese empire during 1895–1945 and contributed to its postwar developments, included the modernization of the agricultural sector, land reform, the establishment of state enterprises, and government bureaucracy such as police state, household registration system, neighborhood association, and legal systems.

After the breakout of the Korean War, Taiwan benefited from its strategic role in checking the expansion of Communist China during the Cold War era. U.S. aid, which covered the gaps between savings and investment, tax revenues, and government expenditures as well as trade deficits at the early stage, was followed by inward foreign direct investments—a topic elaborated by Lin in chapter 4. Twu deliberately explores Taiwan's role in the world economy by examining and re-examining the triangular trade and industrial structures among Taiwan, the United States, and Japan in its postwar development. Students of development economics can better understand the interactions of the three economies and flows of technology by studying Figure 9-3 (chapter 9). Until Taiwan started to trade with and invest in China, which is emerging as a major world market, the triangular axis offers an illuminating scenario of globalization and mutual interactions among the United States, Japan, and Taiwan.

In chapter 10, Chow argues that Taiwan's path of development from dependency to interdependency was accomplished by an "eclectic approach" by dynamically adjusting its trade and development policies in accordance with new internal and external environments. Taiwan did not suffer from development syndromes such as the vicious circle of poverty and the deterioration of terms of trade. Neither did it become marginalized in the world economy for its active pursuit of "outward looking" strategy since the 1960s. On the contrary, Taiwan had an enviable record of "growth with equity."[11] Moreover, in spite of trading heavily with OECD countries, Taiwan enjoyed favorable gains from trade and became a strategic partner for many world-class MNCs in the high-tech industries. So, Taiwan has not encountered "immiserizing growth," nor has she peripherally become a victim of being dependent on the industrialized core in the world economy. Developing countries, if they adopt appropriate trade policies, could trade extensively and intensively with industrialized countries based on their "dynamic comparative advantage" without fear of being exploited by the industrialized core countries, which is what the dependency school had proclaimed.

Chow argues that Taiwan was not indoctrinated by any single set of prevalent development theories. On the contrary, a smooth switch from "import-substitution/inward looking" to "export-promotion/outward looking" strategies was made at an early stage of development. In spite of being an agrarian, Japanese colony, Taiwan did not de-link its trade with its former master country. On the contrary, Taiwan imported substantial technological goods and manufactured intermediates from Japan and traded heavily with industrialized countries—recall the triangular axis described by Twu in chapter 9 and Hsiao and Hsiao in chapter 8. However, the prognostication of trade pessimism did not foretell the path of Taiwan's development either. Taiwan had been enjoying favorable income terms of trade by continually shifting its trade structures; exports from Taiwan were shifted from predominant primary commodities in the 1950s to labor-intensive manufactures in the 1960s and 1970s, and to technology-intensive products in the 1980s. Though further research is needed to determine the factors contributing to gains from trade, econometric tests show that Taiwan has captured the "niche market"—the right customers—in the world in its export destination, and to a less extent has imported the "right commodities"—manufacture intermediates and technological goods to further processing for export. Both have contributed to Taiwan's favorable gains from trade. In any event, secular deterioration of the terms of trade did not occur in Taiwan. By the early 1990s, Taiwan became the third-largest producer and exporter of IT and computer-related products in the world market. Hence, neither the trade pessimism nor the dependency school had played any significant role in Taiwan's development history.

Trade protectionism in industrialized countries was prevalent until Uruguay Round, and developing countries could not anticipate to get much from multilateral trade liberalization under the auspices of the GATT, which used to be ridiculed as a "rich-men's club." Taiwan weathered out trade protectionism better than what had been accomplished in other developing countries. Rather than blame trade protectionism, Taiwan deliberately shifted its trade structures and enjoyed enviable export growth with favorable gains from trade, which obsolesced the "immiserizing growth" hypothesis.

Furthermore, Taiwan's role in the world economy shifted from dependency in the initial stages to interdependency in the late stages of development. Much of Taiwan's trade expansions were led by the growth of intra-industry trade (IIT), especially in manufacture intermediates, which dominated trade flows among industrialized countries. In general, IIT would generate more interdependency between trading partners and make trade frictions much easier to resolve. Chow argues that if trade flow across the Taiwan Strait is to be dominated by IIT after both China and Taiwan access to the WTO, then Taiwan would still be less vulnerable to possible boycott from China than it would be under inter-industry trade.

In addition to the growth of IIT, Taiwan is also allied with OECD countries as a "strategic partner" in many high-tech industries. By echoing Chen and Ku, Chow argues that Taiwan had shifted from a branch of assembly lines to become the "hub of global logistic center" in many consumer electronics, computer, and semiconductor industries. Chow tries to convince policymakers in less developed countries (LDCs) that being a backward, agrarian economy exploited by industrial core countries during colonialization could not preclude them from pursuing appropriate trade and industrial policies for development. Moreover, policymakers in the LDCs must not be indoctrinated by any single set of development models and/or theories. On the contrary, they must be pragmatic enough to adopt suitable development policies in accordance with the dynamic comparative advantages in the world market. Taiwan's "eclectic approach" of adopting pragmatic trade and industrial development policies at various stages of development probably could provide some insightful lessons for other LDCs to map out their future development strategies. While Gold (1986, 17) argues that "specific dependency" in Taiwan led to its development, not underdevelopment, Chow concludes that Taiwan's development path made itself interdependent rather than dependent. Though much of Taiwan's development lessons may be unique and not transferable, they are learnable for developing countries in their struggles for further development.

NOTES

1. For Taiwan's active role in the global production network, see Shin-Horng Chen and Da-Nien Liu (2000).

2. For how Taiwan weathered the Asian financial crisis, see Chow (2000).

3. For Taiwan's democratization, see Chow (2002).

4. From a computable general equilibrium model simulation by Chow, Tuan, and Wang (2001, forthcoming), Taiwan's trade dependency on China's market would increase after both China and Taiwan join the WTO. But, intra-industry trade

would dominate trade flows between China and Taiwan. For the interdependency issue, see chapter 10.

5. The scenario refers to the phenomenon of the branch plants, whose production plans were tied with the FDI from headquarters of the MNCs. As labor cost increased, and or an economic downturn occurred, the MNCs would scale down their branch plants and even withdraw from the host countries.

6. *Taiwan Statistical Data Book, 2000.* Council for Economic Planning and Development.

7. Agricultural economists would like to argue that, just like the importance of the element of calcium to human health is far beyond its relative insignificant weight in the human body, the significant role of agriculture in the economy is not to be evaluated by its relative percentage distributions in total employment and production only.

8. There are less than 2 percent aborigines, and 98 percent of Taiwan's population originated and/or emigrated from Mainland China. Among them, 84 percent of them were Taiwanese by birth, whose ancestors were immigrants from China prior to 1949 and traced back to the seventeenth century, and 14 percent were immigrants from China after 1949 (mainlanders and their descendants).

9. Kojima (1975).

10. See Chow (1999).

11. Fei, Ranis, and Kuo (1979).

REFERENCES

Bradford, Colin, Jr. 1987. "Trade and Structural Change: NICs and Next-Tier NICs as Transnational Economies." *World Development*, vol. 15, no. 3: 299–316.

Chen, Shin-Horng, and Sa-Nien Liu. 2000. "Taiwan's Active Role in the Global Production Network." In *Weathering the Storm: Taiwan, Its Neighbors, and the Asian Financial Crisis*, eds. Peter C. Y. Chow and Bates Gill. Washington: The Brookings Institution Press.

Chow, Peter C. Y. 1999. "Taiwan's Political and Economic Policy toward Mainland China." In *Across the Taiwan Strait: Exchange, Conflicts, and Negotiations*, eds. Winston L. Yang and Deborah A. Brown. New York: Center of Asian Studies.

———. 2000. "What Have We Learned from the Asian Financial Crisis." In *Weathering the Storm: Taiwan, its Neighbors, and the Asian Financial Crisis*, eds. Peter C. Y. Chow and Bates Gill. Washington: The Brookings Institution Press.

———. 2002. *Taiwan's Modernization in Global Perspective*. Westport, Conn.: Greenwood, forthcoming.

Chow, Peter C. Y., Francis Tuan, and Zhi Wang. 2001. "The Impacts of WTO Membership on Economic and Trade Relations Among the Three Chinese Economies: China, Hong Kong and Taiwan." *Pacific Economic Review*, vol. 6, no. 3: 419–444.

Council for Economic Planning and Development. 2000. *Taiwan Statistical Data Book, 2000.*

Fei, C. H. John, Gustav Ranis, and Shirley W. Y. Kuo. 1979. *Growth with Equity: The Taiwan Case*. New York: Oxford University Press.

Gold, Thomas B. 1986. *State and Society in the Taiwan Miracle*. New York: M.E. Sharpe, Inc.

Kojima, Kiyoshi. 1975. "International Trade and Foreign Investment: Substitute or Complement." *Hitotsubashi Journal of Economics*, vol. 16, no. 2: 1–12.

Meier, Gerald M. 1995. *Leading Issues in Economic Development*, Sixth Edition. New York: Oxford University Press.

Ozawa, Terutomo. 1992. "Foreign Direct Investment and Economic Development." *Transnational Corporations*, vol. 1, no. 1: 27–54.

Rodrik, Dani. 1995. "Getting Interventions Right: How South Korea and Taiwan Grew Rich." *Economic Policy*, vol. 20: 55–107

I

Development Path and Lessons of Taiwan's Economy

Lessons from Taiwan's Performance: Neither Miracle nor Crisis

Gustav Ranis

INTRODUCTION

While the world was still admiring the so-called East Asian miracle, the East Asian crisis struck. It is my contention that Taiwan's record—while extraordinary by any comparative less developed country (LDC) standards—can be fully understood and explained and was, therefore, never a "miracle," moreover that her performance since 1997 cannot be characterized as severely affected by the regional crisis. Quite to the contrary, as we trace events in Taiwan over the past half century, we cannot help but be deeply impressed by the consistently high levels of growth and, at least until recently, by the absence of pronounced fluctuations in that performance.

This chapter examines the why's of this unusual record. Though Taiwan has clearly been exposed to contagion or spillover effects in recent years, she clearly was not affected as badly as her neighbors—for example, South Korea, with which she has always been compared internationally and especially within the region. She did so without the benefit of the International Monetary Fund (IMF), and possibly—given the mistakes the IMF made, at least initially—because of the absence of the IMF. The question I wish to address therefore is as follows: Is there something in this particular version of the East Asian performance that protected Taiwan from the worst effects of the East Asian financial crisis?

Let me be clear; I do not believe, looking backward, that policy mistakes were not made in Taiwan, for example, in the financial sector. It is part of the human or national condition. But my basic theme is that Taiwan's historical path made it something of an outlier, even among the so-called "miracle countries." Although no one can ever be inoculated against crisis—and we know there will be future ones as well—Taiwan's particular initial conditions and her particular reinforcement by policy change over time spared her from experiencing the more severe version of recent problems. I endeavor to "explain" why Taiwan has done unusually well over the past half century of development, and—though not without problems—continues to do so to this day. I henceforth discard the term "miracle," because I believe that this was not an act of heaven, but one explainable in terms of a combination of exogenous conditions and acts of good governance.

I briefly review the favorable initial conditions, which were, I believe, instrumental in making Taiwan something of an outlier, even in the favored East Asian context. I then focus on the policy framework that gave Taiwan additional advantages over some of its neighbors over the past four decades.

ADVANTAGES IN THE SHAPE OF INITIAL CONDITIONS

There can be little doubt that the Japanese colonial heritage played an important role in giving Taiwan a long-term advantage in the development race. The colonial administration—if for its own selfish reasons (i.e., its need for sugar and rice)—expended substantial resources on the rural sector, in the forms of roads, drainage, irrigation, and power, as well as on institutional infrastructure, in the form of agricultural research, experiment stations and, most importantly, farmers' associations. All these constituted capital and institutional investments, which together led to a significant Green Revolution in rice long before World War II, with yields rising by 4 percent a year between 1921 and 1937[1]; even more importantly, they laid the groundwork for the full mobilization of the agricultural sector in the postwar era. Taiwan also benefited from rather unusual colonial policies favoring primary education, for example, by the early 1950s, 60 percent of the population was already literate.[2] This respectable initial stock of human capital was, moreover, substantially enhanced by the massive influx of small traders and entrepreneurs who accompanied Chiang Kai-Shek's army moving over from the mainland in 1949.

A second and related substantial initial advantage, shared by only South Korea in the region, was that of a three-step land reform, implemented between 1949 and 1953. Taiwan's reforms, moreover, came on top of Japanese colonial land reforms in 1905. Together they led to an unusually equal distribution of land and proved instrumentally helpful not only in terms of agricultural productivity increases, but also in terms of a redistribution in favor of the lower-income groups.

A third favorable initial condition, strangely enough, was the overall scarcity of natural resources, which (as noted later) not only forced early attention to human capital and the broad enhancement of human development but also helped Taiwan avoid some of the stop–go policies that have bedeviled many other middle-income developing countries.

A fourth, and related, initial condition was the helpful intervention of Taiwan's main outside aid donor in the 1950s and 1960s—the United States. This had three extremely helpful manifestations: First, it helped break the back of the customary deficit/inflation syndrome in the early 1950s via budget support; second, it led to the very helpful announcement in 1961 that although the United States would support the famous nineteen-point reform program, via a ballooning of program lending, economic aid would be cut off by 1965; and third, by establishing a Joint Council for Rural Reconstruction (JCRR)/farmers' association structure, it provided a useful framework for economic democracy in the context of decentralized decision making, the creation and spread of rural credit facilities, and the dissemination of technological information in agriculture and rural nonagriculture.

Finally, I would emphasize the importance of three institutional ingredients, referred to in a conceptual context by Kuznets—secularism, egalitarianism, and nationalism—including the organizational structures that accommodated the policy changes we intend to discuss. Secularism in Taiwan was by no means confined to the elite. The attitude of "stomach first and spiritual values later" was widespread. Egalitarianism, emphasizing equality of opportunity, was reflected in the competitive examinations system inherited from the past, as well as a relatively pronounced tendency to provide equal access in the workplace and in credit markets. Perhaps the most important was the third element, organic nationalism, "a community of feelings grounded in a common historical past," a binding cement felt especially strongly—after some initial hiccups—because of the perceived threat from the mainland during much of the period under consideration. When a system benefits from the existence of organic nationalism, it does not have to first create some synthetic substitute; this means that the government is less likely to overpromise and overcommit and ultimately find itself unable to carry out the major restricted but critical developmental functions, losing its credibility in the process. The subsequent policy choices made in Taiwan clearly did not take place in a vacuum, but have to be related to this favorable overall institutional setting.

ADVANTAGES IN THE SHAPE OF GOOD GOVERNANCE

It is not necessary to recount in detail the history of Taiwan's development from the 1950s onward, passing from the import substitution phase in the 1950s and early 1960s, to an export orientation phase to follow, and concluding with a science and technology-oriented phase beginning in earnest in the 1980s. Today Taiwan finds herself well on the road to mature economy status. But there are certain particular dimensions of policy pursued over those decades that in fact proved critical for Taiwan's ability to avoid some of the worst effects of the East Asian crisis in recent years, which I, nevertheless, think it important to focus on.

The most prominent of these policy dimensions is the fact that, while import substitution clearly was in vogue from 1952 through the early 1960s, it was a relatively mild and relatively short-lived version of the species by any international standard, including in this region.[3] In most developing countries, there exist substantial doubts early on with respect to the adequacy of human resources, people's ability to bear risk and perform vital entrepreneurial functions. This, in turn, frequently leads to a much observed tendency for governments to want to take over these functions on a longer-term basis or, as frequently, to carefully select those individuals, relatively few in number and often closely tied to the government, who would be granted the various required resources and permits, usually at subsidized prices, to take on the necessary industrialization effort. In Taiwan there was no need to cut the colonial tie and to create hothouse infant industry regimes over the longer term. Her initial advantage in human capital and institutional resources and her disadvantage in natural resources undoubtedly helped to mold decisions at the inevitable end of the easy import substitution subphase in the early 1960s, leading to the general rejection of a secondary (more capital-intensive) import substitution regime and the adoption instead of an export-oriented strategy based on an increasingly competitive human resources-based development path.

A critically important companion piece to this industrialization effort was, of course, the early mobilization of the agricultural sector, which provided the required domestic saving and indeed became the first focus of Taiwan's export orientation, built on the shift from rice and sugar to mushrooms and asparagus. These nontraditional crops were much more labor-intensive and subject to labor-using technology change—for example, working days per hectare increased from 170 in the early postwar period to 260 by the early 1960s. Forty-five percent of the growth of agriculture during the 1950s can be attributed to an increase in total factor productivity as a result of government-supported research and technology-diffusion activities.

A very important contributor to this outcome were policies that built on the system's favorable initial conditions by converting the aforementioned Japan-originated farmers' associations into bottom-up institutions, making local infrastructural decisions, creating cooperative banking networks, and helping diffuse both agricultural and food processing-related nonagricultural technology. This stands in sharp contrast, for example, to the way Korea, also a beneficiary of the Japanese farmers' association heritage, used its equivalent, the NACF, for top-down governmental tax and regulatory functions. Indeed, whereas the decentralized nature of the JCRR/farmers' association structure, as well as that of local government generally, have been commented upon, its implications for economic democracy within an essentially nondemocratic one-party government in Taiwan are not always given adequate weight.

Taiwan was, moreover, not satisfied to rest on its colonial era laurels in the general rural infrastructure arena, but made continuous substantial investments in power, transport, and communications throughout the island. There was clearly an absence of the customary rural neglect, with rural and urban electricity rates, for example, maintained at parity so that the power system, while on its own bottoms overall, was subject to internal cross-subsidization.

Booming nonagricultural growth, especially in the rural areas and increasingly export oriented, was of course facilitated by such policy measures as the streamlining of tariff rebates, equal electricity rates throughout the island, the construction of several export processing zones, bonded factories dotting the landscape, and an accelerating learning-by-doing process in the private sector. Taiwan's unusually decentralized rural industrialization effort was assisted by high literacy rates initially and the aforementioned early in-migration of a substantial number of small entrepreneurs from the mainland.

Given the highly equal distribution of land, plus the shift toward more labor-intensive crop mixes and technology, the domestic demand for nonagricultural products was increasingly directed toward these small- and medium-scale rural enterprises. This clearly strengthened the mutual backward and forward linkages between changes in agricultural and nonagricultural output, helping to explain the multidimensional success of the system in terms of growth, employment generation, and enhanced equity. Indeed, the proportion of rural household income earned outside of agriculture rose from 25 percent in 1962 to 43 percent by 1975 to 60 percent by 1980, while the rural income Gini coefficient improved dramatically from about .5 in 1950 to .3 in 1970.

Of course, by the 1960s, all industry, including rural, gradually shifted from food processing to the export of labor-intensive industrial products—for example, textiles, electronic assembly, and others. Agricultural to nonagricultural labor reallocation consistently meant that people were not necessarily leaving rural households; only 17 percent of the so-called migrants had actually departed from rural areas by 1963. Even in more recent years we have seen a remarkable expansion, not only absolutely but also relatively, of rural industry and services; the "chimneys in the countryside" program has had an enduring impact and been of great consequence. Only a few years ago I remember some people in Taiwan complaining about the relative absence of large-scale urban industry in the Korean chaebol or Japanese Zaibatsu style. In the aftermath of the Asian crisis those voices have been stilled.

The two main factors that rendered the rural industrialization phenomenon consistent with an increasingly equal distribution of income, at least into the 1980s, was that initially the smallest, poorest farmers could participate more than proportionally in the economy's booming industrial and service activities. The second was that these rural industries and services themselves could become increasingly labor-intensive, at least until the economy's unskilled labor surplus was exhausted in the late 1960s—the movement of labor was from an egalitarian agricultural sector to an even more egalitarian nonagricultural sector, substantially aiding improvement in the distribution of income. Such balanced growth in the rural areas proved critical not only in terms of "growth with equity" during the 1960s and 1970s, but it also laid the groundwork for Taiwan's enhanced ability to reduce the impact of external shocks in the 1990s, as we shall see.

Even though Taiwan initially adopted the typical import-substitution policy package, including protection, import controls, multiple exchange rates, and substantial government deficits, as well as substantial initial emphasis on public enterprise and government planning, these were all clearly mild versions of the syndrome by all LDC standards. For example, fiscal policy was, from the beginning, deployed to avoid large-scale deficits, initially with the help of foreign aid in the 1950s but increasingly by the high priority given to it by government thereafter. Nearly balanced budgets were early and consistently seen as having important private and public value, a rather unique feature of the Taiwan case. With budgetary surpluses beginning to appear in the early

1960s, it is also interesting to note, for example, that positive real interest rates, very atypical for LDCs, including those in the region, made their initial appearance in Taiwan in the late 1950s and were reaffirmed through most of its development history. After the famous nineteen-point reform package of the 1959–1963 period was adopted, there was indeed a "Taiwan Consensus" in place long before the "Washington Consensus" was unveiled.

Admittedly, government intervention in credit markets remained substantial, and directed credit was in evidence, as was the importance of informal, family-dominated, allocation decisions—now generally maligned as "crony capitalism." But it is also true that the notion came relatively early in Taiwan that money creation was not to be used to shift profits to favored private parties or state enterprises, certainly not to the same extent as practiced in other East and Southeast Asian countries.

It is also clear that import protection and financial intervention remained substantial virtually throughout Taiwan's development experience, although the long-term trend toward gradual liberalization remained clear. Basically, seeing that the increased competitiveness of domestic producers was essential for the ultimate penetration of international markets, but that domestic consumers could continue to be exploited as long as it was politically feasible, can summarize Taiwan's policy. Put in another way, once domestic entrepreneurs had demonstrated their competitiveness in foreign markets, they could be assumed to be less fearful of going head-to-head with foreigners in the domestic market; consequently, by the 1980s and 1990s, protectionism, which had only been marginally reduced earlier, was indeed rolled back substantially for the first time as Taiwan moved in the direction of WTO membership.

All this was aided immeasurably by a flexible government education policy, shifting from compulsory primary to compulsory secondary education and raising the total expenditure on education from 2 percent of GNP and 11 percent of the budget in 1955 to 4.6 percent of GNP and 20 percent of the budget by 1970. The six years of compulsory primary education were extended to nine years in 1968, just when the scarcity of unskilled labor appeared imminent, as shown by the first pronounced rise in unskilled real wages. Another important feature was that vocational training, usually looked down upon in the typical developing country context, increased sixfold between 1966 and 1974, during a time when the nonagricultural labor force increased by 80 percent. Only 40 percent of Taiwan's high school students were in the vocational track in 1963; 70 percent by 1980. Consequently, Taiwan was able to count on a cheap, yet efficient and literate, labor force, flexibly available to meet rapidly changing requirements and make its contribution to a massive export-oriented development drive.

Education as a public sector responsibility has represented a very strong cultural tradition in East Asia, but it is this flexibility—the changing proportions and emphases—that mark off the Taiwan case from some of its neighbors. Even as private sector schooling above the primary level, both secondary and tertiary, increased in relative importance, from 10 percent in 1950 to 60 percent in 1980, demand continued to be strongest for entry into the higher-quality elite public institutions. Expenditures per public school student have run at least twice as high as those in private schools; in public universities the student–teacher ratio has run at 12 to 1 levels, compared to 29 to 1 in private universities. Parents had to pay 50 percent of total costs in private, but only 7 percent in public high schools and universities. This, coupled with the importance of the imperial examinations system in determining entry, rather than the ability to pay or family connections, completes the picture of a relatively meritocratic and flexible educational structure.

Taiwan currently finds herself in what might well be called a science and technology-oriented development subphase. This means that agriculture, having performed its historical mission, is no longer a major catalyst or contributor of savings and has instead become something of a subsidized appendage of the economy. Second, the increasing shortage of labor has caused a marked shift in the output and export mix. Electronics, information science, and technology-intensive exports have soared and now substantially exceed those of traditional textiles, garments, electronic assembly, and other light industries. Foreign direct investment has moved out in search of cheap labor in neighboring countries, and the legal or illegal in-migration of labor has become an important phenomenon. Third, the government has been paying vastly increased attention to infrastructural bottlenecks, transport, environment, and the like, as well as to financing large-scale directly productive activities.

By 1988, expenditures on education had risen to a new high of 5.2 percent of GNP and, at the same time, the percentage spent on primary education had declined from 50 percent to 30 percent and that on tertiary had risen from 15 percent to 30 percent. This shows remarkable flexibility in response to the changing needs of the economy. Within higher education, moreover, emphasis shifted toward engineering and the natural sciences and away from the traditional humanities and agronomy-related concentrations. The government intervened by adjusting entry quotas and by using financial incentives in favor of such new departments as industrial engineering, industrial design, petrochemistry, and so on. Whereas Taiwan tried to prolong the life of its labor-intensive industries by investing in such low-wage neighbors as mainland China and the Philippines, policymakers recognized that the maintenance of substantial total factor productivity change required a gradual shift away from the adaptation of relatively simple imported technologies and toward Schumpeterian-type innovative responses with the help of high-tech manpower as well as investments in R & D. By the 1980s and 1990s, Taiwan increased her formal R & D expenditures to a level in the neighborhood of 2 percent of GNP. Though this is still substantially below mature economy levels, at around 5 percent, it is unusually high by any developing country standard. Moreover, these figures do not capture the substantial informal blue collar, tinkering type of R & D that takes place in the machine shops and factory floors of the many small- and medium-scale establishments that even today still dot the Taiwan landscape. Indigenous patents, although an admittedly imperfect indicator of innovative activity, more than quadrupled during the 1980s, while there had been a tenfold increase in paper citations, a measure of the quality of the basic research output of the mainly government-sponsored institutes and universities.

Although approximately 50 percent of formal R & D takes place in the private sector, government policy has continued to be of considerable importance. In most developing countries, public sector R & D institutes are notorious for their role as white elephants, with objectives tied more to pleasing an international community of scientists rather than to a search for applied usefulness to the domestic economy. Taiwan's entries differed markedly from that general model. A substantial number of research institutes and science parks have been established on the island, predominantly focused on aiding small and medium-size firms, with support increasingly provided via private sector contracts rather than government subsidies.

As a consequence, the volume of technology-intensive exports increased fourfold between 1984 and 1994, and the share of technology-intensive exports of total exports now exceeds 50 percent. Moreover, the reverse impact of exports on domestic productivity levels became increasingly important, either via a feedback effect associated with equipment imports, or via technological licensing and the enhanced flow of direct foreign investment in recent years. This trend was supported by a concerted effort to attract previously brain-drained Taiwanese engineers and scientists from Silicon Valley and elsewhere in the United States to participate in the domestic production and export drive. More than 70 percent of the companies in the Hsinshu Science-based Industrial Park, for example, have been led by returned overseas Chinese.

Paul Krugman, Alwyn Young, and others have emphasized the importance of high investment rates rather than technology change to explain Taiwanese growth performance, but this runs counter to Paul Liu's and others' findings that indicate a fairly high total factor productivity performance, certainly higher than that of Taiwan's neighbors. The widely differing estimates of total factor productivity growth for Taiwan depend very much on the valuation of a heterogeneous capital stock and the particular production function assumed. Moreover, even if—as I agree—high investment rates are part of the story, we would still have to explain why Taiwan has been able to maintain such high savings rates and why, even more to the point, investment has remained so well allocated and not subject to pronounced diminishing returns.

Although, for well-known political reasons, Taiwan has been excluded from the UNDP's Human Development Reports, my own estimates[4] show that her performance has improved steadily and that her Human Development Index level is now just slightly below the average for the industrial countries, occupying twenty-sixth place internationally. The overall Gini Coefficient in Taiwan fell from about .56 in 1950 to .29 by 1970, accompanied by a dramatic reduction in the incidence of poverty. We clearly have a case here of sustained "growth with equity" in income terms and a steady improvement in the quality of life. More recently, income distribution, though still among the most favorable, may have worsened, as is true for most developed countries and for those reaching the mature economy stage, a phenomenon that apparently is related to the growing wage gap between skilled and unskilled labor. However, as T. Paul Schultz has shown, even that recent deterioration may well disappear when we adjust household income by household size.[5]

What we are really interested in is why this combination of initial conditions and policy actions has permitted Taiwan to escape the worst of the East Asian crisis over the last several years. After all, almost all initial transition growth efforts witnessed similar import substitution policies, with substantial government intervention penetrating their mixed economies. And although much of the success of Taiwan has been attributed to its more pronounced external orientation and greater willingness to subject itself to the competitive discipline of the market, this also meant greater risks via greater exposure to the vagaries of international fluctuations, changes in terms of trade, business conditions, and the like.

It is our contention that not only the aforementioned absence of good natural resources, but also the absence of a large volume of foreign capital inflows, for the asking, are part of the reason why Taiwan has escaped the worst effects of the so-called East Asian crisis. We believe that the relatively "steady as you go" monotonicity of performance in Taiwan and the avoidance of the "stop–go" oscillation typical of most developing countries, including many in Asia, can be explained in terms of the previously cited differences in initial conditions that determined the aforementioned policy response mechanisms over time. Consequently, Taiwan finds herself in substantial contrast to the more typical developing country.

Most developing economies, inevitably exposed to shocks emanating from the rest of the world, are tempted, when such external shocks are positive, to attempt to enhance domestic activity through additional monetary expansion and deficit finance; on the other hand, when external shocks are negative, they are tempted to substitute the expansion of the domestic money supply and budget deficits for the decline in externally generated resources. This often leads, ultimately, to the necessity to reimpose controls, or resort to large devaluations, or both. The syndrome is characterized by a general unwillingness to let prices gradually adjust to changing circumstances and instead to try to adjust quantities.

In contrast, the Taiwan case illustrates the tendency to allow growth to follow a more or less natural path over time, dictated by the flexible response to changing factor endowments as well as technological capabilities at home and shifting demand conditions abroad. There clearly has been much less government activism in Taiwan during good times, followed by the desperate attempts to maintain growth when times are relatively bad, as evidenced in other countries. As Kuznets would put it, Taiwan's policies have been much more accommodating rather than obstructive in response to underlying changes, which all societies must adapt to if they are to manage a successful transition into modern growth.

If we look more closely at the basic causes of the so-called East Asian crisis, we realize that most countries in the region had been experiencing a pronounced appreciation of their real exchange rates, having pegged their currencies to a rising dollar. Given the prolonged period of stagnation of the Japanese economy as well as specific negative factors affecting particular industries, especially electronics, a misalignment of exchange rates in most of the region followed. Taiwan, by contrast, was more flexible and, in fact, had devalued earlier.

Why were these countries pegging their exchange rates against the dollar, while Taiwan retained greater flexibility? The earlier experience of the European Monetary System as well as that of many Latin American countries popularized a model in which fixed exchange rates provide the external anchor for a defense against inflation. In the case of the Asian countries, they pursued a policy of a peg against the dollar also to facilitate a continued high-level investment program, financed in part by external capital. As Taiwan's experience indicates, these considerations may well constitute misapplications when transferred to Asia.

It is interesting to note that if you assess the total investment program of the East Asian countries from the 1950s to the 1990s, 60 percent of the total was provided by foreign financing in Korea, whereas, in the case of Taiwan only about 15 percent was financed by foreign capital inflows. Some borrowing abroad to sustain high rates of investment at home is a common feature in any fast-growing developing economy and can be consistent with external solvency. However, during the 1990s there was increasing evidence in most of East Asia that a substantial fraction of the new investments was being directed toward projects in the nontraded goods sector as well as in traded goods areas that were beginning to face slackening demand. Export growth rates were clearly declining in the second half of the 1990s, and there was evidence at the microlevel that new investments were becoming less profitable. The rates of return and the incremental capital-output ratios were moving in unfavorable directions, while nonperforming loans were rising in all parts of the region, including Taiwan. With East Asia generally accustomed to 7 percent or 8 percent growth rates, the effort to try to maintain these by forcing investment into ever less profitable channels proved, I believe, a major contributor to the crisis that followed. Taiwan, though not completely innocent of these tendencies, was much more willing to permit growth rates to move gently downward and for the exchange rate and other prices to reflect this moderation. After all, especially as countries in the region were beginning to approach economic maturity—for example, Korea had become a member of OECD—a willingness to accept 3 percent to 4 percent growth rates, which most developed countries would be happy to live with, would have been preferable to the effort to maintain 8 percent growth rates in the face of slackening demand and falling rates of return.

International financial markets initially responded enthusiastically to the high investment/high growth-oriented policies in the East Asian region. Indeed, capital inflows far exceeded the current account imbalances, leading to an impressive buildup of international reserves in several countries. Most of Taiwan's accumulation of foreign exchange reserves, much higher than those of the other countries in the region, were based on export surpluses rather than on the inflow of short-term foreign capital, a notable difference. At the outset of the crisis, Taiwan had foreign exchange reserves of $86 billion against Korea's $17 billion. Taiwan's total foreign debt was a mere $100 million against Korea's $230 billion. Though both Korea and Taiwan had very high savings and growth rates, the investment rate at 38 percent in Korea was substantially higher than Taiwan's approximately 21 percent. The difference was fueled by the much larger inflows of foreign capital into Korea, mainly of the portfolio variety. This contrast was moreover no accident, because the agricultural sector's contribution to domestic savings in Taiwan was much more substantial than in Korea. Manufacturing sector debt/equity ratios were estimated at 87 percent in Taiwan and at a massive 300 percent level in Korea at the outset of the crisis.

Taiwan's agricultural labor productivity grew at twice the rate of Korea's during the 1960s and 1970s, bolstered by the aforementioned decentralized farmers' association structure, which helped to also spread innovation into rural nonagricultural activities. The decentralized rural-oriented industrialization path of Taiwan meant that although directed credit or "crony capitalism" has by no means been absent, it has been much less pronounced, with the allocation of resources left more to the markets and to family decision making rather than to favoritism by banks. Productivity increases in Taiwan's industry were also substantially higher than in Korea over several decades and, with medium- and small-scale companies the order of the day, labor relations have been less militant and labor markets significantly more flexible.

All these features stood Taiwan in good stead as financial turmoil began to engulf Asia in 1997. Currency traders were unwilling to bet against a currency backed by huge foreign exchange reserves and a foreign debt that was miniscule. Relative to all its neighbors, Taiwan had fewer companies that had overborrowed as a result of cheap official credit or had been protected against bankruptcy by traditional government lending subject to implicit guarantees and the infamous "moral hazard" problem. It should be recalled, for example, that in Korea, by mid-1997, eight of the fifty largest conglomerates were de facto bankrupt. Moreover, as early as 1996, twenty of the thirty largest chaebols showed a rate of return on invested capital below the cost of capital. The situation was much different in the relatively medium- and small-scale industrial sector of Taiwan.

We have already admitted that Taiwan also faced deficiencies in its domestic capital and financial markets. It shared with its neighbors some of the problems of inadequate transparency, inadequate banking supervision, and inadequate bankruptcy laws; but the notion that implicit or explicit public guarantees fully insured investments against all adversity did not prevail in Taiwan to anything like the extent it dominated entrepreneurial thinking elsewhere in East and Southeast Asia. When hit by sizable macroeconomic shocks, including Japan's prolonged slump, the problem of implicit insurance distorting incentives to carry out proper risk assessments in project selection was much less in evidence.

Taiwan, like its neighbors, of course, was encountering some economic problems in the period leading up to the crisis. There was an earlier boom in land, real estate, and the stock market, as high savings rates found their way into more speculative activities and nontraded goods sectors, as opposed to competitive traded goods sectors. But that bubble had burst a few years earlier. At the outset of the crisis in 1997 there was consequently much less speculative investment in international capital markets, and much less accumulation of short-term foreign liabilities. Taiwan's miniscule short-term foreign debt, relative to its foreign exchange reserves, was in stark contrast to both Korea and Thailand, for example. Thus, there had been no inward stampede of short-term capital, and there was no outward stampede once the crisis began. Indeed, the swing in international capital flows, overwhelming in most of the East Asian countries, was modest in the case of Taiwan.

The problems of much of East Asia were, in short, caused by the inconsistent quartet of a fixed exchange rate, unduly early liberalization of capital controls, and growth-promoting monetary and fiscal policies. This was avoided in Taiwan because the exchange rate was kept more flexible, the liberalization of capital controls was not permitted to proceed as fast, and monetary and fiscal policies were more price, rather than quantity, oriented. Taiwan did not take large short-term positions in foreign currency, again in sharp contrast to her neighbors. Instead of investment policies pushing for "full speed ahead" with respect to growth at the macro level, and into additional investments in particular sectors that were showing weakness at the micro level, decisions were more subject to arm's-length rationality, at least in comparative terms. Not until the mid-1990s, as part of Taiwan's drive to become a member of the WTO, was there major liberalization in trade and capital markets; but, although it took four decades to really open up Taiwan, especially to imports, it should also be noted that the direction of the trend has always been clear.

If one looks at the inconsistent policy quartet more carefully, one may note that in two of its four components Taiwan's policies were substantially different and more flexible. The exchange rate was kept more realistic, not as firmly pegged to the dollar; there was more cautious capital account liberalization; and, by virtue of the sharply different level of industrial concentration, public guarantees of private investment as part of the growth-push strategy were much less dominant. Taiwan's relatively small real estate and stock market bubble had burst somewhat earlier, and the lessons had been learned.

Having received much less short-term foreign capital, Taiwan was also much less subject to the rapid reversal of flows—specifically, the Japanese banking crisis and the sudden unwillingness of Japan to roll over Thai and other Southeast Asian debt did not substantially affect Taiwan. Because international lending has an 8 percent (domestic lending has only a 4 percent) bad loans reserve requirement, faced with a squeeze domestically, Japanese banks focused first on the reduction of international lending by suddenly no longer rolling over Thai and Korean short-term debt in 1997. This, plus Japan's continued unwillingness or inability to reflate and thus provide markets for industries that were themselves reaching maturity and undergoing enhanced competitive pressure in neighboring countries, was perhaps the single most important timing trigger for the crisis. Not only was Japan pursuing deflationary policies and slowing its purchase of imports, but, by allowing the yen to weaken, her industry was trying to reclaim market shares that were previously lost to her regional competitors. Here again the impact was heavier on Thailand and Korea than on Taiwan, which had permitted its currency to gradually depreciate.

The aforementioned weakness of Taiwan's natural resource endowment is very much related to the relative mildness of the seemingly inevitable early import substitution subphase and its short duration—that is, there were no resources to keep such an inefficient process going. More importantly, it meant that the large rents usually emanating from the primary sector plus foreign capital inflows and the resulting animated struggle for rents among the various vested interest groups could be avoided. Moreover, because the more plentiful the natural resources, the more exposed the system to exogenous shocks, the "stop–go" phenomenon experienced by so many developing countries—including some of the Southeast Asian countries affected during the so-called East Asian crisis—could be avoided. We may call this the avoidance of an Extended Dutch Disease problem, extended beyond exchange rate inflexibility into decision-making inflexibility.

The significance of the fact that Taiwan could rely on domestic savings and relatively little on foreign capital, and that most of the latter was in the form of long-term rather than short-term inflows, should by now be clear. Moreover, the ability to attract foreign capital is often closely related to the natural resource abundance of a country. As a result, although one would expect changes in the size of various inflows to be countercyclical—positive during bad times and negative during good times in order to ameliorate the political economy effects over the cycle—it is indeed much more likely that foreign investors and foreign donors become more bullish during good times and overdo it, and more depressed in recession times and again overdo it. Not only does the natural resource bonanza attract additional investor interest, but the whole economy is viewed as a better investment opportunity. Thus, capital movements are very likely to reinforce perverse political responses and decision making of the Extended Dutch Disease variety.

Foreign capital, along with natural resource bonanzas, tend to affect the size of the "under the table" rents, which can be reallocated through government-directed credit and "crony capitalist" investment activity and bring with it the aforementioned overreaction to externally originated instability. Once Taiwan had reached its export orientation phase, it was much less subject to this disease. It was able to look at the quantity of money and the quantity of foreign exchange reserves as domestic or international mediums of exchange for transactions purposes, not as instruments to promote growth, with the interest rate and the exchange rate viewed as flexible assists in the face of external shocks.

All this decidedly did not mean a diminished role for government on Taiwan or some sort of laissez-faire policy mix, but a different, perhaps increasingly critical, role for policymakers. Organizational and institutional construction to facilitate the gradual depolitization of economic activity, especially in the monetary and fiscal arenas, is clearly essential, as is appropriate government action to ensure the construction of appropriate institutions, including, as pointed out earlier, time-phased education, R & D, and science and technology-oriented investments. This goes far beyond the customary narrow definition of a government's role in creating physical infrastructure, or even in ensuring the emergence of the kind of nationalism that Kuznets advocated, or to render exports competitive via tax rebates, export processing zones, and so on. The key in Taiwan was clearly institutional change, through the exercise of restraint in the use of expansionary macroeconomic policy over time, accompanied by specific flexible and time-phased resource allocation decisions at the micro level.

Let me, finally, refer to the issue of the democratization of Taiwan, not only as a worthwhile objective in and of itself but also as it relates to the basic question raised in this chaper: Why has Taiwan done relatively well in avoiding the major impact of the Asian crisis and why, if one takes the longer view—that is, over the last forty-plus years—has it undoubtedly been the best performer in the developing world? Whereas there clearly are countries that are both undemocratic and unsuccessful, there are also some that are democratic and unsuccessful. If we accept Robert Dahl's broader definition of democracy—that is, including effective participation by most citizens—we may have to take another look at the Taiwanese experience before the multiparty system came into being. I would, indeed, be prepared to argue that economic democracy, rather than a Westminster-type political democracy, was in place in Taiwan at a relatively early stage. This type of democracy, in the form of group-oriented activity—social capital enhanced by horizontal ties—is certainly helped by ethnic homogeneity, in line with our earlier discussion of an organic nationalism clearly in place in Taiwan from the very early days. The extent to which both development and democracy are based on credibility and explicit, enforceable contracts, it is clearly a function of government to permit reforms to move forward and avoid the "stop–go" pattern so typical of many developing countries.

A strong executive branch within a strong central government was a prerequisite during Taiwan's early import substitution phase, with less reliance on markets and virtually no political democracy. But later on, as decisions became more complicated and a more decentralized market mechanism was needed, this was also associated with increased entry on the political side, as educational levels advanced, civil society gained importance, and not only economic but political participation became possible. We have thus witnessed the natural spillover from economics to the political scene, leading to the now commonly accepted notion that development promotes democracy, at least after some time, associated with the rise of a middle class, a multiparty system, the acceptance of electoral outcomes, and so on. The more difficult question is, Does democracy also promote development?

The intertwining of political democracy and development, both in terms of the vertical and horizontal dimensions of institutional construction, remains a difficult and underexplored subject. Early on, democracy in Taiwan focused heavily on participation in decision making, relying heavily on farmers' associations working with the JCRR at the center, while the bureaucracy was relatively isolated from pressure and bribery. Early on, economic democracy helped growth in Taiwan because it strengthened the existence of organic nationalism. Later on, economic growth could help boost political democracy as the society was faced with an increasingly complicated set of decisions requiring more decentralized mechanisms for resource allocation as well as for well-known dynamic reasons. In Taiwan, income distribution equity and decentralization have proved generally consistent with economic democracy, with political democracy following in more recent years. As political scientists put it, as long as the median voter is satisfied, there is less likely to be a spillover into populism or citizen unrest or militant unionism.

Recent events on the mainland seem relevant to this discussion. After unquestionably strong economic growth in recent years, we are now witnessing something of a slowdown, amidst efforts by the government to maintain high growth rates, even at the expense of falling rates of return on investment activities, accompanied by a worsening distribution of income, all eerily familiar. Whereas, in agriculture, abandoning the commune and resorting to the responsibility system in the early 1980s was a step in the right direction—if now running out of steam—in nonagriculture we have been witnessing a sort of anarchy, with local bodies, townships, and the military carrying out unrecorded and underassessed economic experiments, which the government is now trying to bring under control. Horizontal decentralization in terms of ensuring property rights, regulatory frameworks, the rule of law, and so on, still has a long way to go. The possibility for mutual reinforcement between development and economic democracy still requires many additional steps before it is possible to even consider the next large step, which is toward political democracy.

CONCLUSIONS

The main conclusions of this chapter can be summarized as follows:

1. Because we are able to explain Taiwan's success as a combination of favorable initial conditions and largely induced appropriate policy responses over time, there is no sense to consider the experience a "miracle."
2. The main ingredients of Taiwan's favorable initial conditions that help explain her success were as follows:
   a. A Japanese colonial heritage, which had provided land reform early on and concentrated attention on the provision of rural infrastructure, including of the institutional variety in the form of farmers' associations, agricultural research, primary education, and literacy.
   b. The addition of substantial entrepreneurial talents as well as capital to the system's total resources in 1949.
   c. The virtual absence of natural resources, which forced an early concentration on the importance of human development, eliminated some of the rent-seeking that accompanies land-based bonanzas and, by helping Taiwan avoid the stop-go processes associated with the Extended Dutch Disease phenomenon, ensured the avoidance of "stop–go" fluctuations in response to the inevitable exogenous shocks.
3. The main elements of favorable policy decisions that helped Taiwan avoid the worst of the East Asian crisis are as follows:
   a. Early postindependence land reform, further cementing the foundations for "growth with equity" in the rural areas.
   b. A mild and relatively brief version of the inevitable easy import substitution phase, which avoided the creation of encrusted patterns of rigid prices, deficit finance, protection, and inflation.
   c. Early attention to agricultural productivity increase, permitting that sector to provide the brunt of household saving, labor absorption, and exports.
   d. Continuous and increasing attention to education, marked by flexibility in adjusting to the changing needs of the economy, from primary to vocational secondary to technical junior colleges and, finally, to engineering and science-oriented tertiary

education buttressed by a policy of bringing back high-tech overseas Chinese who had migrated to the United States.

e. A decentralized rural industrialization strategy leading to a workably competitive industrial sector, less subject to the industrial concentration and government-directed credit syndrome of other Asian economies.

f. Modest resort to foreign capital inflows, especially with respect to short-term portfolio capital, while substantial foreign exchange reserves were built up, thanks to mounting export surpluses.

g. A relatively flexible exchange rate regime, with gradual devaluations, preceding the crisis by several years.

h. Large public sector R & D support that, together with a good environment for private innovation, led to large foreign exchange reserves that helped ward off speculative attacks on the currency.

Rapid, relatively steady growth in Taiwan over the last four decades was, moreover, accompanied by the virtual elimination of poverty and—counter to the Kuznets hypothesis—an improvement in the distribution of income, at least until very recently. All this was accompanied by a high level of economic democracy in the early years and a continuously evolving level of political democracy more recently. The necessary adjustments have, moreover, been facilitated by a relatively flexible labor market.

Whenever I have come to Taiwan—and I have paid many visits since the early 1960s—economists and others on the island have emphasized the serious problems they are facing and the dangers and pitfalls that lie ahead. It is quite natural that one should see the inevitable warts more clearly close to home. Yet, given any kind of long-term and comparative perspective, one cannot but be impressed by the remarkably steady and, by any international standard, outstanding overall performance of the system. Though no country's experience can ever be transferred or serve as a reliable guide to another, much can be learned from Taiwan's development experience over the past half century. Her ability to avoid the worst of the Asian financial crisis—without the need or ability to resort to the IMF—moreover, makes one more confident than ever about her future.

NOTES

1. See Yhi-Min Ho, 1966. *Agricultural Development of Taiwan, 1903–1960*. Nashville, TN: Vanderbilt University Press. p. 29.

2. See Paul Morris and Anthony Sweeting, 1955. *Education and Development in Asia*. New York: Garland Publishing, Inc. p. 108.

3. With the exception of Hong Kong, which, of course, was a colony throughout this period and an unusually atypical city-state case to boot.

4. See my "Reflections on the Economics and Political Economy of Development at the Turn of the Century," in *The Political Economy of Taiwan's Development
into the 21st Century*, Essays in Memory of John C.H. Fei, vol. 2, eds. Gustav Ranis,
Sheng-Cheng Hu, and Yung-Peng Chu. Cheltenham, UK: Edward Elgar, 1999.

5. See "Income Inequality in Taiwan 1976–1995; Changing Family Composition, Dying and Female Labor Force Participation," in *The Political Economy of
Taiwan's Development into the 21st Century*.

2

Upscaling: Recasting Old Theories to Suit Late Industrializers

Alice H. Amsden and Wan-Wen Chu

This chapter addresses the question of how latecomers upscale into more technologically complex industries and commercially demanding services.[1] We argue that to understand the process of upscaling in late-industrializing countries, it is necessary to adapt established firm-level institutional theories to suit such countries' structural conditions. Once the theories are revised and the empirical evidence is examined, Taiwan's leading electronics firms and new entrants into liberalized services appear to behave a lot more like leading enterprises in advanced countries ("first movers") than the small- and medium-size heroes of Taiwan's (mythical?) past.

Empirical evidence comes from two sectors in Taiwan: electronics and newly liberalized services, especially finance and telecommunications. The theories subject to adaptation are "first mover advantage" and "networking." The characteristics common to latecomers that warrant theoretical revision are: (1) the maturity of a product when local manufacture begins (which creates standardization, large-scale economies, early concentration in domestic market shares and precocious globalization—off-shore assembly in still lower-wage countries); (2) the emergence of a new type of scale economy related to information and signaling (nationally owned firms must be above a minimum size to win foreign subcontracting orders and to attract the attention of foreign oligopolistic vendors); (3) limits to *domestic* subcontracting (due to competitive imports of active parts and components and restrictions by foreign buyers); and (4) the general absence of cutting-edge skills (which induces a relatively large role for the state). "Second mover advantage" in late-industrializers thus differs from "first mover advantage" in advanced economies, and networks behind the world technological frontier are more dependent on government-led skill formation and import substitution of parts and components than networks that operate at the frontier. The most general conclusion is that trends in the *international* division of labor (between advanced economies and latecomers) and trends in the *national* division of labor (within each latecomer) may not necessarily converge.

THEORETICAL OVERVIEW

Taiwan and other latecomers with fast-growing manufacturing industries, modern services, and real wages must now upscale into still more capital- and skill-intensive sectors. Leading industries such as electronics are already open to foreign competition, and face more competition from lower-wage countries and greater pressure on their profit margins from buyers from advanced economies. Newly liberalized services such as banking and telecommunications, which represent a potential new frontier of profitable enterprise, face intense competition from advanced country service providers, which are themselves attempting to globalize in order to reap economies of scale and expand revenues. How dominant firms in Taiwan are upscaling,[2] and how such firms have managed to grow at extremely fast rates, are the outstanding questions to be addressed.

Market theory correctly predicts a convergence in the industrial structures of early and late industrializers, but it says little about how a latecomer's movement up the ladder of comparative advantage is accomplished at the level of the firm. Whether or not the agent of upscaling is the large or small firm, the new or established firm, or the specialized, vertically integrated, or diversified firm is unspecified. This vacuum has been filled by institutional theories that have addressed the firm-level issue, but mostly from the perspective of advanced industrial economies. Two classic approaches offer conflicting answers about the agent of industrial change. One may be characterized as Jeffersonian and the other as Hamiltonian in perspective.

The former, with antecedents dating back to Proudhon (1809–1865), emphasizes collectivity and cooperation.[3] The relatively small, highly specialized Smithian firm is the agent of progressive change. It is able to cut bureaucratic costs through individual initiative and achieve speed and flexibility in entering new industries by being networked. What it lacks internally it overcomes by being part of a cluster of firms that mutually create "external economies"—as analyzed by Alfred Marshall (1949). Such economies promote innovation and the lean overhead needed to compete abroad. Hamiltonianism, on the other hand, attributes modern manufacturing success to big business and internal economies, with Joseph Schumpeter as one of its earliest partisans (Schumpeter, 1942).[4] It posits that in the course of economic development, as more and more physical and human capital are applied to manufacture, the agent of change becomes the firm that makes a "three-pronged" investment in plants with minimum efficient scale, in managerial hierarchies and proprietary knowledge-based assets, and in global systems of marketing and distribution. The "first mover" to do so enjoys advantages in the form of scale economies, novel products and processes, and the managerial skills and capital to diversify into still newer industries (Chandler, 1990; Chandler and Hikino, 1997).

By far, Jeffersonianism has proved the more attractive of the two theories, championing as it does individualism, cooperation, and democracy. Especially in the United States, whose economic theories tend to dominate in the global marketplace of ideas, the ideology of the small entrepreneur is supreme. This hero is imbued with the attributes of innovativeness, efficiency, and flexibility. Arguably, however, Hamiltonianism has in fact ruled the modern industrial world. The visible hand and internal economies may be said to predominate over the invisible one and external economies (Chandler, 1977). Instead of disintegration and greater specialization, firm-level expansion has increasingly taken the mode of diversification, merger, and acquisition. As an industry matures, it tends to become highly concentrated. Many first movers fall by the wayside, but those that remain also tend to enjoy first mover advantage despite "gales of creative destruction" (Schumpeter, 1942): Hoechst, Bayer, Dow, and DuPont in chemicals; Dunlop, Pirelli, Goodyear, and Firestone in tires; Ford, Fiat, General Motors, and Mercedes in automobiles; Siemens, Philips, Westinghouse, and General Electric in electronics; John Deere, DEMAG, Escher-Wyss, and Olivetti in machinery; Anaconda, Arbed, Krupp, and Nippon Steel in primary metals; IBM, Toshiba, Apple, and Dell in computers, and so on.

In parallel fashion and with similar dissonance, economic success in Taiwan has been attributed mostly to networks and small-scale firms.[5] We argue, however, that reality is otherwise. The small firm may predominate in some industries. But in electronics—the chief example

offered as evidence in favor of network theory—and in modern services—which tend to be neglected altogether in such theory—the relatively big business appears to have acted as the most progressive and
developmental force.

In terms of firm size, although few leading enterprises in any emerging economy appear on *Fortune*'s list of the 500 largest global firms, and
although Taiwan's dominant businesses do not compare in scale or
scope with those of South Korea (size differences, however, decrease
when market segment is controlled for), Taiwan's nationally owned
industrial leaders are among the largest in the developing world. Domestically, Taiwan's 100 biggest business groups have also experienced
a very large increase in their share of GNP. As indicated in Table 2-1,
their share rose from 28.7 percent in 1986, the start of accelerated market
liberalization, to 54 percent in little over a decade. The estimated share
for 1998 might not be sustainable, but even so, a jump from 28.7 percent
in 1986 to almost 43 percent in 1996 is still striking. In the electronics
sector, only 20 percent of output is accounted for by small firms with
fewer than 100 workers. In terms of market concentration, 60 percent of
the electronic industry's output is accounted for by only 160 firms in
total, all with at least 500 employees (the census bureau's highest cutoff
for measuring size) (Amsden and Chu, in process). In individual segments of information technology (IT), the pillar of Taiwan's prosperity
in the 1990s, industrial concentration became extremely high considering relatively modest entry barriers: In 1999 the five-firm concentration
ratio was 72 percent for notebook PCs (personal computers) and 62
percent for desktop PCs (see Table 2-2). The four-firm concentration
ratio was 96 percent for video cards and 62.4 percent for mouses.
Domestic subcontracting was virtually nonexistent, and local sourcing
of parts and components was confined mostly to the supply of passive
inputs. The lion's share of purchases by leading PC companies was
accounted for by imports. Although it is difficult to measure a
company's degree of vertical integration accurately, integration in
Taiwan's leading PC makers appears to have fallen somewhere in
between the extremes set by the world's leading desktop manufacturers
(Hewlett-Packard and Texas Instruments at the integrated end and Dell
and Motorola at the unintegrated end). By the year 2000, six leading PC
manufacturers were making major investments to integrate vertically
into the production of LEDs (liquid electronic displays). In terms of
diversification, entry into new industries was accomplished largely by
existing rather than new firms: The earliest entrants into Taiwan's
cellular telephone manufacturing industry tended to be established
notebook PC-makers with declining profit margins. Diversified business groups, once dismissed as dinosaurs, became the major source of
entry into telecommunication services, nonbanking financial services,

banking, cable TV, private power plants, and a high-speed rail infra-structure project.

Thus, dominant business enterprises in Taiwan (as in Korea) may have started tiny, feeding the myth of the small-scale entrepreneur. But they ramped up to global market size in an extremely short amount of time. They grew fast not because their level of integration was especially low but because their survival depended on exploiting scale economies. Expansion was facilitated by easy access to the inputs required to ramp up fast—mature technology (from established foreign technology sources), capital (savings in Taiwan outstripped investment demand starting in the 1980s), and skills (owing partly to the "reverse brain drain" of Taiwanese Americans).

Nevertheless, none of these findings—which are based on new, un-published data and extensive firm-level case studies—precludes the operation in Taiwan of a domestic "network," meaning transactions among firms that are personally rather than anonymously mediated, as they are in market theory. Simply the nature of a network in an emerg-ing economy operates differently from that specified in established theory; it is much more government-led. By the same token, the "first mover" model must be adapted to suit the conditions of a latecomer before it, too, gains explanatory power. Adaptation is necessary because

TABLE 2-1.   Top 100 Business Groups' Sales as a Percentage of GNP, 1973–1998

					Unit: 10	million NT$
Item/Year	*1973*	*1977*	*1979*	*1981*	*1983*	*1986*
Sales of Top 100 Groups (A)	1326	2364	3819	5076	6337	8402
GNP (B)	4102	8238	11962	17642	21032	29257
Sales/GNP (A/B)	32.3	28.7	31.9	28.8	30.1	28.7
Number of Groups	100	100	100	100	100	100
Groups with Data	111	100	100	100	96	97

					Unit: 10	million NT$
Item/Year	*1988*	*1990*	*1992*	*1994*	*1996*	*1998*
Sales of Top 100 Groups (A)	12193	16881	18654	26630	33334	48526
GNP (B)	36115	44119	54598	65571	77671	89867
Sales/GNP (A/B)	33.8	38.3	34.2	40.6	42.9	54.0
Number of Groups	100	100	100	100	100	100
Groups with Data	100	101	101	115	113	179

Source: Adapted from Amsden and Chu (in process). Data were collected by the China Credit Information Service Ltd (various years). CCIS data usually cover more than 100 groups (except for 1983 and 1986). Data here are recalculated for the top 100 groups only (except for 1983 and 1986).

TABLE 2-2. Market Concentration and Globalization in Taiwan's IT Hardware Products Industry, 1998 and 1999

Product	Industry Concentration (number of firms in parentheses)[+] (%)		Offshore Production (by Taiwan firms) (%)	Value of Production (Taiwan and offshore) (US mil $)	Global Market Share (%)
	1998	1999	1999	1999	1998
Video card	95 (4)	96 (4)	18	33	40
Sound card	87 (2)	90 (3)	65	78	49
Desktop PC	84 (3)	62 (5)	88	7,188	na
SPS	83 (5)	89 (5)	91	1,744	65
Notebook PC	74 (5)	72 (5)	0	10,198	39
CD Rom	72 (5)	—	60	1,740	33
Keyboard	64 (3)	77 (5)	91	512	65
Mouse	62 (3)	62 (4)	89	155	60
Scanner	57 (5)	76 (5)	38	925	85
Motherboard*	55 (5)	58 (5)	38	4,854	66
Monitor	45 (5)	47 (5)	71	9,330	58
Graphics card	40 (5)	53 (5)	65	848	na
TOTAL:	—	—		39,881	—
Weighted Ave.			57		

[+]Concentration is measured in terms of sales. Concentration data are for the second half of 1998 and 1999.
*Excluding those sold as part of a PC system.

Source: Adapted from Market Intelligence Center, Institute for Information Industry, Taipei, as cited in Amsden and Chu (In process).

even at their current stage of development, latecomers' best nationally owned firms continue to lack cutting-edge skills and hence cannot compete on the same terms as first-class American and Japanese innovators. The probability that a dynamic small firm will generate state-of-the-art technology is still lower in an emerging economy than in the United States or Japan. By the year 2000 the most progressive big businesses in Taiwan remained technology borrowers rather than innovators at the world frontier. By definition, a "first mover" in an advanced industrial economy may also access its technology from an external source of supply; it need not be an inventor or technological pioneer. But a first mover is also defined as being in the vanguard of exploiting a truly new technology's potential, before that technology has matured. Hence, we use the term "second mover" to describe dominant firms outside the North Atlantic region and Japan, firms that follow in the wake of genuine first movers. We also refer to "state-led" networking in Taiwan to distinguish the networking model that is the basis for advanced country theorizing.

"SECOND MOVER" ADVANTAGE

The theory of "second mover advantage" may be summarized as follows.

Assumptions

At the outset of production (or provision of service) in a dynamic industry in an emerging economy, the product in question is already *"mature"* (in terms of its rate of technological change), but global demand is still rising rapidly. Hence, the industry may be described as being "mid-tech" (Hikino and Amsden, 1994). We equate maturity with relative standardization in process and product, and we associate standardization with economies of scale, as in the product cycle model (Vernon, 1966). Before standardization, many firms may be assumed to compete for market share. As maturity increases, there is a shakeout. The number of competitors declines, and market concentration rises (Scherer, 1980). The length of time between competitive market entry and high concentration is shorter in a follower country than in a leader because the follower enters the industry when it is already relatively mature, as shown in Figure 2-1.

"Second movers" are firms in latecomer countries that are first to invest in production capacity and management in industries that are "new" to the latecomer in question. By assumption, they are nationally owned. For various reasons, historical and otherwise, this assumption

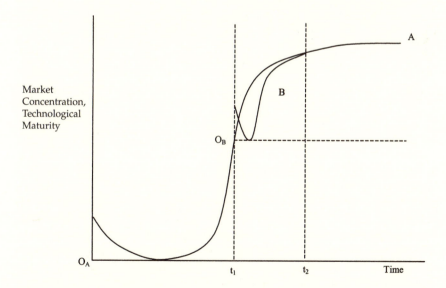

Figure 2-1.   A: Early industrializer; B: Late industrializer.

is not valid for all latecomers (Amsden, 2001). It is, however, valid for Taiwan (as well as for Korea, China, and India). Second movers in the once-protected "old economy" have moved into the modern service sector, either independently or with foreign minority joint venture partners. The survival of nationally owned firms in Taiwan's electronics sector was favored by a strategic policy switch in global operations by first movers in advanced countries. To avail themselves of the cheap labor of latecomers, first movers ceased making direct foreign investments overseas (as they had done in the case of televisions in the 1960s and 1970s). Instead, they began to subcontract production under their own brand name to nationally owned firms (as in the case of PCs in the 1980s and 1990s). American electronics leaders first began to subcontract to other U.S.-based companies. Then their subcontracting shifted to Japan. Finally, as wages rose in Japan, "original equipment manufacturers" (OEMs) and later "original design manufacturers" (ODMs) found subcontractors in the form of nationally owned firms in Taiwan and Korea (and later in Malaysia, Thailand, China, and so forth).

Thus, two key assumptions, mature product and national ownership, suggest an intense upscaling process in latecomers to achieve minimum efficient scale and related managerial and technological skills, and a shorter shakeout period than in advanced economies, where product maturation is more evolutionary and so the rise of high concentration is slower.

Economies of Scale and Scope

To realize second mover advantage requires the exploitation of economies of scale and scope, some of which are unique to latecomers. Three types of economies may be distinguished. Type I concerns the usual production-related economies, with respect to learning-by-doing from longer production runs, cost savings from fuller capacity utilization of fixed capital and managerial resources, bulk purchases of inputs, and so forth. Type II concerns design, a scale economy that may or may not be unique to latecomers. Given fixed costs of design and prototyping, and modularities in designs for different customers, unit costs tend to be lower the greater the output. Type III, unique to latecomers, concerns information, signaling, and risk. To reduce risk and transactions cost, first movers in advanced countries may be hypothesized to prefer relatively large foreign subcontractors (or joint venture partners in the case of services). In the personal computer industry, a subcontractor in Taiwan must typically meet a minimum and maximum percentage of a first mover's total volume of outsourced business. Thus, scale signals a potential subcontractor's eligibility for an OEM or ODM contract, and multiple contracts ease the constraint of a maximum ceiling from a single source of demand (and also reduce design costs). In the case of vendors, scale and scope on the part of a buyer create visibility and a better position in the queue for a new input in short supply. In fact, as first movers around the year 2000 began to demand more products and after-sales service from a single subcontractor ("one-stop shopping"), and as the supply chain became more rationalized (fewer steps in the sequential supply of parts and components to an ultimate final buyer), scale and scope on the part of foreign subcontractors further increased. By the same token, consolidation among service providers in the advanced economies raised the minimum acceptable scale for foreign joint venture partners.

Management and Technology

To ensure the efficient operation of large-scale facilities and thus enjoy second mover advantage, nationally owned firms have to invest internally in managerial and technological skills. In terms of management, second movers can only grow quickly to the extent that they recruit capable salaried managers. They can only survive in the long run to the extent that they solve the succession problem of familial ownership. In terms of technological capabilities, second movers must invest heavily in production capabilities (skills to operate existing facilities at maximum efficiency and quality). Efficiency is critical, given the small margins associated with the manufacture of mature products. To reduce production costs further, they must also invest heavily in design capabilities. R & D in latecomers is devoted initially to improving the basic designs provided by foreign prime contractors. Finally, latecomers must pay special attention to project execution skills. Given that their choice of what to produce is ultimately determined by the exogenous rate and nature of innovation in advanced countries, latecomers must be able to shift production quickly and at low cost from one product to another (otherwise called "flexibility"). Whether in the electronics industry (paths of learning in Taiwan ran from the assembly of radios, then televisions, monitors, or calculators, to the assembly of personal computers, and finally cellular phones), or in modern services (where second movers in the "old economy" diversified into the "new economy"), project execution skills to minimize the cost and maximize the speed of adding capacity and diversifying may be hypothesized to become a latecomer's critical source of competitiveness (Amsden and Hikino, 1994).

Growth Path

At the firm level, the growth path of a second mover may either start with a large or small investment. In the latter case, ramp-up in the face of potential scale economies must be extremely fast. Aside from project execution skills, the rapidity of ramp-up will depend on the availability of debugged technology (which is assumed to exist, given the follower status of a latecomer), capital, and human resources. If these resources are available, aided over time by merger and acquisition, then a firm can grow from small to large in an astonishingly short time period.

It follows that the more an existing firm accumulates competitive assets internally rather than externally, the greater the likelihood that it (or a spin-off from it), rather than a new organic entrant, will be the agent of diversification. Given mature products, subject to large economies of scale and scope, and given internally generated proprietary skill formation, including project execution capabilities, the expectation is the early appearance of high market concentration after the initial growth of a "new" industry (new for the latecomer in question), as well as rising concentration among a small number of diversified firms at the aggregate economy-wide level. Competition may then be expected to occur among second movers with respect to the speed of exploiting new business opportunities.

STATE-LED NETWORKING

The existence of a "network" in latecomers cannot be deduced theoretically. A network (i.e., a locus of transactions among firms that are personal rather than anonymous) is not necessarily an integral part of a latecomer's industrial landscape. To explain, therefore, the presence of what appears to be a network in Taiwan's machinery industries (we focus on information technology), we invoke a central actor, a visible hand. This turns out to be the government. Furthermore, the network that does operate in Taiwan involves almost no local subcontracting (i.e., transactions between firms that are mediated by long-term contract, explicit or implicit). Therefore, we also try to hypothesize the distinct character that a network is likely to assume in the latecomer case.

A network may be hypothesized to flourish under specific conditions that a government may influence but may or may not choose to affect. First, a network tends to arise in a certain type of industry, one whose product is comprised of a large number of discrete parts, each of which must be designed, prototyped, and produced (such as a piece of equipment or a machine). The larger the share of manufacturing in GNP and the larger the share of such sectors in total manufacturing (both of which are partially a function of government policy), the more likely the emergence of a network. Second, under modern manufacturing conditions, the greater the size of an educated elite, and the greater the engineering orientation of such an elite, the greater the likelihood of a network comprising dynamic, learning-based firms. In the case of Taiwan, the share of its manufacturing sector in GNP, and the share of its machinery sector in manufacturing output were both outstanding by latecomer standards. That the government's hand was visible is suggested by the fact that starting in the 1950s and continuing through the 1990s, roughly half of all gross fixed capital formation in Taiwan was accounted for by the government. This share exceeded that of all other latecomers. Moreover, Taiwan's educational attainments and engineering training were especially high, also a function of government support. Third, networking is encouraged by geographical proximity. In the case of Taiwan, its relatively small geographical size and concentration of manufacturing activity in a small geographical area facilitated personal business transactions among a small educated elite.

The activities that occur within a network may be divided into three types, all of which involve "trust" to varying degrees: the subcontracting of parts, components, or steps in an assembly operation for processing by another firm that, as just noted, is premised on a long-term contract (implicit or explicit); the supply of customized inputs (such as tools, dies, and prototypes), which requires close interfirm cooperation; and the local procurement of key peripherals (the monitor and keyboard, for example, in a PC), which represents a soft market for suppliers because of nil transportation costs. Local procurement is the weakest form of networking (and the most prevalent within Taiwan) because the importance of the personal element is unclear; local procurement veers between the personal and the anonymous. In the case of innovators in advanced countries, the key parts, components, peripherals, and customized inputs in a new product tend to be sourced locally in the early stage of a new technology's life because designs are still immature and home-based decision making is critical (Vernon, 1966). A new division of labor then emerges either inside or outside the primary firm. If external, a network forms, as in the American PC industry (Langlois, 1992). A latecomer, by contrast, may import key parts, components, and peripherals, especially those that are technologically complex. Imports dampen or delay the emergence of local high-tech subcontracting and procurement, as evidenced by heavy imports of inputs in the sequential product cycles of Taiwan's electronics industry (first televisions and other consumer durables, then personal computers, then cellular phones). Domestic subcontracting and procurement in a latecomer may thus be expected to emerge more slowly and with less cutting-edge technological content than in an early industrializer. By the same logic, the supply of customized inputs that depend on local proximity (such as tools, dies, jigs, and other fixtures) are likely to emerge first (as they did in Taiwan).

In the face of import dependence, how quickly a network forms partly depends on "import substitution," or the replacement of imports with locally made products. In Taiwan, the government deliberately and systematically promoted domestic manufacture of previously imported inputs. Import substitution was an explicit and long-standing pillar of its IT policies (starting with televisions and continuing through cellular phones). The government's promotion measures included tariff protection (in the case of televisions only), local content requirements for assemblers, subsidized credit, and technical services. Its most spectacular and widely acclaimed success was the formation of a local semiconductor industry, at the heart of which was a state-owned foundry to produce customized chips for PC makers (Mathews, 1997).

Firm size affects the strength of a network because the greater the importance of large, integrated firms, which invest internally in their own proprietary knowledge-based assets, the lower the density of a network and the greater the likelihood of divergence in performance between large and small firms. Divergence is likely unless there is a mechanism to generate external knowledge. Divergence became increasingly evident over time in Taiwan's electronics sector; large firms invested relatively more in R & D, became more efficient (measured by value added per worker), and began to account for an increasing share of total electronics exports. Generally the population of small firms itself may be expected to become more dualistic, with firms led by highly educated and internationally experienced entrepreneurs outperforming firms led by less-educated and parochial entrepreneurs with a "black thumb." Arguably, however, divergence in Taiwan between small and large firms might have been even greater in the absence of the visible hand. The government masterminded and invested heavily in science parks, research laboratories, and joint R & D projects with the private sector. These investments were designed to enhance collective technology and know-how.

Besides influencing firm size through investments in knowledge, governments may affect it through their licensing rules (that tend in latecomers to empower the state to veto new capacity creation), tax laws, commercial codes, and banking regulations (all major financial institutions in Taiwan, until the mid-1990s, were owned and controlled by the government). Because these types of institutions vary by country, theory cannot predict a latecomer's actual distribution of firm size. In Taiwan's case, conservative banking practices are widely believed to have constrained large scale, especially if a loan involved high debt-equity leveraging or multiple industries (Wade, 1990). Less appreciated than banking regulations but also a powerful size constraint (until recently) were government strictures against diversification, merger, and acquisition. These strictures had the effect of strengthening an investment pattern on the part of established, "old economy" firms that favored networking. Instead of (or in addition to) diversifying directly into the highly profitable "new economy" (many business groups, in fact, diversified into IT by establishing organically grown subsidiaries), Taiwan's old groups invested indirectly, by buying equity shares in high-tech startups (majority or minority, active or passive shareholding, on the stock market or privately). Per major established firm, the number of such "reinvestments" and their proportion in total profits have tended to be large. In terms of statistics, if firm size is measured by number of employees or sales, as is typical, passive reinvestments understate actual firm size as measured by paid-in capital. They also underestimate the extent of a firm's diversification into different product markets. Cross-firm financial ownership, however, puts the capital behind the "trust," and so presumably strengthens networks.

The quality of state intervention in networking may be said to depend on how disciplined it is: the more disciplined, the more effective. In the early phase of a latecomer's industrialization, when government wields power over the purse, discipline is created through the imposition of performance standards on subsidy recipients (Amsden, 2001). As firms' technological capabilities, retained earnings, and access to credit rise, dependence on the government weakens. For intervention under these conditions to avoid being a waste of money, the government itself must face some sort of discipline. In Taiwan's case, globalization played the role of disciplinarian. The threat of a "hollowing out," meaning the relocation by firms of their production and other business functions overseas (especially in China), appears to have dominated government thinking. Its strategy to invest heavily in education, import substitution, and science parks was aimed deliberately at upscaling in order to keep industry in Taiwan.

To the extent that globalization involves relocation of labor-intensive operations overseas, in lower-wage countries, then all economic theories are in accord: market and institutional; networking and second mover advantage. Second movers in Taiwan's IT industry, moreover, have relocated their labor-intensive manufacturing overseas (especially to China) far sooner than first movers in their respective product cycles. The two institutional theories part company with each other to the extent that in the network approach, globalization supposedly strengthens networks, while in the second mover approach, it represents a chance for latecomers "to break the chains of networking that bind them" (to their foreign OEM/ODM masters). In the former, the same domestic relations among firms allegedly get reproduced overseas: When one part of a "value chain" (stage of production) goes abroad, other parts follow to replicate the same subcontracting relations (if any) that exist at home (Chen and Chen, 1998). In second mover theory, by contrast, any sizable new market represents a golden opportunity for a national firm to improve its profit margins by developing its own products, building its own distribution channels, and exploiting its own brand name. Globalization enables a second mover to graduate from ODM to OBM status.

By way of conclusion, the theory of second movers and the theory of latecomer networks are not necessarily incompatible. To a degree, both networks and second movers may exist and nurture one another, as they have done in different ways in advanced economies. Nevertheless, we would argue that the dynamic behind Taiwan's upscaling, and hence the explanation behind its rapid growth in the late 1980s and 1990s, was the exploitation of second mover advantage. Competition among second movers for foreign contracts led to the exploitation of scale economies, domestically and globally. This resulted in the emergence of large-scale firms that survived by investing internally in their own proprietary knowledge-based assets, especially in the areas of automation and product design. High levels of concentration were a further consequence, and one that generated the entrepreneurial rents necessary to invest still more internally, in the capacity and especially knowledge needed to expand into still newer product lines and geographical markets.

NOTES

1. This chapter is based on our forthcoming book, *"Second Mover Advantage": Upscaling in Latecomer Taiwan*.

2. By upscaling we mean (1) exploiting a different set of competitive assets than previously, (2) using altered organizational and institutional structures to do so, and (3) subjecting these structures to new mechanisms of discipline and control.

3. "The 'fundamental' law of labour is the law of division (according to Proudhon). There is a further law connected with this—that of 'collective force' as expressed in the 'collective' surplus generated by association, the collective product being the result not of the addition of individual efforts, but of their multiplication when they are brought together in association" (Bartoli, 1987). Pierre Joseph Proudhon *New Palgrave Dictionary of Economics,* vol. 2: pp. 1035–1036, eds. J. Eatwell, P. Newman, and M. Milgate. London, Macmillan.

4. Hamilton himself did not write directly about firm size or scale economies, but he advocated government policies that improved the conditions for both, such as protection from foreign competition and selective subsidies (as well as easy money). See A. Hamilton (1791), *Report on Manufactures* (reprint, Washington: Government Printing Office, 1913).

5. See, among many others, M. Borrus (1997). "Left for Dead: Asian Production Networks and the Revival of US Electronics," in *The China Circle: Economics and Electronics in the PRC, Hong Kong and Taiwan,* ed. B. Naughton. Washington: Brookings; T. L. Chou and R. J. R. Kirby (1998), "Taiwan's Electronics Sector: Restructuring of Form and Space," *Competition and Change,* vol. 2, no. 3: 331–358;

G. G. Hamilton, ed. (1991), *Business Networks and Economic Development in East and Southeast Asia*. Hong Kong: University of Hong Kong, Center for Asian Studies; and I. Numazaki (1997), "The Laoban-Led Development of Business Enterprises in Taiwan: An Analysis of the Chinese Entrepreneurship," *Developing Economies*, vol. 35, no. 4: 485–508.

REFERENCES

Amsden, A. H. 2001. *The Rise of the Rest: Challenges to the West from Late-Industrializing Economies*. New York: Oxford University Press.

Amsden, A. H., and Wan Wen Chu. In process. *Second Mover Advantage: Latecomer Upscaling in Taiwan*. Cambridge, MA: MIT, and Taipei: Academia Sinica.

Amsden, A. H., and T. Hikino. 1994. "Project Execution Capability, Organizational Know-How and Conglomerate Corporate Growth in Late Industrialization." *Industrial and Corporate Change*, vol. 3, no. 1: 111–147.

Bartoli, H. 1987. Proudhon, Pierre Joseph. *New Palgrave Dictionary of Economics*, vol. 3, eds. J. Eatwell, P. Newman, and M. Milgate. London: Macmillan.

Borrus, M. 1997. "Left for Dead: Asian Production Networks and the Revival of US Electronics." In *The China Circle: Economics and Electronics in the PRC, Hong Kong and Taiwan*, ed. B. Naughton. Washington: Brookings.

Chandler, A. D., Jr. 1977. *The Visible Hand: The Managerial Revolution in American Business*. Cambridge, MA: Harvard University Press.

———. 1990. *Scale and Scope: The Dynamics of Industrial Capitalism*. Cambridge, MA: Harvard University Press.

Chandler, A. D., Jr., and T. Hikino. 1997. "The Large Industrial Enterprise and the Dynamics of Modern Economic Growth." In *Big Business and the Wealth of Nations*, eds. A. D. Chandler, Jr., F. Amatori, and T. Hikino. Cambridge, UK: Cambridge University Press: 24-62.

Chen, H., and T. J. Chen. 1998. "Network Linkages and Location Choice in Foreign Direct Investment." *Journal of International Business Studies*, vol. 29, no. 3: 445–468.

China Credit Information Service (CCIS). (various years). *Business Groups in Taiwan*, Taipei.

Chou, T. L., and R. J. R. Kirby. 1998. "Taiwan's Electronics Sector: Restructuring of Form and Space." *Competition and Change*, vol. 2, no. 3: 331–358.

Hamilton, A. 1791. *Report on Manufactures*. Reprint, Washington, D.C.: Government Printing Office, 1913.

Hamilton, G. G., Ed. 1991. *Business Networks and Economic Development in East and Southeast Asia*. Hong Kong: University of Hong Kong, Center for Asian Studies.

Hikino, T., and A. H. Amsden. 1994. "Staying Behind, Stumbling Back, Sneaking Up, Soaring Ahead: Late Industrialization in Historical Perspective." In *Convergence of Productivity: Cross-National Studies and Historical Evidence*, eds. William J. Baumol, Richard R. Nelson, and Edward N. Wolff. New York: Oxford University Press.

Langlois, R. N. 1992. "External Economies and Economic Progress: The Case of the Microcomputer Industry." *Business History Review*, vol. 66, no. 1: 1–50.

Marshall, A. 1949. *Principles of Economics*. London: Macmillan.

Mathews, J. K. (1997). "A Silicon Valley of the East: Creating Taiwan's Semiconductor Industry." *California Management Review*, vol. 39, no. 4: 26–53.

Numazaki, I. 1997. "The Laoban-Led Development of Business Enterprises in Taiwan: An Analysis of the Chinese Entrepreneurship." *Developing Economies*, vol. 35, no. 4: 485–508.

Scherer, F. M. 1980. *Industrial Market Structure and Economic Performance*. Chicago: Rand McNally.

Schumpeter, J. A. 1942. *Capitalism, Socialism and Democracy*. New York: Harper.

Vernon, R. 1966. "International Investment and International Trade in the Product Life Cycle." *Quarterly Journal of Economics*, vol. 80, May: 190–207.

Wade, R. 1990. *Governing the Market: Economic Theory and the Role of the Government in East Asian Industrialization*. Princeton, NJ: Princeton University Press.

3

Coordination Failures and Catch-up: Experiences of Man-made Fiber in Taiwan

Been-Lon Chen and Mei Hsu

INTRODUCTION

The sucessful economic growth and development in East Asian newly industrialized economies (NIEs) after World War II are both remarkable and distinguished. The process of modern economic development is one of industrialization in which less developed economies catch up with the more developed economies. To industrialize, a takeoff at an early stage of economic development is important and necessary. Because takeoff experiences carry messages of great importance for economic development of most, if not all, developing and less developed economies that seek to industrialize and become prosperous and wealthy, this study presents a case study of takeoff experiences.

From a long-run perspective, the dominant feature of the epoch of modern development is the regular contribution of science and technology. This characteristic is shared by mature economies of virtually all types, even though countries may go through a variety of sequences or phases due to varying initial conditions, culture, as well as individual behavior over time. An important aspect leading to success in economic development is the adoption of suitable science and technology. Specifically, if a developing country is able to adopt proper technology, it can move forward and can industrialize gradually and sustain growth.

The textile and apparel industry has played an exceptional role since the industrial revolution in Europe. Since then, the takeoff and early stages of industrialization in many developed countries, including the United States and Japan, have been closely related to the adoption and improvement of their own textile technology. This story applies to two NIEs, Taiwan and South Korea. The production and export of cotton textile/apparel in Taiwan and South Korea expanded very rapidly during the late 1950s and the early 1960s. They then switched to textiles of other kinds such as wool and especially artificial fabrics, leading to the rapid expansion and exports of man-made textiles/apparel. The growth of man-made textiles in turn assisted the growth of many other manufacturing industries, especially the chemical industry. For this reason the role of man-made textiles/apparel was critical to industrialization in Taiwan and Korea, especially during the early stages.[1]

The production of artificial fabrics needs raw material called man-made fiber (hereafter MF). Unlike the textile/apparel industry, which is labor-intensive, the MF industry is not only capital-intensive, but also technology-intensive. A less developed economy in general has no such technology, and moreover it also lacks capability in innovating technology and even adopting technology. Given the difficulties, technology adoption and catching up are very important. This chapter attempts to document and characterize Taiwan's experience in adopting MF technology, emphasizing the development of the whole MF industry. We do not analyze how some particular firm adopted and improved the steps of MF manufacturing, namely polymerization, spinning, and stretching, but instead focus in particular on the initiation of the industry, its growth, the sources of and the forms of technology, and the role of the government. Like Taiwan, South Korea had a similar process of industrialization, switching from cotton textile to artificial fiber and other more skill-sophisticated industries. We also compare Taiwan's MF development experiences with Korea's.

Our basic findings are as follows. First, Taiwan's experience is a catching-up process: it relied completely on foreign technology sources in the 1960s and 1970s, developed its own technology in the 1980s, and finally exported technology in the 1990s. Second, there are more differences than similarities in MF development between Taiwan and Korea due mainly to different colonial linkages and government interventions.

Although several existing works already study the differences in industrial structure and government interventions (e.g., Amsden, 1989; Wade, 1990), the differences in development experience pertaining to MF deserve more deliberate exploration. In a recent work, Chu and Tsai (1999) also studied Taiwan's MF industry. Whereas their emphasis is on the backward linkage effect of the MF in the petrochemical industry, our focus is on the adoption and improvement of MF technology.

Our study is valuable, as the establishment of this industry success-fully renders a transformation from the traditional labor-intensive tex-tile/apparel and food-processing sectors to modern capital- and technology-intensive chemical and other sectors.[2] It demonstrates a case of the initial hesitation of private firms to launch a new industry by themselves under the market forces known as the coordination failures argued in Rodrik (1996) and Chen and Shimomura (1998), among others. As a result, the equilibrium of the economy remained at a low level under which only traditional technology was employed. The government intervention in initiating the new industry via the "dem-onstration/spillover effect" was able to coordinate the investment be-havior of private firms and led the economy to move toward a high level of equilibrium in which modern technology was utilized and the new industry emerged. As will become clear, Taiwan's MF experience was unique in East Asian practices in terms of the way the government intervened and coordinated the investment behavior in the new indus-try. Moreover, our comparison of different development experiences in MF between Korea and Taiwan provides lessons of exceptional values in shedding light on the transition of late industrialization in develop-ing economies.

This chapter is organized as follows. We first describe Taiwan's rapid growth and expansion of textile as well as MF industries and analyze their relationship. Then we document the establishment of Taiwan's MF industry, the sources of and the forms of technology adoption, and the development and catch-up of the MF industry. Next we characterize the development experience of Taiwan's MF industry and compare the differences with South Korea when it is necessary. This chapter closes with concluding remarks and ideas on future research.

TEXTILE/APPAREL, MAN-MADE FIBER, AND THEIR RELATIONSHIPS IN TAIWAN

This section documents Taiwan's growth and expansion in the pro-duction of textiles/apparel and MF and studies their relationship. We start by illustrating how textiles/apparel grew. Figure 3-1 demonstrates the shares of value added of the five major industries in manufacturing, with the five industries either large in the earlier years or later years. The food industry was the largest and the beverage/tobacco industry was also large in the early years (before 1972), whereas both the elec-tronics and chemical sectors dominated in the later years. The only exception was the textile and apparel industries, which have enlarged quickly since their inception after World War II and have always been very important. Indeed, textiles/apparel was the largest in terms of value added after 1970 and before 1985 when it was surpassed by the chemical sector. Moreover, in terms of employee shares presented in Figure 3-2, the critical and unique role of textile/apparel is even apparent: it became the largest as early as 1960 and, except for 1966, that same status continued until 1987.

Although the production of textiles/apparel grew quickly in the early 1950s, their exports remained trivial at the outset. As a result of continuing growth and expansion in production, however, exports of textiles/apparel increased rapidly after 1960 due primarily to the small domestic market and the government's export-promoting policies. Figure 3-3 documents export shares of major industries in total exports. As can be easily perceived from the graph, the share of textiles/apparel reached 15 percent by 1961, became the largest after 1967, and remained above 20 percent until 1983. As Taiwan relied heavily on international markets in obtaining machinery and equipment, energy, as well as raw material, the pivotal role of exporting textiles and apparel for obtaining foreign exchange is thus obvious.

The two principal items of textiles/apparel export in Taiwan are cotton and man-made fiber. The export of textiles/apparel was mainly in terms of cotton at the early stage, whereas man-made textiles/apparel accounted for a larger share during the later stage. Figure 3-4

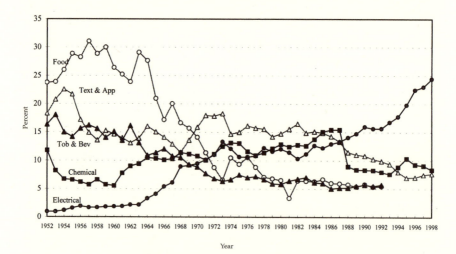

Figure 3-1. GDP share of five major two-digit industries over manufacturing as a whole.

(*Sources:* Calculated based on EPS data bank, except for chemical product of 1988–1998, which is calculated based on National Income, Taiwan District, ROC, 1998, Table 1 in part 2 of chapter 3. Data are not available for food and tob & bev after 1993.)

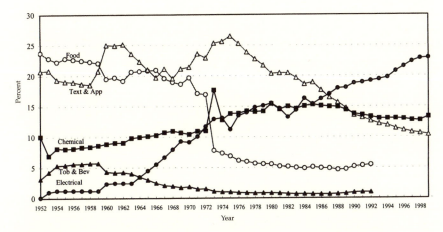

Figure 3-2. Employment share of five major two-digit industries over manufacturing as a whole.

Source: 1952–59, 1960–61: *Industry of Free China*, vol. 18, no. 1, and vol. 19, no. 1 (Council for Economic Planning and Development): 1962–63: *Taiwan Reconstruction Statistics*, no. 9 (Department of Reconstruction, Provincial Government of Taiwan, ROC): 1964–65: by construction; 1966: *General Report on the Third Industrial and Commercial Surveys*, no. 1(1968), no. 3(1986); 1967: *The ROC Report on Industrial and Commercial Census of Taiwan, ROC* (Ministry of Economic Affairs); 1968–72: *Taiwan Industrial Production Statistics Monthly*, no. 48 (Department of Statistics, Ministry of Economic Affairs, ROC); 1973: *Monthly Bulletin of Labor Statistics*, no. 135 (DGBAS, ROC); 1974, 1975–87, 1988–99: *Monthly Bulletin of Earnings and Productivity Statistics*, no. 230, no. 236, and no. 320.

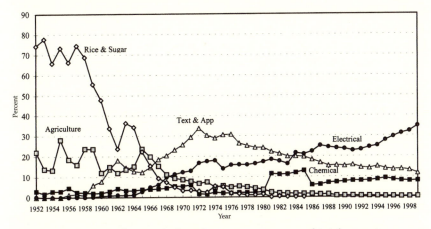

Figure 3-3. Export of major industries as a percentage of total exports.
(*Sources:* Calculated based on *Taiwan Statistical Data Book*, 1984, Tables 10-7a (1952–1983) and 10-13b (1952–1983), except for rice & sugar, which comes solely from Table 10-12; *Taiwan Statistical Data Book*, 2000, Tables 11-7 and 11-11. Data are not available for rice & sugar after 1985.)

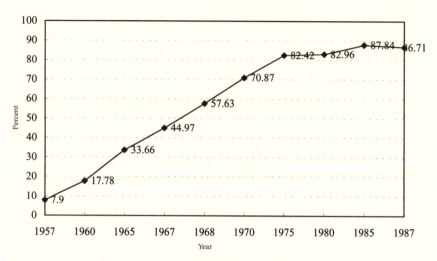

Figure 3-4. Share of Taiwan man-made fiber exports in total exports (selected years).
(*Sources:* Annual report of The Trade of China (various years), Inspectorate General of Customs, Taiwan.)

documents the relative share of man-made textile exports and cotton textiles exports.[3] As can be obviously seen from the figure, although exports of cotton textile dominated in the early years, man-made textiles soon dictated the share. The share of man-made textiles accounted for more than 70 percent by 1970 and more than 80 percent by 1975.

Why did the growth and expansion in production and exports of man-made textiles affect the domestic production of artificial fiber? A simple answer is that it was through the derived demand for inputs. The intermediate inputs of man-made textiles are MF, which generally includes two categories, cellulosic fiber like rayon and noncellulosic fiber such as nylon, polyester, and acrylic. The manufacturing of man-made textiles in Taiwan started shortly after World War II, but the raw material was wholly imported at the beginning. As the domestic production of man-made yarn and fabrics increased to a certain scale, the demand for fibers externally led to the establishment and development of MF locally.[4] Rayon production started in 1957, nylon and polyester in 1964, and acrylic in 1967.

Man-made fiber was developed basically in the direction of backward integration. With the rapid expansion in the production and exports of man-made textiles/apparel after 1968 (refer to Figure 3-4) and therefore its induced demand for MF, the production of MF consequently promptly rose. Table 3-1 demonstrates the production of the four major

TABLE 3-1. Production of Four Kinds of Man-Made Fibers (selected years)

1,000 tons

	1957	1965	1967	1970	1973	1975	1977	1980	1985	1987	1989	1993	1994	1995	1996	1997	1998
Rayon	0.8	19	24	26	50	49	69	78	122	120	153	131	149	105	3	3	3
Nylon	0	0.8	8	42	41	63	77	109	135	174	193	243	270	313	302	331	354
Polyester	0	0.6	2	14	57	136	213	349	755	1,076	1,192	1,753	1,905	1,984	2,121	2,378	2,493
Acrylic	0	0	0.1	6	28	35	63	99	133	141	145	131	155	136	147	152	119
Total	0.8	20.4	34.1	88	176	283	422	635	1,145	1,511	1,683	2,258	2,479	2,538	2,573	2,864	2,969

Sources: Calculated based on *Industry of Free China*, vol. 19 (no. 3); 30(4); 50(3); 59(6); 69(5); 79(3); 84(3); 84(5); 87(3); and 89(3) (Council for Economic Planning and Development).

kinds of MF after their creation. As can be seen, the production of each kind of MF expanded between 1967 and 1987. The production as a whole increased more than thirty-three–fold during this period, while the production of polyester alone expanded even faster, more than eighty-five times faster in this period, and is continuing to increase.

Figure 3-5 illustrates the share of world MF production for selected years after 1965 in six major countries: the United States, Japan, West

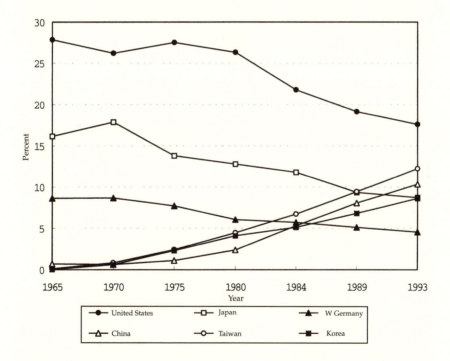

Figure 3-5. World share of man-made fiber manufacturing in major producing countries (selected years).
Sources: Man-made Fibre Handbook (various years), Japanese Chemical Fibre Association.

Germany, Taiwan, Korea, and China. In the 1970s, the United States, Japan, and West Germany were respectively the largest, second largest, and third largest in the world whose share as a whole was larger than 50 percent. Whereas Taiwan only accounted for less than 1 percent before 1970, the share quickly increased to more than 5 percent by the early 1980s. By 1989, Taiwan had outdone Japan and became the second largest producer in the world, second only to the United States, with its global share hitting 12.23 percent in 1993. Japan lost market share partly because the yen appreciated from more than 300 yen per dollar before 1975 to 200.60 yen and 122 yen per dollar in 1985 and 1987 respectively. Moreover, many firms shifted production sites overseas, especially to Korea and Southeast Asia.

Taiwan started the production of MF in 1957, but it has made itself a world giant producer in only thirty years. How was Taiwan able to make itself capable of transcending the traditional large world suppliers of MF, given the fact that Taiwan had no domestic technology of MF in the 1950s? The next section conducts the analysis. As is demonstrated, this accomplishment resembles catching-up processes.

THE MANMADE FIBER INDUSTRY AND CATCHING-UP

The Initiation

The rapid growth in production and exports of cotton textiles from developing economies, especially Hong Kong, Korea, and Taiwan, threatened not only exports but also the domestic markets of North America and Western Europe. This threat finally inspired the emergence of the Long-Term Arrangement (LTA) in 1962 to regulate the expansion of trade in cotton textiles. Because of the LTA, Taiwan switched toward developing textiles using MF.

Foreseeing the threat before the establishment of the LTA, Taiwan's government exercised authority over the creation of a rayon-making plant to make the textile industry diversify away from relying upon cotton fiber in 1954. Under the authorization of the Council for Economic Planning and Development (formerly the Economic Stabilization Board), a state-owned bank called Central Trust Bank of China brought together an American artificial fiber engineering consultant company named Von Kohorn as well as several local textile companies. This project was a part of the first Four-Year Economic Plan in Taiwan (1953–56). Through importing machinery from and licensing agreements with Von Kohorn, the project resulted in a new corporation called China Manmade Fiber Corporation. At the inception of production in early 1957, however, this firm confronted operational and technical difficulties of several sorts. The company could not operate the machine efficiently even with the technical assistance of Van Kohorn. Moreover, the produced rayon fiber did not meet a certain quality standard, so textile manufacturers still preferred using cotton and imported rayon. This company switched to a joint venture in late 1957 with Teijin of Japan, an MF and chemical giant, and the difficulties were then solved.

The pressure of the LTA pushed the government to hasten the speed of restructuring the textile and MF industry. As a part of the second Four-Year Economic Plan (1957–1960), the government asked the China Manmade Fiber Corporation and China Development Corporation, a state financing agency, to create a company to make another kind of fiber, nylon, in 1962. A new company, United Nylon Corporation, was generated under this program. Like the China Manmade Fiber Corporation, the technology of United Nylon Corporation was imported from developed countries, coming through licensing agreements this time rather than through joint ownership. The licensing agreements were with Chemtex of the United States and Zimmer of West Germany. United Nylon Corporation started manufacturing in 1964. At the same time, the China Manmade Fiber Corporation started a joint venture with its Japanese partner in rayon, Teijrin, to establish a new firm to produce the third kind of MF, polyester. This investment venture organized a company called Hualon, which started production also in 1964. In a word, the government had an important role in the initiation of rayon, nylon, and polyester fiber.

Formosa Plastics, Taiwan's first PVC producer, started the manufacturing of the fourth kind of MF in textiles, acrylic, with technology from its own research and development in 1967. However, both quality and quantity did not reach their targets since inception. The company turned to a licensing agreement with Japan's Asahi in 1968, and the problems were then solved. As the establishment of Formosa Plastics was under the government planning program,[5] the opening of acrylic fiber production was therefore indirectly related to the state.

As analyzed here, the development of Taiwan's MF was not very successful at the beginning. The establishment of China Manmade Fiber Corporation in 1957 was the only firm in the MF industry by 1962. This may be partially because of the fact that the labor-intensive cotton textile and apparel industries were the major profitable industries (Been-Lon Chen, 1996). A more important reason is that MF needed more capital and involved a more sophisticated technology, therefore containing larger risks. Without the government interventions, a type of coordination failure problem might have emerged that would settle the economy at such a low level of equilibrium that private firms would not dare to employ modern capital- and technology-intensive technology. The stagnation in the development of this new MF industry, together with the pressure of the LTA, pushed the government to command the China Manmade Fiber Corporation to invest in United Nylon and Hualon in 1962. Nevertheless, even after the establishment of these two new firms, private enterprises did not enter this business immediately. It was not until 1966 when two private firms, Ko Hua and Liang Yu, joined the production of nylon did the turning point occur. After that, Taiwan witnessed a surge of new firms emerging in this industry, with twenty-one companies emerging in the industry by 1970 and thirty-nine by 1976. Table 3-2 is a listing of the names of these thirty-nine firms.

TABLE 3-2. Sources of Technology of Man-Made Fiber Manufacturing in Taiwan by 1976

Product	Name of Firm	Source of Technology	Source of Country	Ching-tao or Shanghai connections	Form of Importation	Year of Importation
Rayon	China Manmade Fiber	Von Kohorn/Teijin	U.S./Japan	yes	Licensing/ Joint venture	1954/57
	Formosa Chemicals & Fiber	Maurer	Switzerland	no	Licensing	1967
Nylon	United Nylon[1]	Chemtex/Zimmer	U.S./W. Germany	yes	Licensing	1962
	Ko Hua[1]	Zimmer	W. Germany	yes	Licensing	1966
	Liang Yu	Dow	U.S.	yes	Licensing	1966
	Formosa Chemicals & Fiber	Zimmer	W. Germany	no	Licensing	1967
	Bao Chen[1]	Zimmer	W. Germany	yes	Licensing	1968
	Jang Dah Nylon[2]	Toray	Japan	no	Licensing	1968
	Dah Ming	Inventa/Luigi	Switzerland/ W. Germany	no	Licensing	1969
	Pacific[2]	Zimmer	W. Germany	no	Licensing	1969
	Ming Bon	Didier/Zimmer	W. Germany/ W. Germany	yes	Licensing	1972
	Jen Dar	Chemtex	U.S.	yes	Licensing	1973
	Hsing Chung	Zimmer	W. Germany	n.a.[3]	Licensing	1974
	Ta Hsing	Chemtex	U.S.	yes	Licensing	1974
	Yeong Jinn	Karl Fisher	U.S.	no	Licensing	1974
	Chung Shing	Chemtex	U.S.	yes	Licensing	1974
Polyester	Hualon[1]	Teijin	Japan	yes	Joint venture	1964
	Nan Ya Plastics	Zimmer	W. Germany	no	Licensing	1967
	Ko Hua[1]	Inventa	Switzerland	yes	Licensing	1968
	Hung Chou Chemical	Holchst	W. Germany	no	Licensing	1968
	Yu-Ho Fibre	Didier	W. Germany	no	Licensing	1968
	Far Eastern Textile	Inventa/Luigi	Switzerland/ W. Germany	yes	Licensing	1969
	Shinkong Synthetic Fiber	Toray	Japan	no	Joint venture	1969
	Dah Ming	Inventa	Switzerland	no	Licensing	1969
	Pacific[2]	Zimmer	W. Germany	yes	Licensing	1969
	Tung-Yun	Chemtex/ICI	U.S./U.K.	no	Licensing	1972
	Tuntex	ICI	U.K.	no	Licensing	1972
	Tainan Spinning	Zimmer/Inventa	W.Germany/ Switzerland	no	Licensing	1973
	Hsing Hsing[1]	Inventa	Switzerland	no	Licensing	1973
	Shi Dai	Inventa	Switzerland	no	Licensing	1973
	Ta Chin	Inventa	Switzerland	no	Licensing	1973
	Ta Hsing	Inventa	Switzerland	yes	Licensing	1973
	Tung Ho Spinning	Zimmer/ICI	W. Germany/U.K.	no	Licensing	1973

TABLE 3-2. (continued)

Product	Name of Firm	Source of Technology	Source of Country	Ching-tao or Shanghai connections	Form of Importation	Year of Importation
	Ta Jiuh	Zimmer	W. Germany	n.a.	Licensing	1974
	Chung Shing	Inventa	Switzerland	yes	Licensing	1976
	Ho Jong	Luigi/Inventa	W. Germany/ Switzerland	no	Licensing	1976
Acrylic	Formosa Plastics	Formosa Plastics/Asahi	Taiwan/Japan	no	R & D/ Licensing	1967/1968
	Tong-Hwa Synthetic Fiber	Mitsubishi Rayon	Japan	n.a.	Joint venture	1970
	Tung Ho Spinning	ICI	U.K.	no	Licensing	1976

Notes: 1. Merged to become Hualon in 1977.
　　　2. Purchased by Full-Point Synthetic Corporation in 1983.
　　　3. n.a. means not available.
Sources: Annual Report of Textile Industry (varous years), Taiwan Institute for Economic Research; Business Groups in Taiwan (various years); and The Largest Corporations in Taiwan (various years), China Credit Information Service Ltd.

The production of all four kinds of man-made fiber had therefore taken off in Taiwan by 1968, all being associated directly or indirectly with the government. Many private enterprises later then joined the industry to get a share of the market once the new industry was introduced. Next we briefly summarize how the new entrants joined, how they introduced technology, and how they expanded before the first oil crisis.[6]

The Development of the Industry Before the First Oil Crisis

Rayon

China Manmade Fiber Corporation was the only producer of rayon before 1967. Its daily capacity was only 5 tons initially and expanded to 10 tons in 1960. As a result, its annual output increased from 800 tons in 1957 to 10,000 tons in 1967. Formosa Chemicals & Fiber Corporation, a member of the Formosa Plastics group, joined the industry in 1967 through a licensing agreement with Maurer of Switzerland and started to produce in 1968, with production capacity at 45 tons per day. Confronted with a strong competition from the new Formosa Chemicals & Fiber Corporation and with a need to lower unit costs via scale economies, China Manmade Fiber Corporation later expanded to a daily capacity of 40 tons in 1969. In light of this, Formosa Chemicals & Fiber Corporation subsequently expanded its daily capacity to 140 tons per day in 1973, increasing from 70 tons per day in 1970. Table 3-3 demonstrates how these two firms expanded the scale over time before 1973. As a result of expansion, Taiwan's rayon production was then

TABLE 3-3. Production Capacity of Rayon before First Oil Shock

	tons			
Year	China Manmade Fiber		Formosa Chemicals & Fiber	
	Daily	Annual	Daily	Annual
1957	55	800	0	0
1960	10	4,000	0	0
1967	n.a.	1,000	0	0
1968	n.a.	n.a.	45	n.a.
1969	40	n.a.	n.a.	n.a.
1970	n.a.	n.a.	70	n.a.
1971	n.a.	n.a.	90	n.a.
1972	n.a.	n.a.	120	n.a.
1973	n.a.	n.a.	140	n.a.

Note: n.a. means not available.
Sources: Chow (1973) and Sun-Ming Chen (1975).

expanded to 45,000 tons in 1975, and 78,000 tons in 1980 (refer to Table 3-1). The output of rayon continued to increase until 1989.

Nylon

Two years after the production of nylon by United Nylon Corporation, two firms were induced to join production in 1966. Ko Hua adopted technology from Zimmer of West Germany, and Liang Yu imported technology from Dow Chemicals of the United States, both through licensing agreements. All three of these firms built a daily capacity of 20 tons at the beginning. In 1967 Formosa Chemicals & Fiber started the production of nylon via licensing agreements with Zimmer of West Germany. Jang Dah Nylon and Bao Chen joined the industry in 1968; Dah Ming and Pacific participated in 1969. Later, Ming Bon and Jen Dar entered respectively in 1972 and 1973; Hsing Chung, Ta Hsing, Yeong Jinn, and Chung Shing appeared in 1974. These fourteen firms constituted the industry of nylon in Taiwan by 1976, with licensing agreements being the only way of technology adoption for all these fourteen firms as illustrated in Table 3-2. Moreover, most technology came from Europe, especially West Germany; the United States was the second source, and Japan accounted for only one source, namely for Jang Dah Nylon.

Production capacity for the five major firms in this industry between 1974 and 1975 is illustrated in Table 3-4. While the total annual capacity of the five firms was over 81,000 tons in 1975, the actual production shown in Table 3-1 was only 63,000 tons, indicating that the firms in this

TABLE 3-4. Annual Nylon Production Capacity of the Five Major Firms in 1974–1975

				tons	
				Formosa	
	United Nylon	Ko Hua	Liang Yu	Chemicals & Fiber	Jang Dan Nylon
1974	7,590	8,250	6,270	9,900	16,500
1975	13,200	14,190	9,900	19,800	24,750

Source: Chow (1973).

industry were competing in enlarging their scale. Taiwan's production of nylon after 1975 was quite fast, as can be seen from Table 3-1. Its annual output increased from 63,000 tons in 1975 to 243,000 tons in 1993, increasing fourfold in less than twenty years. The output has remained on the increase in recent years.

Figure 3-6 presents the world share of nylon production in major countries for selective years. As can be seen, the United States has dictated nylon supply since 1975, accounting for one-third in the world. Taiwan's share increased from 2.5 percent in 1975 to 6.9 percent in 1993, about the same as for Japan and Korea.

Polyester

Three years after the establishment of the first polyester manufacturer, Hualon, Nan Ya Plastics of the Formosa Plastics group entered the industry by introducing technology via licensing agreements from Zimmer of West Germany. Whereas Hualon had an annual capacity of 3,300 tons in 1966, the annual capacity of Nan Ya Plastics was 14,000 tons at its inception, which expanded to an annual capacity of 50,000 tons in 1974. One year after the entrance of Nan Ya Plastics, Ko Hua, Hung Chou Chemical, and Yo-Ho Fiber followed suit. They all used technology from either West Germany or Switzerland via licensing agreements. In 1969, four more firms joined, among which Far Eastern Textile and Shinkong Synthetic Fiber were the biggest. The annual capacity of Far Eastern Textile was 13,500 tons in the beginning year and later expanded to a total of 58,000 tons in 1975; that of Shinkong Synthetic Fiber was 3,700 tons initially and increased to 30,000 tons in 1975. Table 3-5 sums up the production capacity of the four largest firms in the industry before 1975. In the 1970s eleven more firms entered the market (refer to Table 3-2). Thus the total number of firms in polyester rose to twenty by 1976.

Because polyester can be blended with cotton, wool, or rayon and has many applications, it is the most important item among all man-made textiles/fiber. That explains why so many firms entered the polyester

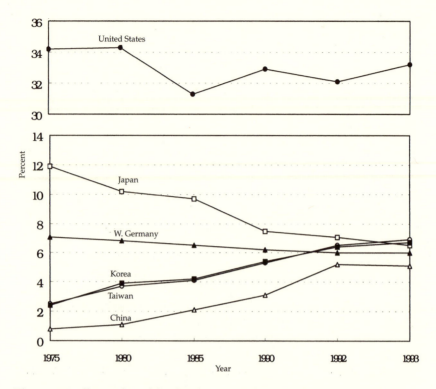

Figure 3-6. Share of world nylon for six major countries (selected years). *Source: Man-made Fiber Handbook* (various years), Japan Chemical Fiber Association

TABLE 3-5. Annual Polyester Production Capacity in the Four Largest Firms before 1975

			tons	
	Hualon	Nan Ya Plastics	Far Eastern Textile	Shinkong Synthetic Fiber
1964	3,300	0	0	0
1967	n.a.	14,000	0	0
1969	n.a.	n.a.	13,500	3,700
1974	13,200	50,000	13,500	3,700
1975	15,510	50,000	58,000	30,000

Note: n.a. means not available.
Sources: Chow (1973) and Sun-Ming Chen (1975).

industry, which made Taiwan's production of polyester increase very fast after 1977. As can be seen from Table 3-1, Taiwan's production of polyester was expanded from barely 2,000 tons in 1967 to 2,493,000 tons in 1998, a compound annual average growth rate of 28.5 percent.

Taiwan's world share in polyester manufacturing is even more astonishing and exceptional. Figure 3-7 is the world share of polyester production in major countries for selected years. As can be seen, Taiwan's share increased from 4.4 percent in 1975 to almost 20 percent in 1993, with Taiwan becoming the world's largest polyester supplier since 1989. With rapid entries and speed of expansion as described earlier, it is not surprising that Taiwan became the world's largest supplier of polyester, surpassing traditional large world suppliers such as the United States, Japan, and West Germany.

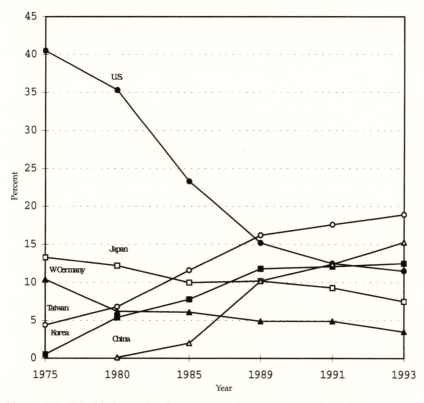

Figure 3-7. World share of polyester in major countries (selected years).
Sources: Man-made Fiber Handbook (various years), Japan Chemical Fiber Association.

Acrylic

Acrylic is a kind of man-made wool. Soon after Formosa Plastics introduced acrylic into production in 1968, it expanded to a daily capacity of 20 tons in 1969. In 1970 another firm, Tong-Hwa Synthetic Fiber, entered the industry using technology from Mitsubishi Rayon of Japan through a joint venture. Its daily production capacity was 15 tons. Table 3-6 reports the subsequent expansion in daily production of these two firms. Facing new competition, Formosa Plastics enlarged its capacity, and by 1976 it had completed a daily production capacity of 155 tons. Tong-Hwa Synthetic Fiber also expanded its daily capacity to 25 tons in 1972, and subsequently to 95 tons in 1977. In 1976 Tung Ho Spinning joined in, employing technology via licensing from ICI of the United Kingdom (refer to Table 3-2). This industry then grew steadily, with annual output increasing from 63,000 tons in 1977 to a peak of 155,000 tons in 1994 (refer to Table 3-1).

The world share of acrylic for major countries is exhibited in Figure 3-8. As can be seen, Japan has dominated acrylic production since 1975, whereas the United States has lost almost a half of its share since 1975. Taiwan's share increased from 2.3 percent to about 6 percent in 1993, close to that of China.

As analyzed previously, the growth of Taiwan's MF was rapid only after 1966 when private enterprises started to enter. The total production of MF was 34,000 tons in 1967, increasing to 178,000 tons by the first oil shock. It is no doubt that foreign technology through either joint ventures or licensing agreements and machinery supplies generated spillovers via staff transfers, buyer–supplier relationship, and other channels, enhancing the entrants and development of the industry.

The first oil shocks severely struck the industry, however. This happened not only because the world market was depressed due to oil shocks, but also because oil waste is a major input in the MF industry, whose higher prices inflated input costs. The numerous entrants and

TABLE 3-6.   Daily Acrylic Production Capacity in Formosa Plastics and Tong-Hwa Synthetic Fiber before 1977

	tons	
Year	*Formosa Plastics*	*Tong-Hwa Synthetic Fiber*
1969	20	0
1970	50	15
1972	55	25
1976	155	25
1977	155	95

Sources: Chow (1973) and Sun-Ming Chen (1975).

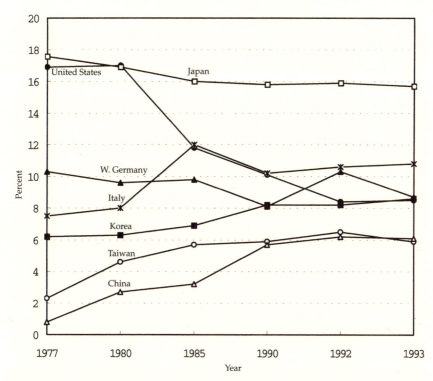

Figure 3-8. World share of acrylic production in major countries (selected years).
Source: Man-made Fiber Handbook (various years), Japan Chemical Fiber Association.

the rapid expansion of MF before the first oil shock and insufficient demand and rising input costs during this oil shock led to losses and difficulties for many firms. In response, many firms either stopped operation or were forced to reduce production temporarily.[7] Some firms even merged.[8] The government also provided policies in stabilizing domestic prices and subsidizing the purchase of domestic MF. Due to proper responses of private firms and the government, when the first oil shock was over, this industry soon recovered rapidly and grew steadily.

The Development of the Industry after the First Oil Crisis

After the first oil shock, Taiwan's production of MF gained a large global market share. The production of MF reached 283,000 tons in 1975, 645,000 tons in 1980, and 2,258,000 tons in 1993 (refer to Table 3-1), with the market share being 2.4 percent, 4.5 percent, and 12.3 percent, respectively (refer to Figure 3-5). Witnessing the growth of MF and other kinds of chemical fiber, the government sequentially introduced policies to establish upperstream fiber in chemical industries.

For industries related to man-made textiles/fiber, the government directed state-owned Chinese Petroleum Corporation to invest in upstream firms to provide raw material for MF. For example, Chung-Tai Chemical was set up in 1976 to make caprolactum (CPL) for nylon, Chinese Amoco Chemical in 1979 to fabricate terephthalic acid (PTA) for polyester, and Chinese Petroleum and Chemical Corporation in 1976 to manufacture acrylonitrile monomer (AN) for acrylic. The government later invested in even upperstream firms (e.g., Naphtha Cracker). This subsequently established Taiwan's vertically related chemical industry, which has since become the second largest in manufacturing in terms of value added since 1990, according to Figure 3-1. It is thus obvious that Taiwan's chemical industry developed in a backward integration, for which the initiation of MF played a critical role.

In the 1980s new entrants of Taiwan's MF no longer relied on imported technology. The first successful cases were made in 1985 when Chi Yuan (now called Cheng Chi) and Fu Jiuh produced nylon and acrylic respectively based on technology from their own R & D. The same story applied to Acelon and ChainYarn, which manufactured nylon based on their own R & D in 1988. Acelon also produced polyester later, based on its own R & D.

By the end of the 1980s, many Taiwanese firms started to develop new materials and new production processes, especially the former. Taiwanese R & D of fine fiber dated back to 1978 when the director of the Plastics and Fiber Research Center (PFRC),[9] Dr. D.-Y. Guo, and the president of Hualon, Mr. Feng-Jang Leu, jointly formed an agreement that these two organizations cooperate to start searching for new and finer fiber. The collaboration began with a breakthrough in getting fine fiber of 75 deniers. Although this joint research project died out after Mr. Leu passed away a few years later, it ignited R & D incentives for many fiber producers. The research in developing new material resulted in a fruitful harvest, especially in generating fine fiber and microfiber. In ten years, the end of the 1980s witnessed some flourishing results of R & D, made either by producers independently or by collaborating with research organizations and universities.

Table 3-7 illustrates selective discoveries of R & D before 1990. In fine fiber, Formosa Chemicals & Fiber Corporation, for example, discovered sequentially fine nylon filament of 1 denier and then of 0.5 denier at the end of the 1980s. Chung Shing successfully uncovered polyester filament of 0.8 denier in 1989 and of 0.5 denier in 1990. Similar discoveries

TABLE 3-7.   Selective Discoveries of Fine Fiber and Microfiber before 1990

Name of Firms	Rayon	Polyester (filament)	Polyester (staple)	Nylon (filament)
Formosa Chemicals and Fibre	0.9 denier	0.5 denier		1~0.5 denier
Chung Shing		0.8~0.5 denier	0.85 denier	
Far Eastern Textile		0.8~0.6 denier (250 ton/month)	0.6~0.8 denier (150 ton/month)	
		0.5 denier (100 ton/month)		
Tainan Spinning		0.8~0.5 denier (24 ton/month)		
Shinkong Synthetic Fiber		0.9~0.5 denier (100 ton/month)	0.12 denier	
Nan Ya Plastics		0.19 deiner (60 ton/month)	0.85 denier (100 ton/month)	
		0.8~0.05 denier (800 ton/month)		

Sources: Textile Industry Yearbooks, 1992, 71–84, 123–165, Taipei: Taiwan Institute for Economics Research, and Chemical Research and Service Organization, ITRI.

have been made by Far Eastern Textile, Tainan Spinning, Shinkong Synthetic Fibre, and other firms (*Textile Industry Yearbook*, 1992, 71–84, 123–165). As for microfiber, the harvest was also tremendous. Nan Ya Plastics, for example, has spent 1 percent of sales in microfiber R & D every year since the early 1980s. In 1987 it discovered polyester filament of 0.5 to 0.2 denier, and the discoveries also obtained patents in Japan, the United States, and other countries. Formosa Chemicals & Fiber Corporation discovered rayon fiber of 0.9 denier, which was the finest in the world at that time.

At the same time, MF and textile producers also strategically formed a vertical alliance. The cooperation between Far Eastern Textile and Hong Ho, the largest textile manufacturer making lady's dresses in Taiwan, started the alliance. In this cooperation, Far Eastern Textile conducted R & D and found micro polyester filament of 0.2 denier. Hong Ho then used this microfiber to produce textiles and apparel. Because the textiles and apparel made from microfiber were of high quality, a large fraction of orders came from Europe and North America and thus the unit value added was high, making profit margins high. This led to incentives for many textile producers to either seek for or enter into a vertical coalition with MF producers, or to join the production of textiles using fine and microfibers. This in turn has resulted in a larger market for fine and microfibers, rendering fiber producers larger incentives to conduct R & D (*Textile Industry Yearbook*, 1992, 71–84, 123–165).

The 1990s have seen many firms exporting a whole plant of MF including technology (i.e., turnkeys). The first case was Tuntex, which invested in a whole plant of polyester to Thailand in early 1989. Other examples include Far Eastern Textile, which invested in several whole plants of rayon to the Philippines in late 1989, and Tuntex, which invested in whole plants of polyester to Indonesia in 1991. The destination of whole plant exports is not confined to less developed countries. Nan Ya Plastics and Formosa Chemicals & Fiber Corporation, for example, invested in whole plants of polyester and of rayon to the United States in 1991 (to North Carolina and to Louisiana, respectively). In the mid-1990s, Tung-Yun invested into whole plants of MF in Thailand and Hualon invested in Malaysia and Northern Ireland. Although relocation of plants abroad may be related to amelioration of rising production costs after New Taiwan dollars appreciated in 1987 and higher tariffs after Taiwan lost the Generalized System of Preferences (GSP) privileges of the United States in 1988, the fact does indicate an important manner that Taiwan's technology of MF has already caught up with those of the developed world as Japanese firms did in the late 1960s and early 1970s.[10]

Although the 1990s have seen rapid growth in Taiwanese electronics, many firms listed in Table 3-2 remained large in the 1990s. For the largest forty firms in terms of sales in manufacturing, Nan Ya Plastics was the largest in 1992, Formosa Plastics was the fifth largest, Formosa Chemicals & Fiber Corporation was sixth, Far Eastern Textile was twelfth, Hualon was thirteenth, Tung-Yun was twenty-first, Shinkong Synthetic was thirtieth, and Chung-Hsing was thirty-second (China Credit Information Service, 1993). Many of the producers became large conglomerates. The Formosa Plastics Group was the largest in Taiwan, and the Far Eastern Group was the fourth-largest in 1993 (China Credit Information Service, 1993). The Shinkong Group, the Chung-Hsing Group, the Tainan Group, the Pacific Group, the Walsin-Lihwa Group (cofounder of Pacific Nylon and Polyester), the Hualon Group, and the Tuntex Group were all large conglomerates. These conglomerates have businesses ranging from chemicals to electronics, retail services, financial services, construction, and other sectors. In the late 1990s, many of these groups entered into the leading areas such as making DRAM and providing wireless communication services. For example, the largest Taiwan DRAM producer, Winbound, is owned by the Huashin-Lihua Group, and the largest private wireless communication company, Taiwan Cellular Corporation or the so-called "Taiwan-Da-Ger-Da," belongs to the Pacific Group. These groups emerging from the MF industry have large economic influence in determining the technological level and in shaping Taiwan's economic structure.

CHARACTERISTICS OF TAIWAN'S MAN-MADE FIBER DEVELOPMENT

This section investigates characteristics in the development of Taiwan's MF. Like Taiwan, South Korea's industrialization and modernization started after World War II and began with the development of the cotton textile industry. Under the restriction of the LTA in 1962, South Korea switched to the production of artificial textiles, thus leading to the development of MF.[11] To highlight the characteristics of Taiwan's MF, we also compare with South Korea.

We briefly describe South Korea's MF development. As early as August 1960, Hanguk Nylon Corporation (now Kolon Nylon), formerly a fiber stretching and finishing producer using imported nylon, was created under the charter and financial support of the government to produce nylon fiber through joint ventures with Chemtex of the United States. It started production in 1963, but the beginning faced some problems due to both a lack of experience and some mistakes in design made by Chemtex. The scale in Kolon was therefore small, and the quality of output was low. Kolon Nylon abandoned stretching nylon yarns in 1964 in order to concentrate on manufacturing nylon. To expand the scale in order to reduce unit production costs, Kolon Nylon later applied respectively to the American Agency for International Development for aid totaling $580,000 in 1964 and the EXIM Bank of the United States for a loan totaling $3,420,000 in 1968, under the endorsement of the government. In 1969 Kolon introduced capital and technology from Toray and started a joint venture with Toray. This joint venture made the production in Kolon Nylon run smoothly. In the same year, Kolon formed another joint venture with Toray to set up the first polyester plant in South Korea. The new firm was called Kolon Polyester and started production in 1971 (Enos and Park, 1988).

Since then, several firms have emerged gradually to produce this and other kinds of MF, also under the charter and support of the state. Table 3-8 records the firms, the forms of technology adoption, and the sources of technology importation in South Korea's MF industry before 1976. The production of MF therefore increased steadily. As can be seen from Figure 3-5, the growth and expansion of MF in South Korea were like Taiwan: It gained global market share after 1975 and expanded rapidly even though the share was less than 1 percent before 1970. The share reached 3.59 percent by 1979, and by 1993 it accounted for an 8.62 percent share, becoming the fifth-largest in the world. For the components, the growth pattern of nylon can be seen in Figure 3-6, polyester in Figure 3-7, and acrylic in Figure 3-8. Like Taiwan, the production of polyester expanded faster; South Korea had only a small global share of 0.52 percent in 1975, but reached 11.26 percent and became the fourth-largest by 1993.

Given these backgrounds, we may compare the similarities, and differences between South Korea and Taiwan. As it turns out, there are more differences than similarities and the differences are mainly due to different colonial linkages and different government interventions. Recently, Suzuki (1999) examined the initiation and the development of the nylon industry in Japan. In Table 3-9 we list the related data compiled from the work in Suzuki (1999). In the following, we also compare with Japan when it is necessary.

Similarities

As discussed previously, the MF industry in Taiwan and South Korea did not emerge automatically. The state in both countries intervened and played an important role in the opening and development of this industry. Both South Korea and Taiwan had a well-developed labor-intensive textile industry before starting the capital-intensive MF industry in the 1960s, and as a result, the absorption capabilities necessary for introducing more capital-intensive and technology-sophisticated MF were equipped as is emphasized by Abramovitz (1986). With few exceptions, all technology of MF came from abroad in the early stages of development as can be seen from both Tables 3-2 and 3-8, with licensing agreements and joint ventures being the two forms.

TABLE 3-8. Source of Technology of Man-made Fiber Manufacturing in South Korea by 1976

Product	Name of firm	Source of Technology	Source of Country	Form of Importation	Year of Importation
Nylon	Kolon Nylon	Chemtex/Toray	U.S./Japan	Joint venture	1960/69
	Tongyang Nylon	Zimmer	W. Germany	Licensing	1967
	Kohap	n.a.	n.a.	n.a.	n.a.
Polyester	Kolon Polyester	Toray	Japan	Joint venture	1969
	Sunkyong	Teijin	Japan	Joint venture	1969
	Cheil Synthetic	Toray	Japan	Joint venture	1972
	Tongyang Polyester	Asahi	Japan	Joint venture	1973
	Sam Yang	Nippon Estel	Japan	Licensing	1968
	Daehan	Chemtex	U.S.	Licensing	1968
	Kohap	n.a.	n.a.	n.a.	1966
	Jeil Synthetic	n.a.	n.a.	n.a.	n.a.
Acrylic	Hanil	Asahi	Japan	Licensing	1964
	Taikyong	Nihon Exlan	Japan	Licensing	n.a.

Note: n.a. means not available.
Source: Tran (1988)

TABLE 3-9. Source of Technology of Nylon and Polyester Manufacturing in Japan by 1970

Product	Name of firm	Source of Technology	Source of Country	Form of Importation	Year of Importation
Nylon	Toray	Du Pout	U.S.	Licensing	1949
	Nippon Rayon (Unitica)	Du Pout	U.S.	Licensing	1953
	Kanebo	Snia Viscosa	Italy	Licensing	1961
	Teijin	Allied Chemical and Dye Corporation	U.S.	Licensing	1960
	Kureha (Toyobo)	Zimmer	W. Germany	Licensing	1960
	Asahi Chemicals	Zimmer/Firestone	W. Germany/ U.S.	Licensing	1960
Polyester	Toray	n.a.	n.a.	n.a.	1949
	Teijin	n.a.	n.a.	n.a.	1949
	Kureha (Toyobo)	n.a.	n.a.	n.a.	n.a.
	Kurary	n.a.	n.a.	n.a.	n.a.
	Nippon Rayon (Unitica)	n.a.	n.a.	n.a.	n.a.

Note: n.a. means not available.
Source: Suzuki (1999).

Initiation of the Industry

The establishment of China Manmade Fiber Corporation was important for Taiwan not just as the start of the new industry, but also because it set the pattern for foreign partners participating in other kinds of MF and other sectors through the 1960s and 1980s, with the government taking the lead in bringing together foreign companies and local producers to fill gaps in the production structure. Because most Taiwanese firms were small or medium in size, the government therefore built public or semipublic enterprises to initiate a new field, attempting to induce private firms to participate in the industry by providing a market with stable prices and by moderately protecting the domestic market from foreign competition through selective tariff policies. By doing so, the state could send signals to private enterprises through "the demonstration effect" that there were indeed not only few risks but also many opportunities in this industry. Other industries of this kind included Hsing-Chu Glass, Naphtha Cracker, China Steel, China Shipbuilding, United Microelectronic Corporation, and Taiwan Semiconductor Manufacturing Corporation, among others.

In contrast, all MF producers in South Korea listed in Table 3-8 were invested by private entrepreneurs from the beginning. The government did not set up public enterprises in the MF industry and even in manufacturing,[12] but rather it assisted the establishment of the industry by providing cheaper capital, better exchange rates, tax incentives, and other benefits and bridged technical cooperation or joint ventures with foreign firms. In the case of cheaper capital, the real interest rates were usually negative, as emphasized in Mckinnon (1973). Moreover, the government established entry barriers to protect existing firms in order to guarantee the industry's growth. By doing so, it of course ran the risk of existing firms' perpetual dependence on such policies. The government may face a dilemma after some period of protection if the local firms under protection have not yet become competitive. If it gives up the protection, local firms that it has nurtured for such a long time may very likely fail immediately; if, on the other hand, protection is postponed, then the lack of discipline provides even fewer incentives for the firms to become efficient. This scenario, however, rarely happened in South Korea.

It is interesting to compare the initiation experience with Japan. Japan started manufacturing nylon in 1949 and polyester in 1958 as the Japanese government intervened in the initiation by picking only Toray in producing nylon and Toray and Teijin in polyester, according to Suzuki (1999). These firms were all private, just like those in South Korea. The government protected these firms by restricting new entries until 1961 and by providing other benefits (e.g., tax exemption and reduction, development loans, and others). Even when new entries were allowed, the capacities of each firm were still constrained by the government. In light of this, the South Korean experience is close to Japan's.

In the process of economic development, initiation and development in the early stages are very important. With a successful first step, a chance is provided for a new industry to grow. As our story reveals, Taiwan's government has consistently played a vital role in the initiation of many new fields in the process of industrialization and economic development. The state began with the establishment of enterprises in some new industries, and then either handed the factories over to selected private entrepreneurs or ran them as public or semipublic enterprises. This intervention attracted private enterprises to join later. One of the underlying reasons may be the inadequate supply of entrepreneurs looking out for new production methods or new ideas in the developing economy, incapable of or unwilling to take the risks of introducing them as argued for many developing economies.[13] But, more important is the coordination failure problem that private firms by themselves dare not risk by switching from the use of traditional technology to the use of modern technology unless other firms have done so. Government initiation or intervention in initiating the new industry is necessary to reduce the risk of departure from traditional production methods, thus coordinating the investment behavior of private firms. Government action has the demonstration/spillover effect, and other firms will follow suit. Once the entrepreneurship is started, it is self-sustaining. The creation of the MF industry is an example, and Taiwan's strategy has proved effective and successful.

Sources of Technology

To establish a totally new industry in a developing country, the first task confronted is to choose proper sources of technology. The sources of technology have two aspects: country level and firm level. For the country level, Taiwan's technology of MF came from all over the developed world, as can be seen from Table 3-2, whereas South Korea's technology was adopted predominantly from Japan, according to Table 3-8. The dominance of Japanese technology in South Korea was usual and perceivable. It may sound unusual at first glance that Japanese technology only played a minor part in Taiwan, whereas technology from West Germany had a major role, given the fact that Taiwan's trade relation with Japan, as well as the United States, has been much closer than that of West Germany and that both Taiwan and South Korea were colonized in history by and close in geography to Japan. Because Japan has been a giant in the chemical industry since the 1960s, Japan's technology would have been the first choice of these two economies when seeking technology overseas. In electronics, for example, a large fraction of firms in Taiwan introduced Japanese technology in early stages of development. There are specific factors explaining partly why many sources of technology in Taiwan came from Europe, especially West Germany.

One of these important factors is entrepreneurs' connections, which are in turn similar to "colonial" linkages. Many entrepreneurs of textiles and apparel were emigrated from mainland China, coming especially from Tsiangtao and Shanghai, where the modern textile and apparel industry had been developed before World War II. Tsiangtao had been colonized by Germany, and Shanghai was colonized by many European countries. As many Taiwanese MF firms were invested in by the immigrating entrepreneurs of textile and apparel, when these entrepreneurs sought technology, their connections with Western countries experienced and built in Tsiangtao and Shanghai provided a channel (refer to Table 3-2).[14] South Korea started to develop the textile industry after World War II (Enos and Park, 1988), and entrepreneurs lacked such connections with Europe and North America. Their early connections were mainly, if not only, with Japan. Colonial linkages therefore dominated the sources.

Another aspect for the source of technology is the type of technology supplier at the firm level. For adopting MF technology, two kinds of suppliers were available: one through manufacturing firms, and the other via engineering consultant firms. Von Kohorn, Zimmer, and Inventa were all old and famous engineering consultant firms, whereas Dow Chemicals, ICI, Teijrin, Toray, and Mitsubishi Rayon were large manufacturing firms. Technology in Taiwan was mainly adopted from engineering consultant firms. Two primary suppliers of technology in Taiwan were Zimmer of West Germany and Inventa of Switzerland, according to Table 3-2, both being engineering consultant firms. In only a few cases was technology in Taiwan adopted from large manufacturing firms.

South Korea, on the other hand, adopted technology mostly from manufacturing firms. Only three cases of technology there were adopted from engineering consultant firms: both Kolon Nylon and Daehan from Chemtex of the United States and Tongyang Nylon from Zimmer of West Germany, and these were the only cases that had technology adopted from countries other than Japan. The South Korean outcome was strongly related to the aforementioned entrepreneurs' connections with West Europe and the United States, making it rely heavily on Japanese technology. It was also related to the fact that South Korea developed textiles later than Taiwan, leading to a larger technology gap between South Korean technology and the world level. For the latter reason, a firm importing technology could lack not only the technology itself but also the production and management-related know-how. It would then choose a manufacturing firm rather than a consultant company as its partner, because only manufacturing firms have that sort of know-how.

Forms of Technology Adoption

There are many forms of technology importation, including joint ventures (direct foreign investment), licensing agreements, production cooperation, original equipment manufacturing, and other informal accumulation of nonproprietary information, among others. Most technology importation in Taiwan took the form of licensing agreements. As is clear from Table 3-2, only four out of thirty-nine firms in Taiwan engaged in joint ventures. Two of these four firms, China Manmade Fiber Corporation and Hualon, were established when Taiwan had no production of rayon and polyester, respectively. Before the establishment of MF, Taiwan's major manufacturing was in textiles with an average firm size very small and the technology labor-intensive and less sophisticated. The creation of MF manufacturing, however, required intensive capital as well as more advanced and complicated technology. These small textile firms did not accumulate enough capital, and more important, they did not have technology and production and management know-how. Moreover, starting a new industry was a risky business even with the assistance of the government. The difficulties that China Manmade Fiber Corporation confronted at the outset via licensing agreements with von Kohorn were such an example.

Joint ventures, on the other hand, not only supplied technology of their needs and shared the risks, but they also provided production and management know-how. In this circumstance, firms were therefore obligated to employ joint ventures as a channel for technology adoption. Once an industry was established, production and management know-how could prevail via transfers of employees and other channels. Together with the facts that Taiwanese preferred ownership (Shieh, 1992) and that Taiwan's saving rate was high and thus capital was more abundant, this made licensing agreements a more popular form of technology adoption.

Both licensing and joint ventures were equally important in South Korea according to Table 3-8. The reasons that joint venture was more popular there can be explained as follows. First, South Korea had less entrepreneur's connections with Europe and North America as mentioned earlier. Second, their savings rate was low, always much lower than Taiwan before 1987,[15] so that South Korea lacked capital. Although the government to some extent may have been able to distribute capital to selective entrepreneurs, the lack of capital became more serious in the 1960s when the United States decided to reduce its aid to South Korea. These factors made South Korea rely heavily on Japanese capital in addition to Japanese technology. Third, it is related to the difference in relative absorption capabilities of technology between Taiwan and South Korea. Taiwan's modern textile industry was developed by domestic capitalists before World War II (including entrepreneurs from mainland China), whereas South Korea lacked that kind of industrial basis. In other words, the technological gap between the domestic industry and international market could be even larger for South Korea. As analyzed previously, firms under this situation would prefer choosing a manufacturing firm as its partner. The manufacturing firm that was supposed to export the technology, however, could not give the know-how for free as its competition existed in the very indecipherable know-how. It is therefore natural to employ joint ventures.

In contrast, when Japan started nylon production, it had a lot of experience in textiles and rayon. As a result, absorption capability was high, and licensing agreements became the only way for technology adoption. In view of this, Taiwan stood between Japan and South Korea.

The inferior situation of South Korea vis-à-vis Taiwan may be seen from the equity shares as well. All local MF companies in Taiwan have held a majority of equity shares since their initiation. Their establishments were carried out wholly or largely by local firms, but this was not the case in South Korea, however. The foreign partners' companies in South Korea's MF industry accounted for more than or equal to 50 percent of the equity shares in many firms. All the partners of this kind were Japanese firms. In polyester, for example, Japanese possessed equity shares of more than or equal to 50 percent in Sunkyong, Kolon, Tongyang, and Cheil Chemical at least up until the mid-1970s. In fact, Japanese companies still held more than 50 percent of equity share in Tongyang Polyester by 1986 (Tran, 1988).

Research and Development

In order to upgrade the industry structure and to catch up with the world frontier level, R & D is necessary. However, the firm size in Taiwan was usually small, and most small business entrepreneurs in Taiwan were conservative toward R & D. Therefore, expenditure on R & D at a firm level is usually smaller than that in Europe, Japan, North America, and South Korea. R & D, however, was so important that Taiwan's government intervened and played an active role. It set up research organizations to conduct industry-specific R & D. This happened not only in the MF and petrochemical industry but also in almost every manufacturing industry. In Taiwan's leading industry of the 1990s, namely the information sector, the case applies. To illustrate an example, although United Microelectronics Corp. and Taiwan Semiconductor Manufacturing Co., two large-scale semiconductor chip manufacturers, have been large companies since the early 1990s and these two companies have conducted their own R & D, a large fraction of new technology was transferred from the Electronic Research and Service Organization (ERSO) under the ITRI in the early stages.

As for public-funded research establishments in Taiwan that conduct specific R & D for MF, there are two major organizations. One is the Chemical Research and Service Organization (CRSO) in the ITRI, which is funded mainly by the Ministry of Economic Affairs, and the other is the China Textile Industry Center (CTIC), also funded by the Ministry of Economic Affairs. The CRSO set up a specific center (called Plastics and Fiber Research Center [PFRC]) to do MF R & D as early as 1975, and the Center has expanded over time. In 1990, for example, the PFRC had twenty-nine permanent researchers among which over 50 percent held a Ph.D. degree. Although the PFRC obtained a regular budget from the Ministry of Economic Affairs, it also sought research contracts from other sources. For example, it has obtained contracts to do research aimed at improving the value added of MF from the Bureau of Industry and the Consultant Office of Technology under the Executive Yuan (i.e., the Prime Minister Office) every year since 1990. In 1991 the total amount of research contracts obtained from the Bureau and the Consultant Office was about $4 million (Taiwan Economic Research Institute, 1991, 24–28). The CTIC was the result of an expansion and was renamed in 1971 from the early Taiwan Textile Testing Center established by the Ministry of Economic Affairs in 1959. In July 1990 the CTIC expanded again. The Ministry gave the Center a total budget of more than $900 million in the period of 1990 to 1995 (Taiwan Economic Research Institute, 1991, 36–43).

Although both the PRFC and the CTIC conducted R & D of MF, they had a kind of division of labor. Basically, the R & D pertaining to the PRFC belonged to more upstream product and process innovations, whereas the R & D in the CTIC was more downstream. The research topics of the PRFC at the end of the 1980s and the early 1990s were mainly on the synthesis of polybutylene terephthalate (PBT) MF, new raw materials of fiber, strengthening of fiber, developing fine and microfiber, speed of spinning, development of fire-free fiber, improvement of dyeing, and others. For the CTIC, it utilized the new materials or new processes discovered by the PRFC and reconducted R & D to improve them. Its focus in the early 1990s was to develop critical technology in improving spinning and stretching, and upgrading man-made fiber textile and apparel manufacturing and others.

All the research outcomes of these two institutions were transferred to entrepreneurs, but the transfers were by no means free. The prices for the transfers were to a large extent market determined and depended on the degree of maturity of the new innovations. If the innovation was less mature, the prices were lower. If it was mature, the outcomes of innovation would be announced to the public. Those entrepreneurs who were interested in the new outcomes then negotiated the prices with the center under consideration. Since 1978, both the PRFC and the CTIC have had many breakthroughs of R & D transferred to MF and textile producers. In 1990, for example, the PRFC transferred the newly discovered microfiber and other raw materials to companies such as Hualon, Shinkong Synthetic Fiber, Far Eastern Textile, Tung-Yun, and Chung-Hsing. These new fibers can now be manufactured using various processes like Un-drawn yarn (UDY), Partial-drawn yarn (PDY), and Spin-drawn yarn (SDY) (Taiwan Economic Research Institute, 1991, 24–28, 36–43).

In contrast, no public counterpart to Taiwan's PFRC or CTIC has been established in South Korea.[16] The firms in South Korea were in general larger in size, and they had large abilities and incentives to do R & D. Using Kolon as an example, it set up the Kolon Technical Research Institute (KTRC) as early as 1975, and its goal was to do testing and improvement of nylon and polyester. In the early era, the KTRC aimed at adopting successfully from Toray more complicated technology and design processes in order to improve output quality and to obtain scale economies, whereas in the later period its goal, like that of the PRFC and firms in Taiwan, was to develop new materials and new processes (Enos and Park, 1988). We must mention that doing R & D is usually a governmental requirement in South Korea as part of the conditions to obtain financial and other supports. An example is Cheil, a member of the Samsung chaebol (conglomerate). In 1979, Cheil founded a central R & D laboratory whose budget in 1983 was $1.7 million (Amsden, 1989). This action was made in response to governmental pressures. In South Korea, if big business groups have been lent long-tern capital at subsidized interest rates (often at negative real interest rates), the government demands that they use the borrowed capital in productive ways. Part of the requirement is to do R & D. In fact, the Technology Development Promotion Act in Korea was passed in 1972 to incorporate legislative regulation making R & D compulsory. This act had little immediate effect in the 1970s because big businesses usually established in-house training institutes to fulfill the requirements. When Cheil set up the central R & D laboratory in 1979, however, the situation changed and many enterprises followed suit. As the government refunded tax credits and sweetened incentives, the number of centralized R & D laboratories rose from 3 in 1967, to 52 in 1980, and to 138 in 1984 (Amsden, 1989).

Industrial Structure

There were as many as thirty-nine firms making MF in Taiwan by 1977, as demonstrated in Table 3-2, whereas the number of firms was much smaller in South Korea, being only a little more than a dozen. Firm size in South Korea tended to be larger than that in Taiwan, and to give evidence, the fourteen Taiwanese nylon producers listed in Table 3-2 manufactured 80,000 tons of nylon in 1973, whereas the three South Korean nylon firms listed in Table 3-8 produced 83,000 tons in that year. In the same year, the nineteen Taiwanese polyester manufacturers as a whole produced 221,000 tons, whereas the eight South Korean firms produced 164,800 tons (*Japanese Fiber Yearbook*, 1980).

As a consequence of large firm size, the market structure was more concentrated in South Korea. To illustrate, in 1985 Tongyang and Kolon had a domestic nylon share in production of 50 percent and 30 percent respectively, whereas Sunkyong, Sam Yang, Cheil Synthetic, and Kolon had a domestic share of polyester in production at 25.4 percent, 20.6 percent, 15.1 percent, and 11.7 percent, respectively, in the same year (Enos and Park, 1988). Of the firms participating in the production of MF in Taiwan, although Far Eastern Textile, Formosa Plastics, Hualon, and Shinkong Synthetic Fiber were large conglomerates in manufacturing, only Formosa Plastics and Hualon were considered as large in the chemical industry. In South Korea, Cheil, Kolon, Sunkyong, Sam Yang, and Tongyang were all large chaebol groups in the chemical industry.

In Japan, the number of firms was also small according to Table 3-9. There were six nylon firms and six polyester firms in Japan, whereas the comparable numbers were fourteen and twenty in Taiwan. It follows that the market structure in South Korea is much closer to that in Japan.

The causes of different firm sizes in Taiwan and South Korea are related to different ways and degrees of government interventions. Political traditions differed in these two countries. In Taiwan an anti–big-entrepreneur philosophy was deep in the minds of economic bureaucrats.[7] As a result of this philosophy, the Nationalist officials were hostile toward large private business in mainland China before retreating to Taiwan and continued to be so in Taiwan at least until 1970. Nevertheless, entries were free in Taiwan, and most private firms were therefore small and medium-sized. In contrast, many existing firms in South Korea were large due to entry and other barriers, and the government, moreover, even promoted the expansion of existing firms using many policies. Indeed, the existence of large chaebols was not seen as a threat to the government regime as it would be in Taiwan. In South Korea a powerful nationalism that arose after thirty-five years of harsh Japanese colonialism supported the notion of the whole South Korean people as a team against the rest of the world.[18] The state and big businesses usually became a coalition in which the state specified the performance requirements on the firms[19] and guided the markets, and in return provided massive assistance using financial, tax, exchange rate, and tariff instruments. Combined with entry restrictions, these factors made South Korean firms large in size.

As an effect of different government interventions and political legacy in Taiwan vis-à-vis South Korea, the market structure became quite different. Taiwan's business groups are smaller and loosely integrated, whereas South Korea's business groups are large and highly central (e.g., Hamilton, Qrru, and Biggert, 1987). Entry barriers in the MF industry were large in South Korea, and thereby only a smaller number of large firms were able to enter, whereas the opposite occurred in Taiwan.

The difference in market structure led to the following results. Taiwan's small firms made them nimble, becoming quite sensitive and responsive to international opportunities and profit margins; Taiwan's numerous niche-seeking firms therefore needed less firm-specific help but had relatively more demand for stable prices and real exchange rates.[20] This in turn made the fraction of SMEs larger over time.[21] These SMEs always cut prices in the international market, leading to a small profit margin but a large international share as a whole. On the other hand, South Korea's small number of large firms helped to sustain a relatively well-developed policy network between the state and these firms, allowing the government to target its industry-specific policies at a smaller number of firms, each capable of a substantial response.

Consequently, the availability of massive assistance encouraged South Korean big firms, for example, to adopt the high-risk strategy of competing head-on with the U.S. and Japanese firms under their own brand names (Wade, 1990, 322).[22] The conglomerates emerged as South Korea's champions through the aforementioned reciprocity (Amsden, 1989).

CONCLUDING REMARKS AND FUTURE RESEARCH

Industrialization and catch-up are important issues in economic development. The inquiry of industrialization can be traced back to Rosenstein-Rodan (1943) and Nurkse (1953). The recently emerged new growth theory has revived the study of this issue under the initiation of Murphy, Shliefer, and Vishay (1989).[23] One of the important policies leading to success in industrialization and catch-up is the adoption and improvement of suitable science and technology according to existing wisdom. Absorptive capability is a prerequisite for transition from traditional sectors to modern sectors, as emphasized by Abramovitz (1986). In general, adopting modern labor-intensive technology is a better strategy at earlier stages, because a developing economy usually has surplus laborers but lacks capital. It has been shown that the textile and apparel industry is the winner to pick in this aspect (Been-Lon Chen, 1996). The switch to capital- and skill-intensive industries is necessary when the technology of textiles and apparel become mature in this economy. A critical point of transition from textiles/apparel to more technology-sophisticated industries is the creation of the MF industry. Successful experiences in adopting technology of MF are useful in providing constructive examples, shedding light on the transition in development. This chapter has as such documented the technology-adoption and catch-up experience in Taiwan.

In characterizing the development experience in Taiwan and comparing it with South Korea, we have found that they shared some common points. Nevertheless, disparities seem to override the two countries. They differed in the initiation of the industry, sources of technology, forms of technology adoption, R & D, and market structure. It is found that the differences are mainly due to different colonial linkages and different government interventions.

We must note the recent experience in China, because it has undergone a dramatic economic transformation since the late 1970s, leading to its rapid economic growth. Among Chinese commodities important in the world markets, textiles and apparel are the most exceptional. In fact, the growth rates of both real value added and exports of textile and apparel in China from 1971–1973 to 1981–1983 have been larger than those of the average of three Asian NIEs (Hong Kong, South Korea, and Taiwan) (Anderson and Park, 1989). The growth of textile and apparel there seems to promote the development of its MF manufacturing. This is evident from the fact that China's global market of MF increased from about 2 percent in 1980 to more than 5 percent in 1984, surpassing South Korea to become a large world producer. Its global market share reached more than 10.35 percent in 1993, being the third largest in the world (refer to Figure 3-5.) It is well known that China attracted a lot of foreign direct investment in the past two decades, especially from Japan and the Asian NIEs, and we believe that their MF technology was adopted from abroad, mainly through joint ventures, although we do not have data available to verify this point. In any case, they are undergoing the important step in industrialization, connecting labor-intensive industries and skill- and capital-intensive industries. The experiences in Taiwan and South Korea are useful for China, as China is now challenging Taiwan's role of MF supply in the international market.

Given the challenge of China, some words should probably be said about the future of Taiwan's MF industry. As China challenges Taiwan in terms of cheaper raw labor, Taiwan surely cannot compete with China for products with large labor intensity. In economic development, the well-known product cycle theory suggests that comparative advantage dictates the flow of international trade and therefore specialization in production. The product cycle theory thus indicates that Taiwan should launch the MF sector into one with an even larger capital and human capital intensity. Italy may be a role model to follow, but that experience explains better for apparel rather than for textiles and MF. For apparel, a kind of final product, what is important is probably its brand name that can attract consumers. For textiles and man-made fiber, two kinds of intermediate inputs, the emphasis should be on the development and invention of newer and finer fiber (a kind of horizontal innovation) and on upgrading the quality of existing products (a kind of vertical innovation). These two ways could generate a larger value added of MF industry, and Taiwan could maintain its market niche even under severe competition from China. They are difficult ways, but there seem to be few better alternatives. Of course, the government, especially the CRSO under ITRI, needs to play a major supporting role.

Let us finally point out some possible limitations of this chapter. We did not distinguish which way of technology adoption of MF was better. Indeed, because both experiences turned out to be successful and remarkable, both are well able to serve as learning models. Nor did we elucidate the process of technology adoption and improvements specific to a firm. We instead focused on investigating the broad picture of the industry. The reason is that this industry involved too many firms, and different firms had dissimilar stages and directions of development. As a result, there were many different firm-specific processes of technology adoption. For our purposes of documenting and characterizing the experiences of Taiwan's MF industry and of making comparisons with South Korea, it suffices to depict a broad picture. Moreover, the picture that we illustrate not only describes this particular industry, it may also apply to other industries from which we can draw more general lessons and lend instructions to latecomers. Nevertheless, a case study of one or two representative firms may be valuable in understanding how it or they made plans to create plants, decided a proper technology to employ, and searched for foreign partners to cooperate. We can make an investigation as to what kind of specific assistance the government has provided in each case. By doing so, it complements the study of the whole industry. This suggests an avenue for further research.

NOTES

1. For the relationship between industrialization and the role of textiles/apparel, see Been-Lon Chen (1996).

2. The share of chemicals in total manufacturing has been used as an indicator of industrial "depth" in production—for example, see Wade (1990).

3. Only exports of cotton and man-made textiles are illustrated here because no data are available for apparel regarding the distinction of cotton and man-made fiber.

4. External economies are one of the major engines of sources of economic growth in recently popularized endogenous growth models pioneered by Romer (1986) and Lucas (1988). For evidence of external economies in Taiwan's two-digit manufacturing industries, see Chan, Chen, and Cheung (1995).

5. The government built a PVC plant first. Although the hard-liners in the Nationalist party fought to have it run as a public enterprise, a U.S. advisor defeated them using the threat of reducing U.S. aid. The government handed the plant over to Y. C. Wang in 1957 to run as a private company (Gold, 1986). Y. C. Wang paid for the purchase, but the amount is not known. This private company was Formosa Plastics. It later grew to become the largest Taiwanese conglomerate in manufacturing.

6. The following summary concerning new entrants draws partially on Chow (1973) and Sun-Ming Chen (1975).

7. Pacific, Jen Dar, and Dah Ming stopped operation. Pacific and Jen Dar were later purchased by Fu-Point Synthetic Corporation, whereas Dah Ming was rented by Hualon.

8. Bao-Chen, Ko Hua, Hsing Hsing, United Nylon, and Hualon were merged and named Hualon.

9. The major public research complex in Taiwan doing applied research for most manufacturing industries is called the Industrial Technology Research Institute (ITRI). ITRI has several organizations, among which is the Chemical

Research and Service Organization (CRSO). The PFRC is one of the centers under the CRSO. We discuss more about the PFRC later in the chapter.

10. As a referee suggested, we could compare the unit value of the four kinds of man-made fiber among Taiwan, South Korea, and Japan to see whether the man-made fiber technology in Taiwan caught up with Japan and was superior than Japan. The data breaking man-made fiber into the four kinds under consideration were available only in the "Output of Principal Industrial Products" table (e.g., see *Industry of Free China*, 1995, 84(5), Table 3, Council for Economic Planning and Development; or *Industrial Production Statistics Monthly*, 1995, Ministry of Economic Affairs; or *Taiwan Statistical Data Book*, 1995, Council for Economic Planning and Development), whose data are in terms of quantity only. Yet, all data available in terms of value are classified into a larger group; they are in either a two-digit category or a three-digit category. When the values are reported, the quantity was not available. As a result, we cannot construct the unit price.

11. For studies in the growth of South Korea's textile industry, see Kim (1980), among others.

12. Among few exceptions in the manufacturing industries is the public Pohang Iron and Steel Co. (POSCO).

13. See Lewis (1955) for a similar argument. For a modern theoretical formulation of this argument, see Baland and Francois (1996).

14. One of the important architects of China Manmade Fiber Corporation, United Nylon Corporation, and Hualon was Mr. Feng-Jang Leu who was born in Jiang-su province and held a college degree in German. The founders of Ko Hua, Liang Yu, Jen Dar, Ta Hsing, Chung-Hsing, Far Eastern Textile, and Hsing Hsing came from Jiang-su province, whereas those of Bao Chen and Pacific were from Sun-ton province and Ho-pei province, respectively. All these firms have Tsiangtao or Shanghai connections.

15. While gross savings in GDP was above 20 percent by 1965, 25.6 percent in 1970, and 31.3 percent in 1981 in Taiwan (Council for Economic Planing and Development, *Taiwan Statistical Data Book*), it was only 14.09 percent by 1965 and 23.52 percent by 1970 in South Korea (Bank of Korea, *Economic Statistics Yearbook*).

16. An exception was the public-funded research institute doing electronics R & D, called Electronics and Telecommunication Research Institute (ETRI). The contribution of the ETRI in upgrading South Korean electronics skill was much less significant than that of Taiwan (Amsden, 1989).

17. This philosophy has descended since the founding of modern China, specified in the book *Three Principles of the People*, written by founding father, Dr. Sun Yat-Sen.

18. See Amsden (1989) and South Korean authors cited therein for this point.

19. Well-known requirements include, among others, performance of production and exports and expenditures on R & D.

20. This is probably one of the reasons that the peripheral equipment of the computer industry and the machinery industry in Taiwan outperformed those of South Korea after the mid-1980s.

21. The employment share of manufacturing SMEs increased over time after the first oil shock, from 35.6 percent in 1970 to 58.65 percent in 1991 as documented in the working paper version of Chen and Hsu (2000), which is available from the authors.

22. For example, the exports of South Korean autos using their own brands expanded rapidly after the late 1980s.

23. Other papers along this line include Matsuyama (1991, 1992), Baland and Francois (1996), Ciccone and Matsuyama (1996), Yanagawa (1996), and Chen and Shimomura (1998).

REFERENCES

Abramovitz, Moses. 1962. "Catching Up, Forging Ahead, and Falling Behind." *Journal of Economic History*, vol. 46: 385–406.

Amsden, Alice H. 1989. *Asia's Next Giant: South Korea and Late Industrialization*. New York: Oxford University Press.

Anderson, Kym, and Young-il Park. 1989. "China and the International Relocation of World Textile and Clothing Activity," *Weltwirschaftlichs Archiv*, 129–48.

Baland, Jean-Marie, and Patrick Francois. 1996. "Innovation, Monopolies and the Poverty Trap," *Journal of Development Economics*, vol. 49: 151–178.

Chan, Vei-Lin, Been-Lon Chen, and Kee-Nam Cheung. 1995. "External Economies in Taiwan's Manufacturing Industries." *Contemporary Economic Review*, vol. 13, no. 4: 118–130.

Chen, Been-Lon. "Picking winners and industrialization in Taiwan." *Journal of International Trade and Economic Development*, vol. 5: 137–159.

Chen, Been-Lon, and Koji Shimomura. "Self-Fulfilling Expectations and Economic Growth: Model of Technology Adoption and Industrialization." *International Economic Review*, vol. 39: 151–170.

Chen, Been-Lon, and Mei Hsu. 2000. "Labor Productivity of Small and Large Manufacturing Firms: The Case of Taiwan." *Contemporary Economic Policy*, vol. 18: 270–283.

Chen, Sun-Ming. 1975. "Manmade Fiber in Taiwan." *Quarterly Journal of Bank of Taiwan*, vol. 20: 255–310.

China Credit Information Service. Various years. *The Largest Corporations in Taiwan*. Taipei: China Credit Information Service Ltd.

———. Various years. *Business Groups in Taiwan*. Taipei: China Credit Information Service Ltd.

Chow, Wen. 1973. "Textile Industry in Taiwan." *Quarterly Journal of Bank of Taiwan*, vol. 18: 95–124.

Chu, Wan-Wen, and Ming-Chu Tsai. "Linkage and Uneven Growth: A Study of Taiwan's Manmade Fibre Industry. In *The Political Economy of Taiwan's Development into the 21st Century*, eds. G. Ranis, S. S. Hu, and Y. P. Chu. Cheltenham: Edward Elgar.

Ciccone, Antonio, and Kiminori Matsuyama. (1996). "Start-up Costs and Pecuniary Externalities as Barriers to Economic Development." *Journal of Development Economics*, vol. 49: 33–59.

Enos, J. L., and W. H. Park. (1988). *The Adoption and Diffusion of Imported Technology: The Case of Korea*. London: Croom Helm.

Gold, T. 1986. *State and Society in the Taiwan Miracle*. Armonk, N.Y.: M.E. Sharpe.

Hamilton, G., M. Qrru, and N. Biggart. 1987. "Enterprise Groups in East Asia: An Organization Analysis." *Financial Economic Review*, vol. 161: 78–106.

Kim, Yang Bong. 1980. "The Growth and Structural Change of the Textile Industry." In *Macroeconomic and Industrial Development in Korea*, ed. C. K. Park. Seoul: Korea Development Institute.

Lewis, Arthur W. 1955. *Theory of Economic Growth*. London: Allen and Urwin.

Lucas, Robert, Jr. 1988. "The Mechanics of Economic Development." *Journal of Monetary Economics*, vol. 22: 3–42.

Matsuyama, Kiminori. 1991. Increasing Returns, Industrialization and Indeterminacy of Equilibria." *Quarterly Journal of Economics*, vol. 106: 617–650.

——. 1992. "The Market Size, Entrepreneurship, and the Big Push." *Journal of the Japanese and International Economics*, vol. 6: 347–364.

Mckinnon, Ronald I. 1973. *Money and Capital in Economic Development*. Washington: The Brookings Institution.

Murphy, Kevin, Andrew Shleifer, and Robert Vishny. 1991. "Industrialization and the Big Push." *Journal of Political Economy*, vol. 97: 1103–1026.

Nurkse, Raganer. 1953. *Problem of Capital Formation in Underdeveloped Countries*. New York: Oxford University Press.

Rodrik, Dani. 1996. "Coordination Failures and Government Policy: A Model with Applications to East Asia and Eastern Europe." *Journal of International Economics*, vol. 40: 1–22.

Romer, Paul. 1986. "Increasing Returns and Long-Run Growth." *Journal of Political Economy*, vol. 94: 1002–1037.

Rosenstein-Rodan, Paul. 1943. "Problem of Industrialization of Eastern and South-eastern Europe." *Economic Journal*, vol. 53: 204–207.

Shieh, Gwo-Shyong. 1992. *Boss Island: The Subcontracting Network and Micro-Entrepreneurship in Taiwan's Development*. New York: Peter Lang.

Suzuki, Tsuneo. 1999. "Industrial Policy and the Development of the Synthetic Fibre Industry: Industrial Policy as a Means for Promoting Economic Growth. In *Policies for Competitiveness: Comparing Business–Government Relationship in the Golden Age of Capitalism*, eds. Hideaki Miyajima, Takeo Kikkawa and Takashi Hikino. Oxford: Oxford University Press.

Taiwan Economic Research Institute. 1991. *Taiwan Economic Research Monthly*, vol. 14: 24–28, 36–43.

Tran, Van Tho. "Foreign Capital and Technology in the Process of Catching Up by the Developing Countries: The Experience of the Synthetic Fibre Industry in the Republic of Korea." *Developing Economies*, vol. 26: 386–402.

Wade, Robert. 1990. *Governing the Market: Economic Theory and the Role of Government in East Asian Industrialization*. Princeton, NJ: Princeton University Press.

Yanagawa, Noriyuki. 1966. "Economic Development in a World with Many Countries." *Journal of Development Economics*, vol. 49: 272–288.

Foreign Investment, Multinational, and Boomerang Effects

Roles of Foreign Direct Investments in Taiwan's Economic Growth

Steven A.Y. Lin

INTRODUCTION

Taiwan's accession to the World Trade Organization (WTO) and recent advancements in information technology[1] facilitate Taiwan's efforts in lifting itself onto a higher level of economic growth. Strategic inward and outward foreign direct investment (FDI) coupled with appropriate economic reforms could provide the means of this transformation. The necessary institutional and policy changes involve further upgrading of its industries, economic privatization, financial sector reform, and the formation of more modern enterprises.

Through inward FDI, Taiwanese firms have received technology[2] and management skills from foreign multinationals, and they have benefited from the multinationals' marketing networks and market information advantages. Thus, Taiwan needs to selectively attract more inward FDI and encourage the formation of more strategic alliances between its businesses and foreign firms. Through outward FDI, Taiwan's businesses have continued to extend their value chain of product supply and increase their foreign trades. The outward FDI needs to be more strategic, and their functions and locations need to be expanded. The government's further encouragement for forming more modern enterprises through acquisitions and mergers would enhance the efficiency of Taiwan's businesses by providing opportunities to capture scale and scope economies as well as providing access to the richer set of resources needed to operate in global markets.

By encouraging strategic alliances and greater private sector participation in research and development, Taiwan would facilitate the upgrading of its industries. The government can help to form larger and more modern enterprises by speeding up the privatization of "state-owned" enterprises. The advantages of larger and more modern enterprises, combined with strategic FDI, would place Taiwan in a better position to catch up with more advanced economies. Taiwan's accession to the WTO and recent advancements in Internet and related technologies would ease this transformation. A healthy financial sector should support and sustain a robust economy as well.

Taiwan faces more challenges in its pursuit of (advanced) industrial country status. In its continuing efforts to promote economic growth through export-oriented policies, Taiwan is encountering pressures from many sides. Until recent years, Taiwan's investment and trade were concentrated in East and Southeast Asia. Its economic dependency on mainland China has been especially high. Consequently, Taiwan's economy is highly exposed to economic fluctuations in Asia and mainland China. In addition, firms in mainland China and the Association of Southeast Asian (ASEAN) countries (Malaysia, Thailand, Indonesia, and the Philippines) are rapidly catching up to Taiwanese firms in terms of manufacturing technology. They have replaced many Taiwanese firms in producing labor-intensive and relatively low-tech products. To be economically prudent, Taiwanese firms need to further diversify their outward FDI. The government should provide more services, encouragement, and incentives on this matter. After its accession to the WTO, Taiwan would have more flexibility in diversifying its outward FDI and still retain some flexibility in managing its levels of economic contact with mainland China.

The challenge facing Taiwan's firms is their ability to continually identify new products or processes that will enable them to maintain respectable rates of growth in exports. Upgrading of its industries has become slower and more expensive in recent years. Further advances in science and technology depend on Taiwan's ability in research and development (R & D). The R & D efforts need not all be on the frontier of research.[3] It is also likely that a certain degree of policy intervention is needed to correct market failures.[4] But the small size of Taiwanese firms is a handicap in this effort. There are distinct scale advantages for large firms in developing or adapting new products and processes. The government needs to encourage greater formation of larger and more modern firms through acquisitions and mergers as well as to speed up privatization of its generally larger "state-owned" businesses.

This chapter is organized as follows: After these introductory remarks, a review of Taiwan's foreign trade and direct foreign investment over recent years is provided, and the changing nature and role of its outward FDI with respect to economic growth is analyzed and discussed. In addition, the helpful role of the WTO and recent advancements in information technology are identified, and policy suggestions for the future are presented. Then Taiwan's increasing economic interactions with mainland China and ASEAN countries are analyzed and their policy implications given. Next the importance of forming more modern enterprises, the privatization of "state-owned" enterprises, the upgrading of industries in Taiwan, and the crucial role of a healthy financial sector are discussed. Lastly, some conclusions are presented.

TAIWAN'S FOREIGN TRADE AND DIRECT INVESTMENT

Inward Direct Investment

Inward foreign direct investment played a key role in integrating Taiwan into the foreign multinationals' international division of labor and aiding in the transference of technology and management skills to Taiwanese firms (Okuda, 1994). The small- and medium-sized[5] enterprises (SMEs) are the mainstay of Taiwan's export-led economy. They also benefited from the multinationals' marketing networks, and superior market information. Taiwan needs to selectively attract more inward FDI and encourage the formation of more strategic alliances between its firms and foreign businesses.

The inward foreign direct investment in Taiwan was very small as a percentage of the country's total capital formation. It fluctuated around a mere 2 percent for the time period between 1965 and 1986. As a percentage of the manufacturing sector's capital formation, the FDI had never advanced beyond 7.5 percent for the same time period (*Taiwan Statistical Data Book*, 1999). However, the foreign sector in Taiwan in the mid-1970s exported 40 to 55 percent of its goods and purchased approximately 50 percent of its materials locally. Foreign firms contributed significantly to the expansion of Taiwan's export capacity (Schive, 1990).

Taiwan drew slightly more foreign direct investment from Japan than from the United States in most of the recent years due to Japan's geographical proximity and because Taiwan is a former Japanese colony (see Table 4-1 and Hatch and Yamamura, 1996). Initial Japanese investment focused on labor-intensive industries and gradually moved into low-end high-tech industries (Kozmetsky and Yue, 1997). From the

1980s, Japan favored investments in East and Southeast Asia for global strategic considerations as well as a means of achieving economies of scale, scope, and networking. By capitalizing on the region's deepening division of labor, Japanese manufacturers used the region in part as a platform for exports to developed markets in the United States and Europe. As a result, most of these host countries, including Taiwan, generated a substantial trade surplus with the United States and deficit with Japan. Asian economies are the most active exploiters of the "trade-as-aid" policy of the United States.

Outward Direct Investment and Trade

Taiwan and South Korean enterprises started to capitalize on the Asian region's deepening division of labor as well in the mid-1980s. This time it was Taiwan's and South Korea's turn to shift production of labor-intensive products to the ASEAN countries and the Peoples' Republic of China (PRC). Before the mid-1980s, Taiwan's pattern of industrialization, outward direct investment, and trade was similar to that of Japan in the 1960s and 1970s. However, unlike South Korea, Taiwan was unable or unwilling to build the heavy industries and conglomerates.

Subsequent to the mid-1980s the SMEs of Taiwan experienced at least two major transformations in this export-led economy. Faced with currency appreciation and rising labor costs, these enterprises ex-

TABLE 4-1.   Taiwan's Inward FDI from Selected Countries, 1993–1998

Country	1993	1994	1995	1996	1997	1998
			($ million U.S.)			
Japan	278	395	572.8	545.8	854.1	539.7
Singapore	63	174.7	75	171	450	239.7
Hong Kong	169.3	250.7	146.6	267	237.1	274.5
United States	235.1	326.8	1,303.90	489.1	491.5	952
Panama	16.7	22.8	24.3	54.5	57.2	49.1
United Kingdom	58.7	30.3	195	36	90.6	75
Germany	33.5	91.5	23.7	37.5	66.6	63.4
France	8.5	15.6	11.3	19.9	12	23.2
Holland	85.8	79.9	75.4	28.5	103.9	125.5
Others	141.4	136.7	32.9	637.7	151.6	1,211.90
Total	1,090	1,524	2,757	2,290	3,879	3,554

Source: Ministry of Economic Affairs, and *Overseas Chinese Yearbook*, Taiwan, 1998. Chung Hung Institution for Economic Research, *Economic Outlook.*

panded scope and depth of the international division of labor in order to lower their costs of production and thus improve their export competitiveness. They stepped into the original design manufacturing (ODM) stage from original equipment manufacturing (OEM) or simple contract manufacturing. They also increased their overseas production platforms with outward FDI in order to improve their export competitiveness. The host countries were initially ASEAN countries and later mainland China. The finished goods were then exported to third countries, usually the United States, or sold in the host countries.

Many of the technologically upgraded enterprises moved into the higher technology industries in the mid-1990s (Industrial Technology Information Services, 1997). They also expanded their activities from primarily manufacturing to include marketing activities, especially the logistic management aspects of marketing. Before this time, marketing was foreign to these enterprises because most of them were contract manufacturers or manufacturers with minor original designs engaged in manufacturing engineering and product development. Starting in the mid-1990s, Taiwan's SMEs were offered the opportunity to extend their supply chain to global logistic management. This function was formerly executed by Japanese and U.S. multinationals, but these foreign multinationals later found it more advantageous to concentrate on the customer end of the value chain than production and the logistic management of marketing (Wise and Baumgartner, 1999). They concentrated on cultivating customer loyalty and on providing technical support services to boost their market shares.

Major high-tech distributors, such as Dell and Compaq, established the international procurement office (IPO) in Taiwan in order to keep their cost low and to secure their supply. Now they have changed by requiring that Taiwanese firms build shipment warehouses at specified locations in order to reduce further their inventory costs and product delivery times. Meeting these demands, the Taiwanese firms have been establishing supply centers near consumer centers in order to secure OEM orders. Establishment of the centers was facilitated by advancements in the Internet and related technologies and logistic businesses such as FedEx and UPS. According to a recent news report in the *Wall Street Journal* (Dec. 14, 1999, A17), more than half a dozen of the Taiwanese Information Technology companies have subsidiaries in the United States, and these subsidiaries' functions went beyond the logistic management of their products.

Many Taiwanese contractors are not content with sitting at the bottom of the economic value chain. Outsourcing and supply chain management has helped many of the better-managed contract manufacturers. Again, according to the *Wall Street Journal* (March 10, 2000, A19), Yue Yuen Industrial (Holdings), Ltd., of Taiwan has a better performance than its biggest customer, Nike, the maker of Air Jordan sneakers. For example, in creating its own brand Air Yue Yuen, the company is outsourcing in China, Indonesia, and Vietnam and has adopted the just-in-time practices originated by the Japanese auto industry. Although Nike would be scared if Yue Yuen said today that it will not supply Nike anymore, many brand-name U.S. companies are trying to get their products to their American customers quicker by manufacturing closer to the United States—for example, in Mexico. Recent advancements in information technology and shipping services (such as FedEx and UPS) helped Taiwanese manufacturers in their global logistic management. However, expanding their outsourcing beyond East and Southeast Asia in order to be closer to consumer markets is needed as well. Several well-known Japanese firms, such as Sony, have factories in Mexico near the U.S. border. These production or assembly platforms are benefiting from low labor costs and tariffs, and they are in close proximity to their consumer markets and subsidiaries in the United States.

Most of Taiwan's foreign direct investments are in mainland China and ASEAN countries for offshore production. They also invested in the United States to acquire their logistic management and to be close to consumer markets. Foreign direct investment in Europe is negligible. Table 4-2 presents Taiwan's outward FDI in selected major countries for the years 1993 through 1998. For the years between 1987 and 1997,

TABLE 4-2. Taiwan's Outward FDI in Selected Major Countries, 1993–1998

	(mill. U.S. $)					
Country	1993	1994	1995	1996	1997	1998
Japan	63.3	22.7	8.8	6.8	32.3	29.6
Hong Kong	161.9	127.3	99.6	59.9	141.6	68.6
P.R.C.	3,168.4	962.2	1,092.7	1,229.2	4,334.3	2,034.6
SE Asia*	275.2	289.4	218.0	486.8	555.8	367.4
United States	529.1	143.9	248.2	271.3	547.4	598.7
United Kingdom	237.9	16.9	8.2	6.1	13.4	9.7
Germany	5.3	1.8	5.2	4.0	3.8	6.4
France	n.a.	0.2	0.9	0.2	0.1	6.5
Holland	10.4	0.3	20.4	0.2	11.1	8.6
Others	1.4	52.3	42.2	100.5	100.6	165.9
Total	4,452.9	1,617.0	1,744.2	2,165.0	5,740.4	3,296.0

* Includes Thailand, Malaysia, Indonesia, and the Philippines.
Source: Ministry of Economic Affairs and Overseas Chinese Yearbook, Taiwan, 1998.

Taiwan made outward foreign direct investments of approximately $20 billion in mainland China. An unofficial estimate is $41 billion by the end of 1998, according to the *Wall Street Journal* (February 3, 1999, A17). The investment in mainland China alone was more than 36 percent of Taiwan's total accumulated foreign direct investment. Investment in Asia is 59.7 percent of its total.

In 1997, Taiwan exports were valued at $122 billion and imports at $114.4 billion. Asia was the most important trading region for Taiwan (50.7 percent of total Taiwan exports and 48.4 percent of total Taiwan imports; see Table 4-3). Next to Asia came North America and then the European Common Market. Ten years earlier, North America was the most important trading region followed by Asia and the European Common Markets. At the end of 1998, Taiwan had a trade surplus (exports value exceeds imports value) of $9.7 billion with the United States; $22.9 billion with Hong Kong; a deficit of $17.7 billion with Japan; and a deficit of $2.32 billion with ASEAN countries (not shown in Table 4-3).

Taiwan's outward FDI induced more exports since the mid-1980s (Schive, 1990). However, as contacts with the host economies expanded and linkages increased, supplies of intermediate components and raw materials have become more localized as well (see Table 4-4 and Schive, 1999). In addition, numerous satellite companies established foreign subsidiaries to supply their core companies that had moved (Schive, 1999).[6] This phenomenon is similar to Japanese FDI in manufacturing (Lipsey, 1998).

Taiwanese firms in recent years have seen increasing geographic fragmentation in their production of high-tech products as well (see Table 4-5). As outward FDI increased, Taiwan's enterprises moved forward along the supply chain to global logistics by distributing purchase orders between domestic and overseas production bases. In 1998, the domestic manufacturing industry allocated nearly 11 percent of its orders to overseas production.

TABLE 4-3.   Regional Distribution of Taiwan's Trade

Export to Region			Import from Region		
	1997 (%)	*1987 (%)*		*1997 (%)*	*1987 (%)*
Asia	50.7	28.2	Asia	48.4	45.0
Hong Kong	23.9		Japan	27.0	
North America	25.5	47.0	North America	21.5	23.7
European C.M.	13.8	13.2	European C.M.	15.3	12.7
Total Export	122 bill. U.S.$		Total Import	114 bill. U.S.$	

Source: Ministry of Economic Affairs and *Economic Outlook* (various issues); Lin (1999).

TABLE 4-4. Sources of Intermediate Inputs of Taiwan's Overseas Subsidiaries

					(% of total by country)					
					Raw Material Supplied					
	Year	*All*	*U.S.*	*Japan*	*P.R.C.*	*Malaysia*	*Singapore*	*Thailand*	*Philippines*	*Indonesia*
Taiwan	1996	50	57	49	50	37	19	32	50	42
	1997	46	55	38	45	34	19	27	52	44
Taiwanese	1996	15	10	16	18	17	10	9	10	9
Subsidiaries in host	1997	18	11	27	21	18	10	10	11	6
country										
					Components Semi-Finished Products Supplied					
	Year	*All*	*U.S.*	*Japan*	*P.R.C.*	*Malaysia*	*Singapore*	*Thailand*	*Philippines*	*Indonesia*
Taiwan	1996	54	63	52	53	38	40	41	65	48
	1997	50	61	50	48	34	40	39	62	47
Taiwanese	1996	16	3	20	19	23	0	12	2	10
Subsidiaries in host	1997	18	5	22	22	25	0	13	3	10
country										

Source: Ministry of Economic Affairs, Survey on Foreign Investment by the Manufacturing Industry, 1999; Schive (1999).

The high-tech industries have higher percentages of overseas production for some intermediate parts. These industries included information electronics, electrical machinery, and precision instruments. We observed a similar phenomenon for U.S. and Japanese multinationals (Lipsey, 1998). Among the major overseas production sites for Taiwan, mainland China shared the highest percentage of production for almost all of the high-tech products, except telecommunication equipment (Table 4-5). Now the high-tech industry is becoming the mainstay of the Taiwanese economy (Industrial Technology Information Services, 1997). Its increasing geographic fragmentation in production calls for the government and businesses to emphasize global logistics management (Schive, 1999).

TABLE 4-5. Procurement Order Sharing in Taiwan's Manufacturing, 1998

		(% of total)						
			Domestic Production		*Foreign Production*			
	Est. Values				*Japan, United States, Mainland*			
Industry	*(million $)**	*Total Order*	*Own Prod.*	*Contract*	*Europe*	*China*	*S.E. Asia*	*Others*
Manufacturing		100	84.95	4.4	2.37	4.42	3.42	0.44
Information electronics	6,351	100	76.97	5.06	4.28	8.83	4.59	0.28
Electronics, electric machinery	6,209	100	76.94	5.12	4.37	8.64	4.66	0.28
Data storage processing		100	68.42	5.05	8.89	10.45	6.92	0.27
Telecom		100	73.86	3.81	0.09	7.14	15.1	0
Electronic components		100	82.06	4.93	1.95	8.15	2.68	0.23
Precision instruments	1,441	100	78.12	2.79	0.61	17.08	1.37	0.03
Metal machinery	4,251	100	92.61	5.01	0.71	1.29	0.26	0.12
Chemicals	4 ,163	100	86/95	2.1	1.44	2.46	6	1.05
Consumer products	3,024	100	88.2	5.3	1.95	2.25	1.63	0.67

* Estimated with the value of exports 1998 (*Taiwan Statistical Data Book*, 1999)
Source: Ministry of Economic Affairs, Statistics Dept., Survey of Manufacturing Activities, July 1999; Schive (1999).

The resale ratio (i.e., exports to elsewhere as a ratio of sales in the host economies) of the Taiwanese subsidiaries differs between small and large enterprises. In 1997 it was at approximately 42 percent for small enterprises; for larger enterprise it was 39 percent. In any case, resale back to Taiwan was highest for information electronics. It could indicate that the outward FDI was made in order to purchase the intermediate components. Concerning the intrafirm division of labor (between the parent and the subsidiary), the overseas subsidiaries produced 32.04 percent of goods identical to their parents (Schive, 1999). These FDIs were made primarily to lower production costs abroad.

INCREASING ECONOMIC INTERACTIONS WITH CHINA AND ASEAN

Mainland China

Taiwan's investment in China through third parties was estimated at more than $41 billion by the end of 1998 based on an unofficial estimate, (*Wall Street Journal*, February 3, 1999, A17).[7] Over 90 percent of these investments produce goods for export. By 1995, China already replaced Taiwan as one of the top-five suppliers to the United States of the following labor-intensive products: apparel and other textile products, leather and leather products, miscellaneous plastic, and so on (Feenstra et al., 1998).

Table 4-6 presents the stock values at year-end 1996 of Taiwan's manufacturing outward direct investments in China by industry. For several industries, the dollar amount investments exceeded half of its total outward FDIs for the same industries. The labor-intensive industries such as apparel, textiles, leather and leather products, and plastic products are among those industries. Based on the average annual growth rate in value added for these labor-intensive industries in real terms for the time period 1991–1995, the average annual growth rates were negatives, ranging from a negative 1 percent to a negative 12 percent. This is an indication of the hallowing out of these industries in Taiwan. Surplus labor, cheap wages, and available land, in addition to cultural and linguistic affinity, made China very attractive for Taiwanese manufacturers of these industries.

We observed a similar phenomenon for the precision instrument industry that is a relatively high-tech industry for Taiwan (see Table 4-6). We find that PRC has the highest percentage of Taiwanese firms' procurement sharing in this industry as well (refer to Table 4-5). Many medium-sized and large-sized companies, instead of the usual small-sized companies, are making investments in mainland China in recent years. Among these enterprises, companies from the electronic and

TABLE 4-6. Stock Values (year-end 1996) of Taiwan's Manufacturing; Outward Foreign Direct Investments in Mainland China by Industry

	Total Outward FDIs[1] ($ million)	Investments in Mainland as % of Total Outward FDIs	Inv. in Mainland as % of Gross Domestic Fixed Capital	Average Annual Rate of Value-add (%)
Food & beverage		66	16.9	3
Textiles	543,041	**43.3	8.1	-2
Apparel	83,069	*68.5	50.8	-11
Leather & leather products	9,194	* 88.9	29.3	-12
Wood & bamboo, etc.	106,253	*68.3	68.9	15
Paper products & printing	230,753	*42.2	3.5	-1
Chemical products	1,141,491	**29.8	5.2	9
Rubber products	217,238	*53.4	20.5	-3
Plastic products	29,263	95.6		
Non-metallic minerals	386,041	**48.3	13	5
Basic metals & metal products	606,740	**50.2	4.3	6
Machinery	39,157	83.3	6.9	5
Electronic & electric appliances	1,898,117	**37.9	8.2	11
Transport equipment	207,841	65.4	7.9	2
Precision instruments	36,066	92.1	78.3	-3

[1] Approved amount, unofficial statistics are more than twice higher.
** Industries not under restriction for outward investment to mainland.
* Industries under restriction for outward direct investments to mainland.
Sources: Ministry of Economic Affairs and *Economic Outlook*, Taiwan (various Issues). Lin (1999). Chung Hwa Institution for Economic Research, *Economic Outlook.*

electric appliances industry are the top investors; personal computer giant Acer, Inc., is an example.

In contrast, we observed the positive average growth rates in value added for the following industries: chemical products, basic metals and metal products, and the electronic and electric appliances industries. They had positive rates of 5 to 11 percent for the time period 1991–1995 (refer to Table 4-6). Thus, FDI in these industries induced complementary effects on the respective industries in Taiwan through division of labor across the Taiwan straits. The dollar amount of Taiwan's investment in China for these industries is close to 50 percent of Taiwan's total outward investments in the respective industries as well. Outward FDIs in China of these industries also exerted pressure for Taiwan to upgrade its manufacturing industries. Investments in the food and beverage, machinery, rubber products, and transportation equipment industries, to a lesser degree, also created complementary effects on the respective industries in Taiwan.

Montgomery and Porter (1991) argue that outward foreign direct investments need to be selective, and certain technologies need to be protected at home base. The high degree of economic dependence on mainland China in terms of investment and trade is alarming. Continual diversification of investment and trade across different countries and continents is a more prudent business strategy. Taiwan could also encourage and assist its businesses to diversify or increase their investments near centers of consumer markets. The importance of marketing research and establishment of marketing networks cannot be over-emphasized.

> In comparison with Japanese industrial structures, Taiwan has quite a lot of similarities due to historical and geographical factors. In one way, Japanese industries have been relocating high cost production offshore except for key materials and components as a part of their global strategic plans. Likewise, some of the industries in Taiwan are also under the pressure of relocating high cost production overseas. However, Taiwan clearly lacks a global strategy and the leverage of controlling the raw materials and components. A consortium of some kind of strategic alliance may be the only solution to survive if the Japanese technology transfers skip Taiwan. (Industrial Technology Information Service, p. 9)

Diversification of Taiwan's outward FDI could be to maximize the businesses' long-term rates of return and to reduce possible risks on a global basis.

Taiwan's overconcentration of investment and trade in Asia and mainland China in particular yielded certain benefits and costs to Taiwan's quest for higher rates of economic growth. The drawbacks became more prominent because the concerned parties at both sides of the Taiwan straits are political rivals (Chow, 1997; Lin, 1999). Taiwan's admission to the WTO will facilitate its further diversification of export and outward FDI markets to the United States and the European Common Market, although any WTO agreement on FDI is still a few years away. A study prepared for the Asia-Europe Economic Ministers' meeting (ASEM) provided a very apt analysis of the economic synergy between Asia and Europe (ASEM, 1999).

ASEAN Countries

Taiwanese businesses invested in ASEAN countries with essentially the same motives as those that currently justify investing in mainland China. Of course, there is not much cultural or linguistic affinity. Encouragement from Taiwanese officials for investment and trade diversification is another motivating factor. The "replacement" and "complementary" effects between Taiwan and the ASEAN countries developed because the investments and the environment are similar to those mentioned earlier with respect to mainland China. These countries replaced Taiwan in producing and exporting labor-intensive products to a third market (mostly North America) while importing parts and equipment from Taiwan as well as purchasing locally for their production (refer to Table 4-4 and Schive, 1999). Taiwan has been running either a small export surplus or deficit with these countries combined at different years (*Taiwan Statistical Data Book*, 1999). The outward investments also exert pressure on Taiwan to upgrade its industries. The top two industries for Taiwan's investment, in terms of accumulated values, are the chemical and textile industries in Thailand, the paper products and textile industries in Indonesia, and the electronics and electric appliances and textile industries in Malaysia.

UPGRADING THE INDUSTRIES

Facing pressure from many sides, one of Taiwan's major challenges is to upgrade its industries' technology. Firms from advanced developed countries had been more willing to license their technology to Taiwan's small-sized firms (Pack, 1992), but Taiwanese firms' next move into new high-tech products or processes will face more resistance, and Taiwan's abilities in research and innovation will become more crucial.

Taiwan's recent progress in science and technology is mainly through the government's involvement. Up until 1993, the government's R & D expenditure exceeded that of the private sector (*Taiwan Statistical Data Book*, 2000, 121–122). The government needs to further foster the economic environment for more private entrepreneurs to participate and compete in technological adaptation and innovation. Bureaucrats may not be as capable as the private sector in choosing technology. The private sector is more responsive to market forces. Larger firms have advantages in entering new product markets or employing new processes due to scale and scope economies. They are more willing and able to invest in human capital and to develop R & D capacity.

The government recognized the disadvantages of SMEs in operating scope, financing, R & D, and marketing. It has promoted the merger of SMEs for more than two decades with little success. Many Taiwanese firms are small and independent. The study of Claessens et al. (1997) indicates that the degree of business affiliation with corporate groups in percentage terms is the lowest for Taiwanese businesses among the East and Southeast Asian countries as well. The government could continue to encourage the formation of larger and more modern enterprises with strong management and world-class corporate governance standards, instead of the family-style enterprises. The government could further privatize the "state-owned" enterprises as well because these enterprises tend to be larger in size.

Taiwan needs to continue its diversification of investments and leapfrog into additional high-tech industries beyond the semiconductor industry in order to moderate the adverse effects of wild business fluctuations as well. Recent policies of the government in promoting biotech and software industries are good examples.

Taiwan's banking institutions are very similar to those of Japan. Lack of tight supervision and of transparency are their drawbacks. In recent years, Japan has engaged in restructuring and reorganizing its financial institutions through mergers in order to improve institutional efficiencies, reduce risks, and revive its economy. Taiwan needs to reorganize and restructure its financial institutions as well through mergers and acquisitions to improve their efficiency and capitalization. A sound financial sector is crucial in supporting its capital market and outward FDIs and in sustaining its economic growth.

CONCLUSION

Accession to the WTO, recent advancements in Internet and related technologies, and facilities for global logistic management would ease the Taiwanese economy's transformation to a higher level of modernization and growth. The means to achieve this transformation are afforded by strategic foreign direct investment and continued upgrading of its high-tech industry. The selective inducement of inward foreign direct investment could partially assist the economy in securing transfers of technology, managerial skills, and marketing networks. Outward direct investment needs to be expanded in terms of functions and locations in order to further stimulate Taiwan's trades, modernization of industries, and economic growth.

In recent years, many Taiwanese firms have evolved from the initial function of contract manufacturing or original design manufacturing to the logistic management aspect of marketing. The dynamics of global competitiveness required the firms in high-tech industries, especially the electronic industries, to build more complex international production networks that extend beyond the boundaries of the firms and country. However, the motivation to reduce costs to offset an erosion of the home country comparative advantage should be no more than a catalyst for choosing the production sites to carry out the assigned functions. Taiwanese firms should consider other important factors, such as where a certain function can be carried out most effectively, where the needs to penetrate important growth markets can be facilitated, and where they can access clusters of specialized capabilities that are necessary to complement their core competencies. In this respect, Taiwan could extend some of their outward FDIs beyond East and Southeast Asia. Taiwan's outward FDI and trade have been overly concentrated in Asia, particularly in mainland China. It could be more diversified. Maximizing long-term rates of return and reducing investment risks, including political risk, through diversification on a global basis could be major goals. Taiwan's accession to the WTO shall facilitate its expansion in trade, investment, and the technological and marketing alliances.

A hollowing-out of some labor-intensive and higher-technology industries was observed in recent years due to the outward direct investments, especially to China. The rather rapid pace and extent of the outward FDIs has been causing a rapidly diminishing comparative advantage of the home supply-base. The primary concern is in the higher-technology industries for its pace of technology outflows and the slowed industry upgrading partly caused by a large sum of capital outflows. Government and industry could pay closer attention in identifying the conditions that are likely to help strengthen and upgrade their domestic production system.

Upgrading Taiwanese industries to the next level faces greater resistance from firms in advanced industrial countries. Further advances in science and technology depend on Taiwan's abilities in research and development. Taiwan could double its efforts in fostering an environment that encourages private firms to compete in the research and development of new products and processes. In addition, Taiwan needs to continue diversifying its investments beyond the semiconductor industry and to leapfrog into additional high-tech industries in order to moderate the adverse impacts of wild business fluctuations as well as facilitating further economic growth.

The small size of many Taiwanese firms is a handicap in the private research effort. There are clear scale and scope advantages in adapting new product or process technologies for larger and more modern firms. This means that the government needs to continue encouraging the formation of larger and more modern enterprises with world-class corporate governance standards through acquisitions and mergers. Taiwan needs to speed up the privatization of its predominantly larger "state-owned" businesses. This privatization effort could contribute to the upgrading of Taiwan's industries. Taiwan's financial institutions need to be reformed in order to improve their efficiency and soundness. A sound financial sector could foster a more robust capital market, outward FDIs, and industry upgrading. Combined with the other policies, they could enable Taiwan's economy to be integrated into the global markets in more significant ways as well.

NOTES

1. For example, the big three automakers in the United States are setting up the "B-2-B net exchange" for parts procurement through the Internet. They are planning to sell their cars through Websites as well.

2. See Okuda (1994) for his analysis of the impacts of inward FDI on productivity growth of Taiwan's industries.

3. Peretto (1999) expounded on the thesis that development and growth are the "stages of a process of structural transformation characterized by changing patterns of capital accumulation, specialization by industries and technological change."

4. Hoppe (2000, 315–338) argues that there may be certain second-mover advantages in adopting technology under uncertainty and the rate of technological progress and the nature of uncertainty shall determine the degree of policy intervention.

5. For the definition of SMEs, see *Small and Medium Enterprises Overview in Taiwan*. For manufacturing, mining, and construction industries, enterprises are classified as SMEs if their paid-in capital is less than approximately $2 million or the number of employees is less than 200 persons. In 1988, for example, the SMEs comprised 98.6 percent of the total manufacturing firms in Taiwan. Also see Chou (1994).

6. For example, the forward linkage relation of a petrochemical company acted as the core company with the downstream plastic producers as the satellite companies. The backward linkage of an automobile manufacturer acted as the core company that assembled parts and components provided by the satellite parts producers and the nonproducers such as a trade company that acted as the core and contracted out production to satellite producers.

7. China's increasing costs of labor had started to deter its inward FDI. See "China's Increasing Costs of Labor Start to Deter Japanese Business," *Wall Street Journal*, December 14, 1999. Taiwan's FDIs were first invested in ASEAN countries, then in mainland China.

REFERENCES

Asia-Europe Economic Ministers' Meeting (ASEM). 1999, October 9–10. *Studies on the Economic Synergy between Asia and Europe*. Berlin, Germany.

Chou, T. C. 1994. *Industrial Organization in a Dichotomous Economy*. Aldershot, U.K.: Avebury.

Chow, Peter C. Y. 1997. "Complementarity and Competitiveness of the Economic Relations across the Taiwan Strait: Problems and Prospects." In *The Republic of China on Taiwan in the 1990's*, eds. Winston L. Yang and Deborah A. Brown. St. John's University, Center of Asian Studies.

Chung-Hwa Economic Research Institute. *Economic Outlook* (in Chinese). Taipei: Republic of China. (Various issues—January 5, 1997, through March 15, 1998. For numerous investments and trade statistics.)

Claessens, Stijin, S. Djankov, J. Fan, and L. Lang. 1997. "Corporate Diversion in East Asia: The Role of Ultimate Ownership and Group Affiliation." World Bank working paper.

Council for Economic Planning and Development, 1998, 1999, 2000. *Taiwan Statistical Data Book*. Taipei, Republic of China. (For various economic statistics.)

Feenstra, R., W. Hai, W. Woo, and S. Yao. 1998, June. "The U.S.–China Bilateral Trade Balance." NBER Working Paper #6598.

Hatch, W., and K. Yamamura. 1996. *Asia in Japan's Embrace*. Cambridge, U.K.: Cambridge University Press.

Hoppe, H. C. 2000. "Second-Mover Advantages in the Strategic Adoption of New Technology under Uncertainty." *International Journal of Industrial Organization*, vol. 18, no. 2: 315–338.

Industrial Technology Information Services. 1997. ROC: "Republic of Computers—Taiwan." Report #9707. Taipei, Taiwan.

Kozmetsky, G., and P. Yue. 1997. *Global Economic Competition*. Boston: Kluwer.

Lin, Steven A. Y. 1999. "Growing Challenges to Taiwan's Economic Miracles." In *The ROC on the Threshold of the 21st Century: A Paradigm Reexamined*, eds. C. C. Chao and Cal Clark. University of Maryland, School of Law.

Lipsey, R. E. 1998. "U.S. and Japanese Multinationals in Southeast Asia Production and Trade." Ninth Annual East Asia seminar on economics, "Role of Foreign Direct Investment in Economic Development," June 25–27, Osaka, Japan.

Montgomery, C., and Michael Porter. 1991. *Strategy: Seeking and Securing Competitive Advantage*. Cambridge, MA: *Harvard Business Review*.

Okuda, S. 1994. "Taiwan's Trade and FDI Policies and Their Effect on Productivity Growth." *The Developing Economies*, vol. 32: 452–463.

Pack, H. 1992. "New Perspectives on Industrial Growth in Taiwan." In *Taiwan: From Developing to Mature Economy*, ed. Gustav Ranis Boulder, CO: Westview Press. pp. 73-120.

Peretto, P. F. 1999. "Industrial Development, Technological Change, and Long-run Growth." *Journal of Development Economics*, vol. 59. no. 2: 389–417.

Schive, Chi. 1990. *The Foreign Factor: The Multinational Corporation's Contribution to the Economic Modernization of the Republic of China*. Stanford: Hoover Institution.

———. 1999, Oct. 25–27. "A Study on Taiwan: High-tech Industries in the Spotlight." Geneva-Hong Kong Conference, Hong Kong.

Wise, R., and P. Baumgartner. 1999. "Go Downstream: The New Profit Imperatives in Manufacturing." *Harvard Business Review*, 512–521.

World Journal, Inc. *World Journal* (in Chinese). New York. (For numerous investments and trade statistics.)

Offshore Sourcing Strategies of Multinational Firms in Taiwan

Tain-Jy Chen and Ying-Hua Ku

INTRODUCTION

Offshore sourcing, also referred to in the literature as import sourcing or international sourcing, has been increasing rapidly since the 1980s (Kotabe, 1992; Monczka and Trent, 1991). Defined as the acquisition of raw materials, components, and subassemblies from international sources for use in fabrication, assembly, or for resale, the primary reason for offshore sourcing has traditionally been in the pursuit of cost reductions (Moxon, 1975; Kotabe and Omura, 1989; Kotabe and Murray, 1990; Encarnation, 1992; Swamidass and Kotabe, 1993). In recent years, however, the role of cost reduction in offshore sourcing has diminished (Kotabe and Swan, 1992), with more weight being given to non-cost considerations, such as marketing strategy formulation, improvements in market performance, increasing the variety of product quality and attributes, acquiring product and process technology from suppliers to achieve worldwide competitiveness, and so on (Swamidass and Kotabe, 1993; Monczka and Trent, 1991).

Offshore sourcing by multinational firms has been an important outlet for Taiwan's exports. Such exports exhibit two characteristics: first, the products are often sold without brands; second, components and parts rather than final products form the mainstay of trade. These characteristics fit very well with Taiwan's industry structure, which is dominated by small and medium firms that have little capacity to build brand names and to establish marketing channels but may serve as offshore suppliers or subcontractors for multinational firms.

The changing motivations for offshore sourcing has important implications for Taiwanese firms who had excelled in cost-based competition but have lost that competitive advantage since the mid-1980s due to rising wages in Taiwan. They can now compete on the basis of flexibility in production and ability to service the global markets. Therefore, if cost-based offshore sourcing is indeed giving way to strategic sourcing, Taiwan's industry should restructure itself to cope with the change. Emphasis of industrial policy should then be placed on strengthening production flexibility and building global supply capabilities.

The conventional literature on offshore sourcing has noted the differences in sourcing strategies embraced by multinational firms of different nationalities. In particular, U.S. multinational firms are said to engage extensively in procurement from external sources, whereas Japanese multinationals prefer intrafirm sourcing, that is, procuring by overseas production (Kotabe, 1996). There is some empirical evidence to demonstrate the advantage of intrafirm sourcing over external sourcing. For example, in Kotabe and Omura's (1989) comparison of market performance of Japanese and European multinational firms operating in the United States, they found the Japanese multinationals superior in performance because they obtained key components and parts from sources within their own organizations. These authors argue that control over the production of key components and parts reinforces the firm's core competence, whereas outsourcing undermines it. However, recent studies of high-technology industries have indicated that Japanese firms' adherence to "key" components and parts may have prevented them from taking advantage of the external capabilities, thus hindering their global competitiveness (Ernst, 1997).

Within the offshore sourcing literature, most studies have used manufacturers as the objects of research, a focus that limits the scope of offshore sourcing within the parameters of foreign direct investment (FDI) where internalization advantages are used to explain the choice of FDI over outsourcing (Swamidass and Kotabe, 1993). Offshore sourcing has in fact assumed an increasingly greater role among merchandisers that possess no manufacturing facilities, such as Nike, Reebok, and Calvin Klein. In addition, many world-renowned manufacturers, though possessing a minor manufacturing capability within their headquarters, rely mainly on offshore sourcing to service the markets.

A common feature among manufacturers and merchandisers in offshore sourcing is their establishment of international procurement offices (IPOs) in their major supply source regions to search, contract, and maintain local suppliers. A survey of eighty large U.S. firms, conducted by the Machinery and Allied Products Institute (MAPI) in 1986, found that almost half the firms surveyed had IPOs located in major supplier-base areas (Monczka and Trent, 1991). These procurement offices assume the responsibility of screening potential suppliers, placing orders, performing quality control, monitoring production schedules, and conveying production-related information to the headquarters. They even perform R & D and product design, in consortium with their local suppliers and contractors, which serve as their "virtual" factories.

This chapter explores the offshore sourcing strategies of multinational firms by surveying ninety-six IPOs located in Taiwan. We may infer from this study the role of offshore sourcing in Taiwan's globalization. The study indicates that the relative importance of cost reduction versus noncost considerations in offshore sourcing depends on whether or not the IPOs are owned by manufacturing firms. IPOs owned by manufacturers are more cost-conscious, whereas those owned by merchandisers are more concerned with noncost advantages. Those multinationals that are most cost-conscious tend to establish their own manufacturing subsidiaries for offshore sourcing. Multinational firms establishing IPOs in Taiwan without any manufacturing functions have become the trend since the mid-1980s.

We also find that the distance between buyers and suppliers matters in the formulation of offshore sourcing strategies. Among the international buyers from different countries, European buyers are inclined to purchase more modern products from Taiwan, allowing more autonomy to their suppliers and maintaining a stable relationship with a single supplier. We argue that distance attenuates the cost advantage of suppliers; therefore, long-distance buyers place more emphasis on strategic considerations than on cost savings when procuring from abroad. Distance also increases the buyer's costs of controlling suppliers and managing the buyer–supplier relationship. Therefore, long-distance buyers look for dependable suppliers with technological complementarity and tend to commit to such a relationship once it is shown to be a working option.

The newly emerged practice of "global logistics" from the late-1980s onward has, however, mitigated the differences between international buyers. New practices call for close cooperation between buyers and the suppliers in the whole range of the supply chain, with the aim of delivering products in a flexible, speedy, and "just in time" fashion. This practice requires a stable supplier–buyer relationship and a mutual commitment from the partners.

OFFSHORE SOURCING STRATEGIES

Offshore sourcing has become an integral part of global competition. Venkatesan (1992) argues that a firm should separate strategic components from commodity components, concentrating on the elements of the strategic components in which the firm can master a leading position in the market while outsourcing the remaining components from independent suppliers. Through outsourcing, the firm can form a partnership with dominant suppliers in the market, sharing their new technology, or processes of production, with them (Swamidass and Kotabe, 1993).

There is, however, the inherent risk of losing long-term competitiveness through excessive outsourcing, either because the company leaks out key technologies to its rivals or because it fails to keep abreast of emerging products or technologies in the industry. Outsourcing from offshore suppliers incurs the additional risk of disruption to supply due to demand fluctuation or coordination failure. Monczka and Trent (1991) argue that a firm should procure from outside sources only if such procurement can be expected to achieve dramatic and immediate improvements in the following areas: (1) cost reduction; (2) quality improvement; (3) exposure to worldwide technology; and (4) product delivery and reliability. Firms identifying themselves with different core competencies should seek improvements in different areas. Firms positioning themselves differently in the market will choose different product strategies, which, in turn, prompt them to take different approaches to offshore sourcing.

It is apparent that manufacturers and merchandisers may identify themselves with different core competencies. With their lack of manufacturing capacity, merchandisers usually establish their core competence in the fields of product design and marketing, outsourcing all their requirements from around the world to service the world market. To the extent that competition in manufacturing equates to competition in terms of cost, cost competitiveness is likely to be considered as a prerequisite by merchandisers in their choice of suppliers. But merchandisers look beyond costs for other capabilities that enhance the value of their design and marketing expertise, such as production technology, proximity to the market, or even after-sales service.

In contrast, manufacturers that identify manufacturing capability as part of their core competence are presumably cost-competitive in certain important areas of production. They will only procure components and parts from other manufacturers in which they lack their own cost advantage. Compared with merchandisers, manufacturers are likely to give more weight to cost competitiveness in their choice of suppliers. Foreign manufacturers that own local manufacturing subsidiaries, in an attempt to internalize the location's cost advantage, are likely to give considerably more weight to cost considerations should they decide to outsource anything from the same location.

Offshore sourcing, whether through internal production or external procurement, entails control mechanisms that coordinate the overseas activities with those conducted at the headquarters. A failure of the control mechanism may result in disruptions in the supply chain and, consequently, damage to the buyers' market position. Distance has an important bearing on the effectiveness of the control mechanism, and on the cost of maintaining such a mechanism. Distance increases the costs of screening, monitoring, and communication, hence, long-distance buyers will engage in offshore sourcing only if sizable benefits are expected, preferring also to establish a stable relationship with their suppliers so that the cost of relationship management is minimized.

THE PURPOSE OF OFFSHORE SOURCING

We surveyed ninety-six international procurement offices (IPOs) in Taiwan owned by multinational firms to unveil their offshore sourcing strategies and to examine the implications for Taiwan's globalization. The sample is derived from a survey of 625 procurement offices listed in *Foreign-Invested Enterprises in Taiwan*, published by Dun & Bradstreet Information Service (1996 edition). Their registered businesses include electronics, machinery products, textiles, sporting goods, footwear, and metal products.

Of the ninety-six IPOs, fifty-three are owned by manufacturers, and forty-three are owned by merchandisers without manufacturing facilities; thirteen of these IPOs are accompanied by a manufacturing subsidiary in Taiwan owned by the same parent firms but operated independently. Goods procured by IPOs are either used for internal functions or for resale; internal functions include internal production and direct sales through headquarters or through other subsidiaries, whereas resale refers to sales to unrelated importers or retailers. Internal functions account for 72.1 percent of procurement by IPOs owned by manufacturers and 54.3 percent by those owned by merchandisers. The sample is first of all grouped according to the country of origin. Those results are presented in Table 5-1.

Of the ninety-six firms, it can be seen that sixteen are based in the United States, thirty-one in Japan, twenty-six in Asian countries other than Japan (hereafter denoted as "Asian firms"), sixteen in Europe (mainly Germany and the United Kingdom), and seven either in the rest of the world or unidentified (hereafter denoted as "others"). We first asked the respondent firms to state their purposes of procurement in

TABLE 5-1. Sample Distribution by Country of Origin

Country of Origin	Number of Firms	Average Employment (Persons)
United States	16	17.6
Japan	31	21.5
Asian	26	29.3
European	16	15.2
Other	7	13.0
Total	96	21.3

Taiwan, tabulating the purposes of procurement into four categories: (1) cost reduction; (2) quality upgrading; (3) capacity supplementation; and (4) flexibility of supply.[1]

The first two purposes are self-evident and are identified by a straightforward question posed to the respondents. Capacity supplementation refers to the purposes of (1) supplementing the shortage of manufacturing capacity at the headquarters or other subsidiaries, and (2) replacing investment in production capacities at the headquarters or other subsidiaries.[2] Flexibility of supply encompasses the following dimensions: (1) shortening the time-to-market, (2) increasing the variety of product mix and product quality offered by the company, and (3) increasing proximity to the markets to be serviced. The questions were designed for multiple answers, and the frequency distribution is listed in Table 5-2.

It can be seen that out of the eighty-eight respondents who provided complete answers to this question, procurement for flexibility in servicing the markets was cited more often than the other three broadly defined purposes. This response was followed by the purpose of cost reduction, then capacity supplementation, and finally upgrading product quality. This result confirms the observation that noncost factors are indeed as important as, if not more important than, cost

TABLE 5-2. Purpose of Offshore Sourcing Frequency, by Country

Country of Origin	Cost Reduction	Quality Upgrading	Capacity Supplementation	Flexibility of Supply	Sample Size
United States	5	2	9	9	15
Japan	9	5	7	9	16
Asian	23	3	7	23	28
European	5	9	7	15	22
Other	5	1	2	5	7
Total	47	20	32	61	88

Note: Purposes of offshore sourcing are multiple.

considerations in recent trends in offshore sourcing (Swamidass and Kotabe, 1993).

Pearson's chi-square statistics indicate that neither American nor Japanese firms are distinctive from the rest of the sample in terms of frequency distribution, as shown in Table 5-2. As a single group, only European firms show a discernible difference in stating their purpose of procurement. European firms indicate that they are more concerned about increasing the flexibility of supply and less concerned about cost reduction compared to the rest of the sample. European firms put more emphasis on flexibility in servicing the markets because they are more distant from Asia and hence need Taiwanese producers to serve as substitutes or second sources of supply to service the Asian markets.

In addition to nationality, firm characteristics may also affect the roles of procurement. Four variables are chosen to represent firm characteristics: (1) whether the IPO is accompanied by a manufacturing subsidiary in Taiwan (a dummy variable); (2) whether the parent firm is a manufacturer or a merchandiser (a dummy variable); (3) the subsidiary's local experience (measured by the number of months of establishment in Taiwan); and (4) the degree of globalization (measured by the number of subsidiaries owned by the parent firm outside of Taiwan). These four characteristic variables, together with country of origin, are employed to perform a canonical correlation analysis of the roles of procurement. The canonical correlation analysis extracts the within-group variations of two sets of variables and measures the correlation between the two extracts. For our purpose, one set of variables contains firm characteristics and country of origin, the other contains the roles of procurement as a portfolio. The results of the canonical correlation analysis are presented in Table 5-3.

Table 5-3 indicates that the first canonical correlation coefficient is 0.5407, suggesting that the two sets of variables are only mildly correlated. The multivariate statistics, whether they be Wilk's lambda, Pillai's trace, or Hotelling-Lawley's trace, indicate, however, that the null hypothesis—that the two groups of variables are uncorrelated—can be rejected at the 5 percent level. The canonical coefficient suggests that predominant factors in determining the roles of procurement are (1) whether an IPO is accompanied by a local manufacturing subsidiary, and (2) whether the headquarters of the IPO maintains a manufacturing capacity. The weight given to country of origin, 0.0235, is virtually negligible, implying that the distinction between manufacturers and merchandisers dominates the pattern of procurement. Nationality, with the exception of European, shows only minor variations in the objectives of procurement; local experience, and degree of globalization, also have only minor influence on the purposes of procurement.

TABLE 5-3. Canonical Correlation between Purpose of Offshore Sourcing and Firm Characteristics

Purpose Variables	Firm Characteristics
Cost reduction	Manufacturing activities in Taiwan
Quality upgrading	Manufacturing activities of parent firms
Capacity supplementation	Country of origin
Supply flexibility	Experience in Taiwan
	Degree of globalization

Canonical Correlation	Multivariate Statistics	Value	Approximate F-statistic	Significance Level
1. 0.5407	Wilks' lambda	0.5641	(1.69)	0.04
2. 0.3479	Pillai's trace	0.5080	(1.66)	0.04
3. 0.2731	Hotelling-Lawley's trace	0.6519	(1.71)	0.03
4. 0.1415	Roy's greatest root	0.4131	(4.71)	0.001

Canonical Coefficient	First Canonical Function
Cost reduction	2.0126
Quality upgrading	1.0534
Capacity supplementation	0.5453
Supply flexibility	0.3017
Manufacturing in Taiwan	1.6756
Manufacturing at parents	0.8342
Country of origin	0.0235
Experience in Taiwan	-0.0101
Degree of globalization	0.0350

The role of manufacturing can be seen from Table 5-4, which shows that if an IPO is accompanied by a manufacturing subsidiary, then cost factors dominate noncost considerations in the purpose of local sourcing, whereas quality upgrading is almost ignored. In contrast, if an IPO is established solely to perform a procurement function, then concerns for supply flexibility dominate cost considerations. Moreover, IPOs owned by manufacturing parents are more concerned with cost reduction than those owned by merchandising parents.

TABLE 5-4. Purpose of Offshore Sourcing Frequency, by Activity

Group	Cost Reduction	Quality Upgrading	Capacity Supplementation	Flexibility of Supply	Sample Size
With manufacturing subsidiaries	11	1	4	7	12
Without manufacturing subsidiaries	30	14	24	43	67
Manufacturer parents	31	8	20	33	51
Merchandiser parents	16	11	12	24	42

PRODUCT CYCLE AND OFFSHORE SOURCING

According to the product cycle theory advanced by Vernon (1966), in manufacturing a product, a country's comparative advantage shifts with the life cycle of the product. In general, as the product matures, the comparative advantage shifts from high-wage to low-wage countries, and a firm operating in countries devoid of the comparative advantage of manufacturing such a product can obtain it through offshore sourcing. The product cycle theory implies that the primary purpose of offshore sourcing is cost saving, and the more mature the product is, the greater the cost savings available by buying from low-wage countries. But as the focus of offshore sourcing moves away from cost to noncost considerations, goods to be procured may also move up the ladder of the product cycle to include more modern products. As elucidated earlier, outsourcing runs the risk of leaking valuable information on technology to suppliers, and the more advanced the products, the more damaging the technology leakage can be. Unless there are substantial benefits to be gained in strategic areas, international buyers usually like to maintain a comfortable technology gap between internal production and production of sourced products. Therefore, only mature products, the production of which involves little sensitive technology, will be procured from low-cost suppliers.

Distance may also outweigh the cost-saving advantage of offshore suppliers because both transport costs and the risk of supply disruptions increase with distance. It is common to observe that cost-minded buyers source from neighboring countries—Americans buy from Mexico, Japanese from East Asia, and Europeans from Eastern Europe. When a buyer procures from afar, cost-saving is usually outweighed by strategic considerations, such as maintaining a flexible source of supply to strategic markets where the buyer is at a locational disadvantage.

In this section, we measure the position of the products to be procured from Taiwan in the product cycle configuration according to its maturity in the market. Four scales are assigned to the maturity level of a product: matured products (scale 1), products over five years old in the market (scale 2), products one to five years old in the market (scale 3), and new products (scale 4). The more modern the products, the higher the scale. The average maturity level in the procurement bundle is tabulated according to the nationality of IPOs. It can be seen from Table 5-5 that European firms procure the most modern products—in the one- to five-year-old range—from Taiwan, followed by American firms, which procure products that average five years old. Japanese and other Asian firms procure similar and most mature products, with the average being products over five years old.

TABLE 5-5.   Maturity of Products Sourced from Taiwan

Nationality	European	Japanese	Asian	United States
Maturity	2.60	1.43	1.48	2.08

Note: Maturity is measured by the following four scales:
    a. Scale 1—matured products
    b. Scale 2—products over five years old in the market.
    c. Scale 3—products one to five years old in the market.
    d. Scale 4—new products.

Since the choice of product cycle may be affected by the purposes of procurement, firm characteristics, and the nationality of the buyers, we ran a logistic regression to distill the factors that determine the maturity level of the products to be sourced. Two variables representing firm characteristics are included in the regression analysis. The first is technology level, which is measured by a composite index formed by the first principal components of the following four indicators of technological capability pertinent to the parent firms: (1) the number of product patents owned by the parent; (2) the number of process patents owned; (3) the number of market-leading products owned; and (4) R & D expenditure as a proportion of sales. The second firm characteristic variable is "globalization level," measured by the number of overseas subsidiaries owned by the parent firm. The results, shown in Table 5-6, indicate that in comparison to the cost-cutting purpose, procurement for the purposes of quality upgrading, capacity supplementation, and supply flexibility all motivate buyers to procure more modern products from Taiwan, as indicated by the negative and significant coefficients associated with these variables. Judging by the magnitude of coefficients, procurement for quality upgrading prompts the buyers toward the most advanced products, followed by procurement for supply flexibility, and then by procurement for capacity supplementation.

In terms of nationality, European firms tend to procure more modern products than the base group, namely American firms. Japanese and Asian firms tend to procure more mature products than the Americans, but the differences are not statistically significant. In other words, European buyers purchase more modern products than the rest of the groups.

In terms of firm characteristics, buyers with a higher level of technology procure more modern products, a confirmation of the technology gap hypothesis. Buyers that are more globalized tend to procure more mature products from Taiwan, but the effect is only marginally significant.

BUYER CONTROL OF THE SUPPLIERS

When sourcing from overseas, the buyers may wish to control the suppliers in terms of the technology to be used in production and the

TABLE 5-6. Logistic Analysis of Product Cycle in Offshore Sourcing—Dependent Variable: Maturity of Products to Be Sourced (ordinal)

Independent Variables	Parameters estimated	
Intercept 1	2.8705**	(6.82)
Intercept 2	3.5656**	(9.64)
Intercept 3	4.8182**	(14.5)
Purposes		
Quality upgrading	-2.1636**	(4.40)
Capacity supplementation	-1.3632*	(2.84)
Supply flexibility	-2.1026**	(4.80)
Nationality		
European	-3.0825**	(7.87)
Japanese	0.4286	(0.22)
Asian	0.5746	(0.23)
Characteristics		
Technology level	-0.9683**	(3.79)
Globalization level	0.0484	(2.52)

Note: Numbers in parentheses are Wald chi-statistics; ** indicates significance at the 5% level; * indicates significance at the 10% level.

brand to be used in marketing. The control on production technology is to ensure that the quality of the procured products are satisfactory and compatible with the other segments of the value chain that are either internally produced or sourced from elsewhere. For example, if multinational firms source computer parts from Taiwan, they need to be certain that the parts will fit into a system or subsystem that incorporates other parts from the rest of the world. Technology control is also important in keeping a strategic linkage between designers and manufacturers when they are geographically separated.

Problems arising from the implementation of production technology or product design can be fed back to designers for improvement, while innovations emerging from the shop floor can be gleaned by the buyers. Venkatesan (1992) argues that when capable subsystem suppliers exist, it is not important for the design and manufacture of the subsystem to be undertaken in-house. What is important is that the one who performs the system integration can specify and control the performance characteristics of the parts that constitute the system. The purpose of technology control is precisely to control the performance characteristics of the parts and components sourced from subsystem suppliers.

Brand control ensures that the procured products fall within the auspices of the brand image and serve to reinforce, rather than undermine, the goodwill established by the brand. Through brand control, good-quality products enhance the value of the brand, the benefits of which are accrued to the buyer rather than the supplier. With brand control, the buyer makes sure that the resources that it invests in improving the product quality of the suppliers is paid off through its brand image. On the other hand, a buyer will be happy to accept the brand of a strong supplier if this enhances the value of the buyer's product (Intel Inside is a prime example).

We measure technology control and brand control by ordinal variables. Technology control is scaled in six levels (1–6, from low to high): (1) no control whatsoever; (2) buyers specifying quality standards and performing inspection on the products; (3) buyers providing technology consultation to suppliers; (4) buyers providing components and parts to suppliers; (5) buyers providing production technology to suppliers; and (6) buyers providing blueprints to the suppliers for fabrication.[3] Buyers may provide multiple services to the suppliers, but the level of control is identified with the highest scale listed here. The higher the scale, the tighter the level of control.

Brand control is scaled similarly in three layers: (1) Supplier's brand name is used; (2) buyer's brand name is used with the supplier's designs (where the supplier serves as an own-design manufacturer, or ODM); and (3) buyer's name and design are used (where the supplier serves as an original equipment manufacturer, or OEM). The higher the scale, the tighter the buyer's control on the brand.

These two dimensions of control are compressed into one single measure of buyer control by the principal components analysis. The loading scores of each observation are then grouped by nationality and compared with each other. The results are presented in Table 5-7.

TABLE 5-7. The Level of Buyer Control

Country of Origin	Mean Loading Score	Sample Size
United States	0.3023 (0.9397)	14
Japan	0.1174 (1.0098)	28
Asian	-0.5260 (1.0310)	19
European	0.0753 (0.8260)	13
Other	0.2136 (1.0293)	7

Notes:
1. Buyer control includes technology control and brand-name control.
2. Numbers in parentheses are standard deviations.
3. Analysis of variance indicates that there are significant differences between the Asian group on the one hand, and the U.S. and Japanese groups on the other, at the 5% significance level. All other pairwise comparisons indicate an insignificant difference at the 5% level.

Table 5-7 shows that the mean loading score is the highest for American buyers, followed by that for Japanese and European buyers, with the Asian group trailing in last place. This implies that American buyers' control of their local suppliers in Taiwan is the most steadfast, probably because of the sophistication of their technology or the strength of their brand image. Asian buyers are the most lax in exerting control over local suppliers, presumably because their technological capability and brand image are the lowest among the four groups.

Our study shows that when technology control and brand control are treated as independent strategy constructs, there is little difference in brand control attributable to the nationality of buyers. In fact, neither nationality nor firm characteristics explain much of the variation among individual buyers in terms of brand control. Original equipment manufacturer (OEM) mode is the predominant arrangement between Taiwanese suppliers and multinational buyers from all origins. On the other hand, nationality and firm characteristics do have some influence over the level of technology control. Table 5-8 presents the results of a logistic regression analysis on the level of technology control, using nationality and firm characteristics as the explanatory variables.

It can be seen that the European dummy yields a positive and significant coefficient, as judged by Wald statistics, implying that European firms tend to allow more autonomy to their Taiwanese suppliers in the choice of production technology, as compared to American buyers, which are treated as the benchmark group. The other country dummies, including those for Japanese and Asian buyers, all yield insignificant coefficients, indicating that they are not significantly different from the American buyers.

Three firm characteristic variables are included in the regression analysis, namely manufacturing subsidiary (a dummy variable indicating whether the IPO is associated with a manufacturing subsidiary), manufacturing parents (a dummy variable indicating whether the IPO is owned by a manufacturer), and the degree of globalization. Only manufacturing subsidiary yields a negative and significant coefficient, implying that multinational firms control their supplier's choice of technology more stringently when they themselves also engage in local production. This is necessary to ensure that goods procured from outside sources are compatible with local production. Manufacturing parents and multinational firms with a higher degree of globalization also tend to control their offshore suppliers more stringently, but the difference is statistically insignificant.

Although, on average, Asian buyers are shown to be most free-handed in terms of technological and brand control (refer to Table 5-7), their control level is not significantly different from the American buyers if other factors are taken into account. Asian buyers are less

TABLE 5-8.   Logistic Regression on the Level of Technology Control—Dependent Variable: Level of Technology Control (ordinal)

Independent Variables	Parameter Estimates
Intercept 1	1.2565 (4.41)**
Intercept 2	-0.2901 (0.26)
Intercept 3	0.3689 (0.42)
Intercept 4	0.8686 (2.27)
European dummy	2.5047 (5.47)**
Japanese dummy	0.2942 (0.24)
Asian dummy	0.5726 (0.65)
Manufacturing subsidiaries	-1.4834 (3.19)**
Manufacturer parents	-0.1983 (0.15)
Degree of globalization	-0.0049 (0.12)

Notes:
1. The level of technology control is scaled as follows:
    (1) No control.
    (2) Buyers provide quality standards and inspections.
    (3) Buyers provide technology consultations.
    (4) Buyers provide components and parts.
    (5) Buyers provide production technologies.
    (6) Buyers provide blueprints for manufacturing.
    (However, level 2 and level 3 are empirically inseparable and are combined as a single level in the estimation.)
2. Numbers in parentheses are Wald chi-square statistics.
3. * indicates significance at the 10% level; ** indicates significance at the 5% level.

globalized and rarely involved in local manufacturing. In contrast, European firms stand out as the most free-handed buyers after controlling the buyer characteristics. Again, we interpret this as a matter of distance, which makes technology control of suppliers costly. To prevent the risk of technological failure for lack of control, European firms will procure from Taiwanese suppliers only if trust can be established, and once this is established, they tend to stick with a single supplier.

BUYER–SUPPLIER RELATIONSHIP

The debate on the American versus Japanese style of the buyer–supplier relationship centers on how close and stable the relationship should be. American-style buyers tend to deal with multiple suppliers at the same time and maintain a high level of competition among these suppliers. For example, contracts are offered on a lot-by-lot basis, often determined by open bidding. Thus, competition among suppliers is the key to ensuring high quality and low price of supply. The drawback of the American system is that it forces individual suppliers to operate in an uncertain environment, making them reluctant to make long-term commitments that may eventually benefit the buyers (Hahn, Kim, and Kim, 1986).

Japanese-style buyers, in contrast, tend to maintain a long-term relationship with a single or small number of suppliers (Taylor and Wiggins, 1997). Japanese manufacturers, which are usually much larger than their suppliers, often invest in their suppliers in the areas of technology development and production facilities (Asanuma, 1992). These relation-specific assets underlie the close coordination and risk-sharing arrangement between buyers and suppliers (Aoki, 1988). As manifested in offshore sourcing, Japanese manufacturers are more likely to depend on intrafirm sourcing, or sourcing from their *keiretsu*-based overseas networks, because relation-specific assets confine the scope of transactions.

In recent years, however, the American and Japanese styles of management seem to have lost country specificity. For instance, the Japanese style of the buyer–supplier relationship has become fashionable among American automakers (Asanuma, 1992). Milgrom and Roberts (1990, 1995) have noted that firms appear to be adopting Japanese-style procurement practices as part of a modern worldwide strategy. On the other hand, Japanese firms are reported to have become more cost-minded and broken loose from the long-term supply relationship in favor of competitive bidding, particularly in the declining industries. Firms may also adopt different supply strategies with regard to different components and parts (Gilbert, Young, and O'Neal, 1994).

In this section, we examine the stability of the buyer–supplier relationship maintained by our sample firms. The stability of the buyer–supplier relationship is measured in three dimensions: (1) the number of parallel suppliers in Taiwan at one point in time; (2) the durability of the supplier relationship (that is, fixed supplier, suppliers subject to regular alternation, suppliers chosen on a lot-by-lot basis, ranked in that order); and (3) whether or not parallel sourcing outside of Taiwan is conducted.[4]

Each dimension is measured by an ordinal variable where a smaller number indicates a more stable relationship. The three dimensions are then compressed into one to construct a single index for the stability of the buyer–supplier relationship, based on the loading score derived from the first principal components. The mean loading scores for various country groups are listed in Table 5-9, which shows that Asian buyers have the highest loading score, followed by American buyers, Japanese buyers, the unidentified group (others), and European buyers, in that order.

TABLE 5-9. Stability of Buyer-Supplier Relationship

Country of Origin	Mean Loading Score	Sample Size	Country of Origin	Analysis of Variance				
				U.S.	Japan	Asia	Europe	Others
U.S.	0.1501 (0.7062)	14	US	-	No	No	Yes	No
Japan	-0.0876 (0.9885)	25	Japan	No	-	Yes	Yes	No
Asia	0.5876 (0.6858)	22	Asia	No	Yes	-	Yes	Yes
Europe	-0.7350 (1.2201)	14	Europe	Yes	Yes	Yes	-	No
Other	-0.5096 (0.8468)	5	Other	Yes	No	Yes	No	-

Notes:
1. A smaller number indicates a tighter relationship.
2. "Yes" indicates a difference in the mean loading score at the 5% significance level;
3. "No" indicates otherwise.

This implies that European buyers maintain the most stable relationship with their Taiwanese suppliers among the five country groups. Analysis of variance (AOV) on the loading scores indicates that there are significant differences between European firms on the one hand, and the other country groups on the other, in terms of loading scores. Japanese firms are shown to maintain a more stable relationship with local suppliers when compared to their American counterparts, but analysis of variance indicates that the differences between the two groups are not statistically significant. Non-Japanese Asian firms are shown to maintain a buyer–supplier relationship similar to the American style, which is significantly looser than the relationships maintained by European and Japanese multinationals.

Holmstrom and Milgram (1994) argue that the buyer–supplier relationship is underscored by a set of institutional factors that condition transactions. Taylor and Wiggins (1997) show that the long-term buyer–supplier relationship of the Japanese type is tied to small orders and self-imposed quality inspection by the suppliers, whereas the short-term, competitive bidding relationship of the American type is associated with large orders and buyer-enforced quality inspection. Firms that maintain Japanese-style supplier relationships emphasize quality more than price and are keen to reduce the cycle time between receipt of materials and their placement into the production process (Gilbert, Young, and O'Neal, 1994).

The Japanese-style relationship, which is stable and durable, entails investment in relation-specific assets that facilitate quick responses and mutual trust. European buyers prefer a stable relationship with their Taiwanese suppliers probably because they operate mainly on small orders and distance hinders their ability to monitor local production and to enforce quality control. When elements of the supply chain are separated by great distance, poor communications and long lead times may incur substantial costs due to supply disruption or extra inventory buildup (Levy, 1995). Maintaining a dependable relationship with a single supplier minimizes these costs.

THE CASE OF INFORMATION PRODUCTS

As a result of rapid developments in Taiwan's information industry, information products have been the major items procured by IPOs in Taiwan. Unlike in the past, when manufacturing subsidiaries dominated the FDI scene, IPOs have become the primary form of multinational operations in Taiwan in recent years. Details of the information products procured by the top twenty IPOs in Taiwan are provided in Table 5-10, clearly showing that the amount of procurement increased rapidly from $11.4 billion in 1997, to $15.6 billion in 1998, and to $23 billion in 1999. The procurement by the top twenty IPOs alone accounted for 40.2 percent of Taiwan's total shipments of information products in 1999, suggesting that IPOs have become a major channel for Taiwanese exports.

The driving force for the booming IPO activity is not only the fierce price competition within the industry but also the increased competition in terms of flexibility and speed. For example, the biggest IPO in Taiwan, Compaq, has introduced the concept of build to order (BTO) to service its customers, replacing the conventional practice of build to forecast (BTF). Under the BTO process, Compaq requires its subcontractors to build personal computers in response to market demand and to deliver the products to end users within the shortest time possible. Compaq imposes a "983" operation formula, which requires its subcontractors to collect 98 percent of the components and parts required for production within three days of the order, and to ship the products within six days. By so doing, the inventory of components and parts will be maintained within three to five days of daily consumption levels. To establish such a rapid response process, subcontractors in

TABLE 5-10.   Information Products Procured by the Top Twenty IPOs in Taiwan, 1997–1999

| | | | $ Millions |
Year	U.S. Firms	Japanese Firms	European Firms	Total
1997	9,030	1,556	816	11,402
1998	13,353	1,262	1,032	15,647
1999	20,140	1,860	1,039	23,039

Note: Top twenty IPOs include ten American firms, five Japanese firms, and five European firms.
Source: Ministry of Economic Affairs (Taiwan).

Taiwan have to operate an efficient "supply chain management" system to coordinate the production and shipping of components and parts in typical "just in time" fashion.

In addition to being fast and flexible, the subcontractors are also required to manage the inventory of final products so that the buyers can concentrate their efforts on product design and marketing. Compaq, for example, requires its subcontractors to maintain manufacturing, warehousing, and after-sales service facilities around the world, in order that the final products can be manufactured near the markets and after-sales service can be provided from proximity. Final products are to be shipped directly to end customers rather than to Compaq's warehouses. The so-called "global logistics" service does away with the inventory burden for Compaq but presents a major challenge to Taiwan's small manufacturers who are under pressure to invest abroad and operate globally.

An alternative approach to global logistics in managing the inventory cost in the information industry is to ask subcontractors to deliver the subsystem, known as "barebone," to the market without the major components such as the central processing unit (CPU). The brand marketer then inserts the CPU at its own assembly lines located near the markets before the shipment of the assembled product. This practice minimizes the risk of price fluctuations associated with the most expensive component of the product, namely the CPU, and also saves on customs duties. The "barebone" manufacturers, although under less pressure to globalize, are also required to maintain a competitive supply chain network.

American computer firms, such as Compaq, Dell, Gateway, HP, and IBM, all operate prominent IPOs in Taiwan without manufacturing capabilities. The products they procure are sold in the world market, although the United States is their major outlet. In recent years, the products they procure have been upgraded from matured to modern ones, and from components and subassemblies to the entire system. In particular, the proportion of notebook computers in their procurement portfolio has increased, while there has been a decline in the proportion of desktop computer monitors, motherboards, and keyboards. This suggests that American firms have totally retreated from assembly activities and opted for one-stop shopping from Taiwan, allowing them to concentrate their efforts on new product definition, setting of standards, system integration, software value-added, distribution, and so on (Borrus, 1997, 157). Some argue that teaming up with Taiwanese manufacturers was the main factor in U.S. computer firms regaining their world competitiveness in the 1990s (Ernst, 1997).

In contrast, Japanese PC firms had insisted on internal production while rejecting outsourcing. When they needed to source from abroad, they preferred to establish manufacturing subsidiaries overseas and produce within their own organizations. This failure to take advantage of local production capabilities is the main reason that Japanese firms fell behind the United States in the electronics industry (Ernst, 1997). Under increasing competitive pressure, the Japanese PC firms—notably Sony, Toshiba, and NEC—have each established IPOs in Taiwan over the past decade. Their procurements, however, concentrated on components and subassemblies such as motherboards and monitors, products that were either shipped back to Japan for assembly into final products or for resale in Taiwan under their own brand names. Procurement of components and subassemblies from Taiwan represented a significant shift in the division of labor between Taiwan and Japan. In the past, Taiwan served as an offshore assembly platform for Japanese products, using Japanese-made components and parts. Later on, Taiwan licensed technology from Japan for its own production. Nowadays, Taiwan provides components and subassemblies to Japanese producers, with very little Japanese content.

European firms are recent entrants to Taiwan's IPO market. Their product mix is diverse and emphasizes flexibility in serving the market. For example, Siemens, one of the largest European IPOs, procures notebook computers, barebones, motherboards, monitors, keyboards, and so on, from Taiwan (*DigiTimes,* September 23, 1999). These products serve a variety of markets, from Europe to the Asia Pacific. However, unlike U.S. firms, the Europeans did not count on Taiwan as their major source of supply, which remains in Europe.

Compared to Japanese and European firms, American firms prefer multiple sources of supply. Most American firms procured from more than three suppliers. But as the procured products were upgraded from matured to modern ones and the "global logistics service" became the norm in contractors' service, the working relationships between American buyers and their Taiwanese subcontractors have been tightened. As more commitments are needed from both sides to share knowledge in the global logistics operation, the value of relation-specific assets increases and it becomes more costly to switch partners. Therefore, relationships become more durable. For example, in the procurement of notebook computers, major American brand marketers, such as Compaq and Dell, have worked with no more than two principal Taiwanese subcontractors and stayed with them.

With the rise of electronic-based supply chain management, entry barriers to the supplier network will become even higher in the future. Therefore, the American style of sourcing will soon give way to a more stable and more interactive buyer–supplier relationship. In fact, the extent of knowledge sharing and the degree of work coordination between buyers and suppliers in the information age lead to them operating like a single enterprise.

As a prime base for international sourcing of information products, Taiwan faces a major challenge from the contract electronics manufacturers (CEMs), which have arisen in the United States. CEMs provide contract manufacturing services just like Taiwanese manufacturers, but they are bigger and more diversified in product lines and location. Major CEMs like SCI and Solectron manufacture almost everything that is electronic, from personal computers, to telecommunications equipment, to medical devices, and have manufacturing plants in places that Taiwanese firms are reluctant to enter, such as Latin America and Eastern Europe. Through the acquisition of manufacturing plants originally owned by brand name producers, CEMs have grown rapidly in recent years. It is estimated that in 1998, about 19 percent of all electronics products shipped by U.S. firms were made by CEMs (*DigiTimes*, January 6, 1999).

Compared with CEMs, Taiwanese manufacturers are smaller in size and more specialized in their product lines. They responded to the challenge of CEMs on two fronts: the first was the enhancement of design capabilities, the other was an increase in manufacturing capacity through investment in China. With their design capabilities, Taiwanese manufacturers provide product designs as well as manufacturing services to international buyers. Because they specialize in small niche areas of the products, their product designs can be considered a subcontracting element of the grand design of the system. On the other hand, Taiwanese manufacturers have also invested heavily in China in order to increase their production capacity, particularly that of standardized products. Aided by low-cost Chinese labor, the Chinese factories are Taiwan's weapons for chipping into world market share. Many Taiwanese manufacturers have aspired to, and actually achieved, the status of the world's top suppliers in the niche products in which they have chosen to specialize. It seems, therefore, that the war between CEMs and Taiwan's contract manufacturers is a war between diversification and specialization, and a war between the Chinese advantage and the global touch.

CONCLUDING REMARKS

In this chapter, we studied the pattern of offshore sourcing by multinational firms in Taiwan. We find that the roles of offshore sourcing differ with the nature of the buyers. Manufacturers tend to emphasize cost saving in overseas procurement, whereas merchandisers that do not hold any manufacturing capacity emphasize flexibility in servicing the global markets. Moreover, manufacturers possessing manufacturing subsidiaries in Taiwan place even more emphasis on cost-saving than manufacturers possessing only procurement offices in Taiwan. The former buyers also exert the highest level of control over their suppliers in terms of technology choice to ensure the compatibility of their products.

Most international procurement offices in Taiwan purchase mature products from local suppliers. However, buyers with stronger technological capability tend to purchase more modern products, indicating the buyers' desire to maintain a technology gap between internal production and outsourcing to minimize the risk of technology leakage. Procurement for the purposes of quality improvement, supply flexibility, and supplementing production capacity at the headquarters tends to target advanced products more often than procurement that is aimed merely at cost saving.

Distance plays an important role in offshore sourcing strategy. In a comparison between the different country groups, Europeans in Taiwan stand out as a distinctive group in terms of sourcing strategy. European buyers purchase the most modern products from Taiwan, provide most autonomy to their suppliers in terms of technology choice, and maintain stable relationships with single suppliers. Distance tends to undermine the benefits of cost advantage, tilting the European buyers toward noncost strategic considerations when sourcing from Taiwan.

The growing trend toward separating design and marketing from manufacturing has witnessed increased sourcing activities by multinational firms in Taiwan. In recent years, more and more IPOs have been established without being accompanied by manufacturing capabilities, and the products sourced by them are increasingly modern, rather than mature ones. Nowadays Taiwanese contract manufacturers provide products to coordinate a full supply chain system to deliver the products to end users in a timely and flexible manner. As well as being cost-effective, they are also required to be speedy and global in their outlook. Investing in foreign locations to build manufacturing, warehousing, and after-sales service capabilities has become a prerequisite for today's contract manufacturers.

The effective management of the supply chain also requires new infrastructure that lies beyond the capacity of individual firms. In response, the Taiwanese government has, for example, invested heavily in the national information infrastructure (NII) since 1995, and has even provided subsidies to private firms building supply chain networks. The Taiwanese government has also recently launched a global logistics center plan aimed at establishing infrastructures that will facilitate the flow of goods, information, and finance. The objective of the plan is to reduce the shipping and handling costs of the entire economy from the current level of 13.1 percent of total value-added to 10 percent, making Taiwan an ideal hub for offshore sourcing (*APROC Newsletter*, August 2000, Council for Economic Development and Planning). The infrastructures envisaged by the plan include airports and seaports, customs procedures, telecommunications, legal provisions for electronic commerce, in addition to NII. In sum, they are the infrastructures that will enable a quick and flexible response network to integrate Taiwan into the world production system in which speed, rather than cost, plays an increasingly important role in market competition.

NOTES

1. Compared to Monczka and Trent's (1992) reasons for procurement, we ignore the reason of "exposure to worldwide technology," which is judged to be unimportant in Taiwan, and delineate the reason of "product delivery and reliability" into capacity supplementation and flexibility of supply. The latter two dimensions are conceptually distinctive and turn out to be important motives for multinational firms' procurement in Taiwan.

2. A respondent firm answering (1) or (2), or both, is recorded as one occurrence of procurement for the purpose of capacity supplementation. The same method is applied to the category of flexibility of supply.

3. Components and parts are considered to be an embodiment of technology transfer (Kotabe and Swan, 1994). But because the supply of components and parts covers only a portion, albeit probably the most important portion, of the technology employed in production, it is treated as a lower level of technology control.

4. Gilbert, Young, and O'Neal (1994) identify six operational characteristics of manufacturers that are actively engaged in the Japanese-style just-in-time production system: (1) high frequency in delivery of materials; (2) small number of suppliers; (3) de-emphasizing the use of low-cost suppliers; (4) long-time commitment to suppliers; (5) small lot size in delivery; and (6) short cycle time between receipt of materials and their placement into the production process. These characteristics are highy correlated. Our measure of the buyer–supplier relationship incorporates the second and fourth characteristics listed.

REFERENCES

Aoki, M. 1988. *Information, Incentives and Bargaining in the Japanese Economy.* Cambridge, U.K.: Cambridge University Press.

Asanuma, B. 1992. "Manufacturer–Supplier Relationships in Japan and the Concept of Relationship-Specific Skills." *Journal of Japanese and International Economics*, vol. 3, no. 1: 1–30.

Borrus, M. 1997. "Left for Dead: Asian Production Network and the Revival of US Electronics." In *The China Circle*, ed. B. Naughton. Washington: Brookings Institution for Economic Research.

Encarnation, D. 1992. *Rivals beyond Trade: America versus Japan in Global Competition*, Ithaca, NY: Cornell University Press.

Ernst, D. 1997. "Partners for the China Circle? The Asian Production Networks of Japanese Electronics Firms." In *The China Circle*, ed. B. Naughton. Washington: Brookings Institution for Economic Research.

Gilbert, F., J. Young, and C. O'Neal. 1994. "Buyer–Seller Relationships in the Just-in-Time Purchasing Environment." *Journal of Business Research*, vol. 29: 111–120.

Hahn, C. K., K. H. Kim, and J. S. Kim. 1986. "Costs of Competition: Implications for Purchasing Strategy." *Journal of Purchasing and Materials Management* (Fall): 2–7.

Kotabe, M. 1996. "Global Sourcing Strategy in the Pacific: American and Japanese Multinational Companies." In *Structural Competitiveness in the Pacific*, ed. G. Boyd. Cheltenham, U.K.: Edward Elgar.

Kotabe, M. 1992. "Global Sourcing Strategy: R & D." *Manufacturing and Marketing Interfaces.* New York: Quorum Books.

Kotabe, M., and J. Murray. 1990. "Linking Product and Process Innovations and Modes of International Sourcing in Global Competition: A Case of Foreign Multinational Firms." *Journal of International Business Studies*, vol. 21, no. 3: 383–408.

Kotabe, M., and G. Omura. 1989. "Sourcing Strategies of European and Japanese Multinationals: A Comparison." *Journal of International Business Studies*, vol. 20, no. 1: 113–130.

Kotabe, M., and S. Swan. 1992. "Offshore Sourcing: Reaction, Maturation and Consolidation of US Multinationals." *Journal of International Business Studies*, vol. 23, no. 1: 115–140.

Levy, D. 1995. "International Sourcing and Supply Chain Stability." *Journal of International Business Studies*, vol. 25, no. 2: 343–360.

Miles, R. E., and C. C. Snow. 1986. "Organizations: New Concepts for New Forms." *California Management Review* (Spring): 515–531.

Milgrom, P., and J. Roberts. 1990. "The Economics of Modern Manufacturing: Technology, Strategy and Organization." *American Economics Review*, vol. 80, no. 3: 511–528.

———. 1995. "Complementarities and Fit: Strategy, Structure, and Organizational Change in Manufacturing." *Journal of Accounting and Economics*, vol. 19: 179–208

Monczka, R., and R. Trent. 1991. "Global Sourcing: A Development Approach." *International Journal of Purchasing and Materials Management*, vol. 27 (Spring): 2–8.

Moxon, R. 1975. "The Motivation for Investment in Offshore Plants: The Case of the US Electronics Industry." *Journal of International Business Studies*, vol. 6, no. 3: 51–66.

Swamidass, P., and M. Kotabe. 1993. "Component Sourcing Strategies of Multinationals: An Empirical Study of European and Japanese Multinationals." *Journal of International Business Studies*, vol. 24, no. 1: 81–100.

Taylor, C., and S. Wiggins. 1997. "Competition or Compensation: Supplier Incentives under the American and Japanese Subcontracting Systems." *American Economics Review*, vol. 87, no. 4: 598–618.

Venkatesan, R. 1992. "Strategic Sourcing: To Make or Not to Make." *Harvard Business Review* (November–December): 98–107.

6

The Boomerang Effects of FDI on Domestic Economy: Taiwan's Agricultural Investment in Mainland China

Jiun-Mei Tien

INTRODUCTION

The economic relationship between Taiwan and mainland China started with trade. As the relationship developed, Taiwanese businessmen were motivated by profit incentives to invest in mainland China. Subsequently, the demand from Taiwanese companies that had invested in mainland China further boosted trade between the two regions. The changes in the industry structure of Taiwanese investment in mainland China over the last few years have two main features. Initially, investment in mainland China was in response to changes in the economic environment in Taiwan; the main emphasis was on exploiting mainland China's cheap labor. However, in the last few years, following the rapid economic development that mainland China has experienced, investment has been concentrated in those industries that have the potential to develop a large domestic market within mainland China. Whereas early investment was mainly in industry, in recent years there has been a rapid increase in investment in agriculture.

In the last few years, Taiwan's agriculture and food-processing industries have had to deal with changes in the overall domestic production environment. With production costs having risen and with products reaching the mature stage of their development, producers in the agriculture and food-processing sectors have been moving production to countries where the production factors that these industries need are more abundant. Taiwanese enterprises have production technology and product marketing advantages that these countries do not. By obtaining raw materials within the countries concerned, producers can reduce both transaction costs and the level of uncertainty between vendor and purchaser. Taiwan and mainland China are separated by only a relatively narrow strait; linguistic, ethnic, and geographical considerations have led many agricultural enterprises to invest in mainland China.

There are significant differences between investment in mainland China by the Taiwanese manufacturing industry and by agricultural producers. Manufacturing firms generally ship intermediate raw materials from Taiwan for manufacture in mainland China, whereas with agricultural investment the Taiwanese producers provide capital and technology, using local agricultural resources to undertake production. The aim of this study is to explore the current status of agricultural investment in mainland China by Taiwanese producers, the Taiwan and mainland China regulations governing agricultural investment, and the impact of investment by Taiwanese businesspeople in mainland China's agricultural sector on Taiwan's economy.

THE CURRENT STATUS OF INVESTMENT BY TAIWANESE BUSINESSPEOPLE IN MAINLAND CHINA'S AGRICULTURAL SECTOR

According to statistics produced by the Investment Commission of the Ministry of Economic Affairs, total reported Taiwanese investment in the agricultural sector in mainland China over the period 1987–1999 came to $1.359 billion, accounting for 79.2 percent of total overseas investment in agriculture over the same period (see Table 6-1). The other main recipients of Taiwanese agricultural investment were Vietnam and Thailand; there was also a limited amount of investment in America, Oceania, Indonesia, the Philippines, Malaysia, and Singapore. Clearly, mainland China has become the main center for overseas investment in agriculture by Taiwanese companies. When one adds to this the investment that has not been reported to the government, the total amount of agricultural investment in mainland China would be several times as large.

Agricultural investment in mainland China involves mainly food and beverage manufacturing. There are many different categories of agricultural investment, and the scale of investment varies markedly. The different types of land use, labor management, financing, and relations with the local community are also more complex than for industrial investment. The regions that have experienced Taiwanese investment in agriculture include Hainan, Fujian, Guangdong, Zhejiang, Shanghai,

TABLE 6-1. Approved Overseas Investment in the Agricultural Sector

| | $ thousand | | | | | | | | | | | | | Total for |
	1987	1988	1989	1990	1991	1992	1993	1994	1995	1996	1997	1998	1999	1987–1999
Asia	0	2,311	401	15,641	39,285	51,090	369,490	196,507	132,475	158,140	443,345	148,616	62,879	1,620,180
Mainland China	0	0	0	0	19,308	46,415	354,558	155,310	119,596	128,802	381,719	91,125	62,879	1,359,712
Singapore	0	0	51	0	0	0	0	0	0	0	0	0	0	51
Philippines	0	400	0	0	40	0	0	0	0	4,968	18,366	1,550	0	25,324
Indonesia	0	351	0	5,898	7,720	675	0	2,717	500	10,526	1,034	815	0	30,236
Thailand	0	1,560	350	9,743	12,217	4,000	9,187	12,048	4,895	13,111	656	7,014	0	74,781
Malaysia	0	0	0	0	0	0	0	72	404	0	0	796	0	1,272
Vietnam	0	0	0	0	0	0	5,745	26,360	7,080	733	41,570	47,316	0	128,804
America	5,000	0	0	15,300	0	0	0	210	20,824	6,320	17,347	1,215	1,025	67,241
Oceania	0	0	0	0	0	0	0	23,300	0	5,151	0	1,368	0	29,819
Total	5,000	2,311	401	30,941	39,285	51,090	369,490	220,017	153,299	169,611	460,692	151,199	63,904	1,717,240

Notes: 1. Agriculture includes agriculture, forestry, fisheries, and food and beverage manufacturing.
2. Where the figure for total annual overseas investment is higher than the combined total for Asia, America, and Oceania, this is because of investment in some other region in that year.
3. In 1993 and 1997 the government permitted retroactive registration of investment in mainland China; as a result, the amount of investment reported for these years is particularly large.

Source: Investment Commission, Ministry of Economic Affairs, Monthly Statistical Report on Investment by Overseas Chinese and Foreigners in the ROC, Overseas Investment, Overseas Technical Collaboration, Indirect Investment in Mainland China and Technology Transfer to Mainland China, December 1999 edition.

Shandong, and Beijing. The different types of production involved include aquaculture, marine products processing, oils, animal feed, fruit, vegetables, livestock breeding, agricultural products processing, tea, flowers, and the like. Agricultural investment is concentrated mainly in Fujian, Guangdong, Shandong, and Hainan. In addition to agricultural investment, Taiwanese businesspeople in mainland China also undertake agricultural technology transfer and international agricultural product market development.

Since 1993, the amount of agricultural investment in mainland China by Taiwanese businesspeople has grown rapidly. Growth has been particularly strong in food and beverage manufacturing, mainly because several of Taiwan's largest food manufacturers have invested in mainland China. Of Taiwan's listed food manufacturing companies, more than half have established operations in mainland China. A common feature of these food manufacturers is that their production is oriented mainly toward mainland China's domestic market. There is also a considerable amount of small-scale direct investment in agriculture, forestry, and fisheries that is not reported to the Investment Commission. This is why food processing accounted for 90.9 percent of approved investment over the period 1991–1999. The average scale of investment per investment project was $520,000; however, there was wide variation in scale (see Table 6-2).

Investment by Taiwanese food manufacturers in mainland China tends to be either independent or in the form of a joint venture with a local company; there are few examples of investment involving collaboration with another Taiwanese company. Investment is normally in the form of cash, although there are also many examples of investment where machinery and equipment are provided in lieu of cash. When food manufacturers first start to invest in mainland China, their main products tend to be similar to those of the parent company in Taiwan; they then begin to make adjustments in line with local market demand. As companies modify their production and sales methods in line with the characteristics of the mainland China domestic market, and as sales gradually increase, the mainland China operations gain more autonomy, and their links with the parent company in Taiwan gradually start to weaken.

TAIWAN AND MAINLAND CHINA REGULATIONS GOVERNING INVESTMENT IN THE MAINLAND CHINA AGRICULTURAL SECTOR BY TAIWANESE BUSINESSPEOPLE

Currently, the principles under which Taiwan permits Taiwanese businesspeople to invest in the agricultural sector in mainland China are as follows:

TABLE 6-2. Distribution by Industry of Taiwanese Investment in the Agricultural Sector in Mainland China (1991–1999)

$ thousand

Industry	Agriculture and Forestry			Fisheries and Livestock Breeding			Food and Beverage Manufacturing			Total		
Year	No. of Cases	Amount	Average Scale	No. of Cases	Amount	Average Scale	No. of Cases	Amount	Average Scale	No. of Cases	Amount	Average Scale
1991	0	0	0	0	0	0	19	19,308	1,016	19	19,308	1,016
1992	0	0	0	0	0	0	27	46,415	1,719	27	46,415	1,719
1993	122	15,740	129	33	14,263	432	791	324,555	410	946	354,558	375
1994	7	2,330	333	6	7,134	1,189	73	145,846	1,998	86	155,310	1,806
1995	4	2,149	537	0	0	0	32	117,447	3,670	36	119,596	3,322
1996	3	1,100	367	0	6,000	0	30	121,702	4,057	33	128,802	3,903
1997	167	39,150	234	43	9,496	221	1,151	333,073	289	1,361	381,719	280
1998	17	14,889	876	8	6,191	774	57	70,045	1,229	82	91,125	1,111
1999	4	3,129	782	1	1,500	1,500	19	58,250	3,066	24	62,879	2,620
Total	324	78,487	656	91	44,584	490	2,199	1,236,641	562	2,614	1,359,712	520

Source: Investment Commission, Ministry of Economic Affairs, Monthly Statistical Report on Investment by Overseas Chinese and Foreigners in the ROC, Overseas Investment, Overseas Technical Collaboration, Indirect Investment in Mainland China and Technology Transfer to Mainland China, December 1999 edition.

1. Investment is permitted for agricultural products that are either not produced in Taiwan or for which Taiwan has a low level of self-sufficiency with a low level of substitutability.
2. Investment is permitted for agricultural products in which Taiwan lacks international competitiveness.
3. Investment is permitted for agricultural products that have high environmental costs in Taiwan.
4. Investment is permitted for agricultural products that are of benefit to the development of agriculture in both Taiwan and mainland China.

Investment is prohibited for the following categories of product:

1. Agricultural products and related production technology the exporting of which to mainland China is either prohibited or restricted by international regulations
2. Agricultural products and related production technology that would have a seriously negative impact on the safety or economic development of Taiwan
3. Agricultural products and related production technology for which the government has invested in research and development, or the development of which the government has actively promoted
4. Fisheries production using the same offshore or coastal fishing grounds as those traditionally used by Taiwanese fishing vessels

The main categories of industry in which investment is permitted in mainland China are the "twilight industries" with high production costs, high levels of pollution, and low international competitiveness. Agricultural products with advanced production technology are among those in which investment is prohibited. As of the end of May 2000, there were 223 agricultural products in which Taiwanese companies were permitted to invest in mainland China. Most of these came under the food and beverage manufacturing sector. There were 10 products in which investment was prohibited, including green tea, hemp, opium, and plant extracts.

Since 1989, the authorities in mainland China have been making a systematic effort to attract Taiwanese companies to invest in the agricultural sector. At first, they concentrated on Fujian, which is geographically and culturally closest to Taiwan. The mainland China government and academia made a major promotional effort that succeeded in attracting the attention of academics, retired government officials, and technical personnel in Taiwan; this in turn stimulated Taiwanese companies to undertake investment. In 1996, the "Cross-strait (Zhangzhou)

Experimental Agricultural Collaboration Site" and "Center for Introducing Agricultural Production and Sales Techniques from Taiwan" were established. In 1997, the "Cross-strait (Fuzhou) Experimental Agricultural Collaboration District" was established. Hainan Province has also been planning similar measures. The authorities in mainland China have provided a variety of incentives to encourage Taiwanese companies to invest in agriculture. These have had a demonstration effect, encouraging the development of agricultural investment by Taiwanese companies in other provinces and municipalities. (See Figure 6-1.)

Mainland China is very protective of its rare strains and breeds and does not permit foreign investment in these products. The government in Taiwan expressly forbids investment in mainland China in hemp, opium poppies, and other drug-related products, as well as in tea production. Investment in the vast majority of other agricultural products is permitted by both Taiwan and mainland China. However, the attempts to regulate Taiwanese investment in the agricultural sector in mainland China by the Taiwanese government have had no practical effect.

THE IMPACT ON THE TAIWANESE ECONOMY OF INVESTMENT IN THE MAINLAND CHINA AGRICULTURAL SECTOR BY TAIWANESE BUSINESSPEOPLE

Mainland China is the main recipient of agricultural investment by Taiwanese businesspeople. At the same time, in diplomatic, political, and military terms, mainland China is hostile to Taiwan. This is a situation rarely seen before anywhere else in the world. Generally speaking, the effects of overseas investment in terms of stimulating

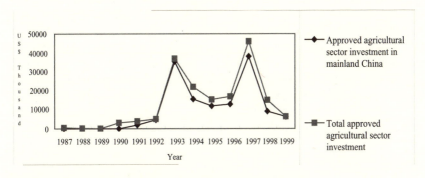

Figure 6-1. Total approved agricultural sector invesment.

trade and causing changes to domestic output depend on the level of technology in the industry in question, the level of connectedness, the sources of raw materials, and the character of and strategy behind the overseas investment.

Initially, investment in mainland China by Taiwanese companies mainly took the form of defensive investment. Companies undertook overseas investment largely because of worsening production conditions at home, with the aim of finding cheaper production factors overseas. Fundamentally speaking, agricultural investment in mainland China by Taiwanese companies also came under this category of defensive investment. However, as mainland China's domestic market has gradually expanded, developing this domestic market has gradually come to be the main consideration in investment decisions.

Defensive investment can affect the domestic economy in the following ways:

1. Squeezing out of investment funds: Funds that would originally have been used for domestic investment are invested overseas instead, reducing the amount of investment in the domestic economy.
2. The impact on domestic output: As production activity moves overseas, there is a commensurate decline in domestic output. The impact of the interindustry multiplier effect can lead to a decline in final output value.
3. Stimulating exports in related industries: When an industry first moves production overseas, a significant percentage of intermediate inputs may be purchased from the home country; this will go some way toward offsetting the loss from reduced domestic output. However, after a period of time has elapsed, the investing companies will usually start to increase local purchasing of intermediate inputs, thereby reducing the intermediate inputs export effect.
4. Competition where goods are exported back to the home country: If the output of overseas investment is exported back to the home country, because the production costs overseas will tend to be lower, this will increase the pressure of competition on domestic industry.
5. International market competition: If the output of overseas investment is sold directly on the international market, it will be in competition with the exports of domestic industry in the home country, and may enjoy a comparative advantage over the home country.

The reduction in output in the home country and the stimulation of exports by related industries will have a direct impact on short-term fluctuations in output in the home country. This type of fluctuation will gradually decrease over time, partly because of the adjustment in supply and demand within the home country, and partly because of the gradual reduction in purchasing from the home country by the companies investing overseas. However, the problems of re-export back to the home country and international market competition will become greater with the passing of time. The more successful the overseas operations of the companies investing overseas, the more obvious this pressure will become, because their products will become more competitive and they may exploit their successes overseas to disrupt the domestic market.

Agricultural investment in mainland China uses mainly local raw materials and local labor as inputs, with the output being sold in both the local market and the international market. The impact of agricultural investment in mainland China on Taiwan is analyzed next.

The Squeezing Out of Funds in Domestic Agriculture

When Taiwanese businesspeople invest in the agricultural sector in mainland China, what they take out of Taiwan is capital, production technology, management methods, and superior crop strains. As far as capital is concerned, most of the Taiwanese businesspeople who invest in agriculture in mainland China had not been farmers engaged in agricultural production in Taiwan; they were entrepreneurs. If these entrepreneurs had not invested in the agricultural sector in mainland China, they would not have invested in agricultural production in Taiwan. This is because of the restrictions on the purchasing of agricultural land in Taiwan, which would make it impossible for entrepreneurs to obtain such land; it would also be difficult to rent a large area of land from farmers. In addition, the profits from agriculture are lower than those that can be obtained from the manufacturing industry and other sectors; most entrepreneurs therefore choose to invest in other industries. In interviews with Taiwanese businesspeople who had invested in the agricultural sector in mainland China, the Taiwanese businesspeople stated that if they had not invested in agriculture in mainland China, they would have used their capital to invest in an industry other than agriculture. Thus, as far as the impact of agricultural investment in mainland China in terms of capital is concerned, investment in mainland China has not directly squeezed out funds that would otherwise have been invested in domestic agriculture. However, it has reduced investment in sectors of the domestic economy other than agriculture.

With regard to investment in mainland China by the food-manufacturing industry, with the decline in agricultural production in Taiwan in recent years, and with the food-manufacturing industry having reached a mature stage of development, as long ago as the 1980s the major food manufacturers had already started establishing factories in mainland China in search of raw materials and markets. If the government had not begun to permit indirect investment in mainland China, these food manufacturers would have invested in some other country rather than expand their plant facilities in Taiwan. However, they might also have moved into other industries, adopting an operational strategy based on diversification.

Impact on Domestic Output of Agricultural Products and Processed Foods

If the companies investing in the agricultural sector in mainland China were involved in the same kind of activity in Taiwan, unless they were unable to maintain their operations in Taiwan, these operations would continue. In other words, they would continue production in Taiwan, and would continue to sell to the Taiwan market. Because investment in the agricultural sector in mainland China does not have a very marked effect on investment in domestic agriculture through the squeezing out of funds, the reduction in final demand output caused by investment in the agricultural sector in mainland China would be limited. However, if the output of the companies investing in mainland China was exported back to Taiwan, because the agricultural products market in Taiwan had already reached saturation point, the addition of further agricultural products would have an exclusion effect on the enterprises that had continued production in Taiwan.

Agricultural Intermediates Transshipment Export Trade Effect

It seems questionable whether investment by Taiwanese companies in the agricultural sector in mainland China will stimulate transshipment export trade in intermediate inputs as investment in manufacturing industry in mainland China has done. If one considers the production technology used in agriculture, although considerable time and effort are required for agricultural technology research and development, once the R & D has been completed, as long as you have possession of the superior crop strains and related production technology, along with a suitable climate and environment, you can then begin large-scale imitative production and enjoy the benefits of the R&D work. It is difficult to keep new agricultural technology secret, or to obtain patents for it. The transshipment export trade effect that could be produced for Taiwan's agriculture through the technology transfer process would probably be limited to the export of seeds, seedlings, and stud animals. Furthermore, even this limited intermediate input export trade would not last long, because crop strains and animal breeds require domestication, and within a few years mainland China would itself have accumulated the necessary strains and breeds. Agricultural investment in mainland China therefore does not require the transshipment export of intermediate inputs from Taiwan as manufacturing investment does, and an intermediate input transshipment export trade effect is therefore not created.

Over the period 1992–1996, the five main agricultural products exported from Taiwan to mainland China via Hong Kong were wood, wool, beverages, compound food products, and food-manufacturing industry waste. The intermediate transshipment export trade and related spillover effect created by agricultural investment in mainland China by Taiwanese companies have thus been very limited.

Exporting of Mainland China Agricultural Products Back to Taiwan

The greatest impact on Taiwan of agricultural investment in mainland China by Taiwanese companies lies in the exporting of agricultural products back to Taiwan and in competition between Taiwanese and mainland China products in international markets. First of all, as far as individual products are concerned, production costs in mainland China are about one third those in Taiwan. Therefore, in addition to being sold in mainland China or on the international market, the agricultural products of some Taiwanese companies investing in mainland China have the potential to be exported back to Taiwan. This is particularly true for products with high added value, or for which there is strong seasonal demand in Taiwan. Exporting this type of product back to Taiwan can yield high profits. The widespread smuggling into Taiwan of mainland China food products such as peanuts, daylily flowers, mushrooms, and fish provides evidence to support this view.

Just how much of the output of Taiwanese companies investing in the agricultural sector in mainland China will be exported back to Taiwan will depend on the volume of production, domestic sales in mainland China, the state of supply and demand in the international market, and the price of agricultural products in Taiwan. The assumption is made that all agricultural products imported into Taiwan from mainland China via Hong Kong in 1995 were produced by Taiwanese companies operating in mainland China. Although reality does not conform entirely to this assumption, under the current circumstances where Taiwan restricts the import of certain mainland China agricultural products, this is the upper limit for exporting of agricultural products back to Taiwan. First, these transshipment imports are broken down into thirty-nine product categories. The spillover effect from domestic interrelation $(I–D)^{-1}$ is then used to calculate the impact on each domestic industry. That is to say:

$(I–D)^{-1}$ • Agricultural products imported from mainland China via Hong Kong = Reduction in output value for each domestic industry

The impact on domestic industry is found to be highest for arable and pastoral farming production. The next most strongly affected industries are, in order, food processing, finance and insurance, commodity trading, fisheries products, and so on. In terms of the level of interconnectedness, the arable and pastoral farming production sector has a level of sensitivity higher than 1, but a level of impact lower than 1. This type of industry tends to develop rapidly when another industry takes off; most of them are vital to the development of other industries. If this type of industry is replaced by goods exported back to Taiwan from mainland China, this is likely to affect the development of other industries. The food-processing industry has a low level of sensitivity but a high level of impact. That is to say, its level of forward interconnectedness is low, but its level of backward interconnectedness is high. This type of industry is unlikely to be affected by other industries, but is very likely to stimulate the development of other industries. The exporting of product back to Taiwan in this industry would affect arable and pastoral farming production. In other words, though the main types of agricultural product that are exported back to Taiwan are arable and pastoral farming products and food products, it is precisely these two domestic industries that are most affected. The reduction in arable and pastoral farming production comes to $207.01 million, approximately 1.36 times the value of the product exported back to Taiwan ($152.56 million) (see Table 6-3). The fall in the output value of food-processing production has been $53.22 million, approximately 5.44 times the value of the product exported back to Taiwan ($9.78 million). The total reduction in output in domestic industry has been $418.30 million, approximately 2.26 times the total value of product exported back to Taiwan ($184.77 million).

Mainland China agricultural products exported to Taiwan via Hong Kong account for only part of total mainland China agricultural product exports to Taiwan. If exports via other channels, such as smuggling, were taken into account, then the total volume of mainland China agricultural product exports to Taiwan would be even higher. The following section discusses the smuggling of mainland China agricultural products.

TABLE 6-3. Simulation of the Economic Effect of Exporting of Agricultural Product from Mainland China to Taiwan

					$ ten thousand	
Sector	Item		Value of Agricultural Products Exported Back to Taiwan (Agricultural Products Imported into Taiwan from Mainland China via Hong Kong in 1995) (1)		Negative Impact on Domestic Industry Output Value (2)	(2)/(1)
01	Arable and pastoral farming	(1)	15,256	(1)	20,701	1.36
02	Forestry		158		214	
03	Fisheries	(3)	847	(5)	1,070	1.26
04	Mining		0		34	
05	Food processing	(2)	978	(2)	5,322	5.44
06	Beverages		21		29	
07	Tobacco		23		23	
08	Textiles	(5)	560		796	
09	Garments and clothing		0		67	
10	Timber and timber products	(4)	633		766	
11	Paper, paper products and publishing		0		301	
12	Chemical raw materials		0		191	
13	Artificial fiber		0		186	
14	Plastics		0		101	
15	Plastics products		0		258	
16	Other chemical products		0		902	
17	Petrochemical products		0		386	
18	Non-metal mineral products		0		48	
19	Iron and steel		0		80	
20	Other metals		0		19	
21	Metal products		0		100	
22	Machinery		0		57	
23	Home appliances		0		5	
24	Electronics products		0		16	
25	Electrical machinery and instruments		0		32	
26	Vehicles		0		36	
27	Other manufactured products		0		26	
28	Construction		0		107	
29	Electric power		0		374	
30	Gas and running water		0		28	
31	Transportation, warehousing, and communications		0		524	
32	Commodity sales		0	(4)	1,287	
33	Financial and insurance services		0	(3)	1,658	
34	Real estate services		0		164	
35	Restaurant and hotel services		0		19	

TABLE 6-3. (continued)

			$ ten thousand	
Sector	Item	Value of Agricultural Products Exported Back to Taiwan (Agricultural Products Imported into Taiwan from Mainland China via Hong Kong in 1995) (1)	Negative Impact on Domestic Industry Output Value (2)	(2)/(1)
36	Commercial services	0	338	
37	Public administration services	0	0	
38	Education and health services	0	35	
39	Other services	0	39	
1–39	Total	18,477	41,830	2.26

Sources: 1995 *Hong Kong Statistical Bureau disk;* 1991 Input–Output Tables, Taiwan area. The Republic of China, February 1995.

When one compares Taiwan's (ROC) Customs import and export trade statistics and the mainland China customs statistics, one would expect them to be in conformity with one another. In reality, every year there has been a disparity between the value of agricultural product imports from mainland China reported by Taiwan's (ROC) Customs and the value of agricultural product exports to Taiwan reported by the mainland China customs authorities. If one takes the higher figure in each case, then over the period 1997–1999 Taiwan imported approximately $260 to $360 million worth of agricultural products from mainland China, with down, medicinal plants, timber, and shavings being the biggest single import items. Over the same period, Taiwan exported $130 to $160 million worth of agricultural products to mainland China, with plywood, charcoal, shuttle-woven fabric, and miscellaneous compound food products being the biggest export items. Taiwan thus had a trade deficit in agricultural products with mainland China.

The Smuggling of Mainland China Agricultural Products into Taiwan

In accordance with the Regulations Governing the Authorization of Trade Between Taiwan and Mainland China, mainland China agricultural products imported into Taiwan must conform to the following two requirements: (1) They must not be injurious to national security, and (2) they must not have a negative impact on related industries. There are currently over 480 types of agricultural products the importing of which from mainland China is permitted, including live eels, live finless eels, dried cashew nuts, coffee, millet, frozen sardines, cane sugar, and so on. The economic impact model for the exporting of mainland China agricultural products to Taiwan given previously was based on these regulations. If the regulations were relaxed or abolished, the volume of agricultural products imported into Taiwan from mainland China whould increase significantly, as is made clear from the widespread smuggling of mainland China agricultural products into Taiwan. Although investment by Taiwanese companies in the agricultural sector in mainland China is not directly related to smuggling, it does increase mainland China's ability to smuggle agricultural products. The increase in smuggling of agricultural products increases supply in Taiwan's domestic agricultural products market, causing the price of agricultural products to fall. Because farmers cannot achieve a reasonable level of profit by producing the products in question, production contracts.

For several years now, a wide variety of different agricultural products have been smuggled into Taiwan from mainland China, including arable and pastoral farming products, forestry products, and fisheries products. The smuggling in of agricultural products from mainland China not only threatens national security, affects the supply and demand of agricultural products, and causes the price of domestic agricultural products to fluctuate, it also threatens consumers' health. Infectious diseases are widespread in mainland China, and smuggled agricultural products are not subject to health inspections. The data in Taiwan's *Annual Customs Report* show that, over the period 1989–1998, the types of smuggled mainland China agricultural products seized by Customs included fresh fish and other marine products, black melon seeds, peanuts, mushrooms, cows' stomachs, cows' tendons, daylily leaves, fir boards, alcohol, and other products. The total amount of smuggled goods seized each year during this period varied between approximately $120,000 to $3,170,000 (see Table 6-4); the quantity of smuggled agricultural products destroyed every year came to approximately 2,000 tons.

According to the Chung-Hua Institution for Economic Research Studies *Analysis of Competition and Complementarity between Taiwanese and Mainland China Agricultural Products* (Chiu, Tien, and Tuan, 1994; Chiu, Tien, and Chen, 1995), the cost of producing one kilo of pork in Taiwan is approximately three times the cost in mainland China, and as a result the price of pork in Taiwan is approximately three times as high as in the mainland. If mainland China pork can be successfully smuggled into Taiwan, the profits could be very high. The production cost per hectare of rice in Taiwan is around twelve times as high as in mainland China, and the market price for one kilo of rice in Taiwan is around seven times as high as in the mainland. Here again, substantial profits

TABLE 6-4.   Seizure of Mainland China Agricultural Products Smuggled into Taiwan, 1989–1998 ($ Thousands)

Year	Amount	Year	Amount
1989	235.2	1994	3172.3
1990	185.9	1995	2983.4
1991	167.8	1996	1169.9
1992	119.4	1997	664.7
1993	681.8	1998	306.3

Source: Annual Customs Report.

could be made from importing or smuggling in rice. The cost of raising a chicken is around twice as high in Taiwan as in mainland China; the production cost for mushrooms is around three times as high, and the price of red beans in mainland China is around one third the price in Taiwan. Because of the disparities in terms of production cost and price between agricultural products in Taiwan and mainland China, regardless of whether agricultural products are imported legally or smuggled in, high profits can be made.

Competition between Taiwanese and Mainland China Agricultural Products in the Japanese Market

There can be no doubt that agricultural investment by Taiwanese companies in mainland China has an indirect effect on Taiwanese agricultural products' export markets. Although there is no direct evidence to prove this relationship, one can look at the growth and decline of Taiwanese and mainland China agricultural products in international markets in the last few years. Although there may be some degree of complementarity between these production factors, when a consumer is buying a particular product, the products become substitutable with one another. When the manufacturers send these substitutable products to the market, they compete with one another—competition that expresses itself in the form of market share. The higher the market share, the more competitive the product. Thus, regardless of whether there is complementarity in terms of factor inputs, the final goal of the product is consumption. As soon as the product appears in the consumer market, it will come into competition with any substitutable product. In other words, although factor complementarity may occur during the production process, once the product is on the market, competition develops.

Over the last five years, the import value for agricultural products in Taiwan has increased every year, whereas the export value has fallen every year. Overall, Taiwan's trade deficit in agricultural products is getting bigger. By contrast, mainland China's agricultural product exports are increasing rapidly, while at the same time the value of agricultural product imports in mainland China is also increasing steadily year by year. Overall, mainland China has been maintaining a trade surplus in agricultural products (see Figure 6-2).

If one compares the twenty leading agricultural product import and export items for Taiwan and mainland China, over the years Taiwan's main import products have been corn, soya beans, cotton, timber, tobacco, and fishmeal. The biggest source of imports has been the United States, accounting for over 90 percent of agricultural product imports. Taiwan's main agricultural export products are pork, frozen tuna, down, and eels. The main recipient of these exports is Japan, which accounts for over 90 percent of Taiwan's agricultural product exports. In the past, mainland China's main agricultural product imports were wheat, vegetable oils, and so on. However, in recent years cotton has become the main agricultural import product. In 1993 and 1994, mainland China's main agricultural export product was corn. However, by 1995 corn was no longer being exported. Instead, the main agricultural export product was now tobacco. In 1999, mainland China's main agricultural export products were meat, fish, and meat and fish products. Exports of these products have developed strongly from 1995. It can reasonably be assumed that the steady diversification in mainland China's agricultural exports products over the last few years is closely related to agricultural sector investment in mainland China by Taiwanese and foreign companies.

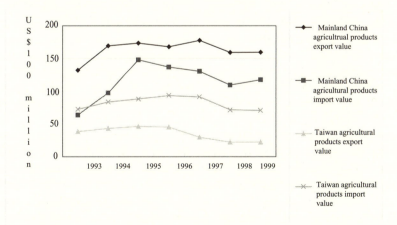

Figure 6-2. Import and export value trends for Taiwan and Mainland China. *Sources:* The Taiwan (ROC) Customs Import and Export Trade Statistics; The Mainland China Customs Statistics.

Japan is the largest market for both Taiwanese and mainland China agricultural products. In 1996, Japan was the main market for twenty-one out of thirty of Taiwan's leading agricultural product export items. Furthermore, for eleven of these products Japan accounted for 90 to 100 percent of total exports. The data for 1992–1996 show that during this period Taiwanese agricultural products remained stagnant in the Japanese market, remaining at around the $3 billion level. Over the period 1997–1999 there was a dramatic fall; by 1999 total Taiwanese agricultural product exports to Japan had fallen to only $1.04 billion. The main export items were fish, down, vegetables, and edible roots.

Turning to the status of mainland China agricultural product exports in the Japanese market, these grew from $1.976 billion in 1990 to $3.51 billion in 1993, $5.818 billion in 1996, and $5.43 billion in 1999. The main export items were fish, meat, fish and meat products, vegetables, edible roots, and their products. There was particularly rapid growth in meat and fish. These are precisely the products in which Taiwan has seen exports to Japan fall off in recent years. Clearly, competition between Taiwanese and mainland China agricultural products in the Japanese market is already quite marked, and Taiwanese agricultural products are at a disadvantage compared to mainland China products.

In addition, in the last few years Taiwan and mainland China agricultural product imports from Japan have been increasing. However, mainland China's agricultural product imports from Japan have been increasing at a faster rate than Taiwan's. Overall, both Taiwan and mainland China have a trade surplus with Japan with respect to agricultural products, and there is considerable overlap in the type of agricultural products that Taiwan and mainland China export to Japan. However, there are differences in the types of product that they import from Japan (see Figure 6-3).

CONCLUSION AND POLICY RECOMMENDATION

Conclusion

Agricultural sector investment in mainland China by Taiwanese companies got off to a later start than industrial investment, and the amount of investment is less. In recent years, economic reform in mainland China has stimulated economic development. Per capita income has risen, and consumption has risen with it. In particular, there has been a significant increase in demand for food products. As a result, foreign companies have been impressed with the potential of mainland China's domestic market. In addition, as reform has progressed, it has become increasingly less likely that mainland China will return to a command economy; this has made foreign companies more willing to invest in the

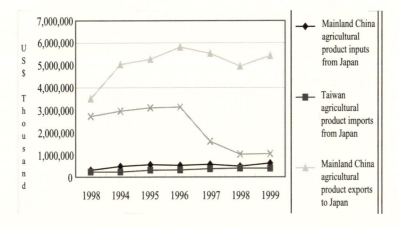

Figure 6-3. Growth and Decline of Mainland China and Taiwan Agricultural Products in the Japanese Market.
Sources: The Taiwan (ROC) Customs Import and Export Trade Statistics; The Mainland China Customs Statistics; The World Trade Atlas Disk.

complex agricultural sector. In addition, as far as overall resources are concerned, mainland China possesses land and labor resources available for development, which is a necessary precondition for agricultural sector development. As a result, in the last few years there has been vigorous foreign investment in mainland China's agricultural sector; investment by Taiwanese companies has been equally pronounced.

Investment in mainland China by Taiwanese companies is motivated by the desire for the profits that can be secured by exploiting mainland China's cheap raw materials and extensive markets. Although many companies have made profits in mainland China, many others have been forced to pull out, and other companies are still waiting to see how things develop before investing there. There are two categories of Taiwanese businesspeople who have invested in the agricultural sector in mainland China. The first is those who were already involved in agriculture or a related industry in Taiwan. The second is those who were impressed by the possibilities offered by the mainland China market. The first category of investors are in a position to provide agricultural technology; the second category of investing provide only capital.

As far the mainland China economy as a whole is concerned, the increase in agricultural sector investment by Taiwanese companies has provided an additional source of capital, superior technology, and superior strains and breeds. It has created a virtuous circle whereby production has increased, farmers' incomes have increased, villages have grown more prosperous, the supply of agricultural products has increased, consumption levels have risen, agricultural exports have increased, and foreign currency income has increased. As a result, both in the present and in the future, agricultural sector investment by Taiwanese companies is proving beneficial to agricultural development in mainland China.

Regarding the impact of agricultural sector investment in mainland China by Taiwanese companies, given the current regulatory framework, there are six main points that can be made. (1) Agricultural sector investment in mainland China by Taiwanese companies has not squeezed out investment in Taiwan's domestic agricultural sector. (2) There has been little impact on the level of output of domestic agricultural products and processed foods. (3) Because Taiwanese companies investing in the agricultural sector in mainland China have little need to import intermediate from Taiwan, the intermediate transshipment export trade effect that can be created for the agricultural sector in Taiwan is limited. (4) Currently, Taiwan imposes considerable restrictions on the importing of agricultural products from mainland China, while at the same time there is currently strong demand for agricultural products and products made from them in mainland China's domestic market. As a result, the impact of lawful exports of agricultural products back to Taiwan has not been great; however, the producers all hope that they will be permitted to export their products back to Taiwan. (5) The differences in production cost and price between agricultural products in Taiwan and mainland China mean that considerable profits can be made from smuggling. As a result, smuggling of agricultural products from mainland China is rampant. (6) Agricultural investment in mainland China by Taiwanese companies has speeded up the rate of improvement in technology and the accumulation of capital in mainland China's agricultural sector, thereby increasing the competitiveness of mainland China agricultural products on international markets, and creating a situation where agricultural products from mainland China and Taiwan are in competition in these international markets.

Although the government in Taiwan has adopted a "no haste, be patient" policy of attempting to slow the development of investing links with mainland China, they have not been able to restrain the enthusiasm of Taiwanese businesspeople for investment in the mainland. Add to this the various measures adopted by the authorities in mainland China to encourage agricultural sector investment by Taiwanese businesspeople, and there has been a steady stream of Taiwanese food manufacturers establishing themselves in mainland China. Under these circumstances Taiwan's policy for the overall development of the agricultural sector needs to be adjusted so that Taiwanese agriculture can continue to develop and farmers' rights can be protected.

Policy Recommendation

Besides agriculture, other Taiwanese industries have also invested in mainland China. Estimates by various government agencies indicate that, as of October 2000, total Taiwanese investment in mainland China had already reached $50 to $70 billion, of which agricultural sector investment accounted for only around 3.5 to 5 percent. Thus, even if this capital had not been invested in the agricultural sector in mainland China, it is unlikely that it would have been invested in agriculture or other industries in Taiwan; it would probably have been invested in some other sector in mainland China.

Although Taiwanese investment in agriculture in mainland China has benefited a handful of Taiwanese businesspeople, there are several problems related to the limited profits that have been made—some latent, some already starting to make themselves felt. Examples include the wasting of large quantities of personnel and material, the lack of protection for consumers with respect to smuggled products, the harm caused to agricultural producers in Taiwan, and the way in which the transfer of agricultural technology from Taiwan has increased the competitiveness of mainland China agricultural products on international markets, and so on. At the same time, while demand for imported agricultural products is high in Taiwan, mainland China can provide only a limited part of this. From the point of view of Taiwanese agriculture as a whole, therefore, the negative impact of Taiwanese investment in the agricultural sector in mainland China far outweighs the benefits.

At present, Taiwanese agriculture is a relatively weak sector. The government has adopted various protective measures and regulations with respect to agricultural products and imports; once Taiwan joins the WTO, these measures will have to be reduced steadily gradually. The reduction of tariffs and market opening will have a negative impact on those agricultural products that are currently protected. In addition, we also have to take into consideration the impact of agricultural imports from mainland China. Currently, trade in agricultural products between Taiwan and mainland China is restricted by the political environment, with only indirect trade being permitted. However, smuggling has continued to exist. Taiwanese agricultural investment in mainland China has been concentrated in the foods sector; government regulations prevent these products from being exported back to Taiwan. However, if, after mainland China and Taiwan join the WTO mainland China products are able to enter the Taiwan market, their low cost will constitute a serious threat to Taiwanese agricultural products.

If the problems affecting Taiwan's agriculture are to be solved, production of noncompetitive agricultural products will have to be reduced, with a speeding up of the transfer of some agricultural sector resources (including farmers and agricultural land) to the manufacturing or service sectors. In order to make this adjustment in the use of agricultural resources in Taiwan, the government agencies with responsibility for agriculture must be reorganized and streamlined, and appropriate measures taken in response to the development of international competition in agricultural products and the technology transfer that can result from Taiwanese investment in agriculture in mainland China. Taiwanese agriculture needs to switch over to capital-intensive, technology-intensive forms of agricultural production that are not easily imitated, and regulations must be established to control the diffusion of the results of R & D work in these high-tech areas; this is the only way to guarantee the future of Taiwanese agriculture.

REFERENCES

Works in Chinese

Chiu, Yi, Jiun-mei Tien, and Chang-chen Chen. 1995, June. *An Analysis of Competition and Complementarity between Major Agricultural Products in Taiwan and Mainland China, Part Two.* Chung-Hua Institution for Economic Research.

Chiu, Yi, Jiun-mei Tien, and Chiao Tuan. 1994, June. *An Analysis of Competition and Complementarity between Major Agricultural Products in Taiwan and Mainland China.* Chung-Hua Institution for Economic Research.

Directorate General of Budget, Accounting and Statistics, Executive Yuan. 1995, February. *Industry Interconnectedness Table Report for the Taiwan Region, 1991.*

Directorate General of Budget, Accounting and Statistics, Executive Yuan. 1995, December. *Fixed Price Industry Interconnectedness Table Report for the Taiwan Region, 1986, 1989 and 1991.*

Hsu, Wen-fu, and Jiun-mei Tien. 1997, August. *Agricultural Sector Investment in Mainland China by Taiwanese Businesspeople.* Department of Agricultural Economics, National Taiwan University (research project commissioned by the Mainland Affairs Council).

Tien, Jiun-mei. 1996, July. "A Comparison of the Agricultural Products Trade Structure in Taiwan and Mainland China." *Taiwan Economics and Finance Monthly*, vol. 32, no. 7: 55–68.

———. 1998, March. "Investment in the Mainland China Agricultural Sector by Taiwanese Businesspeople, 1991–1996." *Economic Monographs*, no. 33. Chung-Hua Institute for Economic Research.

———. 1998, June. "Investment in Mainland China: A Case Study of Yuan Tsu Enterprises Ltd.," *Cross-strait Trade News*, no. 78: 33–37.

———. 1998, September. "An Analysis of Agricultural Sector Investment by Taiwanese Businesspeople in Fujian Province and Hainan Province." *Explorations in Cross-strait Relations*, no. 11: 138–158.

Yang, Feng-suo. 1997, November. "Investment in Mainland China by Taiwanese Food Manufacturers and the Implications of the Division of Labor." *Taiwan Economic Research Monthly*, vol. 21, no. 11: 60–69.

Yen, Tsung-ta, and Hui-chin Li. 1990, June. *Investment in Mainland China by Taiwanese Businesspeople and Its Impact on Taiwanese Industry.* Chung-Hua Institution for Economic Research, June 1990.

Works in English

Agmon, I. 1979. "Direct Investment and Intra-Industry Trade: Substitutes or Complements? In *Economics of Intra-Industry Trade*, ed. H. Giersch. Tubingen: J.C.B. Mohr.

Caves, Richard. 1971. "International Corporation: The Industrial Economics of Foreign Investment." *Economica*, vol. 38, no. 149: 1–27.

——. 1974. "Causes of Direct Investment." *Review of Economics and Statistics*, vol. 56, no. 3: 279–293.

General Administration of Customs of PRC. *Commodity Classification for China Customs Statistics*, 1992 Edition.

III

Taiwan's Economy in Global Perspective

7

Taiwan's Role in the World Market

Henry Wan, Jr.

INTRODUCTION

Taiwan is fascinating to researchers in many fields. Typically, this island has displayed a significance disproportional to its size: 13,900 square miles in area (one-third of the state of Ohio), and just 21 million in population. In anthropology, it is believed to be the ancestral home of all Austronesian speakers, from Hawaii to Madagascar, and from Malaysia and Indonesia to New Zealand (see Bellwood, 1985). In history, Dr. Shih Hu, born in Taiwan, was the prime mover of the vernacular revolution to all Chinese communities (see Grieder, 1970).

Significance disproportional to size is also the case of the Taiwanese economy.

The significance of an economy is reflected by its interaction with others. A fair measure is export. Manufactured export is even better: It represents the stage of development, and not natural wealth. Thus one may start with the world market share of manufactured export. Because Crisis 1997 was quite disruptive and the years leading to it may also be atypical, we use the data of 1992. The world market shares of Taiwan and Korea in manufacturing exports, that year, are suggestive (see Sadli and Thee, 1999).

	Korea	Taiwan
Overall	2.6	2.8
Low skill	4.1	4.7
High skill	2.1	2.2

For perspective, the Korean population is much less than 1 percent of the world total. But as an economy that is not traditionally viewed as advanced, Korea has a share much higher than 1 percent in the area of manufacturing. In boxing, "punching above one's weight" is how the English would characterize it. Now Taiwan's population is less than half of Korea's. Yet in 1992, Taiwan's shares were larger even than those of Korea. Of course, these are not particularly large shares relative to Japan or America. But as one shall see, there is more here than meets the eye.

To students of economic development, Taiwan has played a fivefold role in the globalized economy. First, it is the source for key supplies. When an earthquake interrupted Taiwan's output for a week or so in September 1999, the world price was affected for microchips, a commodity with ubiquitous presence in modern life. The way Taiwan becomes such an important source is revealing. Some examples make the point. When General Instruments established a factory in Taiwan, it recruited workers from Thailand because of the lower Thai wages. The decision to locate such an operation in Taiwan is due to the quality of Taiwan's engineers, whose preference to work close to home wins respect. When TSMC became the world's largest chip foundry, its distinct advantage is its decision to concentrate in fabrication, and not to conduct activities that may be used later to compete against its current clients (like Japanese firms had done). The skill of its labor force and the thoughtfulness of its entrepreneurs as trading partners are the source of Taiwan's importance in the world market.

Second, it is a channel for technology diffusion. It is well known that the Taiwanese investors had transplanted various export industries to mainland China. To visualize its potential impact, consider the somewhat earlier migration of industries from Hong Kong to mainland China. When manufacturing employment fell from 900,000 to 400,000 in Hong Kong, the number of Chinese workers serving Hong Kong–owned firms in the mainland went to about 4,000,000. Investors from Taiwan, an economy thrice more populous than Hong Kong, provide a much broader spectrum of industrial skill than their Hong Kong counterparts, who specialized in the labor-intensive sectors. See, for example, the description by Chung (1997) of the electronics industry. Although large may be the impact of technology transfer from Taiwan to mainland China, this in itself is still far from the whole story. According to Sadli and Thee (1999), Salim Group of Indonesia relied upon Taiwanese technology to compete against the Japanese in the American consumer electronics market. According to Kim (1997), Hyundai of Korea repeatedly acquired its DRAM technology from Vitelic, Taiwan.

Third, it is a significant strategically. In the 1990s, according to Borrus (1997), the Taiwanese electronics industry, along with other members in the "China Circle," had helped the successful revival of the American electronics industry (once "left for dead") against its Japanese rival. Guided by the overall architectural design of their American allies, what Taiwan subcontractors have contributed are good quality and competent design at competitive cost, with a much faster delivery than the Japanese firms. Again what these China Circle allies offered is not cheap labor but an edge (speed) that large Japanese firms cannot match.

Fourth, it is an important source of investment fund. Taiwan's prominent role in the mainland Chinese economy as well as Southeast Asian countries from Vietnam to Malaysia to the Philippines is well known. Take 1990, for example; at 36 percent, Taiwan was the largest source of foreign investment in Malaysia, more than the share of either America or Japan (see Tan, 1997). But again numbers do not tell the full story. The fact that such investment often took the form of joint ownership or equity rather than short-term loans or stock ownership is important. These investors are not fair-weather friends. By their risk-sharing during Crisis 1997, such foreign investment has contributed to the superior resilience of the Malaysian economy, in comparison with its Southeast Asian neighbors.

Last but not least is Taiwan's potential as a role model in economic development. For decades, various East Asian economies have enjoyed sustained, rapid growth, each following a somewhat different industrial policy. In our view, among the various strengths of the Taiwanese economy, what is most worthwhile for emulation is that it has prospered, not as a prima donna, but as a team player.

This is especially important today, when more and more developing economies strive for rapid growth, and many of them are at a similar phase of technical achievement with each other. To win popular support, charismatic leaders often mobilize national resources to achieve the dazzling and spectacular. Examples are not hard to come by. In Malaysia, the Perusahaan Otomobil Nasional (Proton) is still just the assembler after seventeen years, with neither scale, nor brand name, nor a chassis or engine designed on its own. Yet, it bought an 80 percent share of the Lotus Corporation of Britain. Before the 1997 crisis, Indonesia did not have a strong automobile industry, yet it started to develop a civil aircraft industry. In the case of Korea, both the entry into shipbuilding and the effort to become the world's second largest pro-

ducer after taking losses for twenty successive years seem to be motivated by noneconomic objectives. In contrast, although Taiwan supplies 80 percent of the world's need in motherboards for personal
computers, clearly profit, and not glamour, is the attraction. The fact is
the stage of world trade can simultaneously accommodate many successful team-players, but not many successful superstars.

After all, the financial crisis of 1997 was brought on by the deteriorating terms of trade against Thailand, Indonesia, and Korea. Such
change in the world prices was in turn the result of industrial over-
expansion in several economies.

The institutions and experience of Taiwan have always been the focus
of attention of many developing economies. To see how far-reaching is
this influence, one can point to Mauritius. When Hong Kong textile
merchants sought out Mauritius as a supply base for knitwear, their
factories were given by the host government the status of "export zone
companies," which are exempt from the bureaucratic regulations. As
Findlay and Wellisz (1993) observed, such institutions were promul-
gated with their Taiwanese counterparts as the blueprint. Interestingly,
unlike in the case of many Southeast Asian economies from Vietnam to
Malaysia and Philippines, Taiwanese capital has played little part in
Mauritius. This fact neatly separates Taiwan's function as a role model
from all the other four. In this function, size does not matter. Today,
Mauritius is the most successful case of development in either all of
Africa or in the Indian Ocean basin.

The rest of this chapter is devoted to three topics: the pattern of
production specialization of Taiwan, the relationship of government
policy to such a pattern, and what economic theory can say about such
a policy. Each item is considered in brevity. A few concluding remarks
close the chapter.

NICHE MARKETS AND THE TAIWANESE FIRM

At the present stage, the Taiwanese economy resembles most small
European economies. Each firm seeks its own living space to survive
and thrive, according to no master plan. Many types of firms coexist. In
particular, four categories are active in the export market:

1. There are creatures of the product cycle, like suppliers of plastic
   products, footwear, and garments. They arose when the local labor
   was cheap, and they migrated overseas (many to the Chinese
   mainland) when labor cost became too high.
2. There are commodity producers, like those exporting nails, bolts,
   and fasteners. Such firms use standard technology, have devel-

oped their competence, and managed to earn a normal margin of profit.

3. There are exporters whose strength is their flexibility and punctuality. They supply goods from machine tools to bicycles. In general, these are associated with neither state enterprise, nor business groups, nor multinational firms.

4. There are also firms in the high-tech sectors, more in electronics than in bioengineering. Here, the government efforts seem to have played a beneficial role, as we shall see. In each of these industries, most of the Taiwanese firms have found their niche. Typically, their competitiveness is not based on their size. Yet, occasionally, some of these firms have also become the largest in the world, like bicycle producer Giant Manufacturing Company. (See Crown and Coleman, 1995.)

The bottom line is that among the developing world, the living standard of Taiwan is already quite high today. If the ultimate goal for development is (only) to achieve a high living standard, then Taiwan is already quite successful by that criterion. For example, using a battery of socioeconomic indices, Thorbecke and Wan (1999) concluded that the living standard appears to be higher in Taiwan than in Korea, at the present.

On the world market, the industries Taiwan specializes in are neither particularly capital intensive nor strongly dependent on the economy of scale. As a consequence, there is less need to compete for market share, nor, for that matter, the urge to tap foreign saving for domestic investment.

Much of Taiwan's output, employment, and trade rests with the small and medium enterprises. They form clustered subcontract networks, adjusting their product mix by their overseas orders. There is a high rate of capacity utilization and considerable flexibility in their structure of labor cost.

This is a mode of development to live and let live, but not one of competing to become the next America or Prussia. It is also a strategy of progress through stability. For decades, the rates of unemployment and inflation are consistently lower than not only the United States or Europe but also Korea, an economy at a similar phase of development. There is little foreign debt, and the ratio of domestic public debt to national income is low by OECD standards.

According to Adelman (1999), in their heavy-chemical industry (HCI) drives, Korea relied upon inflationary finance, foreign borrowing, and the starving of small to medium enterprises of credit, but Taiwan adopted none of these expediencies.

Compared to other economies, Taiwan's more conservative policy means (1) a more stable pace of growth over an extended period (see

Amsden, 1992) as well as (2) less damages from external shocks, both during the period of oil shocks, 1974–1982, and the 1997 financial crisis. According to James, Naya, and Meier (1989), from data for selected non–oil producers in 1974–1982, this is as follows.

Economy	Percent loss of GDP
Hong Kong	26.7
Korea	13.3
Philippines	14.5
Singapore	46.3
Taiwan	12.7
Thailand	15.3

We can also list the real GDP growth for selected Asian economies in 1996 to 1998:

Economy	1996	1997	1998
China	9.7	8.8	7.8
Hong Kong	4.9	5.3	-5.1
Indonesia	7.4	5.5	-13.7
Korea	7.1	5.5	-5.8
Malaysia	8.6	7.7	-7.5
Philippines	5.8	5.2	-0.5
Singapore	6.9	7.8	3.5
Taiwan	5.7	6.9	5.0
Thailand	5.5	-0.4	-9.4

There appears to be no compelling reason that this trend cannot continue further, allowing the people to live even longer and better, and converging to the growth paths of the Benelux or the Scandinavian states. These latter economies have never adopted an active industrial policy like those of Japan and Korea. Yet, their living standards are also among the highest in the world. They are the home of some of the world's largest firms, such as Philips, Unilever, and Royal Shell of the Netherlands, producing goods with the most prestigious brand names.

STATE POLICY BY EVOLUTION

During the 1950s, the public sector dominated Taiwanese industries. Gradually, the private sector has overtaken the public sector, even though the privatization of state enterprises remains incomplete. State trading and the import substitution regime were eased out over a considerable amount of time. Reforms are gradual but sustained.

Quite contrary to what many economists (especially those from Korea) believe today, the policymakers in Taiwan early on had no great expectations about small and medium enterprises. Minister K.Y. Yin (1954) stated:

> It is only too common to find in Taiwan today, industrial units whose equipment is antiquated, whose scope is exceedingly small, whose technique is inferior, whose management is inefficient, whose enterprises completely devoid of the modern enterprising spirit, often seek short-term advantages but ignore the long range advantages of their own enterprises.

This sentiment was almost a mirror image to what was conveyed by President Park of Korea: "Mammoth enterprises . . . play . . . a decisive role in the economic development and the elevation of the living standards."

Yet, the difference is quite stark. The Korean government under Park was born out of a military coup, amid a desperate population valuing effective governance over chaotic democracy. It felt free to create the mammoth enterprises by controlling the banks and granting short-term policy loans—at negative real interest—to formerly jailed business leaders under the Illicit Wealth Accumulation Act. In Taiwan, the ruling Chinese Nationalists led a government-in-exile, which was bound by its own decades-long ideology, laws, history, and hierarchy that could not be dismissed at will without risking further alienation of its followers. Yin himself was temporarily removed from office in 1955 under the alleged charge of attempting to favor a "third party" (crony associate) (see Wade, 1990).

At any rate, in Taiwan, the State certainly did not favor the small and medium enterprises. As a backseat driver with a vastly different background, Yin was probably ignorant about how difficult it was for local Taiwanese firms at that time to operate, let alone to follow his "ideals."[1] Even today, the attrition rate among the Taiwanese firms is still high. Yet, under benign neglect, the Darwinian process works wonders.

The announced government policy in Taiwan is usually to assure that a list of strategic industries is established. This list for industry targeting includes steel, petrochemicals, shipbuilding, automobiles, semiconductors, and civil aircraft. At the outset, efforts were made to form a State-led consortium, with major local business groups as participants. With few exceptions, the latter had shown great reluctance. Unlike Korea, the government neither committed sufficient public resources as inducement (in Korea: short-term policy loans, at negative real interest) nor forced the hand of the local business groups against their wish (in Korea: through threatening to ruin them by calling back the loans). In the cases of the mass production automobile industry and the civil aircraft industry, the projects were shelved. In the cases of steel and shipbuilding, the government went ahead alone. In the cases of petro-chemicals and semiconductors, foreign partners were brought in.

To some observers, in Taiwan and abroad, this record reflects the lack of resolve of the government. On the other hand, the more resolute Korean policy under President Park also drew criticisms first from Korean economists (e.g., Yoo, 1990; Sakong, 1993; Hong, 1995 and recently, many observers, after Crisis 1997).

There is also a possible alternative interpretation about Taiwan's policy stance. In particular, the process of government decision making in Taiwan may be characterized as "open to a long period of debates," and "adaptable within a rapidly evolving environment." The develop-ment of the electronics industry may serve as a useful example.

When the government set up the Industrial Technology Research Institute (ITRI), the purpose was to provide research and development services for the private industry, perhaps like the Batelle Memorial Institute. It soon became apparent that researchers were interested in a more visionary agenda, to bring to Taiwan more advanced technology. In contrast, the private firms were much more pragmatically oriented, often hoping to get help in reverse-engineering existing foreign prod-ucts.

The launch of the spin-off firms by former research staff from ITRI was the outcome of the mismatch of purposes between the existing Taiwanese firms and the researchers at the ITRI. Eager to see the fruits of the government-sponsored research getting applied, the government did provide some finance for certain start-up firms. At the same time, the government had neither the intention to encourage a mass exodus from ITRI, which might erode the operation of the latter; nor the intention to shoulder the full market risk in case the spin-off firms become nonviable for any number of reasons; nor the appetite to launch fully owned state enterprises (like China Petroleum, China Shipbuild-ing, and China Steel) in the risky environment of the high-tech sector.

Some of such spin-off firms, such as UMC, TSMC, and Windbond (see, for example, the description in Hobday, 1995), become highly successful in the world market. Not all projects are successful. Van-guard, for example, is now taken over by TSMC.

Jones and Sakong (1980) characterized the making of Korean eco-nomic policy under Park as "bold initiatives, with ready reversals." In contrast, the development policy of Taiwan often seems to be made by piecemeal evolution, which is altogether a different mode of operation. In the lending policy of the government banks (see Cheng, 1993) and the frustrated plans in promoting the large trading corporations (see Fields, 1995), the decision process of the state in Taiwan presents a similar picture.

FROM THE PERSPECTIVE OF ECONOMIC THEORY

By an evolutionary process, the economic policy of Taiwan has developed several features that are both innovative and effective. Two examples are provided here.

(1) Setting up industrial parks, from the Export Processing Zones to the Science Based Industrial Parks. As Li (1988) explained, from the initial proposal in 1956 to the establishment of the first export zone in 1966, it took a decade-long policy debate. Such industrial parks serve three purposes:

(a) Firms inside the park operate in a streamlined regulatory environment of a duty-free port, like Hong Kong. On imported inputs used for exported outputs, firms outside the park must pay duty first, and ask for its rebate later; firms inside the park can import the inputs duty-free.

(b) Firms in the park are given assistance to acquire a plant site (sometimes built according to specification), with ready access to shipping, public utility, labor supply, as well as those supporting services attracted to the site.

(c) A plant site in a park is rented only for a fixed duration and after prior approval. Thus the government can screen the applicants and exercise some control. The industrial policy of a government can be exercised in some limited way, at much lower transaction costs than the allocation of directed credit by the Korean government under Park. Such costs include the concentrated industrial structure favoring the business groups and the piling up of nonperforming debt at the financial institutions. (For details, see Sakong, 1993.)

Under the neoclassic assumption of a frictionless world, the advantage of such industrial parks has been evaluated by economists, like the benchmark contributions of Hamada (1974). On the other hand, when the information of foreign investors is imperfect about the host economy (the regulatory complexities, the availability and reliability of such local inputs like labor and plant building), a well-administered industrial park eliminates much cost and uncertainty in their searching process. According to the communications from a former manager at General Instrument, such an arrangement has ameliorated Taiwan's initial disadvantage relative to Hong Kong in attracting foreign investment. One can argue that the industrial policy of Singapore also operates on such a basis.

From the viewpoint of "political economy," a total liberalization that transforms Taiwan into another Hong Kong would be politically impossible in one single step. According to Li (1988), as it was, such industrial parks emerged only after much debate and compromises over ten years, in order to overcome the objections of various entrenched interests. But we argue here that actually an industrial park may be even better than a duty-free port.

It would be wrong to claim that the planners in Taiwan had the knack in picking the winner. This clearly was not the case. Initially, the three export processing zones were designed to attract industries for garments, electronics, and precision equipment. Although the first zone at Kaohsiung was an instant success, the utilization rates of the second and third zones were initially lower than expected. The electronics industry has succeeded beyond expectations, but the progress of the precision equipment industry was much slower.

Two points may be made.

First, what transpires is that under effective administrators and after careful planning, the institution of the industrial park in Taiwan was a success. It provided the effective antidote against the usual coordination failure: Foreign investors are deterred by the perceived transaction cost due to the lack of suitable supporting inputs; various indigenous inputs (land, labor, and public utilities) lack the opportunity to earn their shadow value, in terms of coveted foreign exchange. From that time on, export zones were set up in many different economies, including the successful development of Subic Bay in the Philippines, after the American withdrawal.

Second, in both Hong Kong and Singapore, the limited size of the local market would force foreign investors to concentrate on the world market. In Taiwan, the regulation for the export zone serves the same purpose. In contrast to firms catering to the less affluent local clientele (like those in large economies such as Brazil and India), firms focusing on the world market must pay greater attention to the quality of product and the punctuality of delivery. Quality control and production scheduling are such skills that are important for various export operations. For the inexperienced local producers they are also standards costly to maintain, at a high level. Hence, for the sake of diffusion of such multipurpose technology, it is highly desirable for the host economy to have foreign firms employing local workers and operating export activities in their midst (see Van and Wan, 1999). Because the local Taiwanese market is larger than Hong Kong and Singapore, it may take the stipulation of export requirement in industrial parks to channel foreign firms toward the world market.

Finally, according to Li (1988), the successful operation of such industrial parks had further provided much-needed publicity for Taiwan—that Taiwan is hospitable for foreign investors, even outside such industrial parks. Moreover, the unexpected fast expansion of foreign

investment in those parks also had its demonstration effect in government circles, for improving the regulatory environment for foreign
investment and trade. Because the provision of such information is
clearly another beneficial externality, it justifies the efforts to set up such
parks with suitable infrastructure. In a real world with information
imperfection, the aspect of social product must be considered. Hence
the case for the successful outward-oriented policy is not equivalent to
the neoclassical justification for the laissez-faire.

(2) The establishment of the semiconductor industry. Take the Taiwan
Semiconductor Corporation (TSMC), for example. It has utilized
Taiwan's comparative advantage in two types of human capital,
namely, both a pool of senior technical personnel who were educated
and had worked in North America and an adequate supply of engineers
trained in local technical colleges, on top of the financial capital from
government-controlled banks. It also suits several local conditions, in
the following sense:

(a)   Constrained by the extant law and regulations, the traditional
        form of state-owned enterprises (like China Steel) lacks the
        flexibility in recruitment and decision making to compete in the
        fast-moving world market for high-tech goods.
(b)   Feeling more at home in petrochemicals and consumer electron-
        ics, the local business groups were reluctant to test waters in
        information technology. Likewise, the government was unwill-
        ing to finance such ventures in similar terms like what Korea
        extended to Samsung and Lucky Star-Gold Star.
(c)   With its human and financial capital, Taiwan found that there
        was no need to leave all leadership to multinational firms, like
        what Singapore does.

Ultimately, TSMC became a highly successful joint venture between
the government and Philips, Canada. It is now the world's largest chip
foundry. Eventually, the local business groups entered the field, almost
a decade later. This is another case of the demonstration effect, where
government action is justified by the presence of social cost.

From the viewpoint of economic theory, the local private firms lacked
information to make competent feasibility studies to enter the market
and thus understandably hesitated to shoulder the cost of potential
failure on their own, just to develop the data that are accessible to other
private firms. In contrast, foreign private firms knew all along the ripe
time for entry. Thus, a joint venture with foreign firms is a desirable
move by the government, not only from the viewpoint of the profit and
loss statement of that particular venture, but also from the viewpoint

of providing the public good information, through the partly public-owned joint venture.

The petrochemical industry in Taiwan was initially started in similar circumstances by the government (see Chu, 1994).

A parallel was the founding of the Yahata steel works by the govern-ment of Meiji Japan, when private firms declined to enter. This ended in losses, because public ownership was unsuitable. It forced the gov-ernment to privatize in haste, but then the private buyer made the operation a success, contributing to the industrialization of Japan (see Morishima, 1982).

CONCLUDING REMARKS

The importance of Taiwan is significant beyond its size. Its most profound role is to serve as a role model for development. Today six East Asian economies are remarkable for their economic performance, yet four of these six are so special that they can only serve as a source for insight, but not a template for emulation.

Japan started the process of industrialization in the late nineteenth century, when the world was a vastly different place, in both politics and technology. Its economic precondition is closely entwined with its fourteen years of warlike activities leading to the debacle of August 1945.

The Chinese mainland is a class by itself, because of its size and its political institutions.

Significant portions of the economies of Hong Kong and Singapore are associated with their positions as regional financial centers as well as world-class entrepôts. Surely, not every economy can earn their daily bread in like fashion.

Thus, Korea and Taiwan are left as the two more typical cases for the rest of the developing world.

Both Korea and Taiwan are showcases of development, though they are as different from each other as, say, France and the Netherlands: partly due to their differences in size, but also partly due to history.

Korea industrialized five or ten years later than Taiwan, though it has grown since at slightly faster average rates with much more variability. Per capita consumption of Taiwan remains still somewhat ahead in most dimensions, after forty years. The decisiveness of Korean policymakers (notably Park) and the ambition of Korean business leaders had apparently great appeal to development econo-mists like Lall (1996).

With their relative sizes, neither Korea nor Taiwan is likely to be another England, America, or Japan on the world stage, for any foreseeable period.[2] But as role models, both can have very significant impact, and interestingly, their impact will be quite different.

Both economies became what they are due to their outward orientation. Both are likely to enjoy prosperity, as those economies in West Europe.

Yet, as this chapter shows, because of the relative weights of increasing returns industries (shipbuilding, automobiles, steel, etc.) in these two economies, their influence as role models to other developing economies is not the same. Many "Taiwans" can prosper together. In contrast, the Korean economy deserves to be left to thrive in isolation. The emulation of Taiwan can be mutually advantageous to all. The widespread emulation of Korea either will be unsuccessful or is likely to lead to such unexpectedly keen competition among these entrants as well as with Korea.

Because Japan, Korea, and Taiwan constitute "Northeast Asia," a comparison including Japan may be fruitful. During its rise as an industrial power after World War II, Japan expanded its market share rapidly, but usually offers something special in its products, from machine tools to cars to camera and computer, such as high quality, high durability, and user-friendliness. Low price at high volume was rarely the only, or even the major, edge for Japanese goods. Where Japan excels in superior design and technical virtuosity, Taiwan delivers in flexibility and speedy service. Never for once have either Japan or Taiwan financed export promotion by inflation or raising foreign debts. Trade balance is consistently favorable, and foreign exchange reserves rise and rise.

The Korean gains in market share were often based on the economy of scale and hence competitive pricing. Trade balance turned now positive, then negative, and foreign reserves fell after rising. Occasionally, inflation spells and foreign debt were harnessed for the sake of development. Success comes mostly from dedication, resourcefulness, and hardihood, but sometimes also partly because the would-be competitors offer Korea a wide berth rather than mutually assured destruction (MAD). As it stands, take the four firms in the automobile industry, for example. Besides Hyundai, all the other three, Kia, Daewoo, and Samsung, ran into difficulties in the aftermath of 1997, seeking foreign takeovers. After years of state support, Hyundai is left alone with shallow pockets in a world auto market with world-class behemoths like Chrysler-Mercedes.

We can all celebrate that the economic recovery of Korea is now in apparently fine form. But there is also a time to draw lessons from what happened for development economics. Evidence suggests that, in the trading world, Taiwan is the more practical if less "heroic" role model.

NOTES

1. The author is grateful for the kind comment of the discussant, Professor Frank S. T. Hsiao, regarding this point.

2. As Professor Hsiao correctly pointed out, Scandinavia and Switzerland are the role models of the average Taiwanese.

REFERENCES

Adelman, I. 1999. "State and Market in the Economic Development of Korea and Taiwan." In *Taiwan's Development Experience: Lessons on Roles of Government and Market*, eds. E. Thorbecke and H. Y. Wan, Jr. Boston: Kluwer Academic Press.

Amsden, A. H. 1992. "Taiwan in International Perspective." In *Taiwan Enterprises in Global Perspective*, ed. N. T. Wang. Armonk, NY: M.E. Sharpe.

Bellwood, P. S. 1985. *Pre-history in the Indo-Malaysian Archipelago.* Sydney: Academic Press.

Borrus, M. 1997. "Left for Dead: Asian Production Networks and the Revival of the American Electronics." In *The China Circle: Economics and Electronics in the PRC, Taiwan and Hong Kong*, ed. B. Naughton. Washington: Brookings Institution.

Cheng, T. J. 1993. "Guarding the Commanding Heights: The State as Banker in Taiwan." In *The Policy of Finance in Developing Countries*, eds. S. Haggard and Tung-Jen Cheng. Ithaca, NY: Cornell University Press.

Chu, W. W. 1994. "Import Substitution and Export-led Growth: A Study of Taiwan's Petrochemical Industry." *World Development*, vol. 22, no. 5: 781–794.

Chung, C. 1997. "Division of Labor across the Taiwan Strait: Macro Overview and the Electronics Industry." In *The China Circle: Economics and Electronics in the PRC, Taiwan and Hong Kong*, ed. B. Naughton. Washington: Brookings Institution.

Crown, J., and G. Coleman. 1995. *No Hands: The Rise and Fall of the Schwinn Bicycle Company, An American Institution.* New York: Henry Holt.

Fields, K. J. 1995. *Enterprises and State in Korea and Taiwan.* Ithaca, NY: Cornell University Press.

Findlay, R. E., and S. Wellisz, eds. 1993. *Five Small Open Economies.* New York: Oxford University Press.

Grieder, J. B. 1970. *Hu Shih and the Chinese Renaissance: Liberalism in the Chinese Revolution, 1917–1937.* Cambridge, MA: Harvard University Press.

Hamada, K. 1974. "An Economic Analysis of the Duty-free Zone." *Journal of International Economics*, vol. 5, no. 3: 225–241.

Hobday, M. 1995. *Innovation in East Asia: The Challenge to Japan.* Brookfield, VT: Edward Elgar.

Hong, W. 1995. *Trade and Growth: A Korean Perspective.* Seoul: Kudara International.

James, W., S. Naya, and G. Meier. 1989. *Asian Development: Economic Success and Policy Lessons.* Madison: University of Wisconsin Press.

Jones, L., and I. Sakong. 1980. *Government, Business and Entrepreneurship in Economic Development: The Korean Case.* Cambridge, MA: Harvard University Press.

Kim, L. 1997. *Imitation to Innovation: The Dynamics of Korea's Technological Learning.* Boston: Harvard Business School Press.

Lall, S. 1996. *Learning from the Asian Tigers: Studies in Technology and Industrial Policy*. Houndsmill, Basingstoke, Hampshire, U.K.: MacMillan.

Li, K. T. 1988. *The Evolution of Policy behind Taiwan's Development Success*. New Haven, CT: Yale University Press.

Morishima, M. 1982. *Why has Japan Succeeded?: Western Technology and the Japanese Ethos*. Cambridge, U.K.: Cambridge University Press.

Sadli, M., and K. W. Thee. 1999. "The Relevance and Comparability of Taiwan's Development Experience to Indonesia." In *Taiwan's Development Experience: Lessons on Roles of Government and Market*, eds. E. Thorbecke and H. Y. Wan, Jr. Boston: Kluwer Academic Press.

Sakong, I. 1993. *Korea in the World Economy*. Washington: Institute for International Economics.

Tan, K. Y. 1997. "China and ASEAN: Competitive Industrialization through Direct Foreign Investment." In *The China Circle: Economics and Electronics in the PRC, Taiwan and Hong Kong*, ed. B. Naughton. Washington: Brookings Institution.

Thorbecke, E., and H. Y. Wan, Jr. 1999. "Some Further Thoughts on Taiwan's Development." In *Taiwan's Development Experience: Lessons on Roles of Government and Market*. eds. E. Thorbecke and H. Y. Wan, Jr. Boston: Kluwer Academic Press.

Van, P. H., and H. Y. Wan, Jr. 1999. "Emulative Development through Trade Expansion: East Asian Evidence." In *International Trade Policy and the Pacific Rim*, eds. J. Piggott and A. Woodland. Houndsmill, Basingstoke, Hampshire, U.K.: MacMillan.

Wade, R. 1990. *Governing the Market*. Princeton, N.J.: Princeton University Press.

Yin, K. Y. 1954. "Adverse Trend in Taiwan's Industrial Development." *Industry of Free China*, vol. 2, no. 2: 1–6.

Yoo, J. H. 1990. "The Industrial Policy of the 1970's and the Evolution of the Manufacturing Sector in Korea." KDI Working Paper 9017. Seoul: KDI.

8

Taiwan in the Global Economy: Past, Present, and Future

Frank S.T. Hsiao and Mei-Chu W. Hsiao

INTRODUCTION

> The spirit of the "child of Taiwan" reveals to us that even though Taiwan, Penghu, Kinmen and Matsu are tiny islands on the rim of the Pacific, the map of our dreams knows no limits. The map extends all the way to the horizon as long as our 23 million compatriots fear no hardship and move forward hand in hand. Long live freedom and democracy! Long live the people of Taiwan!

Thus concluded the inauguration speech of the newly elected Taiwanese President Chen Shui-bian on May 20, 2000. It culminated Taiwan's "double miracles" in politics and economy during the past century of hard work and struggle.

In this chapter, we would like to show that Taiwan has come a long way.

The development of Taiwan's economic and political events are influenced and shaped by its geographical position as a relatively small island at the center of the northwest side of the Asia-Pacific region[1] (Figure 8-1). With almost the same altitude as Hawaii, Taiwan is surrounded by several large countries in the world, "large" in one way or another (Table 8-1). To the west, there is China, the most populous

TABLE 8-1. Taiwan in the World Economy

Unit Country	Area 1000 km² 1995	Rkg	%tle	Pop millions mid-95	Rkg	%tle	Pop Density person/km² 1995	Rkg	%tle	GDP $ billion 1995	Rkg	%tle	GNP per capita 1995	Rkg	%tle
Taiwan	**36**	**113**	**16**	**21**	**39**	**71**	**589**	**4**	**97**	**260**	**19**	**86**	**12,396**	**25**	**81**
Singapore	1	133	1	3	114	15	3,000	2	99	84	37	72	26,730	8	94
H.K.	1	134	0	6	85	37	6,200	1	99	144	28	79	22,990	13	90
Korea, Rep	99	89	34	45	23	83	454	6	96	455	11	92	9,700	27	80
Malaysia	330	56	58	20	40	70	61	65	51	85	36	73	3,890	36	73
Thailand	513	42	69	58	17	87	113	37	72	167	25	81	2,740	52	61
Philippines	300	61	54	69	14	90	229	20	85	74	41	69	1,050	78	42
Indonesia	1,905	13	90	193	4	97	101	42	69	198	23	83	980	79	41
Japan	378	51	62	125	8	94	331	9	93	5,109	2	99	39,640	2	99
China	9,561	3	98	1,200	1	99	126	32	76	698	7	95	620	93	31
India	3,288	7	95	929	2	99	283	11	92	324	15	89	340	108	19
USA	9,364	4	97	263	3	98	28	96	28	6,952	1	99	26,980	6	96
Netherlands	37	112	16	16	48	64	419	7	95	396	12	91	24,000	11	92
Canada	9,976	2	99	30	29	78	3	129	4	569	9	93	19,380	15	89
Australia	7,713	6	96	18	43	68	2	131	2	349	13	90	18,720	17	87
U.K.	245	67	50	59	16	88	239	18	87	1,106	5	96	18,700	18	87
Spain	505	43	68	39	25	81	78	57	57	559	10	93	13,580	24	82
Portugal	92	91	32	10	66	51	108	40	70	102	33	75	9,740	26	81

Sources: Taiwan, from TSDB, 1996. All other countries, from WDR, 1997.
Shaded countries have values (or ranking or percentile) equal to or smaller than Taiwan.

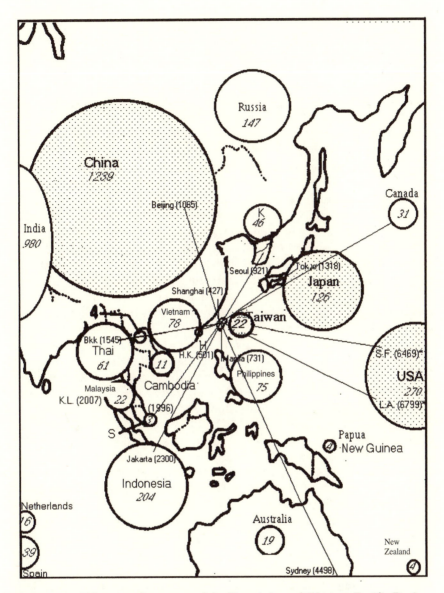

Figure 8-1. Taiwan as the center of the East Asia and Western Pacific Region.
Sources: Population (in millions) in italic, taken from *WDR*, 1997.
Distance (in miles) in parentheses. (See Note 1.)

country with the third largest landmass (although one of the lowest per capita GNP countries) in the world. Japan is in the northeast, the world's second largest country both in terms of its economic size (the GDP level) and its standard of living (the GNP per capita level). To the east beyond the Pacific Ocean, there is the United States, the largest economy with the third largest population, the fourth largest area, and the sixth highest GNP per capita country in the world. In addition to these three great Pacific powers, Indonesia is far down in the southwest, with the fourth largest population in the world. Sandwiched among these giants, those who are inclined to the Chinese position of chauvinism and irredentism tend to consider Taiwan too small to be a country.

Thus, we first address the question of whether Taiwan is "small" in the global economy. We have shown that either from the size of population, the GDP level, the GDP per capita level, or from the volume of production and export items, Taiwan ranks very high compared with other countries in the world. Taiwan's central position in the northeast side of the Asia-Pacific region lured the Europeans, the Chinese, the Japanese, and the Americans to the island. Thus, we next review Taiwanese history with emphasis on the interactions among these peoples during the past 400 years.

Then we briefly examine Taiwan in the global economy before the nineteenth century. The Dutch as well as the Spanish formally colonized Taiwan from 1624 to 1662 to trade with China and Japan. The Kingdom of Cheng followed from 1662 to 1683, and traded with the Japanese, the English, and others, but not with China and Holland. Ch'ing conquered Taiwan in 1683 and held it until 1895. From 1683 to 1760, Taiwan was virtually under the autarky system, and from 1760 to 1860, Taiwan traded exclusively with China. Taiwan was reintroduced to international trade after 1860, only to be ceded to Japan in 1895.

The modernization of the Taiwanese economy and society came during the Japanese period after 1895. We next show that Taiwanese agricultural production reached its apex and ranked very high in the world by the end of the 1930s, and massive industrialization started in earnest during that time with the help of resources imported from Japan, China, and Southeast Asia.

As the chapter continues, we show that, after a postwar interruption, Taiwanese industrialization continued, especially after the mid-1960s when the Pacific trade triangle among Taiwan, Japan, and the United States was formed. The trade triangle sustained the rapid Taiwanese economic growth. Rapid economic growth was also helped by the inward direct foreign investment from Japan and the United States, especially in the 1970s and the 1980s. In the 1990s, Taiwanese outward direct foreign investment rose rapidly, about half of which was invested in China. Next we show that, despite severe setbacks in the international political arena, Taiwan's national competitiveness for the future has never been stronger. However, the military threat from China has overshadowed Taiwan's bright future. Thus, we also analyze the economic and political relations between Taiwan and China and conclude with some final remarks.

Numerous papers have been written on Taiwanese economic development. The most recent and comprehensive reviews are contained in Thorbecke and Wan (1999, 3). To our knowledge, however, few works examine Taiwanese economic development from the historical, geographical, and comparative perspectives. Systematic studies of Taiwanese economy under Japanese colonialism and Japanese influence in the postwar period have not been written. Links between the prewar and postwar economic development, Taiwan–Japan–United States trade nexus, and the changes of inward and outward direct foreign investments after the lifting of Martial Law in 1987, and its consequence of facing complicated relations with China economically and politically also are lacking. This chapter brings these topics together with the benefit of our previous works, and provides some overviews of a new area of research. Thus, the chapter could supplement the main features left out in Thorbecke and Wan (1999) and help in future efforts in the new direction of long-run Taiwanese economic development and prediction.

TAIWAN IS A LARGE COUNTRY IN THE GLOBAL ECONOMY

In fact, Taiwan is not a "small" country in many aspects as compared with other countries. Table 8-1 shows Taiwan's rankings of area, population, population density, the GDP level, and the GNP per capita level with 133 other countries listed in the *1997 World Development Report* published by the World Bank. Although Taiwan's area is only 36,000 km^2, ranked 113rd, it is about the size of the Netherlands. Its population ranked 39th, at the 71st percentile, slightly larger than Malaysia and Australia, and about half of that of Spain and South Korea. Its population density ranked 4th, at the 97th percentile. Its GDP level ranked 19th, at the 86th percentile. Thus, its aggregate economic activities surpassed any of the ASEAN countries, Portugal, Mexico, Sweden, and Denmark, and are only slightly less than Belgium and Argentina. Few people are aware that Taiwan's economic size is as much as 80 percent of that of India, and 75 percent of that of Russia and Australia. Its GNP per capita ranked 25th, at the 81st percentile, and is comparable with some OECD countries like Portugal and Spain. If 55 other "smaller" member countries of the United Nations, not listed in the *1997 World*

Development Report, are considered, Taiwan's area and population percentiles will improve to the 40th and 79th percentiles, respectively, and its percentiles for the GDP level and the GNP per capita level will increase to whopping 90th and 87th percentiles, respectively.

In the field of international trade, Taiwan's achievement is indeed more staggering. The Taiwanese economy advanced steadily from exporting agricultural goods and agricultural processed goods (rice, sugar, canned foods, etc.) to low-technology manufactured goods (textile, metal manufactures, machinery), and then to high-technology manufactured goods (electronic products, electrical machinery products, information and communication products, etc). In the 1960s, Taiwan was the number one country in exporting mushrooms and asparagus to the world market. In the 1980s, Taiwan could claim more than two dozen exporting items as "Taiwan is Number One" in the world. In 1983, Taiwan exported 520 million pairs of plastic shoes, one pair for every nine persons in the world; 11 million dozen umbrellas, one for every 40 persons in the world; and more than 6 million tennis rackets. In addition, it exported 3.16 million sets of sewing machines, having 80 percent of the world sewing machine exporting market; 240 million units of minimotors, having 70 percent of the world minimotor exporting market; 80 million bicycle tires, having 50 percent of the world bicycle tire exporting market.[2]

By 1986, Taiwan produced the world's largest number of computer terminals, printed circuit boards, monitors, recreational boats, electronic calculators, telephones, and the like (Ministry of Economic Affairs [MOEA], 1991, 239). In 1993, Taiwan supplied 76 percent of the world's exports of handheld scanners for personal computers, 62 percent of motherboards, 51 percent of monitors, 25 percent of sewing machines, 29 percent of ABS fiber, 9 percent of bicycles. All ranked number one in the world. The achievement is indeed staggering. In that year, there were ten items ranked number one, including those just mentioned, three items number two (desktop scanner, PTA, machine mold), and five items number three (PS petrochemical, personal computer, lighting diode, printed circuit board, and desk-top scanner) in the world export markets.

The most noteworthy achievements in the 1990s are in the area of personal computers and integrated circuits. In fact, in 1995 Taiwan produced more than 10 percent of the world's personal computers, and its production of keyboards and motherboards ranked number one in the world (Nikkei, February 11, 1996). In 1998, the global production shares by volume of the scanner (85 percent), case (75 percent), motherboard (66 percent), SPS (66 percent), keyboard (65 percent), mouse (60 percent), monitors (58 percent), sound card (49 percent), video card (40 percent), notebook PC (39 percent), and graphics card

(31 percent)—all ranked number one in the world. There is no ranking of the world share of CD-ROMs (33 percent) and desktop PCs (16 percent), but its ranking should also be high. Taiwan in 1998 ranked "the number three producer of information technology world wide, only behind the United States and Japan."[3] Indeed, as we will explore further later in this chapter, Taiwan is certainly a very large country in the world in almost all categories except its land area.

AN OVERVIEW OF EARLY TAIWANESE HISTORY
FROM AN INTERNATIONAL PERSPECTIVE

Taiwan's geographical position also determines its historical relations with the surrounding countries. Before the seventeenth century, Taiwan was initially inhabited by nine ethnic groups[4] of Malay-Polynesian origin. While some claim that Chinese population on Taiwan may trace back to the third century (A.D. 230, the Period of Three Kingdoms),[5] a recent study indicates that a reliable Chinese account on Taiwan appeared only in 1349.[6] From the sixteenth century on, the Han people began arriving in the western part of Taiwan from the coastal area of southern China. They were fishermen, pirates, criminals, or tax evaders. Some were Japanese pirates (Vertente, Hsu, and Wu, 1991, 49). Most of them made no efforts to settle permanently, and the Ming government of the time never extended its rule on Taiwan (ibid, 34; see Figure 8-2A[7]). Thus, when the Dutch from the Dutch East India Company[8] in Batavia of Indonesia occupied and settled in the southern part of Taiwan (see Figure 8-3) in 1624 as the base of entrepôt trade with Japan (Su, 1980, 57) and monopolizing

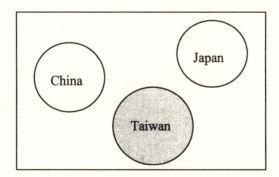

Figure 8-2A. International Relations of Taiwan—Before the Seventeenth Century.

its trade with China (Vertente et al., 1991, 69), the Ming government did not protest or interfere.[9]

The Dutch built Fort Zeelandia in Tainan area and ruled Taiwan for thirty-eight years from 1624 to 1662. They had a shortage of labor and brought in "Han serfs" from China (Su, 1980, 69–74; 1986, 13). Meanwhile, the Spanish in the Philippines felt the threat of the Dutch and tried to expel them from Taiwan. They landed and settled in Santiago near Keelung (see Figure 8-3) in 1626 (Su, 1980, 79). In the following year, the King of Spain declared that Formosa belonged to the Spanish crown (ibid., 80). However, the Dutch eventually expelled the Spanish from Taiwan in 1642 and controlled the northern and southern parts of the island (ibid.; see Figure 8-2B).

The shortest distance from Taiwan to China is only 110 miles, and so Taiwan has been often influenced by events in its neighbor. In 1661, the Manchus overthrew the Ming government, a foreign tribe that invaded China from the north and established the Ch'ing Dynasty. Ming's defeated general, Cheng Ch'eng-kung (Koxinga), fled to Taiwan and drove away the Dutch.[10] The family of Cheng ruled Taiwan and expanded its territory in the southern part of Taiwan (see Figure 8-3), while fighting with the Manchus, for 23 years from 1662 to 1683 (Vertente, et al., 1991, Chapter 5). During this period, trade with other countries, except China, flourished (see Figure 8-2C). Taiwan then came under the Ch'ing government, which lasted 212 years in Taiwan from 1683 to 1895.

The Ch'ing government ruled Taiwan with indifference and passivity (ibid., 130) and continued the discriminatory and prohibitive

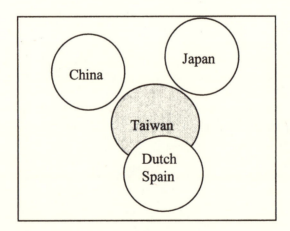

Figure 8-2B. The Dutch and Spanish Period (Dutch, 1624–1662; Spanish, 1626–1642).

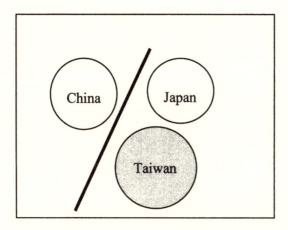

Figure 8-2C. International Relations of Taiwan—The Cheng Period (1662–1683).

rule of the Dutch colonial system with added "decadent feudalism of China" (Su, 1980, 118–246; 1986, 23–24). By the end of its rule, its territory had expanded to the coastal flatland area of western Taiwan (Figure 8-3). The government controlled only major cities, and its rule did not extend to the vast mountain area and the eastern part of Taiwan (Figure 8-3). Being keenly aware of its limitations, for almost 100 years the Ch'ing government banned immigration and emigration between Taiwan and the mainland lest people should run into the mountains and revolt against its rule. Thus, Taiwan was isolated from China and other parts of the world for 78 years from 1683 to 1760 (see Figure 8-2, D and E).

Despite the precaution, the settlers frequently rebelled against the Manchus.[11] The Taiwanese economy expanded only slowly, and its trade was confined exclusively to China. Only after the mid-nineteenth century when the English and French forced open the ports of Taiwan (Vertente et al., 1991, 136–137), other European powers followed, and Taiwan re-entered the world trading system (Su, 1986, 34–35; Huang and Chen, 1995, 312, 321).

At the end of the first Sino-Japanese war, China ceded Taiwan and the Pescadores to Japan "in perpetuity" by the Treaty of Simonoseki in 1895.[12] After crashing the short-lived Democratic Republic of Taiwan established by the local people,[13] for the first seven years, the Japanese still had a hard time eradicating the sporadic armed rebellion against its rule. Even by 1901, a Japanese government survey drew[14] along the center of Taiwan dividing east and west "the approximate boundary

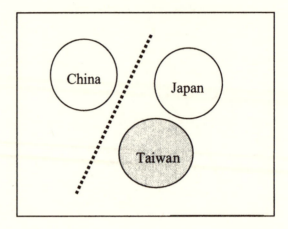

Figure 8-2D. Interantional Relations of Taiwan—The Ch'ing Period, I (1683–1760).

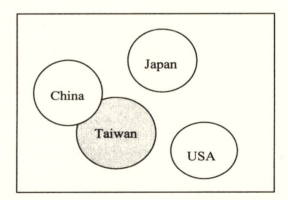

Figure 8-2E. International Relations of Taiwan—The Ch'ing Period, II (1760–1895).

line separating savage district and territory under actual control of Japanese administration." In fact, it was only in 1930 that the Japanese administration, for the first time in Taiwanese history, actually controlled and integrated all of Taiwan with iron fists.[15] By the 1920s, Taiwan had been placed into the Japanese economic domain exclusively (see Figure 8-2F) and was trading almost entirely with Japan. Ironically, under Japanese colonialism, Taiwan started modern economic and social development, building the foundations for rapid postwar economic growth.[16]

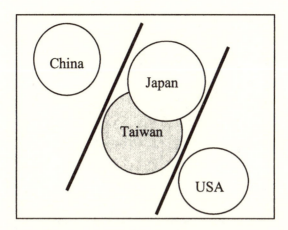

Figure 8-2F. International Relations of Taiwan—The Japanese Period (1895–1945).

Japanese influence continued even after World War II. Similar to the Cheng period in the seventeenth century, the Nationalist Republic of China was overthrown by the communist People's Republic of China in 1949, and the defeated Generalissimo Chiang Kai-shek fled to Taiwan where he established the Republic of China on Taiwan (although he pretended that he was still the ruler of China). China was off limits for the Taiwanese from 1949 up until the end of the Cold War in the late 1980s (Klintworth, 1995, 28). At the same time, China itself was isolated economically and politically from the global economy.[17] As we will see in later details, during this Cold War period Taiwan was able to ally with Japan and the United States (Figure 8-2G) and to form a trade triangle with these two powerful countries. Thus it catapulted itself to rapid economic growth.[18]

After the death of Chiang, the authoritarian regime of Taiwan started to thaw, culminating in the lifting of thirty-eight-year-old martial law in 1987 (Hsiao and Hsiao, 2001) and the democratic election of the first president in 1996. The termination of the "Period of Mobilization for Suppression of the Communist Rebellion" in 1991 also ended the almost half-century-old enmity with China. The event also coincided with China's reform and open-door period from 1989 until the present (Ishida, 2000, 277–279). This stimulated Taiwanese outward direct foreign investment in China and negotiation between the two countries. When the world experienced the end of the Cold War in 1991, Taiwan entered the new era of internationalization and globalization (Figure 8-2H).

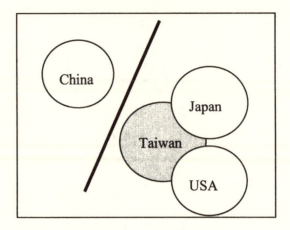

Figure 8-2G. International Relations of Taiwan—The Cold War Period (1945–1991).

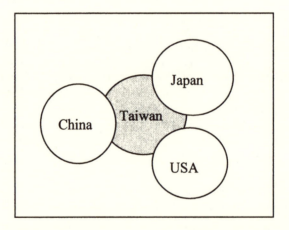

Figure 8-2H. International Relations of Taiwan—Post–Cold War Period (1991–).

THE TAIWANESE ECONOMY BEFORE THE NINETEENTH CENTURY

We now examine briefly the position of Taiwan in the global economy before the nineteenth century. As we have seen previously, although sporadic Han Chinese immigrants and the aborigines lived on the island before the seventeenth century, the Dutch, and, for a very short period, the Spanish in northern Taiwan, formally colonized Taiwan in 1624. Modern Taiwanese economic history should start from the Dutch period.

The Spanish Period
(1626–1642)

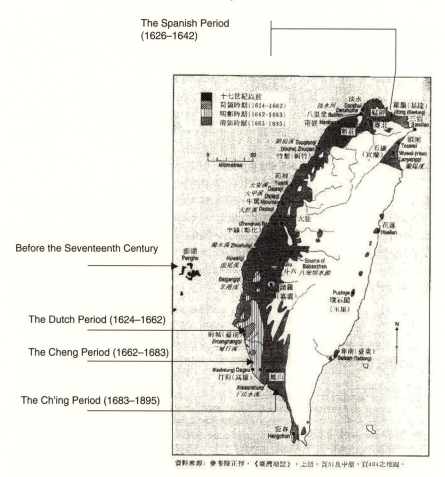

Before the Seventeenth Century

The Dutch Period (1624–1662)

The Cheng Period (1662–1683)

The Ch'ing Period (1683–1895)

Figure 8-3. Han settlement on Taiwan—a historical perspective.
Sources: Taken from T. Liu (1995, 297, also in T. Liu 1998, 166). Originally taken from Chen (1959–60, vol. I, 31 and vol. II, 404).

The Dutch Period—Global Trade in the Seventeenth Century

The original purpose of the Dutch and the Spanish in coming to Taiwan was to use it as the trade entrepôt between China and Japan. Later, they found that they might also gain by colonizing Taiwan and trading native products with Japan and China. Thus, the Taiwanese economy was already export-oriented in the seventeenth century.[19]

As early as the second half of the sixteenth century, Europeans, Chinese, and Japanese were known to come to Taiwan either for transferring commodities to the third countries[20] or for trading with the Taiwanese aborigines with agate, cloth, salt, copper, and so on for buckskin (Nakayama, 1959, 24–25). In order to trade with China, the Dutch colonized the southern part of Taiwan in 1624. Its influence spread to the northern area like Keelung and Tamsui by the 1650s (Su, 1980, 74; Chang et al., 1996, 48). At the beginning, they traded the daily necessities for buckskin and venison supplied by aborigines. Later, they brought in Chinese agricultural laborers (Han serfs, as characterized by Su, 1986, 13), and encouraged Han immigrants and aborigines to cultivate sugar cane and paddy rice to be refined for exports (Hsian-wen Chou, 1957).

The Dutch exported buckskin, venison, dried fish, and sugar to Japan in exchange for Japanese silver. From 1634 to 1661, the magnitude of the exports of buckskin was simply amazing: It ranged from the high of 151,400 pieces in 1638 to the low of 19,140 pieces in 1642. The Dutch then exported Japanese and European silver, along with venison, antlers, rice, sulfur, and dried fish, which were produced in Taiwan, to China in exchange for raw silk, silk and satin, herbal medicine, porcelain, and gold. These precious commodities, along with spices, which were purchased from Southeast Asia, were then shipped to Holland from Taiwan. Some of the raw silk and silk products were also re-exported to Japan (Su, 1980, 78–79; Hsian-wen Chou, 1957, 61).

Another important trading partner under the Dutch regime was Persia. To Persia, Taiwan exported tea and much of its sugar output, along with camphor and copper, which were imported from Japan, and ginseng, which was imported from China. As usual, Han immigrants and native aborigines produced buckskin, sugar, and rice; the Dutch collected the commodities, and monopolized the export business. During the Dutch occupation from 1624 to 1662, the trading activities in Taiwan were very lucrative. In accounting for the total profits in Asia in 1649, the Dutch reported once that, among the nineteen trading posts in Asia, the trade with Taiwan alone earned 25.6 percent of the total Asian profits, only next to the trade with Japan (38.8 percent) (Su, 1980, 80).

The Cheng Period—Continuation of Global Trade

In 1662, after being defeated by the ascending Ch'ing dynasty, the Ming general Cheng Ch'eng-kung and his troops fled to Taiwan, drove away the Dutch, and established the Kingdom of Cheng (Chang et al., 1996), or the Kingdom of Formosa as it was called by the British (ibid., 90). The Cheng government adopted the Dutch economic system. Its major concern was to "return to China," rather than develop Taiwan for the benefits of the Taiwanese. The government welcomed trading with all countries except China and Holland (Chou, Tsao, and Lai, 1959). The Ch'ing government also closed and banned the coastal area for travel to and trade with Taiwan, although illegal trade relations between Taiwan and China persisted.

Trading with Japan continued to prosper. Every year, eight to fifteen Taiwanese ships sailed to Japan for trade. Taiwan exported sugar, buckskin, silk products, and herbal medicine to Japan, and on the return trip imported copper, lead, weapons, and other military materials (Chang et al., 1996, 92).

The Cheng government also increased trade with Southeast Asian countries. Every year, one or two Taiwanese ships sailed to Luzon, Indochina, Cambodia, Thailand, Malacca, and Batavia. The British took the place of the Dutch in Taiwan's trade with the Europeans. From 1670 to 1680, the British and the Cheng government had three commerce treaties, and in 1671, the British established a trading house in Taiwan. However, until the end of the Cheng Kingdom in 1683, that business did not flourish (ibid.).

In general, during the Cheng period, Taiwan continued to trade with foreign countries. The government mainly conducted the trade, and the commodities imported were mainly military materials.

The Ch'ing Period—From Autarky to Bilateral Trade and the Development of Taiwanese Capitalism

The Ch'ing government conquered the Kingdom of Cheng in 1683. To avoid future insurgence against China using Taiwan as a base, it proclaimed a strict ban of immigration from the coastal cities in China to Taiwan. Trade between both sides of the Taiwan Strait was restricted and discouraged. The policy changed several times after 1732 and was revoked for good only in 1760 (Su, 1980, 128–129; 1986, 26). As a result, Taiwan's economy was forced into an autarky system. It stagnated for a long period as it retreated from the global scene.

From 1760 to 1860, Taiwan traded almost exclusively with China, mostly with people in Fujian. Taiwan exported agricultural products like rice, sugar, jute, rattan, and camphor wood to China, and imported manufactured products like cotton fabric and cloth, silk, paper, porcelain (Huang and Chen, 1995, 320), agricultural equipment, and wine. In one account, during 1741, Taiwan produced slightly more than 100 million dans[21] of rice, half of which was exported to China (Oh, 1970, 77).

After 1860, Tamsui and Anping in Taiwan were opened to the Europeans under the Peking Treaty between China and England. The Europeans came to trade with Taiwan, and Taiwan was reintroduced to the global economy.[22] As might be expected, the openness of trade reduced the importance of China as Taiwan's trading partner and restructured Taiwan's trade composition. Taiwanese rice lost its competitiveness to Southeast Asian rice in China, and with a rapid increase in Taiwanese population, rice export was greatly reduced (Huang and Chen, 1995, 322, 331). Furthermore, Taiwanese sugar was gradually replaced by local sugar in China, and more of it was, instead, exported to Hong Kong, Australia, the United States, Japan, and others.

Meanwhile, Taiwan's tea replaced sugar to become the largest export item. In 1895, more than 81 percent (16 million pounds) of Woolong tea was exported to the United States (ibid., 331), the rest went to Europe. Taiwan also became the world's largest producer of camphor. In 1868 (and 1895), Taiwan exported 1.6 (and 6.9) million pounds of camphor, 2.6 (and 2.3) times larger than the second largest exporter, Japan (ibid., 334). Coal was one of the new export items, mainly sold to China.

At that time, unfortunately, more than 50 percent of total imports was opium. Other imports consisted of manufactured goods, like cotton and its products, woolen fabrics, kerosene, metals (especially lead for sealing sugar boxes), matches (100 percent from Japan), and other miscellaneous goods, which increased importance over the years. However, like the other periods, there had been trade surpluses every year since 1872, and the surpluses increased until the end of the Ch'ing period (ibid., 337–339).

Before 1860, various Taiwanese export associations controlled most of Taiwan's trade with China (ibid., 354; Twu, 1975, 373). After 1860, they lost in competition to foreign traders, especially the British, who set up trading houses in Taiwan. The old-fashioned export associations simply could not compete with the Western management system. Although the profits in coastal trading were very high, about 30 percent per annum on average, due to political instability in China and market fluctuation, the trading was highly speculative and risky, and many ventures went bankrupt (Hao, 1986, 346, and Chapter 10).

As time went by, some Taiwanese merchants were able to learn management practices from the Europeans and started their own trading companies. Toward the end of the 1890s, some Taiwanese trading companies even excelled over the European trading houses.[23] In the tea trade, for example, in 1874, the export volume of tea by Taiwanese traders exceeded twice that by foreign traders. By 1881, about 90 percent of Taiwanese tea was exported by Taiwanese merchants (Huang and Chen, 1995, 361). They also dominated in exporting camphor and sugar, as well as importing opium and textiles (ibid., 361–364). In general, we submit that, before the Japanese occupation in 1895, Taiwan had experienced a Commercial Revolution,[24] which, in England, was considered to be a prelude to "Industrial Revolution."[25]

Like merchants in England, the sign of transition from the commercial revolution to the industrial revolution in Taiwan had already appeared before the Japanese occupation in 1895. Some Taiwanese merchants, like the Lin Pun-yuan family of Pangchiao, traded domestically and internationally, and even established local banks and money exchange houses to lend money to tea producers (Huang and Chen, 1995, 364; Su, 1980, 320). Some sugar traders also financed sugar producers (Twu, 1975, 380). In general, by the end of the nineteenth century the Taiwanese merchants were able to dominate trade and to accumulate wealth through commercial relations with China, England, and the Netherlands. Eventually, the merchants also became moneylenders to the local producers.[26] It was reported that by 1895 at least four Taiwanese families had wealth of 10 to 40 million taels, and there were seventeen Taiwanese millionaire families.[27] Indeed, Taiwan had the makings of a classic "bourgeois-nationalist revolution."[28]

TAIWAN IN THE GLOBAL ECONOMY DURING THE JAPANESE PERIOD

The victory of Japan in the first Sino-Japanese war in 1895 over the Ch'ing government and over Taiwanese uprisings distorted the "natural" development along the path to full-blown Taiwanese capitalism.[29] Japanese capital flooded into Taiwan and suffocated, so to speak, the Taiwanese native capital from creation of large-scale modern banks and factories.[30]

Because Japanese capitalism was still in the infant period, the new colonial government at first tolerated the existence of the local Taiwanese capitalists. Except sugar and those commodities under national monopoly (opium, salt, camphor, tobacco, etc.), few restrictions were imposed on the production and distribution of daily necessities (Twu, 1975, 397). At the same time, the government drove away the European and Chinese commercial capital by setting up a discriminatory tariff system, establishing the Bank of Taiwan (1899) to substitute foreign financial control, instituting a monopoly system, and helping Japanese merchants to overtake the foreign monopoly of the sugar trade (Yanaihara, 1929, 43–48; Azuma, 1941, 93–95; Su, 1980, 338).

By the 1920s, however, Japanese capital flooded into Taiwan, and the larger and modern Japanese-owned firms overshadowed the Taiwanese-owned firms. Led by the sugar companies, all the major, larger firms and banks were held by Japanese private capitalists.

However, small Taiwanese enterprises also flourished. In 1936, there were about 7,000 Taiwanese manufacturing firms.[31] At the end of 1938, some 310,000 to 410,000 Taiwanese farms and landlords produced and sold paddy rice, which was refined into rice by about 3,300 local Taiwanese millers.[32] Among them, 732 firms bought rice for exports. In the late 1930s, about 90 percent of the rice exported to Japan was monopolized by four major trading companies (Kawano, 1968, 129). Taiwanese firms remained small and numerous. Similarly, from 1936 to 1937,

127,000 small farms cultivated sugar cane (about 30 percent of total farmers), which was sold to forty-nine Japanese sugar factories in Taiwan (ibid., 92). During the same period, four major sugar companies exported nearly 88 percent of the sugar produced in Taiwan to Japan (ibid., 87–88). Thus, the production of sugar and the distribution of sugar and rice, and other exports and imports, were almost completely under the control of the Japanese. There was little room for the Taiwanese to engage in export businesses. Native development of commercial capitalism gave way to the Japanese.

Taiwanese Agriculture in the World Production

Under colonialism, Taiwanese were mostly farmers and toilers.[33] At least until the mid-1930s, the major emphasis in economic development was in agriculture. In fact, Taiwan developed agriculture with handicaps. It is not only small in land, but also not all of this small land is suited for developing agriculture. Only 31 percent of the area has an elevation below 100 meters. The rest has an elevation either between 100 and 1,000 meters (37 percent), or above 1,000 meters (31 percent) (Chen, 1963, 89). It is "one of the most mountainous islands in the world" (ibid., 87). "There are more than 20 peaks with an altitude of more than 3500 meters. . . . This is very seldom found . . . in the whole world, considering the small size of the island" (ibid., 88). The arable area, mineral resources, and sites suitable for hydroelectric generation are severely limited. The island is exposed to monsoons, typhoons, earthquakes, and even droughts. Heat and rain washed away nutritive soil elements (like phosphorus and potash), leaving mostly acidic soil.[34] Furthermore, because Taiwan is located in a subtropical zone, plant diseases and bugs are prevalent (Ping, 1947, 64).

Despite these natural disadvantages, Taiwan's subtropical location enables it to produce quite different crops. It is this geographical advantage that made Taiwan unique in the Japanese Empire, and the Japanese saw the comparative advantage of developing agriculture in Taiwan (Frank S. T. Hsiao, 1997). To cope with the natural disadvantages, the Japanese developed Taiwanese agriculture by intensive research and development,[35] and organized rural institutions (Ho, 1978, 57–65). They kept systematic and meticulous meteorological records since 1896 (Tang, 1947, 16; Chen, 1963, 121); conducted soil surveys and agricultural experimentation; invested heavily during the 1920s in extensive flood control and modern irrigation systems (Ho, 1978, 36–37); introduced or improved new breeds of plants and crops that withstood weather changes, diseases, and bugs (Tang, 1947, 12–14); used fertilizer extensively (Ishikawa, 1967, 102–105); and improved cultivation methods (Tang, 1947, 14–19).

By 1938, the utilization rate of the arable land in Taiwan was 24 percent (59,000 hectares),[36] higher than Korea (20 percent) and Japan proper (17 percent); lower than major countries like Denmark (62 percent), India (57 percent), Italy (49 percent), and England (46 percent); but much higher than that in any province in China (Tang, 1947, 1). The total area of cultivated land has remained almost constant between the prewar and the postwar periods (*Taiwan Statistical Data Book* [*TSDB*], 2000).

By 1944, ninety-six field crops were planted in Taiwan (Ping, 1947, 75). The six major crops were paddy rice (41.8 percent of the value of total agricultural production),[37] sugar cane (18.1 percent), sweet potatoes (6.7 percent), bananas (4.1 percent), pineapples (2.2 percent), and tea (1.9 percent) (ibid., 76). Rice, sugar cane, and sweet potatoes have been consistently the major agricultural produce of Taiwan during the prewar and early postwar periods.

The increase in Taiwan's agricultural productivity was remarkable. Between 1905 and 1909, per hectare output of Taiwan's agricultural production was only about half that of Japan, but it caught up to about 80 percent by the end of the prewar period, and reached the same amount between 1960 and 1964 (Shinohara and Ishikawa, 1972, 18). By another measure, however, output per farm family of agricultural products in Taiwan during 1935 to 1939 was already about 50 percent higher than that of Japan[38] (ibid., 19). Through irrigation and agricultural and biological innovation, Taiwan became the most advanced rice-producing country in the whole of Asia during the 1930s and the 1950s (ibid., 19; Han-yu Chang, 1957). Similar statements can be made for other crops.

Rice production increased steadily over the years. In 1938, the maximum amount of production reached 6 times that of 1900. Similarly, sugar cane production increased 31 times, sweet potatoes 9 times, bananas 36 times, peanuts 5 times, tobacco 66 times, and pineapples 20 times. Note that all crops, except tea, increased steadily, and reached maximum production by the end of the 1930s. After 1940, agricultural production started to level off and decreased giving way to industrial production following Japan's plunge into the Pacific War.

The magnitude of agricultural production was staggering when we compare Taiwan's achievement with the world. From 1934 to 1938, Taiwan on average produced 1.3 million tons of rice per year. This is about 1 percent of the world rice production, compared with about 8 percent in Japan, and 34 percent in China, and ranked about tenth in the world.[39] Although Taiwan's production was small when compared with these two large neighboring countries, if we consider the size of Taiwan's area and population, we find immediately that Taiwan stands out. In 1940, Taiwan produced more than 50 times its fair share of rice in terms of its proportion of total world area, and 3.3 times of its share in total world population.[40]

The international statistics of two cash crops are available, and they are even more staggering. During 1934 to 1938, Taiwan on average produced 2.4 percent (0.04 million tons) of the world's tea and 2.2 percent of the world's bananas per year. Taiwan's tea production was the sixth largest in the world (next to India, Ceylon, Indonesia, Japan, and China [YS43, 140]) and its banana production was the third largest in the world.[41] This means that Taiwan produced tea and bananas more than 120 times of its share in terms of its area and more than 8 times its share of total world population!

Most of the output of rice, tea, and bananas was exported. During 1934 to 1938, on average about 51 percent (0.7 million tons) of rice per year and about 62 percent of bananas was exported to Japan (Hsian-wen Chou, 1958, 37, 48). In contrast, about 80 percent of tea was exported, mostly to countries other than Japan (TEY41, 144–146), and consisted of about 3 to 4 percent of Taiwan's total exports (SS51, Tables 324, 326). The amounts are awesome if we consider the world export market. Taiwan's exports of bananas (0.15 million tons, including exporting to Japan) constituted about 5.4 percent of the world exports in 1937 and 1938, competing for first or second place in the world banana export market (YS43, 144). Taiwan's exports of tea (9.7 kilotons) from 1936 to 1939 were, on average, about 2.2 percent of total world exports (447 kilotons) during the same period, competing for the sixth largest tea exporting country in the world (YS43, 139). This pattern of exports continued long after the early postwar period (TSDB, 1985).

Sweet potato, used as a secondary food staple in villages, feeds for hogs, and raw material for producing alcohol, was the third important crop. During 1934–1938, Taiwan produced 1.7 million tons of sweet potatoes, a whopping 3.7 percent of world production, ranked fourth in the world, next to China, Japan, and the United States (1.8 million tons). Despite large production, most of them were used domestically. On average, only 2.6 percent of its production was exported to Japan (Hsian-wen Chou, 1958, 46). Taiwan's sugar production was indeed very impressive. From 1938 to 1940, Taiwan produced on average 1.2 million tons of sugar per year, which is almost 7 percent of the world sugar production during that period (17 million tons), ranked fourth among the sugar-producing countries, only next to India (2.9 million tons), Cuba (2.7), and Indonesia (1.5) (YS43, 130).

We note that 70 to 80 percent of pineapple production in Taiwan was canned (Ping, 1947, 78) and, along with tea, exported to Japan and other countries. From 1936 to 1938, Taiwan produced on average 1.2 million boxes of canned pineapple per year, a whopping 7.5 percent of the world production (16 million boxes), ranked third in the world, next only to Java (12 million boxes) and Malaya (2.6 million boxes) (YS43, 145).

During the Ch'ing and Japanese periods, salt production was a monopoly of the government and was one of Taiwan's major products and exports. In 1938, Taiwan's salt production was about 0.241 million tons, which was about 0.5 percent of the world production (37 million tons), and ranked thirteenth in world production. Its importance continued even after World War II. In fact, from 1951 to 1960, Taiwan produced on average 0.3 million tons of salt per year: 63 percent of the output was exported, with 85 percent exporting to Japan.

Before World War I, Taiwan and Japan were the only two countries in the world producing natural camphor (YS41, 365). From 1891 to 1895, the world annual camphor exports were about 31 kilotons. Taiwan exported on average 56 percent of the world annual exports (Chen, 1963, 422). After World War I, Germany developed synthetic camphor, and Taiwan's production fluctuated and decreased. By 1939, it was estimated that Taiwan still produced about 50 percent of natural camphor, or 30 percent of the world production (ibid., 428), although the importance of its value in Taiwan's total production and exports decreased considerably.

Thus, by the end of the 1930s, Taiwan already was the world's major producing country of bananas (third), canned pineapples (third), sugar (fourth), sweet potatoes (fourth), tea (sixth), rice (tenth), peanuts (tenth), and salt (thirteenth). Unlike many other colonies, Taiwan was by no means a "monoculture" country. To produce so many different agricultural products in such large quantities, the infrastructure of the society—like transportation, communication, and education—must have been built to accommodate such massive development. In the early 1940s, based on this agricultural accumulation and the basis of wealth,[42] the Japanese were able to develop industry in Taiwan quickly and massively, although it was too late.

When the war ended in 1945, Taiwan already had a highly advanced agricultural sector. The war damage to Taiwan's agriculture was minimal (slightly less than 50 percent) as compared with other industries, and it recovered quickly by 1950 (Kai and Chu, 1951, 61). After 1949, when about 2 million Chinese refugees and soldiers flooded Taiwan, every 3 Taiwanese farm laborers had to support 1 Chinese soldier, and every 1.1 farm laborer supported 1 nonproducing Chinese soldier, refugee, or bureaucrat (Hsiao and Hsiao, 1996, 228). The Chinese civil war and refugees induced chaos and extreme poverty during the early postwar era. The misery had nothing to do with Japanese colonialism, although the Chinese contend otherwise. This real burden for the Taiwanese occurred when the Chinese came to Taiwan after World War II. Without prewar development of the agricultural sector, as we have already stated, the Taiwanese economy would have collapsed. Elsewhere we have seen the upsurge in agricultural productivity during the early postwar period (Hsiao and Hsiao, 1996, 240–242). We submit that, unlike many other developing countries, the very foundation and potentiality of such a postwar take-off to higher productivity were laid in the prewar period.

Industrial Development—Taiwan in the "Great East Asia Co-Prosperity Sphere"

By the second half of the 1930s, Taiwanese agriculture had reached its limit: The arable land was exhausted. Agricultural technology and its research and development had also reached their ceilings. At the same time, rapid industrialization, militarization, and scarcity of resources in Japan proper also forced industrialization and a readjustment of Taiwan's economic structure (Kusui, 1941, 508; 1944, 159–170). It all started after the completion of the Sun-Moon Lake hydraulic power plant in 1934, tripling Taiwan's electricity output to 150,000 kilowatts (Takahashi, 1937, 420). The power plant was followed by the development of an aluminum factory (in 1935), an iron alloy factory (in 1935), a shipping yard (in 1936), and other industries like pulp (in 1935), fertilizer (in 1937), and oil and fats (in 1935) (Kusui, 1944, 69–74).

From mid-1937 on, as the Taiwanese economy entered the war stage, the emphasis was on metal processing and refinery, machinery (including weapons, airplanes, and automobiles), and the petroleum, chemical, and pharmaceutical industries (Kusui, 1944, 158, 168). They are mostly defense-related industries. At the same time, light industries of daily necessities, such as lightbulbs, glass, ink, pencils, porcelain, radios, leather, nails, and agricultural machinery, and so on, were developed for wartime self-sufficiency (Sumiya, Liu, and Tu, 1992, 21), independent of Japan proper. Thus, Taiwan entered the import-substitution phase of economic development, which continued after the war until the mid-1960s. By 1939, the value of industrial output exceeded that of agricultural output for the first time.[43] Taiwan was no longer an agricultural society.

As we have seen, Taiwan is a natural resource–poor country. The most important mining product was coal (0.22 percent of world coal output in 1941), followed by a limited amount of gold (0.06 percent of world gold production in 1941), crude oil, and natural gas.[44] Only those industries producing soda, nitrogen, cement, carbide, or glass could manage to use domestically produced industrial salt, limestone, and natural gas (shown in the callout box in Figure 8-4). To develop heavy and chemical industries as well as machinery industry, Taiwan had to rely on foreign resources. Figure 8-4 shows the major sources

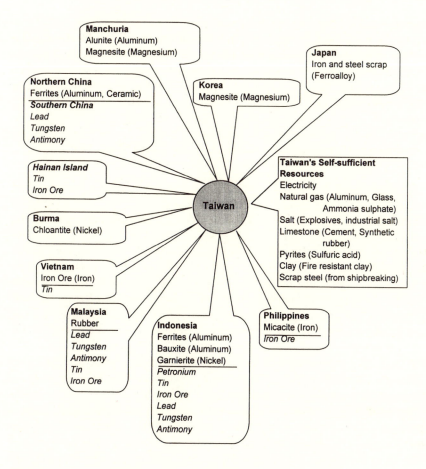

Figure 8-4. Taiwan's prewar industrialization and resources.

of resource imports. The item in parentheses shows the product that was actually produced during 1939–1940 (Chang, 1980, 109–111), and the items in italic were planned sources of imports (TEY41, 518–519; also Kusui, 1944, 177–178). All of them could be imported "from the 'Japan-Manchuria-China bloc' and the Southeast Asian countries close to Taiwan" (TEY41, 519). The figure illustrates the strategic role and the regional position of Taiwan in Japan's prewar "Great East Asia Co-Prosperity Sphere." In fact, Japan's "southward movement policy" would have been inconceivable without Taiwan (Yano, 1975, 149). Taiwan was envisioned as having a lofty mission,[45] to exploit the rich resources of South China and South Seas (Nanshi Nanyo) for the prosperity of Japan and "all the previously oppressed people" living in the region.[46]

Though Taiwan's prewar industrialization was too late and most industries were just burgeoning, a wide range of light and heavy industries, including all the basic industries for future industrialization, had been established on the island. They stabilized the postwar economy and paved the way for rapid postwar industrial development in the mid-1960s. Because initial conditions before economic take-off play an important role in the growth process, as often asserted by the new growth theory, Taiwan was probably one of the few countries that had the most favorable initial conditions among all the developing countries in the postwar period. In this sense, we submit that there is no "miracle" in Taiwanese economic development after the war.

POSTWAR TAIWAN IN THE GLOBAL ECONOMY

After World War II,[47] the Chinese Nationalist (Kuomintang, KMT) Government confiscated and combined Japanese-owned firms and banks, and converted them into fifty or so public enterprises.[48] Non–Taiwanese-speaking Chinese bureaucrats and managers replaced non–Taiwanese-speaking Japanese capitalists. Lacking resources and technical ability to engage in new industries, the government had to rely on the old industrial base left over by the Japanese. At the end of the war, the Japanese left behind basic metal, chemical, and other "heavy" industries, which were relatively capital-intensive in those days. As seen in Figure 8-4, most raw materials for these heavy industries had to be imported, and their finished products had a limited market in the war-torn Taiwanese economy. Thus immediately after the war, the KMT government had difficulty in deciding whether to spend scarce capital and precious foreign exchange to restore the war damage and to maintain these white-elephant industries (Chi-yuan Lin, 1968, 296). However, internal and external political developments around 1949 and 1950 altered the picture virtually overnight. The civilian and military industries built by the Japanese in Taiwan to take advantage of resources in South China and the South Seas to fight the Allied Forces were now utilized by the KMT government to fight Chinese communists in the defense of Taiwan. Essentially the KMT perpetuated the Japanese-controlled wartime economy and industries (Hsiao and Hsiao, 2001; Twu, 1975, 499), though on a larger scale due to massive U.S. aid that supported the influx of Chinese refugees and 600,000 Chinese soldiers at that time (Hsiao and Hsiao, 1996).

Taiwanese firms remained small and fragmented, and "a broad movement from below upward" was also severely limited. Until the end of the 1970s, banks and financial institutions, insurance, stock exchange, education, transportation, communication, utilities, public media, and the like were either highly or completely restricted. Nowhere could

Taiwanese small-and-medium enterprises (SMEs) enter the businesses of even local transportation, newspapers, shipping, aviation, gas, electricity, and so on.[49]

But there are important differences in the postwar period. The Japanese had exploited Taiwan's agricultural and industrial resources without Taiwanese initiative, and capital and technology were almost completely under their control.[50] Nevertheless, when the Japanese left Taiwan in 1945, they also left behind physical plants and the people who assisted them in managing and operating the plants. More importantly they left behind technical know-how, new skills, human capital, and a whole set of social and economic infrastructure. In addition to an extensive irrigation system, effective farm organizations, pervasive educational systems, massive electricity-generating facilities, and extensive transportation and communication networks (Hsiao and Hsiao, 1996, 219–221), they also left behind the changes of customs and habits for modern industrial society,[51] such as appreciation of manual labor,[52] propensity to innovate,[53] the habit of keeping time and being on time, the concept of law and order,[54] and respect for ruling by law and following instructions. In other words, the social, cultural, and psychological environments for economic take-off—despite the fact that some of them were undoubtedly coerced by the colonial government for the sake of the mother country and military purposes—were already created in the 1930s and the early 1940s. Using the modern terminology, Taiwan's "institutional reform" was completed long before the end of World War II. The reform enabled the prewar rapid development of agriculture and industry, and also has been essential, but often ignored in the literature, to postwar rapid economic growth.[55]

Other important differences are foreign influences and international markets. The U.S. advocacy of free market and free trade, and the U.S. influence on KMT government policies through the U.S. Aid Program, nurtured the Taiwanese small-and-medium enterprises (Hsiao and Hsiao, 1996, 238–239). The rapid rise of postwar Japanese capitalism ironically stimulated the Taiwanese entrepreneurs and helped the Taiwanese SMEs (ibid., 284–285). The postwar technological innovations of product-life-cycle commodities promoted Taiwanese enterprises. In terms of trading practices, however, there is an important similarity to the prewar situation. Until the early 1980s, foreigners, especially Japanese trading companies, have dominated the trading business.

Major Trading Partners

Figure 8-5 and Figure 8-6 are area diagrams that dramatically characterize major Taiwanese trading partners.[56] Both figures show

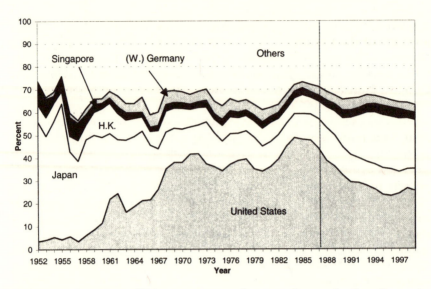

Figure 8-5. Direction of Taiwanese exports (country shares of real total exports, 1986 = base year).

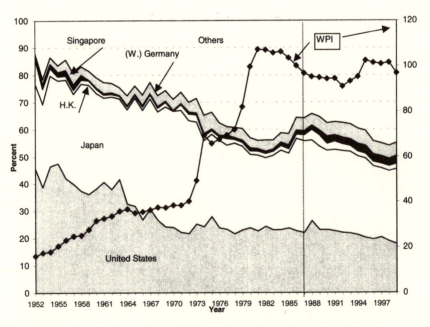

Figure 8-6. Direction of Taiwanese imports (country shares of real total imports, 1986 = base year).

that the United States and Japan are the two largest trading partners throughout the postwar period until the end of the 1980s. Figure 8-5 shows that Japan was the largest export market for Taiwan until 1966. Japan's share in total Taiwanese exports ranged from 60 percent in 1955 to a mere 8.4 percent in 1998. After 1967 the United States became Taiwan's largest export market. The U.S. share of total Taiwanese exports ranged from 49 percent in 1984 to 29 percent in 1992. Since 1990, Taiwanese exports to Hong Kong, as the entrepôt to China, have exceeded exports to Japan. In 1999, Hong Kong's share was 21 percent and Japan's share only 10 percent. Up to 60 percent of Taiwanese exports to Hong Kong were re-exported to China.[57] Like the United States, Taiwan has a hard time breaking into Japanese domestic markets. Despite Taiwanese efforts in attaining a diversification of trading partners, Figure 8-5 shows that the relative export shares of Singapore, which is the entrepôt to the ASEAN countries, and of West Germany, which is the gateway to Europe, and of others remain almost unchanged, although exports to these countries have accelerated since 1985 (*TSDB*, 2000). This means that trade with these countries has increased only at the same pace with trade with Japan and the United States. Throughout the 1980s and the 1990s, Taiwan was one of the most active exporting countries in the world. The total exports in 1980 were about $20 billion, ranking 20th among the 133 countries listed in WDR,[58] and in 1995 were about $112 billion, ranking 21st in the world.

The major importing partners, however, are just the reverse of the major exporting partners. Figure 8-6 shows that prior to 1963 Taiwan imported primarily from the United States. Japan was busy with its economic reconstruction, and the United States was the only major partner helping Taiwan's reconstruction with a huge aid program. The roles of the United States and Japan were reversed in the mid-1960s when the U.S. economic aid program was terminated. After 1964, imports from Japan became dominant. Japan's share in Taiwanese imports ranged from 45 percent in 1971 to 25 percent in 1982. The U.S. share in total Taiwanese imports ranged from 48 percent in 1955 to 18 percent in 1999. It has decreased gradually. Taiwan's total imports in 1980 were $20 billion, ranking twenty-first in the world, and in 1995, total imports increased to about $104 billion, ranking fifteenth in the world.[59]

Through the postwar era, imports from the United States and Japan alone ranged from 45 percent (1998) to 80 percent (1954) of total Taiwanese imports, and exports to these countries also ranged from 34 percent (1997) to 64 percent (1955). Here lies the dependency criticism of Taiwanese economic development.[60] Both Japan and the United States constantly played very important roles.

Taiwan, Japan, and the United States Nexus

Figure 8-7 dramatizes Taiwan's trade relationship with the United States and Japan.[61] The trade volume and the deficits with both countries from 1952 to 1974 become invisible when the scale is in billions of dollars. Thus we have plotted the data from 1952 to 1965 in units of $10 million (the left panel), and from 1966 to 1975 in units of $100 million (the middle panel), and after 1975, in units of $billion (the right panel). As shown in the lower part of the diagram, from 1952 to 1999 Taiwan's real imports from Japan (M in the lower part) are consistently higher than Taiwan's real exports to Japan (X in the lower part). This means that Taiwan consistently had a negative balance of trade with Japan since 1953 (except 1955). The dark solid bars in the lower part show this.

The situation is quite different with the United States. Before 1967, Taiwan also had trade deficits with the United States every year. After 1968, however, Taiwan's real imports from the United States (M in the upper part) have been consistently lower than its real exports to the United States (X in the upper part), bringing about real trade surpluses. The empty bars in the upper part of the figure show this.

Since 1968, both deficits with Japan and surpluses with the United States have increased over time with the progress of Taiwan's industrialization. In Figure 8-7, this is illustrated as an explosion to the two sides

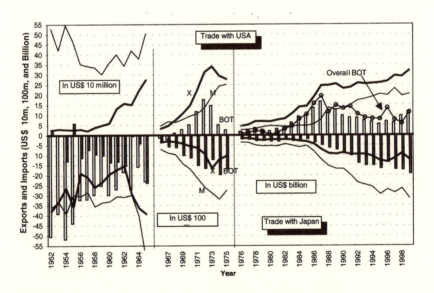

Figure 8-7. The structure of the Pacific trade triangle (real exports, imports, and balance of trade).

of the horizontal axis like a broom. After 1988, exports to the United States slowed down under the watchful eyes of the U.S. government under the Omnibus Trade Competitiveness Act passed in the U.S. Congress in 1988 (Hsiao and Hsiao, 1995). At the same time, imports from the United States increased considerably, narrowing down the bilateral trade surpluses. With devaluation of the U.S. dollar and upward revaluation of the Japanese yen, Taiwanese exports to Japan jumped up greatly between 1985 and 1988 but ran out of steam and flattened out afterward. Real commodity imports from Japan, however, continued to accelerate, indicating that the more Taiwan tries to increase its exports, whether to the United States or other countries, the more Taiwan has to rely on imports of materials and capital equipment from Japan. Despite almost desperate efforts by the KMT government,[62] Taiwan simply cannot elude its dependency on Japan!

Real trade surpluses with the United States peaked at $17 billion in 1987 and then started to decline, while trade deficits with Japan continued to increase, although with a slower pace. The deficits with Japan reached an all-time high at $19.3 billion (at the 1986 price) in 1999. However, Taiwan still has managed to achieve a huge surplus in its overall real balance of trade every year since 1976. For example, Taiwan had an overall surplus of $11.3 billion in 1999. Figure 8-7 shows that Taiwan's real balance of trade, shown as the marked line with circles, tends to move closely with the real trade surpluses with the United States, implying that the latter is the main source of Taiwan's trade surplus.

A Pacific Trade Triangle

From these discussions, we may derive several characteristics of the Taiwanese economy in the postwar period:

1. Taiwanese trade relies very heavily on the United States and Japan. Taiwan relies more on the U.S. markets for exports, and on Japan for imports.
2. In the 1980s, Taiwanese trade with both the United States and Japan bloomed significantly. Its increase in exports to the United States was paralleled by the increase in imports from Japan and, to a lesser degree, from the United States.
3. Since 1968, Taiwan has persistently had real trade surpluses with the United States and trade deficits with Japan, although the overall trade balance with all traded partners is consistently positive since 1976. Despite many serious attempts to reverse the trade deficits with Japan,[63] the Taiwan government has never succeeded. Figure 8-7 illustrates this point. In real terms, the deficits with Japan have worsened greatly in recent years after the

Taiwan government has emphasized the development of high-
tech industries in the late 1980s.

4. From Figure 8-7, the following trade patterns emerge. Taiwan
   imports intermediate goods and raw materials mainly from
   Japan[64] and exports manufactured goods mainly to the United
   States. These triangular relations among Taiwan, Japan, and the
   United States are the backbone of the rapid growth of the Taiwan-
   ese economy.

Elsewhere (Hsiao and Hsiao, 1996, 258–262) we have shown that
textile products in the 1960s and the 1970s, as well as machinery products and electrical products in the 1980s and in the 1990s, were the
leading export items. Taiwan's industrialization also centered on these
three leading commodities. There has been a huge expansion of exports
in machinery products and electric equipment. Exports to the United
States and imports from Japan are especially dramatic. A less dramatic
increase in exports can also be observed for basic metals and articles,
and chemicals. The machinery products and electric equipment are
significant in both exports and imports in the 1980s and the 1990s.

On Sustained Growth

Many economists contend that Taiwan was fortunate (meaning the
government was wise enough) to adopt an export-promotion policy in
the mid-1960s, which pushed the economy to rapid growth. However,
as we have shown in the Appendix, the export-promotion policy itself
does not ensure rapid growth. With risk of some repetitions, here is the
answer to the important question of how Taiwan's outward-oriented
strategy has been sustained. It is due to special geographical and historical circumstances.

Taiwan was already an export-oriented country under the Japanese
regime. The Taiwanese were very much accustomed to the notion of
"production for exports" for living and profits. As soon as the Taiwanese economy recovered from war damages and the society recuperated
from the terror[65] of the February 1947 Incident, Taiwan started exporting traditional agricultural products like sugar, rice, bananas, tea, and
canned foods to Japan. When the KMT government started its export-
promotion policy in the mid-1960s, the Taiwanese already had more
than two generations of successful experience with exports as a modern
business practice.

In the early 1960s, textile products, lumber and timber products,
plywood, electrical and machinery apparatus, chemicals, and basic
metals were added to rice, sugar, and bananas for exports (TSDB, 1975,
190–191). The postwar rapid economic development is the continuation

of the prewar agricultural and industrial development, which was interrupted by World War II and China's civil war (Hsiao and Hsiao, 1998, 2001). Much to the dismay of the Chinese bureaucrats in Taiwan (Shi and Li, 1978), the historical tie between Taiwan and Japan persisted and strengthened in the postwar era: First Japan as the number one export market for Taiwan, then as the number one country from which Taiwan imports intermediate goods and capital goods.

One of the major hurdles of an export business is international marketing. A country may produce goods, but may not find a market in which to sell the products. We have seen that, except during the last part of the Ch'ing rule of Taiwan, Europeans and Japanese conducted most of the foreign trade. After World War II, even during the 1970s and the 1980s when the KMT government encouraged the establishment of local "large trading companies," 60 percent of total exports was handled by either foreign-owned, or foreign-and-Taiwanese-jointly-owned, trading companies. Furthermore, the majority of these foreigners were Japanese. The remaining exports were divided almost evenly: 20 percent by the manufacturers and traders and the government-owned Central Trust, and 20 percent by 36,000 Taiwanese small trading companies (Yajima, 1986, 107). It was also estimated in 1981 that the Japanese Shoshas[66] alone, directly or indirectly, handled 40 to 50 percent of Taiwanese foreign trade (Bang-Li Liu, 1996, 145). Another government survey in 1984 showed that 75 percent of total exports (in terms of value) were controlled by foreign businesses. Most of them were Japanese companies (ibid.). Through Japanese joint ventures and trading companies, Taiwanese firms were able to solve most of their marketing problems. The reason is simple. In addition to geographical proximity and historical ties in the early postwar period, many older Taiwanese entrepreneurs spoke and read Japanese. Japanese customs and habits were not completely alien to them. This undoubtedly removed major hurdles[67] of technological transfer and facilitated trade between Taiwan and Japan after the war.[68]

This venue of marketing through foreign companies also proved successful for conducting trade with the United States and other countries. In 1973, Taiwan replaced Japan in the U.S. shoe market, and in 1976, Taiwan replaced Italy to become the world's largest exporter of shoes. By 1980, shoe manufacturing was Taiwan's third largest exporting industry, following only textiles and electronics (Skoggard, 1996, 55–56). However, ten or so foreign branch offices or agencies handle two thirds of the shoe export business (Bang-Li Liu, 1996, 130).

In a recent paper, Coe, Helpman, and Hoffmaister (1995) have shown that opening trade with industrial countries is effective in increasing the total factor productivity (TFP) of a developing country. They also found that which country is selected is also important. "A developing country whose trade is more biased towards industrial countries that have large cumulative experiences in R&D has higher productivity." And among the developed countries, "the United States has by far the largest domestic capital stock, . . . about five times as high as Japan, which is the country with the second largest effect." Thus, by historical coincidence and geographical proximity, as shown in Figure 8-1, both Korea and Taiwan are indeed very fortunate to be associated with the United States and Japan as their major trading partners, and as we have seen earlier, Taiwan's trade with both countries has been about 50 percent of total trade since 1952.

Factors other than the pacific trade triangle, such as availability of cheap labor, the rise of multinational companies, and international division of labor, the Vietnam War, long prosperity and growth in the world economy, especially in Japan and in the United States, and advocacy and encouragement of free trade and free markets by the world organizations like the International Monetary Fund and the World Bank, government macroeconomic policy and planning, all helped make Taiwan's drive to export a great success. However, we consider that these amenities were of secondary importance, because they were also available to all other countries. Thus, we submit that the outward-looking propensity of the Taiwanese people and the Chinese bureaucrats in Taiwan, along with the triangle relationship with Japan and the United States, spurred by the decreasing value of the New Taiwan dollar against the U.S. dollar, have sustained the outward-looking strategy of Taiwan, and made it a success even until today.

Direct Foreign Investment and Economic Growth

Japan and the United States are not only Taiwan's most important trading partners, but their manufacturers also invested directly and heavily in Taiwan, supplementing Taiwan's domestic investment at the beginning of its industrialization and throughout the postwar period.

An Overview of Inward DFI in Taiwan

In the early 1950s,[69] when the newly independent former colonies, and semicolonies such as China, were still recovering from the horror of exploitation and imperialism,[70] Taiwan was probably the only country in the world that invited much-suspected direct foreign investment (DFI) with open arms.[71] Seeing Taiwan's success, Korea followed suit, along with other developing countries, China, and the ASEANs in the 1980s.

Figure 8-8 shows the increase of the approved amount of DFI in Taiwan from 1952 to 1999. As in the case of trade statistics, we have

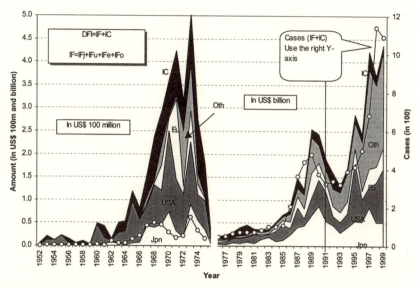

Figure 8-8. Real direct foreign investment in Taiwan (cases and amount approved).

converted the data into real terms,[72] using the 1986 wholesale price index as the base. Overseas Chinese investment (IC) is shown in the upper dark band in Figure 8-8. The rest of the chart shows the (non-overseas Chinese) foreign investment (IF), consisting of investment from Japan, the United States, Europe, and other countries (IF = IF_j + IF_u + IF_e + IF_o). IC consists of investment from those overseas Chinese mostly residing in Hong Kong and Japan. Before 1965, IC was an important source of DFI. However, the weight of IC in total DFI decreased after 1965, taken over by IF from the United States. After 1982, IC's weight in total DFI decreased drastically, and became negligible after the mid-1980s. IF from the United States started in 1953, and was superseded by investment from Japan most of the time after 1982 until 1995. In any case, as with trade relations, Japanese and American investments dominated DFI in Taiwan from 1966 to 1995. Though investment from Europe is also increasing, after 1995 "other sources" of foreign investment have exceeded all others.

The main areas in the "other sources" category are British territories in Central America,[73] which include the Virgin Islands, Bermuda, Belize, and British West Indies. The diagram shows two facts that indicate the resilience of Taiwan in the global economy: the two oil shocks in 1973–1974 and 1979–1980 eventually spurred, rather than depressed, DFI, and that Taiwan still can attract and even increase continuously the American and Japanese investments despite strong competition from China and elsewhere in recent years. In fact, as shown in Figure 8-8, the record amount of DFI (IF+IC) was reached just recently in 1999 at $4.23 billion in real value with 1,089 cases.[74] The Taiwanese economy has never been so strong.

Altogether, from 1952 to 1999, 11,111 cases (shown by the solid line with circles in Figure 8-8) with the amount of $37 billion (in nominal values[75]) of DFI were approved for IF and IC. Among IF, Japan is the largest contributor with 3,230 cases ($8.3 billion), followed closely by the United States, accounting for 1,694 cases ($8.7b), Europe, for 928 cases ($4.1b). Other countries were responsible for 2,562 cases ($12b). The bulk of DFI has occurred only recently (TSDB, 2000, 260).

In general, from 1952 to 1999, 26 percent of Taiwan's DFI has been in electronic and electric products, totaling $9.4 billion in 1,544 cases. This is followed by other products, 13 percent, $4.8 billion in 1,927 cases; banking and insurance, 13 percent, $4.6 billion in 502 cases. None or very few DFI were in agriculture, fisheries and livestock, paper and paper products, and construction (TSDB, 2000, 261). Among the foreign investment (IF), the lion's share goes to electronic and electric products ($9.2b/1,339 cases), followed by chemicals ($3.7b/470 cases), services ($3.2b/1,229 cases), foreign trade ($2.5b/1,754 cases), and machinery, equipment, and instrument ($1.6b/431 cases) (ibid.). Indeed, through forward and backward linkages, foreign capital has helped build Taiwan as the kingdom of electronics and computer,[76] and had a significant positive effect on the real growth of Taiwan's GDP.[77]

The Active Role of Taiwanese in the Global Economy—Outward Direct Foreign Investment

As the Taiwanese economy matures, it has started investment in foreign countries. The spurt of outward investment occurred after the mid-1980s, mainly due to dollar depreciation against the New Taiwan dollar and yen, rising wage rates and labor shortage in Taiwan, and the lifting of martial law[78] in 1987 that was followed by acceleration of economic and political liberalization, which in turn invigorated environment protection activities and labor movements. Like Figures 8-6 to 8-8, Figure 8-9 shows Taiwanese outward investment in real values (1986 = base year) by area: American, Asian, European, and other regions. We also added Taiwan's investment in China, which will be explained in detail in the following section. Taiwan's outward investment (not including China, same below in this section) was rather irregular and small before 1987, and increased steadily and sharply from a mere $0.1 billion with 45 cases in 1987 to $3.4 billion with 774 cases in 1999, an amount that was the maximum yearly investment in

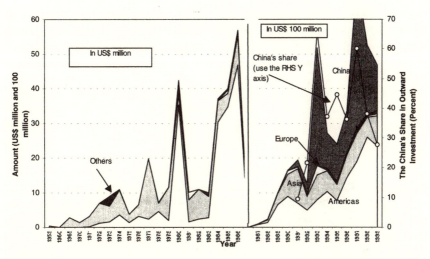

Figure 8-9. Taiwanese outward investment (in real value [1986 = base year]).

real value ($3.3 billion in nominal value). In 1999, Taiwan's outward investment was about 80 percent of its inward direct foreign investment that year.[79]

In fact, Taiwan's outward investment practically started[80] only in 1965, and from 1952 to 1999, total outward investment amounted to US$ 21.9 billion in nominal value[81] with 5,426 cases (*TSDB*, 2000, 262). According to the Investment Committee (2000) report, two thirds of total outward investment went to the American region (63 percent), followed by Asia (32 percent) and Europe (3.3 percent, mostly in Germany). Oceania (in Australia) and Africa (Liberia and South Africa) consisted of only 1.6 percent. As high as one third (32 percent) of the total outward investment went to British Territories in Central America ($6.9b/690 cases), followed by the United States (21 percent, $4.6b/2,075 cases), Malaysia (6.4 percent, $1.4b/239 cases), Singapore (5.4 percent, $1.2b/276 cases), and Hong Kong (4.9 percent, $1.1b/528 cases). We suspect that most of the larger Taiwanese investments in British territories transferred to China.[82] Investment in Japan is very disappointing, consisting of only 1.4 percent ($0.4b/195 cases) of the total. Like exports to Japan, Japanese markets are very hard to break.

By industrial categories, 37 percent of Taiwanese outward investment goes to banking and insurance ($8.1b/830 cases), followed by electronic and electric products (17 percent, $3.7b/1,484 cases), others (8 percent, $1.7b/712 cases), foreign trade (7 percent, $1.6b/881 cases), and chemicals (6.1 percent, $1.3b/211 cases). "Electronic and electric products" was the largest item (26 percent) of inward direct foreign investment. It appears that the electronic and electric-product industry has a dual structure in Taiwan: The high profit margin and high-end part of the industry stay in Taiwan, and the more labor-intensive part of the industry moves out to China via British Territories, also to Malaysia, Singapore, and Hong Kong, circumventing the increase in wages in Taiwan.

Trade and Investment in China

As shown in Figure 8-2, the enmity between Taiwan and China separated both countries from 1949 to 1987, when the thirty-eight-year-long martial law was lifted. Whereas China started attracting trade and investment from Taiwan after its implementation of the reform program in 1979, the Taiwanese government lifted its strict restriction on travel to China only in 1987. In 1988 Taiwan granted indirect imports of some fifty Chinese agricultural and industrial raw materials through third countries, and only after 1990 indirect exports and indirect investment were permitted.[83] Indirect contact with China made official statistical data hard to collect.[84]

The columns of the left-hand-side panel of Figure 8-10 show Taiwanese data[85] on exports to China ($Xt/2$, filled column) and imports from China ($Mt/2$, the empty columns) (both figures are divided by 2 so that all the data may be presented in one diagram). The lines show the Chinese data on Taiwanese exports to China (Xc, the dotted line) and Taiwanese imports from China (Mc, lower solid line) for 1980 and 1990 to 1995. Apparently, the Chinese data consistently underestimate export and import figures by more than 50 percent compared with those of Taiwan. In any case, both data show a very rapid increase in Taiwanese exports to China and a very slow increase in imports from China, resulting in a large trade surplus for Taiwan every year since 1981. The trade surplus in 1997 was $18.5 billion, more than enough to offset Taiwan's total trade deficits of $17.3 billion that year (TSDB, 2000, 210). Most of the items exported to China were fur and its products, pulp and papers, textiles, printings, chemicals and their products, and so on (Yu, 1996).

The right-hand-side panel of Figure 8-10 presents Taiwan's investment in China. The solid line (Cases_t) and the light filled column (Approved_t) on the left side of the three-column group show Taiwan's data on approved investment to China in nominal value.[86] We also show the approved investment in real value on the right-hand side of Figure 8-9. The rather irregular trend of investment in China probably reflects the unpredictable political relation between the two countries, and the large bumps in both the amount approved and the cases in 1993 and 1997 are the results of passing two new laws that set the deadline

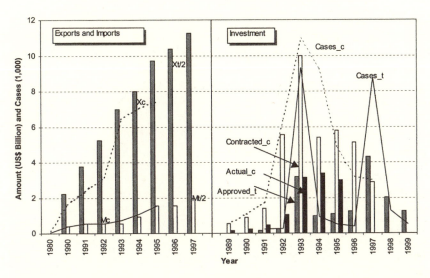

Figure 8-10. Taiwan–China trade and investment relations (in nominal values).

for Taiwanese firms to register their China investment or face fines (Morrison and Cooper, 1999, 125; Ishida, 1999, 158).

Aside from these two years, Figure 8-9 indicates that Taiwanese investment in China has been not only increasing alarmingly, but also becoming so large that it consists of almost one third to more than one half of Taiwan's total outward investment in recent years (see the marked line in the right-hand-side panel, which is measured on the right Y-axis). In fact, the outward investment to China from 1991 to 1999, the period for which the Taiwan government has data, consists of 44 percent of total outward investment from 1991 to 1999. It is more alarming in terms of cases: The approved cases for investment in China from 1991 to 1999 is a whopping 83 percent of the accumulated cases, which was 26,687 cases. More and more small and medium-sized enterprises in Taiwan are investing in China, and there is a sign that larger enterprises are following suit. Most of the projects went to South China, in the categories of electronic and electric appliances, food and beverage processing, basic metals and metal products, plastic products, and so on (*TSDB*, 2000, 264–265). It all started from low-end labor-intensive industries. However, in recent years, more and more capital-intensive and high-technology industries also move to China. For national security reasons, the Taiwan government has tried to limit and regulate China investment and to promote the "Southward Policy," that is, to invest in Southeast Asia.[87] Even so, in 1999, investment in China still amounted to 28 percent ($1.3 billion, 499 cases) of the total outward investment that year.

To show the discrepancies in collecting the data, we also illustrate the Chinese data[88] on Taiwanese investment in China. The middle empty columns (Contracted_c) show the contracted investment, which is far larger than the actual investment (Actual_c in filled dark columns), indicating the potential problem of using "approved" investment statistics of Taiwan. The dotted line (Cases_c) shows the Chinese data on the (contracted?) cases. The Chinese data may be 1.2 times (1993) to 24 times (1992) greater than the Taiwanese data.[89] It is not clear why the Chinese data also have a large bump in 1993 and 1997, as the new Taiwanese laws should not affect Chinese statistics. This may cast the reliability problem of Chinese data.

TAIWAN AND THE GLOBAL ECONOMY IN THE 21ST CENTURY

During the past 100 years, the Taiwanese economy has followed the classical case of development: from traditional feudal society to modern agricultural development. It went through the typical stages of exports of agricultural and processed goods, and then industrial development through the phases of import substitution, export promotion, and high-tech industrialization.

One of the popular views about Taiwanese economic development is that it started after the war "from a state of extreme poverty and political and social backwardness" (Lai et al., 1991, 1), implying that Taiwan's economic success is a case of the "rags to riches" dream in less than forty years. Even a chapter of a book is devoted to this title and theme (Chan and Clark, 1992). Similar views are abundant among many economists. However, according to Maddison's data (1995), the real GDP per capita of Taiwan measured in 1990 Geary-Khamis dollars reached the prewar highest level of $1,522 in 1942, and then plummeted to $693 in 1944, a year before the end of World War II. According to Maddison's data, the figure in 1944 was well below[90] the real GDP per capita in 1904 and 1905 ($712). The change can be perceived roughly from Figure 8-11, which shows the ten-year moving average of real GDP per capita in 1990 Geary-Khamis dollars for Taiwan, South Korea, and some OECD countries in the logarithmic scale. Apparently, here are the "rags," as the Taiwanese standard of living plunged below its 1904 level! Even in 1952, the real GDP per capita ($1,020) is only comparable to that of 1924 ($1,034). The early postwar poverty, slow recovery, and the deprivation of the Taiwanese were the results of the civil war in China carrying over by the Chinese to Taiwan. It is not a consequence of colonialism. It was a temporary setback for the long-run economic development,[91] which started in 1895 up to the early 1940s, and was

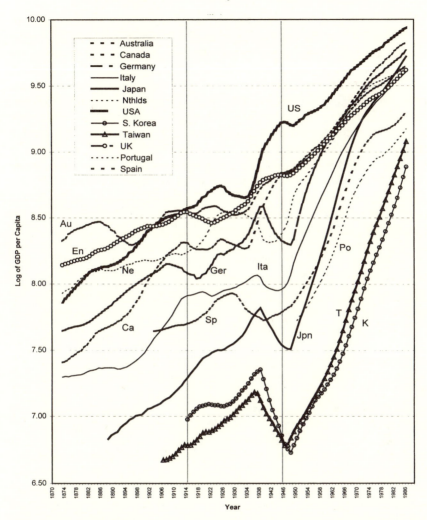

Figure 8-11. Real GDP per capita of Taiwan, Korea, and some OECD countries (ten-year moving average).

interrupted for more than two decades and then continued only after the mid-1960s.

As we have elaborated in this chapter and elsewhere, it is simply unreasonable, if not wrong, to ignore prewar development and consider only the "miracle" of postwar Taiwanese economic development. In fact, according to the same Maddison's data, Taiwanese real GDP per capita growth rate (1.97 percent) ranked third or fourth in the world during the prewar period, following Japan (2.64 percent) and Korea

(2.03 percent), and almost tied with that of Norway (1.98 percent), as can be seen from the slope of the curves in Figure 8-11. By the early 1940s, its real GDP per capita level was higher than other Asian countries, except Japan[92] and Korea (Figure 8-11). In fact, the "Taiwan miracle" already started in the prewar period (Hsiao and Hsiao). Due to an influx of the Chinese refugees, government mismanagement of the economy, and wartime mobilization to fight against the Chinese communists, the Taiwanese real GDP per capita recovered to the prewar peak only in 1963 (at $1,612).[93]

After the transition period, the economy took off to steady growth in the mid-1960s. It grew faster than any country in Asia including Japan, and even faster (the lines are steeper) than all the advanced countries in the postwar period (Hsiao and Hsiao, 2000, 2001). Although, compared with Japan, its real GDP per capita decreased after the war until 1970, Taiwan started to catch up with Japan after 1970 (ibid.). In terms of real GDP per capita, as shown in Figure 8-11, Australia and Canada, some of the former British colonies, already caught up with the United Kingdom by 1990. Likewise, by 1990, in terms of nominal GNP per capita, Taiwan came very close to Spain and Portugal, its former colonial powers. Eventually, Taiwan (at $12,333; *TSDB*, 2000, 332) surpassed Portugal ($10,690) and came very close to Spain ($14,080) in 1998 (World Bank, 2000, 231). If Taiwan continues its current track of progress, it is not inconceivable that Taiwan may even surpass the Netherlands and Japan.[94]

Competitiveness Indexes

After the 1997–1999 Asian financial crisis, we are reasonably optimistic about the future of Taiwan. Figure 8-12 and Figure 8-13 show Taiwan's international competitiveness in global economy as evaluated by two international organizations: The World Economic Forum (WEF) and the International Institute for Management Development (IMD). WEF defines national competitiveness as the capability of maintaining a high economic growth rate of a nation for the coming five to ten years. As shown in the lower row of the X-axis of Figure 8-12, it consists of 179 variables (in 1998), which are classified into eight categories. They are then weighted to derive the national competitiveness index and ranking (Wen-po Chang, 1998). In 1999, WEF evaluated fifty-nine major trading countries. Taiwan ranked fourth, superseded only by Singapore, the United States, and Hong Kong. Figure 8-12 also shows that Japan ranked fourteen, Korea, twenty-two, and China, thirty-two, out of fifty-nine countries (WEF, 1999, 11). The four columns in each category show the ranking of each index from 1996 (the empty column) to 1999 (the darkest filled column). Taiwan's competitiveness ranking has

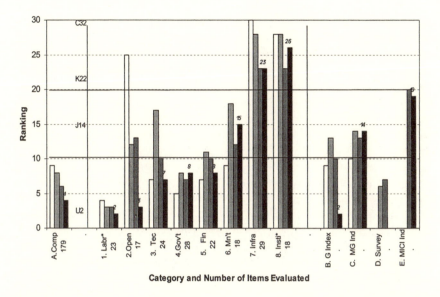

Figure 8-12. Taiwan's competitiveness in the global economy (WEF data, 1996–1999).

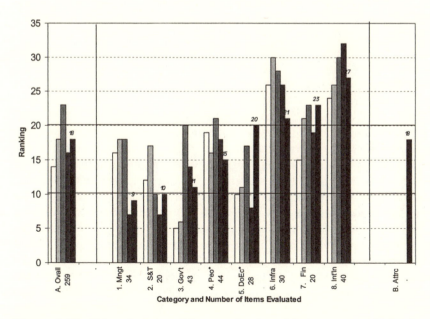

Figure 8-13. Taiwan's competitiveness in the global economy (IMD data, 1995–1999).

been improving consistently since 1996 (from ninth, to eighth, to sixth, and to fourth).

Taiwan's 1999 ranking in the eight categories are Labor, second, Openness, third, Technology, seventh, Government, eighth, Finance, eighth, Management, fifteenth, Infrastructure, twenty-third, and Institution, twenty-sixth (ibid.). In response to the financial crisis from 1997 to 1998, Taiwan's openness improved considerably. So also did its finance sector, to some extent. Among the Asian countries, Taiwan is well-prepared for the next phase of the new economy of information technology (EPA, 2000, 105). Its computer hardware production in 1998 ranked third in the world, next only to the United States and Japan (ibid.). As much as 80 percent of families in Taiwan own cable TVs, even exceeding that of the United States (ibid). Taiwan's labor performance is consistently the best among the fifty-nine countries, including work ethic (fourth), unemployment insurance (fifth), social welfare system (sixth), and so on (WEF, 1999, 205). This may be the reason that Taiwan can still attract massive inward direct foreign investment even though its wage rate is higher.

Taiwan's "institutions" have the worst performance. According to WEF's national competitiveness balance sheet (ibid., 205), the culprits are product liability (thirty-sixth), judiciary independence (thirty-sixth), organized crime (thirty-seventh), legal corruption (thirty-seventh), and litigation costs (forty-first). Although Taiwan's "infrastructure" has been improving during the past years, it still ranked twenty-third in 1999, mainly due to the lack of private investment in infrastructure (thirty-first), road indicator (forty-first), and cellular telephones (forty-second). Other liabilities include foreign access to capital markets (fifty-sixth), government influence (fifty-eighth), and insider trading (fifty-eighth).

In addition, the WEF also adds four more aggregate indexes (the last four categories in Figure 8-12). The "growth index (G)" predicts the average growth rates from year 2000 to 2008 based on the experience of the last eight years. Taiwan faired exceptionally well in this prediction: 4.29 percent, only second to Singapore, 5.02 percent, among the fifty-nine active countries in the world. In terms of the "market growth index (MG)," which is the predicted growth rate times the size of the economy to measure each country's contribution to world economic growth, Taiwan ranked fourteenth. Instead of the competitive survey of company CEOs, a new index, the "microeconomic competitive index (MECI)," which measures the microeconomic foundations of economic development, was substituted in 1998. For this, Taiwan ranked nineteenth in 1999. In general, the most important indexes are competitiveness and growth, in both of which Taiwan ranked near the very top.

Taiwan's rankings in the IMD annual reports are somewhat inferior but still respectable. Like WEF indexes, IMD's Overall Competitiveness index "ranks nations' environments and analyzes their ability to provide an environment in which enterprises can compete" (IMD, 1999, 14). It has 288 variables, which are also grouped into eight Competitiveness Input Factors, as shown in Figure 8-13. Six categories are similar to those of the WEF, and "Labor" and "Institutions" are substituted by "People" and "Domestic Economy," respectively. The IMD indexes seem to emphasize competitiveness of firms and so reflect more on short-term conditions of the economy. In the case of Taiwan, most of the indexes worsened during 1996 and 1997, and improved in 1999, which are shown by the darkest filled columns.

In 1999, the IMD evaluated forty-seven industrialized and emerging countries. The overall competitiveness index for Taiwan in 1999 was eighteenth, still better than most of the active countries, although lower than Singapore (first), the Netherlands (fifth), Hong Kong (seventh), Canada (tenth), Australia (twelfth), Japan (sixteenth), but much higher than all the other ASEAN countries and China (twenty-ninth) and Korea (thirty-eighth). Its ranking of the eight categories are Management, ninth, Science and Technology, tenth, Government, eleventh, People, fifteenth, Domestic Economy, twentieth, Infrastructure, twenty-first, Finance, twenty-third, and Internationalization, twenty-seventh. Compared with the WEF rankings, both evaluations agree on high rankings in Technology and Government, a similar ranking in Finance, but quite different in five other categories. IMD also has an extensive list of strength and weakness of items in each category (IMD, 1999, 313). In addition, it has added three new Location Attractiveness Rankings in 1999 to "show which countries are the most attractive for locating or relocating Manufacturing, R&D, and Services and Management activities" (ibid.). In this, Taiwan ranked eighteenth overall, which consists of Manufacturing, ninth, R&D, nineteenth, and Services and Management, nineteenth (ibid., 311). The high ranking on attractiveness of manufacturing activities again substantiates the recent increase of inward direct foreign investment that we saw in Figure 8-8.

Economics and Politics with China—Some Concluding Remarks

As we have stated in this chapter, geography and history determine the economy and politics, and politics and economics are closely interwoven. Examples are trade frictions, tariff negotiations, regulations on inward and outward foreign investments, or even the gunboat diplomacy of yesteryear.[95] For the future of the Taiwanese economy, however, the most urgent problem it faces today is, unfortunately, the basic problem of nation-building, which other countries already experienced a long time ago, and the ensuing military threat from China for "unification."

We have seen the tremendous growth of Taiwan's trade and outward investment in China in the 1990s. Taiwanese firms are the second largest foreign investors in China, next to Hong Kong, in the early 1990s,[96] and are probably the largest investors throughout the 1990s if Taiwanese indirect investment through Hong Kong is considered. The growth and magnitude up to now probably indicate complementarities of economic relations between the two countries. As the world competitiveness indexes have shown, although the future prospects of Taiwan in the global economy have been excellent and bright, they hinge greatly, if not crucially, on Taiwan's political relations with China. Any discussions of Taiwan in the global economy in the future cannot, and should not, avoid its problem with China. The basic problem is China's territorial claim on Taiwan and the threat of the use of military force. But China's territorial claim is tenuous at best, and both countries would benefit by a peaceful resolution of the dispute in a civilized manner.

As we have seen, while it is true that some Han people from China visited Taiwan and some might have settled there, and there were some sporadic but vague records of Taiwan in old Chinese and Japanese literature, no nation claimed Taiwan as its territory until the early seventeenth century. Despite its proximity, the Ming Dynasty was relieved and content when the Dutch claimed Taiwan, instead of Pescadores, as its territory in 1624. It was the Dutch and the Spanish who introduced Taiwan to world trade as far away as with Southeast Asia and Europe in the seventeenth century, a prelude to Taiwan's global position in the twentieth century after World War II. The Dutch were replaced by the Kingdom of Cheng, which continued global trade but imposed a trade ban on China. Taiwan then came under the Ch'ing regime after 1683, and became a formal Chinese province only in 1886. The history certainly belies the Chinese claim today that "Taiwan has been 'an inalienable part of China since ancient times dating back 1700 years.'"[97]

Ch'ing ruled Taiwan with indifference and inefficiency. It considered that "Taiwan is a trifling place—taking it would add nothing, relinquishing it would not be a loss."[98] It ruled Taiwan loosely, and its power had never extended to the vast mountainous region of Taiwan. The Japanese saw the strategic position of Taiwan. Thus, Taiwan was ceded to Japan in the 1895 Treaty of Simonoseki after the first Sino-Japanese War.[99] Note that Taiwan was certainly not "stolen from China," as was claimed in the 1943 "Cairo Declaration." During the Chinese resistance against the Japanese invasion of China in the 1930s and early 1940s, the Chinese Communist Party and the KMT Government in China were aware of the treaty, and fully supported the independence of "the Taiwanese nationality," along with the Koreans, before World War II (Hsiao and Sullivan, 1979). The 1928 and 1931 Political Theses of the Taiwanese Communist Party[100] also proclaimed the "national liberation movement" and Taiwan independence, which were supported by the USSR's Comintern (Communist International), the Japanese Communist Party, and the Chinese Community Party (Hsiao and Sullivan, 1983).

Only after 1943, however, the KMT, and subsequently the People's Republic of China in 1949, has asserted that Taiwan be "returned" to China in accordance with the "Cairo Declaration" (ibid., 1979). The fact is, the "Cairo Declaration" was merely a news release of the U.S. government that was not signed by any Allied leaders, and as such it does not provide the international legal base of the Chinese claim. The peace treaties between Japan and the Allies (1951), and even between Japan and the Republic of China (1952), which formally ended World War II, also did not specify the legal status of Taiwan. Because the People's Republic of China (PRC) has never governed Taiwan even for one moment, and because Taiwan has its own effective territory, government, army, and people, Taiwan has never been an integral part of the People's Republic of China, quite contrary to the Chinese claim.[101] In fact, as we have seen in this chapter, Taiwan has thrived when Taiwan was, and is, politically independent from China.[102]

Historical facts aside, it is anachronistic and unacceptable to claim territory by foolishly contending ancestral kinship and geographical proximity.[103] Cooperation or unification between Taiwan and China, if there is any, must be based on the consensus of the people of Taiwan through peaceful and civilized negotiations between the two countries, not by finger wagging or bullying and the threat of force. As we have shown in this chapter, although Taiwan may be small in terms of its landmass and population compared with those of China, it is large in many other respects, including its per capita and aggregate GNP, trading prowess, foreign exchange reserves, inward and outward foreign investments, and its national competitiveness, especially in the new-economy fields of information technology. The win–win situation for both Taiwan and China can be achieved only when China recognizes Taiwan as an independent country,[104] which is exemplary for China to achieve its own economic and political miracles in the new century. Whereas for China, as we have just seen, this recognition is not unprecedented, it will tremendously enhance the position of Taiwan and China in the global economy and politics.[105]

APPENDIX: EXPORT PROMOTION POLICY MAY NOT BE SUSTAINABLE

The general theme on the literature of Taiwanese economic development is that export-oriented policy works (for an example, see the latest papers in Thorbecke and Wan, 1999). This is not at all true, although the notion is so popular that many economists take it for granted. Here is a simple counterexample. Let the national income model be

$$Y = C + I + G + (X - M) \tag{1}$$

where, as usual, Y is national income, C is consumption, I is investment, G is government expenditure, X is exports, and M is imports. Let's assume the simplest economic behavior:

$$S = Y - C = sY, I = K', S = I, X' = gX, M = mY, N' = nN, \text{ and}$$
$$Y = AK^aN^{1-a}$$

where S is savings, K is capital, N is population, $X' = dX/dt$, etc., and s, g, m, and n are positive constants. Then, the model reduces to per capita magnitude as

$$k' = (s + m)Ak^a - gh\ e^{(g-n)t} - nk$$

where $k = K/N$, $h = X(0)/N(0)$.

This is Solow's fundamental equation of economic growth if $g = m = 0$. It shows that, when t is sufficiently large, per capita capital decreases if the growth rate of exports, g, is larger than the growth rate of population, n, $(g > n)$. This condition is satisfied in most of the developing countries, and certainly is the case for Taiwan, Korea, and Japan. Furthermore,

$$\partial k'/\partial g = -hg^2 e^{(g-n)t} < 0.$$

Thus, increase in the growth rate of exports (g) will decrease capital accumulation at any moment in time. Hence, in this model, export-oriented policy results in decumulation of per capita capital, quoad hoc, decrease in per capita GDP. It is by no means "common sense" that exports necessarily promote growth.

After all, if that is indeed the case, every country may just do so to achieve economic development. In fact, in the late 1970s, OECD (1979) designated ten Newly Industrializing Countries (NICs) as the fast export expanding countries. In less than two decades, only the four Asian NICs have remained. There is nothing "fortunate" or "wise" about government policy changes in Taiwan (and Korea) in achieving rapid growth. Their economies may decline also.

NOTES

*We are indebted to Professors Teruo Asamoto, Shinichi Ichimura, Hiroshi Ishida, Chung H. Lee, Ts'ui-jung Liu, Yuzin Chiautong Ng, Eric D. Ramstetter, Jaw-yann Twu (Muraoka), Henry Wan, Jr., and Wen-hsing Wu for generous sharing of their publications at various stages of writing this chapter. Our special thanks go to Mr. Pao-Jui Chen for rushing a copy of the new *TSDB 2000*, to Professor Hiroshi Setooka for sending valuable new data, and to Professor John P. Powelson for comments and making the paper more readable. We also appreciate the editor, Professor Peter C. Y. Chow, for his successful conference arrangement, patience, and encouragement. All errors of omission and commission are ours.

1. The distance is mainly taken from a Web site, "How far is it" http://indo.com/distance/. The original map was taken from Yano, 1990, 685. Also see Klintworth, 1995, 9. Ohsono (1998, 151) uses a similar diagram to show Hong Kong to be the center of East Asia.

2. Duan, 1989, 313. No sources of data are given. Note that this is a Chinese text, which generally say nothing good about Taiwan.

3. Underwood, 1999, 22. *Source:* Institute for Information Industries, Market Intelligence Center, Taiwan. "Taiwan IT companies produced more than US$19 billion in hardware products in 1998. Adding offshore production, the total reached US$32 billion, an increase of 8.4 percent over 1997" (ibid.).

4. There are several suggestions on classification (see Su, 1980, 16–17).

5. Chuong-da Wu, 1958, 5. Most politically oriented Chinese adopt this point of view. For details, see Su, 1980, 20–35.

6. A book by Wang Ta-yuan, *Brief Account of the Island Barbarians*, 1349. Wang mentioned Penghu, Liu-chiu, and P'i-shi-yeh, "which probably refers to Taiwan." See Vertente et al., 1991, 26. Many old chronicles could not distinguish among Ryukyu Islands, Taiwan, and Penghu (Pescadores) islands, which are a group of tiny islands located between Taiwan and the mainland (ibid., 39; also Su, 1980, 21).

7. Figure 8-2 is an extension and refinement of Figure 1 in Klintworth, 1995, 4. We use a solid line to denote the separation of the two countries, and a dotted line to show weak relations between Taiwan and China. Figure 8-2 reinforces the falseness of the Chinese claim that "Taiwan was part of 'the sacred territory of China since ancient times,'" as quoted in Klintworth, 1995, 5.

8. The Dutch gained independence from Spain and established The Republic of Holland in 1579. They "allied themselves with England . . . in an attempt to wrest hegemony over the European seas from Portugal and Spain . . . and sent warships to . . . the Asian seas, occupying and plundering colonies." "For this purpose, the Dutch monarch established the Dutch East India Company in 1602 . . . and . . . establish(ed) a permanent residence in Batavia (Su, 1986, 11).

9. It seems that the description about the events leading to the Dutch occupation of Taiwan is clearer in Su (1980, 58) than that in Vertente (1991, 58 or 74). Su wrote that after eight months of bloody battle with the Dutch, the Ming government agreed on two conditions for peace. If the Dutch would retreat from Pescadores, which China considered its territory, the Ming would not interfere with Dutch occupation of Taiwan, and that trade with China could be tacitly tolerated. In discussing why the Dutch came to southern Taiwan instead of the northern part, Ang (1999, 58) did not mention the agreement specifically.

10. Actually, an official peace treaty between Cheng and the Dutch was signed on February 1, 1662 (Vertente et al., 1991, 104).

11. According to Hsu (2000), during a period of 212 years from 1683 to 1895, there were 107 rebellions against the Ch'ing government and at least fifty-one armed conflicts among the local ethnic groups. The Taiwanese were not known to be submissive to the government authorities.

12. Article II of The Treaty of Peace between Japan and China in 1895 states, "China cedes to Japan in perpetuity and full sovereignty . . . the island of Formosa, together with all the islands appertaining or belonging to said island of Formosa" (Cohen and Teng, 1990, 103). However, the so-called "Cairo Declaration," November 22–26, 1943—attended by Roosevelt, Churchill, and Chiang—stated, "It is their purpose that . . . all the territories Japan has stolen from the Chinese, such as Manchuria, Formosa, and the Pescadores, shall be restored to the Republic of China." The word "stolen" is wartime language, which does not reflect the fact. Furthermore, it is worth noting that the Cairo Declaration is merely a news release or bulletin of the State Department of the United States and was *not* signed by any of the attending heads of state. Thus it does not have any legal standing. For the latest discussion, see Chiang (2000).

13. Vertente et al., 1991, 154–156. It was the first republic in Asia. For details, see the doctoral thesis by Ng (1970), and also the Ph.D. thesis by Hsiu-zheng Huang (1987).

14. Vertente et al., 1991, 155. James W. Davidson compiled the map in 1901.

15. In 1930, when Japan started exploiting mountain resources, the aborigines revolted against the Japanese (the Wushe Incident). The revolt was savagely suppressed, and new policy for the mountain regions and aborigines was put into effect (Vertente et al., 1991, 159). We submit that the incident was significant for Taiwan's national "unification." The fact belies the Chinese claim that "whole" Taiwan was part of China, because the local Chinese government never ruled the mountainous regions of Taiwan even during the Ch'ing period.

16. Jacoby, 1966, 71; Ho, 1978, 90, 100–101; Klintworth, 1995, Chapter 2; Hsiao and Hsiao, 1996, 219–221, 234–235, 240–242.

17. The years from 1949 to 1989 correspond to China's self-reliance period (1949–1978) and economic adjustment period (1979–1989). See Ishida, 2000, 274–276.

18. Twu, 1975; Hsiao and Hsiao, 1996, 264–267, 273–276, 282–285; M. Hsiao, 1992.

19. The following three sections on the Dutch, Cheng, and Ch'ing periods are taken partly from Hsiao and Hsiao, 1999a, 481–489.

20. Nakayama, 1959, 25; Su, 1980, 77–78. In a 1554 map by the Portuguese, Taiwan was called Ilha Formosa (Chang et al., 1996, 60).

21. 1 dan = 1 hectoliter

22. For a specific aspect of globalization of Taiwanese trade through an English company during this period, see Fu-san Huang (1999).

23. "The Chinese merchants by and large out competed Western traders because of their familiarity with local conditions, their ability to dispense with additional middlemen and their satisfactions with a relatively small profit margin" (Hao, 1986, 346). The relation and relative influence of local and foreign capital are still unclear, and more research is called for.

24. Commercial Revolution in the Middle Ages in Europe occurred in the period 950–1350 (Lopez, 1971), that in England, "from the English Restoration to American Independence," 1660–1776 (Davis, 1967, 3–4), and in China "along the coast from the 1820s to 1883" (Hao, 1986, 338).

25. Davis, 1967, 24. The importance of international trade continued even during the Industrial Revolution (see Hobsbawn, 1968, 38).

26. From the Marxists points of view, this process is important in the development of capitalism (see USSR Institute of Economics, 1955, vol. 1, 87–88; vol. 2, chapter 12, "Commerce, Credit, and Money Circulation."

27. Twu, 1975, 381. However, there are some conflicting observations on the Taiwanese economy before 1895. Yanaihara observed that until the very end of the Ch'ing period in Taiwan, "no single modern bank, modern corporation, modern factory existed. . . . All the establishments of capitalist enterprises in Taiwan came only after Japanese occupation" (1929, 55). More research is needed.

28. The Taiwanese Communist Party observed this point in 1928 on the development of Taiwanese capitalism. For details, see Hsiao and Sullivan (1983), 278.

29. This is also the argument presented in the 1928 Political Thesis of the short-lived Taiwanese Communist Party (1928–1931). For references, see Hsiao and Sullivan (1983). We adopted their line of arguments for different reasons. The thesis is influenced by the political and economic principles of the Japanese Communist Party in the 1920s along the line of the Marxist theory of capitalism, which emphasizes the internal (like domestic saving) rather than the external (like commercial) factors of capital accumulation. In Japan, it is known as the Ohtsuka Proposition (Ohtsuka Shigaku) (Kakuyama, 1980, 22–23), and was propagated in early postwar Taiwan by Han-Yu Chang, 1974.

30. Economic development under the Japanese regime may be divided into five periods (Hsiao and Hsiao, 1998; 1996, 215–221): The initial period (1895–1905); the intermediate period (1905–1931); the quasi-war stage (1931–1937), which covers the period from the Manchurian Incident to the beginning of the Sino-Japanese War; the first war stage (July 1937–1941), which covers the Sino-Japanese War and the beginning of World War II; and the second war stage (1942–1945), which covers World War II until the end of the war. The first two periods are based on the classification of Sumiya, Liu, and Tu (1992, Chapter 1), and are rather well documented. The last three periods are given in Kusui (1944) and correspond to the period of Japanese militarism.

31. Calculated from Table 1a in Hsiao and Hsiao, 1999a, 495. The existence of small and medium-size manufacturing enterprises in Taiwan is not at all a postwar phenomenon.

32. Mizoguchi and Yamamoto (1984) counted that Taiwanese millers consisted of 94 percent of total millers in 1929 and 93 percent in 1939. We submit that this is the origin of the postwar Taiwanese small-and-medium enterprises (Hsiao and Hsiao, 1999a). Note that, in colonial Korea, unlike Taiwan, the Japanese dominated the rice milling business in 1939 (ibid).

33. This section is taken partly from Frank S. T. Hsiao, 1997.

34. Chen, 1963, 137; Ping, 1947, 62–63; detailed soil analyses for the local area can be found in SS51, 517–520.

35. Japanese studies and research on Taiwan started long before their occupation (Wen-hsing Wu, 1995), followed by intensive "explorations" immediately after the occupation (Wen-hsing Wu, 1997).

36. The sources of data are not given. We think it is taken from TEY41, 120–124.

37. From Ping, 1947, 76, which is taken from the 1944 Taiwan agricultural yearbook. Note that the value of total agricultural products includes 9.7 percent of hog and 2.4 percent of chicken production.

38. Note that this is different from the comparison of per farm family disposable income (Ping, 1947). Hayami and Ruttan (1970) argues that in Japan, there was a rapid growth in agricultural output and productivity from 1886 to 1920, followed by a much slower growth in the 1920s and 1930s, due to the rice imports from Taiwan and Korea, and decline in technological progress.

39. Korea produced 3.6 million tons in 1937 (YS43, 103). According to YS43 (101), Taiwan's rice production in 1937 was 1.8 million tons, and world production was 93.8 million tons. Hence, Taiwan's share was 1.9 percent of the world production.

40. In 1940, Taiwan comprised an area of about 0.02 percent of the world area, and 0.27 percent (5.7 million) of the world population (Frank S. T. Hsiao, 1997, 498). In other data, on average from 1937 to 1940, the percentage of Taiwan's rice production ranges up to 1.9 percent of the world rice production (93 million tons), ranked ninth in the world (see YS43, 101).

41. No data are available for two other major producers, India and Ecuador (see Y91, 206). Thus Taiwan might be either fourth or fifth during 1934 to 1938.

42. It has been said that industrialization in colonial Taiwan was not so much financed by the large capitalists from Japan proper, but much more by local saving in Taiwan (TEY41, 81; Ho, 1978, 84).

43. Kusui, 1944, 157; also see Sumiya et al., 1992, 21. In real terms, they came very close to each other (NT$435 million vs. NT$412 million) in that year. The proportion for the three industries—agriculture, manufacturing, and services— in real terms were 33 percent, 31 percent, and 36 percent, respectively, in 1939 (Wu, 1995, 635).

44. See Frank S. T. Hsiao, 1997, 503–504.

45. In addition, over 300,000 Taiwanese youth went overseas as volunteer workers or soldiers, or "industrial soldiers" (Ji-wen Lin, 1996, 225). The "lofty mission or calling" also manifested itself in Taiwan's marching songs, like the songs of the Taiwanese Army (Taiwangun no Uta), The Honor of Taiwanese Volunteer Corps (Homare no Taiwan Shiganhei), Marching to the South (Nanshin no Uta), Marching of the Emperor's People (Komin Koshin Kyoku), and the like (Nampokensha, 1943?, 124–133. In the title of the book, the cherry flower is Japan's national flower). Part of the last song has been translated in English in Lai, Myers, and Wei, 1991, 30–31.

46. Kusui, 1944, 287, and various literature published at that time. The Taiwanese (and the Japanese) activities in Southeast Asia are coming out only recently (see Schneider, 2000). As much as we oppose any Chinese military threat on Taiwan, we do not condone any aggression of war. However, the historical facts about Taiwanese activities in the past should not be buried and unrecognized. Just like the Japanese, the Taiwanese have learned that military aggression does not pay. Both learned in the postwar period that without resorting to force, both countries and all people in South China and South Seas can achieve "co-prosperity" by trading, a lesson for China today.

47. This section is mainly based on Hsiao and Hsiao, 1996, 262–268.

48. Taiwan's postwar economic development may be divided in six stages (Hsiao and Hsiao, 1996): The Chaotic Period (August 1945–1949); the Transition Period (1950–1953); Recovery and Import Substitution Period (1953–1963); Take-off and Export Promotion Period (1964–1973); Second Import Substitution Period (1974–1980); Accelerated Growth and High-Tech Industrialization Period (1980–   ).

49. Tian-Cheng Chou, 1992, 99. Private electric companies and factory-owned private electric plants once thrived during the Japanese colonial period (see Ping-yan Lin, 1997).

50. Using these points, the Chinese economists tend to "miniaturize" the economic and social development in Taiwan during the Japanese period (see Tsong-han Chang, 1980, 112, 255; Hsian-wen Chou, 1958).

51. Economists often ignore these points. Other customs and habits include the ban of foot binding for women, pigtail hair dressing for men, cleanness, and maintenance of private and public hygiene (Wen-hsing Wu, 1999). The last change includes "ventilation and lighting of a house, building of a lavatory inside the house, . . . the habits of bathing, washing hands after relieving, a waste basket and waste disposal arrangement for every house, spittoons and garbage cans in public places, . . . set a certain date for house cleanings and village cleanings, etc." (see ibid., 6; also, Tsurumi, 1977, 154–155). These cannot be taken for granted and need vigorous enforcement. In considering modernization, Ishida (2000, 268) reports from his fieldwork in 1993 at Liaoning University, a major university in China, that "even at the Liaoning University, people spit on staircases and hallways, garbage are all over the place, the toilets are not hygienic, the smell floats in the air up to hallways and classrooms. The student dining room has few tables and chairs. Students eat rice and side dishes from one small enameled eating ware like a face-washing bowl, standing. I wonder whether this is really the place for research and education at the highest academic institute." The first author of this chapter had a similar experience in Beijing in the mid-1980s.

52. The Confucian ethic of despising labor must be eradicated. As early as 1907, in "the revised Common School Regulations . . . agriculture, commerce, and manual arts became compulsory in schools which offered them. The teaching of these subjects was designed to fight the deep-rooted repugnance literate Taiwanese felt toward manual labor" (Tsurumi, 1977, 50). In a confidential memo, the Japanese wrote that "the [upper class] Taiwanese . . . despised manual labor and had nothing but contempt for honest and useful occupations which required physical skill or exertion" (ibid., 51). Thus the teacher's responsibility was to "make the next generation of native leaders less prejudiced against agricultural, commercial, and manual occupations" (ibid.). Undoubtedly, this attitude toward labor and work ethics has contributed tremendously to the growth of rural industry in Taiwan (Hsiao and Hsiao, 1999a, 512–513).

53. As we noted earlier (Hsiao and Hsiao, 1996, 240, note 32), ex-President T. H. Lee, then a member of Joint Committee of Rural Reconstruction (JCRR), a U.S. Aid organization, once remarked in 1959–1960 to a group of his graduate students at National Taiwan University that the Taiwanese farmers read Japanese magazines, even before the JCRR experts, to diversify and improve their farming methods. (About Japanese language in rural Taiwan, see Tsurumi, 1977, 154.) This is in contrast with the report that, at the beginning of the Green Revolution (introduction of Ponlai rice) in Taiwan during the early 1920s, the Japanese used police force to enforce the use of new seeds of rice among Taiwanese farmers.

54. Tsurumi (1977, 156) gives an interesting episode: Around 1969, "a remark made . . . by a mainlander resident of Taiwan in his fifties: 'Those stupid Taiwanese. All they learned under the Japanese was to line up in queues.'"

55. More elaborate and same argument can be found in Cho and Kim, 1991, 6–7.

56. Figure 8-5 and Figure 8-6 are in real terms calculated from the nominal values in *TSDB*, 1989, 210–212; 2000, 210–214, divided by the wholesale price index (WPI) in *TSDB*, 2000, 179. The base year of the WPI published in 2000 *TSDB* is 1996. Thus, to compare with our previous calculation (Hsiao and Hsiao, 1996, 263–265, Figures 8, 9, 10), we have converted the base year to 1986. The conver-

sion to real values is important because when the dollars are exchanged in NT Dollars, we want the values of NT Dollars to have the same purchasing power over the years. Because Taiwan's WPI has been generally stable (see the line in Figure 8-5), especially in the 1990s, the general shape and trend of all figures in real values have similar shape and trend as those in nominal values.

57. Ishida, 1999, 161. His data is based on *Monthly Economic Statistics of Two Sides of the Strait*, no. 71, July 1998, 19–20. However, his data on exports to and imports from Hong Kong do not match those in *TSDB*. Morrison and Cooper (1999, 120) even estimate up to 88 percent.

58. The calculation is based on WDR, 1997, 242, and *TSDB*, 2000, 210.

59. See note 58.

60. However, Taiwan is not unique, and nothing to be alarmed about, in one-sided trade relations with other countries. Even in 1998, 31 percent of Japanese exports and 24 percent of Japanese imports were to and from the United States, while the corresponding figures for Taiwan were only 27 percent and 19 percent, and for Korea were 17 percent and 22 percent, respectively (see Economic Planning Agency [EPA], 2000, 314, 320).

61. Calculation of Figure 8-7 is the same as for Figure 8-5 and Figure 8-6. Balance of trade (BOT) is commodity exports X (in heavy solid line) minus commodity imports M (in lighter solid line) in Figure 8-7.

62. The following episode is illuminating. In February 1982, to reduce $3.2 billion trade deficits with Japan, Taiwan surprised the world by unilaterally banning imports from Japan of more than 1,500 commodities for an indefinite time, and heavy trucks and diesel engines for one year. Tokyo threatened to cancel Taiwan's preferential tariff and trade status. The ban inflicted serious damage to Taiwanese exports and its national economy. As Tokyo also could not wage a trade war simultaneously with the United States and the EEC, both sides reached a compromise and the ban on half of the goods was lifted by November that year. For details, see Arnold (1985); Aoki (1985).

63. See reports by Shi and Li (1978); Liu and Jian (1983). In addition to the desire to be independent of Japan, anti-Japanese feeling of the Chinese officials also played in these attempts.

64. Because Taiwan has perpetual trade deficits with Japan, the Taiwan government discourages importing consumer goods from Japan.

65. For the effects of the February 28 incidents, see Frank S. T. Hsiao, 1992; Lai et al., 1991; Hsiao and Hsiao, 1996, 223–224.

66. In addition to marketing, Sogo Shosha also helps in financing, foreign exchanges, organizing, and consulting (Steven, 1990, 70). There seems to be no study of their actual operations in Taiwan.

67. According to a survey, barriers to exporting are culture, language difference, special customs requirements, market information (particular markets, availability, usefulness, awareness), product design and specification requirements, government policy, and the like (Brooks and Frances, 1991, 102).

68. A forty-six-year-old Taiwanese president of a sewing machine company stated that "about forty years ago, Singer set up an affiliate in Taichung. This firm encouraged and helped the local people to build factories to produce sewing-machine parts. In 1972, I started to run this business. . . . Techniques from Japan and a bunch of brave young people are what made Taichung the sewing-machine capital of Taiwan. Although our technology . . . originated in Japan, we're now totally independent of it, thanks to our own R&D" (interview by Hwang, Chung, and Chang, 1998, 30).

69. This subsection is partly based on Hsiao and Hsiao, 1996, 269–272.

70. China's unequal treaties ended only in 1943, and Chiang Kai-shek published *China's Destiny* "to show the harm they had done to China" (Fairbank, 1967, 62).

71. We reasoned that this was because the émigré regime of the Republic of China on Taiwan had no roots in Taiwan and wanted to break its isolationism internationally and domestically.

72. All data are divided by Taiwan's WPI with 1986's wholesale price being taken as 100 (*TSDB*, 2000, 179, 258, 260).

73. Investment Commission (2000), April. We suspect that these so-called DFI may be Chinese (mainland) capital registered in Central America, and pose a grave security problem for Taiwan.

74. In terms of nominal values, the maximum amount was reached two years earlier, in 1997, at $4.27 billion (*TSDB*, 2000, 258).

75. In real value of 1986 prices, the total amount of DFI comes to $40 billion.

76. We have examined the effect of DFI on technology transfer, DFI and Taiwan's television industry in Hsiao and Hsiao, 1996, 273–276, and M. Hsiao, 1992.

77. In a previous paper (M. Hsiao, 1992, 151), it is shown that, using the 1967–1987 data set, when the real growth rate of DFI increases by 1 percent, it may generate a 0.11 percent increase in the growth rate of Taiwan's GDP.

78. For the acceleration of economic and political liberalization after the lifting of martial law in 1987, see Hsiao and Hsiao (2001).

79. However, according to Se and Asamoto (1999, 175), if outward investment is measured from balance of payment statistics instead of the approval base, outward investment already exceeded inward foreign investment every year since 1988. For the relation between inward and outward investment using Investment-Development Path analysis for Taiwan, see Van Hoesel (1996) and Se and Asamoto (1999).

80. The total outward investment for 1952 to 1999 was $21,879 million (*TSDB*, 2000, 262), and that for 1965 to 1999 was $21,872 million, a difference of about $7 million, which accounts for the outward investment from 1952 to 1964.

81. In real value, it is $22.4 billion. The difference is almost negligible.

82. According to the "Principal Statistics of Approved Direct Mainland Investment via Third Countries," the total investment in China from 1991 to 1999 is $14.5 billion, 22,134 cases (*TSDB*, 2000, 264). The difference in the number of cases seems to indicate that, for political and security reasons, most of Taiwan's private large investment goes through the third countries in British Territories or Hong Kong (Ishida, 1999, 169).

83. Ishida, 1999, 139–140; Morrison and Cooper, 1999. Yu (1996) divides the trade and investment relationship between Taiwan and China in four periods: the frozen period (1949–1978), the defrosting period (1979-1987), the warming-up period (1988–1995), and the period after 1996. The Chinese data in Morrison and Cooper are based on those "supplied by the Chinese Embassy, Washington, D.C.," and the Taiwanese data are from the "Taiwan Ministry of Economic Affairs." We have tried to identify the data from published sources.

84. There are some discrepancies in trade data, and we are unable to make more useful analysis.

85. Morrison and Cooper, 1999, 123; Ishida, 1999, 157. Ishida is based on *Monthly Economic Statistics of the Two Sides of Strait*, no. 71, July 1998. Morrison and Cooper's data, 1990–1995, are the same as Ishida.

86. Morrison and Cooper (1999, 125) listed up to 1995. We extended the data to 1997 by *TSDB*, 2000, 264. Both data are also the same as Ishida's (1999, 158), which is taken from *Monthly Economic Statistics of Two Sides of Strait*, ibid.

87. Indeed, history repeats for Taiwan. The problem with Taiwan today is that it has no institutes like the Research Institute of People and Culture of the South (Nanpo Jinbun Kenkyujo), which belonged directly to the Governor-General of Taiwan to study Southeast Asia during the Japanese period.

88. Morrison and Cooper, 1999, 124; Ishida, 1999, 158. Both data sets are consistent.

89. The Taiwanese data tend to understate because firms may be reluctant to register to avoid government control, and the Chinese data tend to overstate because some foreign firms may register under a Taiwanese name to take advantage of the preferential treatment afforded to the Taiwanese firms in China (Morrison and Cooper, 1999, 120).

90. Wu presents the real GDP per capita in New Taiwan dollars from 1920 to 1971, as measured in 1937 prices (Wu, T., 1991). It increased from NT $142 in 1920 to NT $213 in 1931, and reached the prewar maximum of NT $225 in 1939. It then started decreasing and plummeted to a mere NT $45 in 1945. The recovery was very slow. Wu's data also show that until the mid-1950s, it dipped even below the 1920 level. It recovered to a mere 56 percent of the 1939 prewar level (NT $225) in 1952, still way below the 1920 level.

91. Using the Perron tests of time-series analysis, we have shown that the plunge of GDP per capita in 1944 was indeed temporary (Hsiao and Hsiao, 1999b).

92. This is corroborated by actual observations at that time. In a report to the U.S. Congress, Conlon Associates (1959, 139) wrote that "Taiwan did not enter the post war era without advantages. Progress under Japan had been extensive. Prior to World War II, the Taiwanese had a standard of living second only to that of Japan itself in Asia. The people had acquired many industrial and agrarian skills. The years immediately after 1945, however, were years of chaos."

93. For the early postwar economic conditions of Taiwan, see Hsiao and Hsiao, 1998.

94. We have discussed this in Hsiao and Hsiao, 1998, 1999b.

95. In fact, we have pointed out that the true "miracle" is that Taiwan achieved rapid economic growth without government protection in foreign economic relations (Hsiao and Hsiao, 1996, 288). Ichimura (1995) discusses economics and politics of Japan extensively. His discussions and suggestions for Japan also apply to Taiwan.

96. EPA, 2000, 142. In 1998 and 1999, Taiwanese investment in China was exceeded by Hong Kong and the United States, and almost the same, or slightly less than, Japanese investment in China.

97. As repeated in Klintworth, 1995, 264.

98. These are the words of the Ch'ing Emperor K'ang Hsi (1662–1722), as quoted in Vertente et al. (1991, 130).

99. After the Treaty of Simonoseki, through the interference of Russia, France, and Germany, China retained Liaodong Peninsula in southern Manchuria. Understandably, the Chinese side preferred to cede Taiwan to Japan, rather than to raise the question on Taiwan to reverse the Japanese decision to return Liaodong Peninsula to China. Faced with the alternate, the Chinese negotiators were so eager to cede Taiwan to Japan that they even advised the Japanese how to eradicate the Taiwanese rebels who rose against the secession (Ng, 1970, 25–26; Hsiu-zheng Huang, 1987, 73). In addition to the three countries, England, Spain, and the United States were also interested in Taiwan but never interfered with Japan's acquisition of Taiwan (Ng, 1970, 36–39; Hsiu-zheng Huang, 1987, 83–87).

100. In keeping with the "One Country, One Party" principle, Comintern recognition, as well as the Chinese and the Japanese Communist Parties' acceptance, of the "Taiwanese Communist Party" "as an independent communist party in 1931 also provided tacit backing for Taiwan's eventual political autonomy from China" (Hsiao and Sullivan, 1983, 286),

101. Klintworth (1995, 14) observed that "Taiwan has been under the effective administrative control of a government in Beijing for no more than one of two decades in the last several centuries. Taiwan was China's for a few years in the 1660s and from 1887 to 1891. For most of the rest of its time in modern history, Taiwan was controlled by the Dutch, the Japanese, or the Americans, or largely neglected by the mainland Chinese." By the Chinese logic, because China was once a part of the Mongol Empire for ninety years (1279–1368), China should be an "inalienable integral part" of the Mongolian People's Republic.

102. Klintworth, 1995, 8. Taiwan has been "lucky" by not falling into the fate of China's Hainan Island in the past 100 years (ibid., 55; Frank S. T. Hsiao, 1987; 1997, 507, note 36). "Agricultural Taiwan, Industrial China" was the future plan for Taiwan by the Nanking Nationalist (KMT) Government in 1946 (Frank S. T. Hsiao, 1997, 507; also see Kirby, 1995).

103. Even China's "leading scholar" on Taiwan, Li Jiaquan (the former Director of Institute of Taiwan Studies, Chinese Academy of Social Sciences) holds such a view, unable to give one good reason for unification. See the quotation in Klintworth (1995, 265). If "Socialist Theory of Market" is China's "philosophy of poverty," the dogma of territorial claim is the telltale of China's "poverty of philosophy." Its poverty was just recently demonstrated again fully in Wei (2000), in a vivid contrast to Chiang (2000), the lead article in the same issue of the journal. It is not coincidental that China has to resort to force.

104. This may be a dream, but so were the collapse of the "Great East Asia Co-Prosperity Sphere," German Nazis, the Soviet Union, and democratization of Taiwan during our lifetime. If the Taiwanese are persistent, the dream will come true. The first sign of thawing and the test of civility should come by China's blessing of Taiwan's membership in the United Nations. When the day comes, its impact on world economy and politics will far exceed the unification of the two Germanys or the two Koreas.

105. Just consider the fact that, in 1998, the foreign exchange reserves for Japan was $212 billion, China, $141.1 billion, Hong Kong, $88.4 billion, and Taiwan, $84.4 billion, ranking first to fourth in Asia (Taiwan Briefs, 1999, 14). Twu (1997, 168) observes that "Taiwanese money" is the reason China wants "unification" with Taiwan under the cover of fanatic Chinese nationalism, and warned that it might rekindle the fear of "yellow peril" in the region.

REFERENCES

Statistical Data Sources

Fifty-one Year Statistical Summary of Taiwan Province (SS51) (Taiwan Sheng-51 Nianlai Tongji Tiyao). Statistics Department of Taiwan Province Governor-General, December 1946.

Investment Commission (2000). *Monthly Statistics on Overseas Chinese and Foreign Investment, Outward Investment, Outward Technical Cooperation, Indirect Mainland Investment, Guide of Mainland Industry Technology*, April. Taipei, Taiwan: Ministry of Economic Affairs.

Taiwan Economic Yearbook (TEY4x) (Taiwan Keizai Nempo), vol. *x*, 194*x* (x denotes the year of publication). Taipei: Taiwan Keizai Kankokai.

Taiwan Statistical Data Book (TSDB), 1975, 1985, 1993, 2000. Council for Economic Planning and Development, Republic of China.

Yano, I. 1991. *100 Years of Japan, Viewed by Numbers* (Y91) (Suji de miru Nihon no Hyakunen). Tokyo: Kokuseisha.

Yano, K., and K. Shirazaki, *Illustration of Japanese National Achievements* (YS*xx*) (Nihon Kokusei Chosa), yearly since 1927 (xx denotes the year of publication).

Articles

Ang, Ka-im. 1999. "Commerce, Trade, and Aborigines in the Northern Taiwan in Early Era" (in Chinese). In *Taiwanese Commercial Traditions, Collected Papers (Taiwan Shangyeh Chuangtong Lunwenji)*, eds. Fu-san Huang and Ka-im Ang. Taipei: The Preparatory Office of the Institute of Taiwanese History, Academia Sinica.

Aoki, T. 1985. *The Pacific Era and Japan.* Tokyo: Yuhi Kaku (in Japanese).

Arnold, W. 1985. "Japan and Taiwan: Community of Economic Interest Held Together by Paradiplomacy," chapter 11 in Ozaki, R. S., and W. Arnold, *Japan's Foreign Relations.* Boulder, CO: Westview Press.

Azuma, K. 1941. "Taiwanese Economy before the Economic Control" (in Japanese). In Chapter 3 of *Showa 16 Nenhan Taiwan Keizai Nempo* (1941 Taiwan Economic Yearbook).

Brooks, M. R., and A. Frances. 1991. "Barriers to Exporting: An Exploratory Study of Latin American Companies." In *Export Development and Promotion: The Role of Public Organizations*, eds. F. H. R. Seringhaus and P. J. Rosson. Norwell, MA: Kluwer.

Chan, S., and C. Clark. 1992 *Flexibility, Foresight, and Fortune in Taiwan's Development: Navigating between Scylla and Carybdis.* London: Routledge.

Chang, Han-yu. 1957. "Technical Development of Taiwan's Rice Agriculture during the Japanese Period" (in Chinese). *Quarterly Journal of the Bank of Taiwan, 9*(2), September. Also in: *Collected Works of Dr. Chang Han-yu* (Vol. 1, 363–393). Taipei: San-min Bookstore, 1974.

——. 1974. *Economic Development and Economic Thoughts, Essays of Dr. Han-yu Chang* (in Chinese), vol. 2. Taipei: Committee of Publishing Essays of Dr. Han-yu Chang.

Chang, Sheng-yen, Wen-hsing Wu, Zheng-hua Wen, and Bao-tsung Dai. 1996. *The Development of Taiwan* (in Chinese). Taipei: National Kong-Chung University.

Chang, Tsong-han. 1980. *Prewar Taiwan's Industrialization* (in Chinese). Taipei: Lian-jin.

Chang, Wen-po. 1998. "The Meanings and Implications of National Competitiveness." *Industry of Free China*, vol. 88, no. 12 (December).

Chen, Cheng-hsiang. 1963. *An Economic and Social Geography.* Taipei: Fu-min Geographical Institute of Economic Development.

——. 1959–1960. *A Geography of Taiwan* (Taiwan dizhi), Two volumes. Taipei: Fu-min Geographical Institute of Economic Development.

Chiang, Y. Frank. 2000. "State, Sovereignty, and Taiwan." *Fordham International Law Journal*, vol. 23, no. 4 (April): 959–1004.

Cho, Lee-Jay, and Yoon Hyung Kim. 1991. "Political and Economic Antecedents to the 1960s." In *Economic Development in the Republic of Korea*, eds. Lee-Jay Cho and Yoon Hyung Kim. Honolulu: University of Hawaii Press.

Chou, Hsian-wen. 1957. "Exploitation Economy in Taiwan during the Dutch Period" (in Chinese). *Volumes on Taiwan Studies*, no. 40. Taipei: Bank of Taiwan.

———. 1958. *Taiwanese Economic History in the Japanese Occupation Period* (in Chinese). *Taiwan Studies*, no. 59. Taipei: Bank of Taiwan.

Chou Hsue-pu, Yong-he Tsao, and Yong-hsiang Lai. 1959. "Historical Documents on Trade between Taiwan and England" (in Chinese). *Volumes on Taiwan Studies*, no. 57. Taipei: Bank of Taiwan.

Chou, Tian-Cheng. 1992. "Small-and-Medium Enterprises on the Fringe of the Power" (in Chinese). In *Dissecting Taiwanese Economy: Monopoly and Exploitation under an Authoritarian Regime*, eds. Hsin-huang Hsiao et al. Taipei: Taiwan Research Fund.

Coe, D. T., E. Helpman, and A. W. Hoffmaister. 1995. "North-South R&D Spillovers." NBER Working Paper Series, No. 5048, March.

Cohen, Mark J., and Emma Teng. 1990. *Let Taiwan Be Taiwan, Documents on the International Status of Taiwan*. Washington: Center for Taiwan International Relations.

Conlon Associates. 1959. *United States Foreign Policy: Asia*, Studies No. 5, Prepared at the request of the Committee on Foreign Relations, United States Senate. Washington: U.S. Government Printing Office.

Davis, Ralph. 1967. *A Commercial Revolution, English Overseas Trade in the Seventeenth and Eighteenth Centuries*. London: The Historical Association.

Duan, Zheng-pu, ed. 1989. *Postwar Taiwanese Economy*. Beijing: China Social Science Publishers.

Economic Planning Agency (EPA), ed. 2000. *Asian Economy 2000* (Ajia Keizai 2000). Tokyo: Ministry of Finance Press.

Fairbank, John K. 1967. *China, The People's Middle Kingdom and the U.S.A.* Cambridge, MA: Harvard University Press.

Hao, Yen-p'ing. 1986. *The Commercial Revolution in Nineteenth-Century China, The Rise of Sino-Western Mercantile Capitalism*, Berkeley: University of California Press.

Hayami, Y., and V. W. Ruttan. 1970. "Korean Rice, Taiwanese Rice, and Japanese Agricultural Stagnation: An Economic Consequence of Colonialism." *Quarterly Journal of Economics*, 84 (November): 562–589.

Ho, Samuel P. S. 1978. *Economic Development of Taiwan, 1860–1970*. New Haven, CT: Yale University Press.

Hobsbawn, E. J. 1968. *Industry and Empire, An Economic History of Britain since 1750*. London: Weidenfeld and Nicolson.

Hsiao, Frank S. T. 1997. "Colonialism or Comparative Advantage?—On Agricultural Development in Colonial Taiwan." *Proceedings of the National Science Council, Part C: Humanities and Social Sciences*, vol. 7, no. 4 (October): 497–513.

———. 1992. "The Economic and Cultural Backgrounds of Taiwanese 2-28 Civil Strife—An Application of Social Expectation Theory" (in Chinese). In *Proceedings of 1991 Conference on Research on 2-28 Civil Strife*, ed. Yong-hsing Chen. Taipei, Taiwan: The U.S.-Taiwan Cultural Exchange Foundation, 2-28 Citizen's Study Group, and Modern Research Foundation, 77–113.

———. 1987. "The Effects of Direct Foreign Investment—The Taiwanese Experience and Its Implication to China" (in Chinese). In *Proceedings of the Second International Conference on the Future of Taiwan*, Xiamen, China, August 1985, edited by Huan-qui Quo and Fu-san Zhao, cosponsored by the Institute of Taiwan Studies, Chinese Academy of Social Sciences, Simon Fraser University, and Institute of Taiwan Studies, Xiamen University. Beijing: China Friendship (Yuo-yi), 69–118.

Hsiao, Frank S. T., and Mei-chu W. Hsiao. 2001. "Economic Liberalization and Development—The Case of Lifting Martial Law in Taiwan." Forthcoming in *Change of an Authoritarian Regime: Taiwan in the Post-Martial Law Era.* Taipei: Taiwan Studies Promotion Committee, Academia Sinica, January. University of Colorado, Department of Economics, Discussion Paper 99-29.

———. 2000. "International Comparison of Taiwanese Economic Growth—A Long-Run Perspective." Working Paper, Department of Economics, University of Colorado.

———. 1999a. "The Historical Traditions of Taiwanese Small-and-Medium Enterprises." In *Taiwanese Commercial Traditions, Collected Papers* (Taiwan Shangyeh Chuangtong Luwenji), eds. Fu-san Hugan and Ka-im Ang. Taipei: The Preparatory Office of the Institute of Taiwanese History, Academia Sinica, 465–524.

———. 1999b. "Catching Up but Falling Behind in the Long Run—On Capitalistic Development of Taiwan and Korea." Working Paper No. 110, Economic Research Center, School of Economics, Nagoya University, Japan.

———. 1998. "Colonial Linkages in Early Postwar Taiwanese Economic Development." In *Harvard Studies on Taiwan: Papers of the Taiwan Studies Workshop, volume 2,* eds. William C. Kirby and Michael S. Weiss. Harvard University, John King Fairbank Center for East Asian Research.

———. 1996. "Taiwanese Economic Development and Foreign Trade." In *Comparative Asian Economies,* ed. J. T. Kuark in *Contemporary Studies in Economic and Financial Analysis* (vol. 77, part B). Greenwich, CT: JAI Press, 211–302. Originally published in Fairbank Center Discussion Paper No. 9, 1994, Harvard University, and also in *Harvard Studies on Taiwan: Papers of the Taiwan Studies Workshop, Volume I,* eds. William Kirby and Megan Greene. John King Fairbank Center for East Asian Research, Harvard University, 1995.

———. 1995. "Globalization of the Taiwanese Economy and U.S.-Taiwan Trade Relations." In *Advances in Pacific Basin Business, Economics, and Finance,* vol. 1, ed. C. F. Lee. Greenwich, CT: JAI Press, 197–214.

Hsiao, Frank S. T., and Lawrence R. Sullivan. 1979. "The Chinese Communist Party and the Status of Taiwan, 1928–1943." *Pacific Affairs,* vol. 53, no. 3: 446–467.

———. 1983. "A Political History of the Taiwanese Communist Party, 1928–1931." *Journal of Asian Studies,* vol. 52, no. 2 (February): 269–289.

Hsiao, Hsin-huang, Yun-pong Chu, Jia-dong Hsu, Zhong-ji Wu, Tian-Cheng Chou, Ji-li Yan, Yun-han Chu, and Zhong-chen Lin. 1992. *Dissecting Taiwanese Economy: Monopoly and Exploitation under an Authoritaran Regime.* Taipei: Taiwan Research Fund.

Hsiao, Mei-chu W. 1992. "Direct Foreign Investment, Technology Transfer, and Industrial Development—The Case of Electronic Industry in Taiwan." In *Research in Asian Economic Studies,* ed. M. Dutta in *Asian Economic Regime: An Adaptive Innovation Paradigm* (vol 4, part A) Greenwich, CT: JAI Press, 145–64.

Hsu, Wen-hsiung. 2000. *Social Organization and Disorder in Taiwan.* Taipei: Lien Ching. (Summarized by Ching-shih Chen in forum@natpa.org, July 19, 2000.)

Huang, Fu-san. 1999. "The Change of Jardine, Matheson & Co. Trading Practice toward Taiwan When Taiwan Opened Ports." *Taiwanese Commercial Traditions, Collected Papers (Taiwan Shangyeh Chuangtong Lunwenji),* eds. Fu-san Hugan and Ka-im Ang. Taipei: The Preparatory Office of the Institute of Taiwanese History, Academia Sinica, 83–105.

Huang, Fu-san, and Ka-im Ang. 1999. *Taiwanese Commercial Traditions, Collected Papers* (Taiwan Shangyeh Chuangtong Lunwenji). Taipei: The Preparatory Office of the Institute of Taiwanese History, Academia Sinica.

Huang, Fu-san, and Tsu-yu Chen. 1995. "Business Development" (in Chinese). In *Modern History of Taiwan, Volume on Economy.* Taipei: Taiwansheng Wen Hsian Wei Yuan Hui.

Huang, Hsiu-zheng. 1987. *Secession of Taiwan and 1895 Resistance against Japanese.* Ph.D. thesis, Institute of History, National Taiwan Normal University, Taipei.

Hwang, Jim, Oscar Chung, and Violet Chang. 1998. "Voices from the Heartland." *Free China Review*, vol. 48, no. 1 (January).

Ichimura, Shinichi. 1995. *Economic Development of Japan and Her External Economic Relations.* Translated in Chinese by Wen So, et al. Beijing: Beijing University Press.

International Institute for Management Development (IMD). 1999. *The World Competitiveness Yearbook.* Lausanne, Switzerland.

Ishida, Hiroshi. 2000. *The Strategies for Social and Economic Development in Rural China* (Chiukoku Noson no Kaihatsu Senryaku—Nohmin wa "Yutaka" ni Nattanoka). Economic and Political Studies #117. Osaka, Japan: Kansai University, Institute of Economic and Political Studies.

———. 1999. *The Structure of Taiwan Economy and Its Dynamics* (Taiwan Keizai no Kozo to Tenkai). Tokyo: Ohtsuki Shoten.

Ishikawa, Shigeru. 1967. *Economic Development in Asian Perspective.* Economic Research Series, No. 8, Hitotsubashi University, The Institute of Economic Research. Tokyo: Kinokuniya.

Jacoby, Neil H. 1966. *U.S. Aid to Taiwan, A Study of Foreign Aid, Self-help, and Development.* New York: Frederick A. Praeger.

Kai, Chang Kuo, and D. B. Chu. 1951. "Compilation of Taiwan's Production Index and Survey of Taiwan's Production Trends" (in Chinese). *Finance and Economics Monthly*, vol. 1, no. 9 (August): 58–62.

Kakuyama, Sakae, ed. 1980. *Studies on Western Economic History* (Koza: Seiyo Keizaishi), volume 1. Tokyo: Dobunkan.

Kawano, Shigeto. 1968. *Taiwan's Rice Economy*, 1941, translated into Chinese by Ying-yen Lin. *Taiwan Studies*, no. 102. Taipei: The Bank of Taiwan.

Kirby, William C. 1995. "Planning Postwar Taiwan Industrial Policy and the Nationalist Takeover, 1943–1947." In *Harvard Studies on Taiwan: Papers of the Taiwan Studies Workshop*, vol. 1, eds. William C. Kirby and J. Megan Greene. Cambridge, MA: Harvard University, Fairbank Center for East Asian Research.

Klintworth, Gary. 1995. *New Taiwan, New China, Taiwan's Changing Role in the Asia-Pacific Region.* New York: St. Martin's Press.

Kusui, Ryuzo. 1944. *A Study of the War-time Taiwanese Economy* (Taiwan Senji Keizairon). Taihoku: Nampo Jimbun Kenkyujo.

———. 1941. "Problems in Taiwan's Industrialization" (Taiwan Kogyka no Shomondai), Chapter 3 in TEY41.

Lai, Tse-han, Ramon H. Myers, and Wou Wei. 1991. *A Tragic Beginning: The Taiwan Uprising of February 28, 1947.* Stanford, CA: Stanford University Press.

Lin, Chi-yuan. 1968. "Industrial Development and Changes in the Structure of Foreign Trade, The Experience of the Republic of China in Taiwan, 1946–66." *IMF Staff Papers*, 25 (July): 290–321

Lin, Ji-wen. 1996. *Studies of War Mobilization System during the Last Stage of Japanese Ocupation Period (1930–1945)* (in Chinese). Taipei: Tao-Hsiang.

Lin, Ping-yan. 1997. *The Beginning of Taiwanese Experience: The History of Taiwan Electric Power Inc.* (in Chinese). Taipei: The Resource Center of Taiwan Electric Power Inc.

Liu, Bang-li. 1996. "The Structure of Post-war Taiwanese External Trade Network" (in Chinese). *Quarterly Journal of the Bank of Taiwan*, vol. 47, no. 1: 125–150.

Liu, Tai-ying, and Jin-chaung Jian. 1983. *The Economic Effects of Japanese Business Investment in Taiwan* (in Chinese). Report to the Committee on Research, Development, and Assessment, the Executive Yuan, submitted by the Taiwan Economic Research Institute.

Liu, Ts'ui-jung. 1998. "Han Migration and the Settlement of Taiwan—The Onset of Environmental Change." In *Sediments of Time, Environment and Society in Chinese History*, eds. Mark Elvin and Liu Ts'ui-jung. Cambridge, U.K.: Cambridge Univeristy Press. (Reprint of the Chinese version, Taipei: Institute of Economics, Academia Sinica, 1995.)

Lopez, Robert S. 1971. *The Commercial Revolution of the Middle Ages, 950–1350.* Upper Saddle River, N.J.: Prentice-Hall.

Maddison, Angus. 1995. *Monitoring the World Economy 1820–1992.* Paris: Development Centre, OECD.

Ministry of Economic Affairs (MOEA). 1991. *White Paper on Small and Medium-Size Enterprises.* Taiwan: Small and Medium Enterprises Bureau, Ministry of Economic Affairs.

Mizoguchi, Toshiyuki, and Y. Yamamoto. 1984. "Capital Formation in Taiwan and Korea." In *The Japanese Colonial Empire, 1895–1945*, eds. R. H. Myers and M. R. Peattie. Princeton, NJ: Princeton University Press.

Morrison, Wayne M., and William Cooper. 1999. "China-U.S.-Taiwan Economic Relations." In *Asian Economic and Political Issues*, vol. 2, ed. Frank Columbus. New York: Nova Science.

Nakayama, T. 1959. "Taiwan's Buckskin Production and Its Exports to Japan in the 17th Century" (translated into Chinese). *Volumes on Taiwan Studies*, no. 71. Taipei: Bank of Taiwan.

Nampokensha. 1943(?). *Military Songs for Young Cherry Flowers* (Wakasakura Gunkashu). Taipei: Nampokensha.

Ng, Yuzin Chiautong (Ko Sho-do). 1970. *A Study of the Republic of Formosa, 1895, A Chapter in the History of Taiwan Independence Movement.* Tokyo: The University of Tokyo Press.

Nikkei, *Nikkei Sangyo Sinbun* (Japan Economic and Industry Daily), various issues.

Oh, Iku-toku. 1970. *Taiwan, Its History in Agony* (Taiwan, Kumon suru sono Rekishi). Tokyo: Kobunsha.

Ohsono, Tomokazu. 1998. *Maps for Seeing Asia, New Edition* (Shin, Ajia o Miru Chizu). Tokyo: Kodansha.

Organization for Economic Cooperation and Development (OECD). 1979. *The Impact of the Newly Industrializing Countries, on Production and Trade in Manufactures.* Report by the Secretary-General. Paris: OECD.

Ping, R. 1947. "Characteristics of Taiwanese Agriculture" (in Chinese). *Journal of the Bank of Taiwan*, vol. 1, no. 1 (June): 55–86.

Schneider, Adam. 2000. "The Taiwan Development Company and Indochina: Subimperialism, Development, and Colonial Status." In *Taiwan Historical Research*, vol 5, no. 2. Taipei: Academia Sinica, 101–33.

Se, Akio, and Teruo Asamoto, ed. 1999. *Studies on Taiwanese Economy* (Taiwan Keizairon). Tokyo: Keiso Shobo.

Shi, Ji, and Zheng-zhong Li. 1978. *A Study of the Methods of Improving Trade Deficits and Imports between Taiwan and Japan* (in Chinese). Research Report submitted to the Ministry of Economic Affairs, Taipei.

Shinohara, Miyohei, and Shigeru Ishikawa. 1972. *Taiwanese Economic Growth* (Taiwan no Keizai Seicho). Tokyo: Aziya Keizai Kenkyujo.

Skoggard, I. A. 1996. *The Indigenous Dynamic in Taiwan's Postwar Development, The Religious and Historical Roots of Entrepreneurship.* Armonk, NY: M.E. Sharp.

Steven, R. 1990. *Japan's New Imperialism.* Armonk, NY: M.E. Sharp.

Su, Bing. 1980. *400-Year History of the Taiwanese People* (Taiwanren Subai-nien-shi). San Jose, CA: Paradise Culture Associates.

———. 1986. *Taiwan's 400-Year History, The Origins and Continuing Development of the Taiwanese Society and People.* Washington, DC: The Taiwanese Cultural Grass Roots Association.

Sumiya, Mikio, Shin-kei Liu, and Chau-yen Tu. 1992. *The Taiwanese Economy* (in Japanese). Tokyo: Tokyo University Press.

Taiwan Briefs. 1999. In *TOPICS, The Magazine of International Business in Taiwan,* vol. 28, no. 10 (December 1998/January 1999). Taipei: The American Chamber of Commerce in Taiwan.

Takahashi, Kamekichi. 1937. *A Study of the Modern Taiwanese Economy* (Gendai Taiwan Keizairon). Tokyo: Chikura Shobo.

Tang, W. T. 1947. "Taiwan's Agriculture and Its Research" (in Chinese). *Quarterly Journal of the Bank of Taiwan,* vol. 1, no. 3 (December): 1–19.

Thorbecke, Erik, and Henry Wan, Jr. 1999. *Taiwan's Development Experience: Lessons on Roles of Government and Market.* Boston: Kluwer.

Tsurumi, P.E. 1977. *Japanese Colonial Education in Taiwan, 1895–1945,* Cambridge, MA: Harvard University Press.

Twu, Jaw-yann. 1975. *Taiwan under Japanese Imperialism* (Teikoku Shugika no Taiwan). Tokyo: Tokyo University Press.

———. 1997. *Hong Kong, Taiwan, and Greater China, Arrival of the New Century of Three China?* Tokyo: Jiji Tsushin Sha.

Underwood, Laurie. 1999. "The Park That Chips Built." *TOPICS, The Magazine of International Business in Taiwan,* vol. 29, no. 3 (April). Taipei: The American Chamber of Commerce in Taiwan.

USSR Institute of Economics, Academy of Sciences. 1955. *Textbook on Economics,* translated into Japanese by the Association of Marxism-Leninism Dissemination, vols. 1 and 2.

Van Hoesel, Roger. 1996. "Taiwan: Foreign Direct Investment and the Transformation of the Economy." In *Foreign Investment and Governments: Catalysts for Economic Restructuring,* eds. J. H. Dunning and R. Narula. New York: Routledge.

Vertente, Christine, Hsueh-chi Hsu, and Mi-cha Wu. 1991. *The Authentic Story of Taiwan, An Illustrated History, Based on Ancient Maps, Manuscripts and Prints.* Knokke, Belgium: Mappamundi: Taipei: S.M.C.

Wei, Su. 2000. "Some Reflections on the One-China Principle." *Fordham International Law Journal,* vol. 23, no.4 (April): 1169–1178.

World Bank. 1997; 2000. *World Development Report (WDR).* New York: Oxford University Press.

World Economic Forum (WEF). 1999. *The Global Competitiveness Report.* Cambridge, MA: Harvard Institute of International Development.

Wu, Chuang-da. 1958. *Development of Taiwan* (Taiwan de Kaihua), in Chinese. Beijing: Ke-Hsueh.

Wu, Tsong-min. 1995. "Long-Run Fluctuations in Aggregate Outputs of Taiwan and Changes in Economic Structure" (in Chinese). In *Modern Taiwanese History*, ed. Kuo-ji Li. Taipei: Taiwan Sheng Wenshian Weiyuanhui, 609–36.

Wu, Wen-hsing. 1995. "Japan's Investigations and Studies on Taiwan before the Occupation" (in Chinese). In *The Proceedings of the First Academic Conference on Taiwanese Local Culture*. Taipei: Center of Education and Humanity Studies, National Taiwan Normal University.

———. 1997. "Tokyo Empire University and the Evolution of 'Academic Explorations' of Taiwan" (in Chinese). In *100 Years of Taiwanese Historical Studies—Reviews and Studies,* Taipei: Institute of Taiwanese History Preparation Office, Academia Sinica.

———. 1999. "Transformation of Taiwanese Society under Japanese Colonialism and Its Historical Implications" (in Chinese). In *The Proceedings of the Fourth Conference of East Asian History Education*. Tokyo: Society for the Camparative Study of History and History Education.

Yajima, Kinji. 1986. *The Complete Scope on the Taiwanese Economy* (Taiwan Keizai no Subete), 2nd edition. Tokyo: Nihon Keizai Tsushinsha.

Yanaihara, Tadao. 1929. *Taiwan under Imperialism* (in Japanese). Tokyo: Iwanami Shoten.

Yano, Tooru. 1990. *A Cyclopedia of Asia/Pacific, New Regionalism and the Role of Japan* (Jiten, Azia Taiheiyo—Atarashii Chiekizoh to Nihon no Yakuwari). Tokyo: Chuo Keizai Sha.

———. 1975. *Genealogy of "Southward Movement"* (Nanshin no "Keifu"), Chuko Shinsho, 412. Tokyo: Chuoh Koronsha.

Yu, Tzong-shian. 1996. "Relations between Two Sides of the Strait and the Taiwanese Economy." *Industry of Free China*, vol. 86, no. 6 (December).

9

Colonization and NIEs'lization of Taiwan's Economy Blending with Japan's Globalization: A Global Perspective

Teruzo Muraoka (Jaw-Yann Twu)

INTRODUCTION

In this chapter, we raise three questions for discussion. First, it is about the Taiwan economic problem brought on by colonization under the control of Japanese imperialism. We mainly discuss the features of Taiwan's economic structure as a colony of Japanese imperialists in the prewar period of about fifty years. It is important to assess the formation of colonial economic structure as well as its effect on the success of industrialization as NIEs (newly industrialized economies). Second, it is about the impact of Japanese economic rejuvenation and globalization on the Taiwan economy as well as the issue of growth transferring in the postwar period. We analyze the relationship of Taiwan economic NIEs'lization with Japanese economic rejuvenation, rapid economic growth, and external investment as well as yen appreciation. Third, it is about the interrelationship of colonization, NIEs'lization, and modernization in Taiwan economy. This issue is certainly related to the first two questions.

JAPANESE IMPERIALISM AND THE COLONIZATION OF TAIWAN

"The Last Empire" and "The Initial Colony"

In this chapter, Japan is regarded as "the last empire" and Taiwan is "the initial colony."

Japan's military and economic modernization began with the Meiji Reformation in 1868. After less than thirty years, it sought external expansion and perpetrated aggression against other countries. With the Sino-Japanese War of 1894–1895 launched by Japanese imperialists to enter and invade the Chinese market, Taiwan was first occupied and became the first colony of Japan. In the view of world history, Japan was the last empire compared with the other European and American imperialist countries because Japanese imperialism embarked upon the political venture and joined big powers for contention in the world market relatively late.[1] Because no other countries became the imperialists after Japan, we can certainly regard Japan as the last imperialist in the rank of big powers. We analyze the impact of this historical feature on the ruling and management of the Taiwan colony later.

As far as Taiwan as "the initial colony" is concerned, we may review the process of Japanese imperialism in its external expansion and aggression. Taiwan was for the first time to be a colony of Japanese imperialism. After Taiwan was occupied and became the colony of Japan, Japanese imperialists launched the Russo-Japanese War (1904–1905) and occupied the Korean peninsula. With the implement of Japanese colonial policy, the Korean peninsula became the number two colony of Japan. Then twenty-six years later the September 18th Incident occurred, which was the seizure of Shenyang in 1931 by Japanese invaders as a step toward their occupation of the entire northeast of China. Thereafter, three provinces in northeast China (Hilongjiang, Jilin, and Liaoning province) became the number three colony of Japan, which was called Manchuria.

Further reviewing history, we find the important meaning of the economic linkage between "the last empire—Japan" and "the initial colony—Taiwan." First let us look at the different styles and the changes for Japanese imperialists ruling and managing the colonies. In the colonial period of Taiwan, the Japanese followed Western European imperialism and adopted a direct rule and control policy over Taiwan. A governor-general administration, the direct ruling system, was established in Taiwan in May 1895 by Japanese imperialists. With such a system Taiwan had been entirely and directly controlled by Japanese imperialists. However, the ruling and control system was different in the number two colony, the Korean peninsula. In the Korean peninsula, Japanese imperialists adopted the policy of annexation as a result of the Russo-Japanese War. With such annexation, the Korean peninsula was in substance put under the protection of Japanese imperialists and lost its own regime within five years. Furthermore, the Korean army was disbanded. Finally, the governor-general administration of Korea was established in October 1910. As for the creation of Manchuria, founded in March 1932, it further revealed the dirty tricks directed by Japanese imperialists. It set up a puppet regime as an intermediate base and access to the big Chinese market.

Then why did Japanese imperialists adopt three different ruling and managing systems in these three colonies? Because few people have discussed this issue, I would like to explore the reasons briefly as follows.[2]

In the late nineteenth century, the big powers, mainly the European and American imperialists, scrambling for the world market and ruling the colonies, had centered on setting up the direct ruling system. However, upon entering the twentieth century, such direct ruling systems had no longer kept up with the trend of the times and this stage came to an end for the big powers scrambling for the world market. Under such circumstances, Japanese imperialists had to adopt the method of annexation for occupying the Korean peninsula. So-called annexation was just based on a nominal equal. Both Korea and Japan signed a formal agreement for annexation as one country treaty (The Treaty of Japanese Annexation of Korea, August 1910). However, in substance, the Korean peninsula (the Lee Dynasty) was put under the protection of Japanese imperialists and became a colony.

Since the early 1930s, the evolution of the times could not allow the Japanese imperialists to adopt the tactics of annexation for occupying the three provinces in northeast China. After World War I (1918), nationalism was rising. The American president, Thomas Woodrow Wilson (1913–1921), advocated a national self-determination for solving the colonial problems. The League of Nations was established. Thereafter, the ideological trend of national self-determination became the mainstream. In such a situation, Japanese imperialists had to adopt a new ruling system, namely to set up a puppet regime. So-called Manchuria was such a puppet regime. It was just a nominal independent country. In substance, it was under the jurisdiction of the Japanese central government. As the number three colony of Japanese imperialism, Manchuria had no independent and no self-determinant power in dealing with its domestic and diplomatic affairs.

Studying these three forms of a ruling system, we can find a common characteristic: All these three colonies were under the complete control of Japanese imperialists. With such power, Japanese imperialists can be mainly distinguished from the European and American imperialists. This point is worth exploring in studying the colonial history of Japanese imperialists.

The Direct Ruling System and Surplus Accounting in the Taiwan Colonial Economy

For ruling and managing the Taiwan colony, Japanese imperialism was based on the principle of "direct ruling and the surplus accounting." Having learned from European and American imperialists, Japanese imperialists imposed direct ruling in Taiwan political and economic affairs, but did not bear any financial burden. It required the Taiwan governor-general administration to realize a "local procurement," set up "a special account system for the Taiwan governor-general," and reach the "balance of local annual revenue and expenditure" without "financial subsidies" from the Japanese central government.[3] With such policy commitment, the Taiwan colonial economy started to increase exports to Japan since 1908, which exceeded the amount of import from Japan. Although there was a temporary trade deficit due to a 1911–1912 storm hitting Taiwan agriculture and industry, the trade surplus further increased since 1913 and reached its peak by 1923–1924. As a colony of Japan, Taiwan could not receive any income from Japan, such as foreign exchange for its trade surplus. Such trade surplus only represented the tribute goods (sugar in the mid-1920s and rice in the second half of the 1930s) presented to the Japanese imperialists. Compared to the contribution of the Korean peninsula, Taiwan provided a huge physical contribution to Japan.[4]

The situation on the Korean peninsula was quite different. The trade balance of the Korean peninsula to Japan was not too bad before 1927 and there was some trade surplus, particularly in 1924. However, since 1932 the trade surplus became the trade deficit, and the situation was getting worse and worse. In 1939 the trade deficit even reached 3 million yen. With an increasing trade deficit, the entire economy of the Korean peninsula could not be kept in a state of equilibrium. Therefore, how to make up the trade deficit became a serious problem.[5]

With the huge trade surplus of Taiwan to Japan, the serious shortage in the resources of the Korean peninsula was made up. Therefore, it was Taiwan's trade surplus to Japan that helped the Japanese imperialists to complete the colonization of the Korean peninsula, which further became a base for Japanese imperialists to expand and occupy the three provinces in northeast China.

We can therefore get a clue for understanding the economic significance of the Taiwan colonial economy to Japan as follows. First,

Japanese imperialists occupied Taiwan as its first colony and forced Taiwan to contribute a huge trade surplus to Japan. Then Japanese imperialists used that surplus as the financial input to support the colonization of the Korean peninsula and Manchuria. Furthermore, Japanese imperialists were able to expand to northeast China and establish the Manchuria puppet regime. Finally, it constructed a heavy chemical industrial base in Manchuria in order to further scramble for the entire Chinese market and realize a subcolonization in China. Therefore, we can say that the economic significance of the Taiwan colonial economy lies in providing its trade surplus to Japan for supporting the colonization of the Korean peninsula and Manchuria.

After reviewing these series results in colonial history, we need to discuss how the colonization of Taiwan progressed.

Monoculture Pattern and Multistructure Colonization in the Taiwan Economy

The Taiwan colonial economy was mainly based on the "monoculture pattern and multistructure." In other words, such a pattern can be regarded as the basic condition for Taiwan managing its colonial economy and increasing its trade surplus to Japan. Monoculture means to set up a mono-production system and provide the mono-exported-commodity for meeting the needs of the Japanese imperialists. Initially, Taiwan mainly produced sugar-related products. The production series was from the culture of sugarcane to the sugar refinery, which was for exporting sugar to Japan. Starting from 1905 this process lasted about 17 or 18 years until 1922. In 1920 only sugar occupied 65.8 percent of total exports to Japan that accounted for 83.7 percent of total exports from Taiwan. Then from about 1922 to 1938, Taiwan started to produce Japonica rice (improved by the Japanese) for exporting to Japan. In that period, more than half of the cultivated land was used to plant Japonica rice (see Figure 9-1). Finally, since 1939 Japanese imperialists regarded Taiwan as the "base for southern-expansion" and moved its military industry, oil processing, shipbuilding, and machinery into Taiwan for taking advantage of Taiwan's human and natural resources. It was considerably noticeable that three military-related industries such as the metal-working industry, machine industry, and chemistry industry increased their production suddenly in and after 1939 (see Figure 9-2).

Referred to as the "base for southern-expansion," which was set out of military action by the Japanese government on July 22, 1940, colonial Taiwan was also the base of the so-called "Great East Asian Co-Prosperity Sphere" being announced on August 1, 1940. Taiwan possessed infrastructure facilities, especially on power resources (150,000 to 200,000 kw), built to work in the 1920s for the demands of industrial

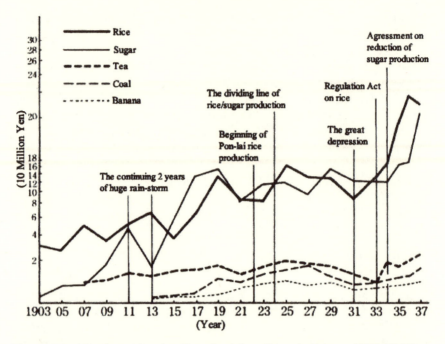

Figure 9-1. Development of major colonial products in Taiwan (1903–1937).
Source: The Editorial Board, Bank of Taiwan, "Forty Years History of Bank of Taiwan" 1939, Taipei, pp. 182–183, in Japanese, quoted from Twu's book "Taiwan under Japanese Imperialism" (in Japanese), University of Tokyo Press, 1975, p. 89.

production. This was a very exceptional case of power infrastructure investment in a colonial region in the world. Why the Japanese imperialists made overhead investments in the colonial region is not only a very interesting issue but also a vital problem for understanding the characteristics of Japanese capitalism as well as Taiwan's modernization in the postwar.

We are confirmed that the monoculture pattern became a multistructure, and the Taiwan colonial economy changed from planting to military industry in the latter part of the 1930s. This was an inevitable outcome with the combination of the last empire—Japan—and the initial colony—Taiwan. Such consequences were not too complicated compared to the case of the Korean peninsula.

The colonial process of the Korean peninsula economy was based on a simultaneous process of rice production in the southern island and military supplies from the northern island's underground resources. Therefore, the economic structure in these two regions was obviously different. The south was an agricultural base for producing Korean rice,

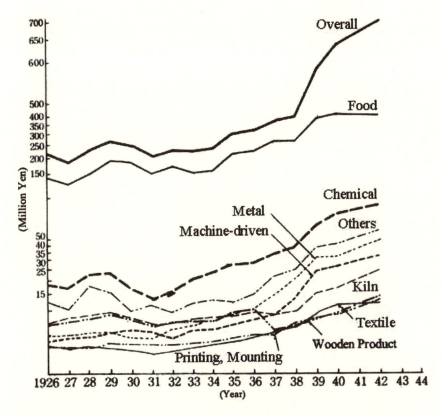

Figure 9-2. The transition of industry output by category (1923–1942).
Source: Bureau of Business Management, The Taiwan government-general, "Commerce and Industry Statistics" and Bureau of Administration, The Ministry of Finance, "Taiwan Industry" (vol. 2, no. 4, Taiwan section) in "Historical Investigation into Japanese Activities Abroad," 1946(?), pp. 213–214, in Japanese, quoted from Twu's book "Taiwan under Japanese Imperialism" (in Japanese), University of Tokyo Press, 1975, p. 148.

and the north was a base for providing military supplies. Then why did such different patterns not occur in Taiwan? To answer this question, we have to consider the need for Taiwan to create the "surplus," and we have to consider the different geographic location. That is to say that Japanese imperialists had to force Taiwan to create a surplus (in trade to Japan) so as to make up for the trade deficit of the Korean peninsula to Japan. Therefore, the Taiwan economy was not allowed to separate its regional structure and produce a "deficit" as the Korean peninsula economy was. This point is very important for understanding the economic process of the Taiwan colony and is worth exploring further.

The "monoculture pattern and multistructure" had certainly brought about a further influence on Taiwan's postwar NIEs'lization. We may see this point more clearly from the following analysis.

The Base for Japanese Southern Expansion and the Consequences of the Surrender of Japan to the United States

As we all know, the final destiny of the last empire—Japan—and the initial colony—Taiwan—was that Taiwan became the base for Japanese southern expansion. We also know that Japan was defeated and surrendered to the United States. What is the significance of this historical process on the formation of Taiwan's postwar economic framework?

First, we should point out that the purpose of the Japanese imperialists changing Taiwan into a base for southern expansion was to attack and occupy China and the Southeast Asian market. With a two-way war operational strategy committed to by Japanese imperialists, Taiwan was mainly used as a relay base.

Second, after the Japanese imperialists joined the big powers in contention for the world market, they launched the Sino-Japanese war in 1894–1895 and the Russo-Japanese war in 1904–1905 along the route of the Sea of Japan. Taiwan, as the initial colony of Japan, is also located along the corridor of the Sea of Japan. We can therefore see that the Japanese imperialists were in an overlord position along the Sea of Japan before being defeated by the United States. Japan's surrender to the United States represented a failure in contention with the United States for the Southeast Asia market along the Sea of Japan.[6] We should emphasize that Japan was defeated by the United States, not by China or European big powers—an important historical inspiration in promoting Japan's rejuvenation and new development and Taiwan's economic NIEs'lization in the postwar period.

Let us discuss the important meaning of the defeat of Japan for Taiwan. In July 1945, the Postam Declaration did not stipulate the return to Taiwan to China. With U.S. manipulation, Japan was not able to deal with its initial colony Taiwan. However, the United Kingdom and the United States did not require Japan to take responsibility for the offense to Taiwan. Consequently, Taiwan was arranged by the United States to be a strategic base against the Chinese communists and put on a lever for international political contention. This situation was closely correlated with the change of international orders, such as the East-West Cold War and Pax Russo-Americana.

In short, Japan was a defeated nation, and surrender to the United States brought about a chance for Japan to approach the Chinese market again under subordination to the United States in the postwar period. Japan's subordination to the United States and being under the American umbrella resulted from its surrender to the United States, not to China. This point is also the key for exploring and understanding the postwar economic relationship of Japan and Taiwan. It was a result of Japan's defeat and surrender to the United States that Taiwan stepped onto a new stage of economic development under the American and Japanese umbrella.

To sum up Taiwan's colonial inheritance, Japanese imperialism managed Taiwan for fifty-one years. Determing which policies are positive and which are negative for Taiwan's modernization in the postwar period is not so easy. Substantially speaking, the colonial policies adopted by the great powers including Japan in the prewar mostly stand up against the storm of academic criticism in the developing countries. Apart from such generalization, we are able to recapitulate how the colonial legacies affect Taiwan's modernization.

First of all, the "monoculture pattern and multistructure" had certainly brought about the rising productivity of the agriculture sector by dint of exporting commodities with sugar and then rice on the one hand, and building up the labor group by the sugar industry and then by the munitions factory on the other. Food production offered a broad base of capital formation, plundering from farmers in the 1950s,[7] and creating a labor group provided a basic condition of industrial development, such as the spinning industry as well as the plastics industry in their initial stages.

Second, the pressure a mass of Japanese big firms and medium and small enterprises being launched into colonial Taiwan put on Taiwanese indigeous business cycles resulted in a decline of Taiwanese inherent economic strength and influence in urban areas as well as rural district.[8] This was hard to ignore in the sense of land reform as well as state-owned enterprise clusters springing up in the postwar. In fact, the native landlords were basically without political power to resist land reform that was carried out by the new imported Kuomintang (KMT) regime in 1949–1952 on one side while entire Japanese enterprises moved to the stated-owned enterprises free of charge on the other side. The great power of the KMT regime penetrated into every corner in rural society, as well as in an initial dual industry structure of big state-owned enterprises together with small private businesses built in the Taiwan economy all over in the early postwar period.

Third, the strong centralizaion of administrative power of the Japanese colonial systems—including a police state, family register, neighborhood association (group unit), bureaucratic government, legal system of law ruling—those colonial legacies were almost left to the KMT-imported regime alone as an inheritance in the postwar. On this point, we are sure that the "dictatorship development" of the Chang family (1945–1987) was built in the Japanese colonial legacy of the ruling system. As a result, with the aid of anti-communist strategy anchored by the United States, the necessary preconditions for NIEs'lization were assembled.

NIEs'LIZATION WITH COLONIAL INHERITANCE

The Cold War System in the Postwar Period and Taiwan's Economic Independence

To discuss the NIEs'lization of Taiwan, we need first to know the basic conditions for Taiwan to reach its economic independence after the war. There are two basic conditions for forming an independent national economy: having a self-determinant power for tariff, and ability to issue national currency. The former depends on the country's trade and commerce policy, and the latter depends on its foreign exchange policy and monetary policy. Taiwan has not only the sovereignty of administering its tariff but also the sovereignty of issuing its own currency and setting up the foreign exchange rate. Therefore, from the point of view of economics, Taiwan has an independent and self-determinant national economy.

It actually happened by chance that Taiwan came to possess these two conditions. First, due to the civil war between the KMT and the CPC (Communist Party of China) in the late 1940s, the KMT government was not even able to fend for itself and therefore had no time to take care of Taiwan's economy and finances. In that stage, Taiwan had not even had many economic and trade contacts with mainland China, and it took care of itself by a self-reliant economy. Second, due to a later confrontation between the United States and the USSR and the Korean war (in June 1950), the Chinese communists were not able to dispatch troops to attack Taiwan.

Therefore, the internal war of the KMT and the CPC and the East-West Cold War forced Taiwan to step into its economic independence. Fortunately, Taiwan had rice and sugar for export so as to earn foreign exchange and support its economy. Before the materials of U.S. support arrived in Taiwan in 1952, it was the export of rice and sugar that saved Taiwan from an economic collapse.

In this regard, Taiwan was much luckier than Korea. Similar to Taiwan, Korea was also put on the frontier of the East-West Cold War and divided into a separated south and north by the three-year Korean war. In that time Korea did not have enough commodities to export to earn foreign exchange.

Before accepting U.S. support in 1952, Taiwan exported rice and sugar to Japan to earn foreign exchange. Since the economic and trade relationship between Japan and Taiwan was stopped in the 1940s, rice and sugar were still the primary products of monoculture. As analyzed previously, the monoculture system, an inheritance of colonization, impacted the sound development of the Taiwan economy. However, such colonial products became the export-demanded goods for rescuing Taiwan.[9]

On the other hand, the foreign exchange for Japan to pay for the imported rice and sugar made in Taiwan also came from the U.S. support for Japanese rejuvenation (based on the agreements of GARIOA, Government and Relief in Occupied Areas, and EROA, Economic Rehabilitation in Occupied Areas; both total about $2 billion of U.S. support funding provided to Japan from 1945 to 1952). Therefore, Taiwan's foreign exchange income also came from U.S. support indirectly.

In short, Taiwan's economic independence was actually supported by the United States. Let us look at more cases of such U.S. support. On just the third day of the Korean War (June 27, 1950), the United States dispatched its Seventh Fleet to the Taiwan Sea and claimed the Taiwan Sea area as a neutral zone to avoid Chinese communist attacks on Taiwan. Then during the Korean War itself (February 1951), the United States and Taiwan signed a "Mutual Security Treaty between the U.S. and the Republic of China." After another agreement signed in December 1954 ("Mutual Defense Treaty between the U.S. and the Republic of China"), Taiwan joined the United States to implement the policy of "containing China." Therefore, with the U.S.'s policy against communist China, the Taiwan national economy was able to be supported and got the chance for rejuvenation.

The Base for Anti-Communism and the Colonial Inheritance

In fact, Japanese postwar rejuvenation and the formation of the Taiwan national economy had to be kept consistent with U.S. strategic benefit in the world. In that time, U.S. strategic benefit in the world was focused against communism. In Asia, it was focused against and on containing Chinese communism. Because Chinese communist infiltration into the Asian neighboring countries and its incitement to revolution threatened U.S. ruling power and benefit in Asia, the United States surged a movement against communism—McCarthyism—from 1950 to 1954. In Taiwan, the economic structure inherited from the colonial economic system and the KMT political dictatorship was consistent with the U.S. strategy against communism and China.[10]

Relying on its relationship with the United States and Japan, Taiwan was able to form and develop its national economy. With its position against Chinese communism, Taiwan was able to enjoy U.S. support (including military support). With the openness of the U.S. domestic market, Taiwan was able to export its products to the United States and therefore step into NIEs'lization. At the same time, the demand of export to the United States brought about another demand for production equipment, which needed to be imported from Japan. Japan providing capital and technology to Taiwan was actually an inheritance from Taiwan colonial time. With the increase of export to the United States and import from Japan, Taiwan gained a huge trade surplus to the United States but had a trade deficit to Japan. Therefore, there was a triangle structure between the United States, Japan, and Taiwan. As a periphery of the United States and Japan, Taiwan relied on both of them to realize its NIEs'lization. We can therefore say that Taiwan's NIEs'lization was a product of anti-communism and inheriting the colonial system.

Triangle Framework and NIEs'lization

Here we should point out that the formation of the triangle framework was not based on any principle of equal and mutual benefit. As already mentioned, Taiwan's economic development had to be kept consistent with U.S. anti-communism and based on colonial inheritance from Japan. Another important condition for the formation of the triangle framework is that the United States was in a core status, Taiwan (or the four small dragons of Asia—Taiwan, Korea, Hong Kong, and Singapore) was on the periphery position, and Japan was the intermediate. Without Japan as the medium axis, small axis Taiwan would not be able to resist any external impact, particularly from the large axis—the United States (see Figure 9-3).

Generally speaking, developing countries were easily trapped by the following syndrome of openness in their process of introducing foreign capital and implementing export-oriented policy: (1) Depreciation of its own currency due to the increase of trade deficit; (2) Rapid currency inflation; (3) Unequal distribution of income and widened income disparity; (4) Unbalanced central governmental revenue and expenditure and increased financial deficit due to the rapid increase of financial burden for improving urban infrastructure and supporting a large amount of urban migrants; (5) Increase of external debts due to a vicious cycle of elements (4) and (1); (6) The seriousness of unemployment, social upheaval, and credit loss of ruling system. Consequently, the introduction of foreign capital and export-oriented policy had to be given up halfway.

As the intermediate, Japan helped the periphery regions like Taiwan get relief from such a syndrome of large openness. This point was very important in improving the efficiency of the triangle framework and promoting Taiwan NIEs'lization.

Having the relationship with Japan and the United States, Taiwan started to implement the policy of introducing foreign capital and

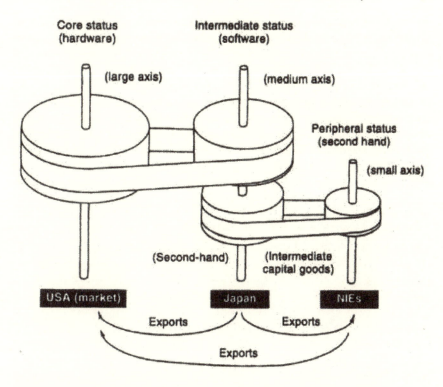

Core status
(hardware)

Intermediate status
(software)

(large axis)

(medium axis)

Peripheral status
(second hand)

(small axis)

(Second-hand)

(Intermediate
capital goods)

USA (market)   Japan   NIEs

Exports   Exports

Exports

Figure 9-3. The flow of technology with triangle mechanism (1980s).

Note: Cores status: opening up of domestic market, development of basic technology, providing of means of settlement (finance), overseas investment, acceptance of foreign labor, etc.

Immediate status: opening up of domestic market, introduction of technology (applied machine), transfer-out (second-hand), overseas investment, etc.

Peripheral status: export dependence, introduction of technology (second-hand), economic development (development dictatorship), introduction of foreign capital (foreign system reform, land reform), etc.

promoting export-oriented industrialization from the mid-1950s to the mid-1960s. Confronted with the Chinese communists' land reform, the KMT government also started land reform in Taiwan by reducing the rent of land in 1949 (previously more than 50 percent of output, now the rent of land was reduced to 37.5 percent) and providing "Land to the Tiller" from 1950 to 1953. In the mid-1950s, due to a depression in the textile industry, transferring from the Taiwan domestic market to export was under consideration and the relevant foreign exchange reform was finished in 1958–1963 (changing the multiple exchange rate into a single exchange rate system). These two reforms (land reform and foreign exchange reform) in Taiwan were five to seven years earlier than those in Korea, and they laid a solid foundation for the success of Taiwan's NIEs'lization. Of course, all these policies were based on the national policy of anti-communism and U.S. support (world strategy). Therefore, we can say that the prerequisite of NIEs'lization was consistent with the ideology of "anti-communism" and "U.S. support." In such an international environment, Taiwan stepped onto the initial stage of postwar development.

Because Taiwan started to implement the industrializing policy of introducing foreign capital and export-dependence earlier than Korea, it enjoyed more benefit from an international division with its special relationship with Japan and the United States. Probably, Taiwan was the luckiest one among the four small Asian dragons. Of course, it was not without conditions that Taiwan was in connection with Japan and the United States and enjoyed the benefit of international division of labor. Whenever an economic conflict or a change of coalition in safeguard between Japan and the United States occurred, Taiwan was the major one to be affected. On the other hand, Taiwan was easily impacted by any policy change of Japan and/or the United States in dealing with Chinese affairs. Taiwan also faced increasing pressure from the speed of Chinese economic reform and openness. The competition in foreign capital introduction, commodity export, and international market between Taiwan and mainland China was serious. In addition, the Taiwan economy has no third way out. It has to orient toward internationalization and seek to survive from the world market. Therefore, it cannot avoid frequent impact from the international economy. Because Taiwan (before January 1902) had no seat in international economic institutes like IMF, WTO, or World Bank, it had to maintain the trade surplus and guarantee the income of foreign exchange through self-reliance. Such seriousness and isolation facing Taiwan was very different from other INEs like Korea.

Indigenous Economic Power Blending with Japan's Globalization

Tracking the developmental process of Taiwan's capitalism and looking into its future, we need to further analyze how its indigenous economic power blends with Japan's globalization.

First, let us see the actual strength and dynamics of Taiwan's indigenous economic power. In Taiwan's capitalist society, there are three large economic forces.

The largest force is the state-owned enterprises group. Most of Taiwan's key industries, like the heavy chemical industry, the finance and banking industries, and the transportation and communication industries (called high commanding height) have already become state-owned enterprises, which are under the direct control of central government. The foundations of these industries were left by the large Japanese enterprises in the colonial period. The Taiwan government acquired them without paying any compensation. In a broad sense, the huge KMT enterprises group possessing $30 billion in assets in the high commanding height, can be included in this state-owned enterprises group.

The second largest force is the Taiwan indigenous enterprises group. Originally, the sources of this force came from the capital of landlords, agri-business, and commercial agriculture, as well as money lending. Later these indigenous enterprises stepped into the route of "introducing foreign capital and export-oriented" industrialization. With the connection and cooperation with foreign enterprises, particularly the Japanese enterprises, the Taiwan indigenous economy started from middle and small labor-intensive enterprises and gradually changed into the capital-accumulated machinery industry, chemical industry, and even electronics and automobile industry. In this group, there are some enterprise blocs and even large enterprises; however, the large parts are still the middle and small enterprises.

The third force is the foreign capital coming mainly from Japan and the United States. The capital from overseas China can also be included in this group. Starting in the 1960s, gradually growing in activity in the 1970s and 1980s, and becoming hot in the 1990s, this group is mainly concentrated in manufacturing and the information technology industry.

Among the three forces, the progress and competitive ability of indigenous enterprises are worthy of notice. Before Japanese imperialists occupied Taiwan in 1895, Taiwan's indigenous economy already had commercial and trade contacts with mainland China as well as the world market (Europe, the United States, and Australia), and therefore a certain primary industrial base was already established. It also exported some sugar and camphor to the world market. In the colonial period, Taiwan's indigenous landlord system and tenant farming system did not collapse at all. Postwar land reform forced landlords to invest in commerce and middle and small enterprises. "Foreign capital introduction" also provided the opportunity for indigenous capital to cooperate with foreign capital. In this aspect, Korea was not able to catch up with Taiwan.

Korea was not that active in introducing foreign capital because of the worry that foreign capital might control the management power of enterprises and even the key of the entire economy of Korea. The situation in Taiwan was different. With a huge state-owned enterprises group, Taiwan was not afraid to be controlled by foreign capital. Besides, the basic idea of the Taiwan indigenous enterprise group is to make money. So they would take the opportunity whenever it came and in whatever form it took—direct foreign investment, technological cooperation, or direct technology transfer. Unlike Korea, the Taiwan indigenous enterprise group was concerned more about the benefits of foreign investment.

As mentioned earlier, Japanese imperialists before World War II did not destroy Taiwan's indigenous landlords and merchants. In the postwar period, Japanese capitalists staged a comeback and invested in Taiwan again. Because Japanese investment in Taiwan provided the opportunity for pursuing their own interests, it was acceptable to Taiwan indigenous enterprises. With Japanese investment and transferred technology, Taiwan's indigenous enterprises developed from labor-intensive production series to OEM (original equipment manufacture) and further joined in international division and benefited from the world market. Such mercantilism and benefit-taking attitude were the traditional style of Taiwan's indigenous capitalists. With such traditional style and rich experience for making money as well as the relationship with Japan, Taiwan's indigenous capitalists were able to handle their economic activities smoothly.

For a long period of time, the trade surplus to Japan was an important economic source and regarded as a lifeline by Taiwan's indigenous capitalists. Although Taiwan's trade to Japan became deficit in the postwar period (the trade deficit to Japan was $17.11 billion in 1995, $17.68 billion in 1998, and accumulated to $191.4 billion from January 1971 to September 1999), the basic situation and original form for making money and accumulating capital did not change and even became more important. This implies that it is difficult for Taiwan to break away from its colonial economic structure.

CONCLUSION

Based on about 100 years' history, we discussed Japan's and Taiwan's relationship. From this review we can see that Taiwan colonization and Japanese imperialism happened in almost the same historical period. After the war, Japan was able to rally its forces under the Pax-Americana system, and Taiwan was also involved in the united front of the United States and Japan for another fifty years. For Taiwan, this whole period meant more than just being compared with other developing countries' history of colonization. Taiwan wants to be a very vital part of history for studying in the world.

Taiwan's NIEs'lization was following the steps of the United States and Japan. However, where will be its destination still remains to be seen. Tracking the historical process, we can see that the background of Japan occupying Taiwan was due to the existence of the China market as an axis of rotation. All the development and change in Japan's and Taiwan's relationship before World War II was around such an axis. Even after the Cold War, this historical axis is still important and unchanged. Therefore, the maintenance and development of Japan's and Taiwan's relationship must always be based on a consideration of the China market. In this regard, it is important to deal with Japan's and Taiwan's relationship by looking at new international orders in multilateral relationships, not just a bilateral relationship between Japan and Taiwan.

Of course, the position of modern China is different from that in the prewar period. Since 1978, China itself began an economic reform and an openness for promoting economic development, entering the world market and becoming a big economic and political power in the world. With this point, we could say that the development of Japan's and Taiwan's relationship has stepped onto a different stage.

In short, Japan's and Taiwan's relationship is very important to both of them. To Japan, the relationship with Taiwan was an important and indispensable part for its imperialism development in the colonial period. To Taiwan, the relationship with Japan means the first step of forming Taiwan capitalism. We can therefore say that it was in the modern historical process that Taiwan and Japan formed a close and inseparable relationship with which no other countries, even Korea, can compare.

As for the future evolution of such a relationship, it would depend on the development and change of the China market. Therefore, further study in Chinese market economy would become equally important as the studies in the history of Japanese imperialism and Taiwan colonization. To achieve this difficult task, a joint study and cooperation from worldwide economists are certainly desirable earnestly.

NOTES

1. An initial argument of the "the last empire—Japan" was advocated by Professor Tsutomu Ouchi, 1962, *Nipon Keizai Ron* (*Analysis of Japanese Economy*, volume 1), Tokyo: University of Tokyo. But professor Ouchi made no mention of "the initial colony—Taiwan," neglecting a vital point.

2. Some books of achievement, such as Su Yamamoto Yuzo, 1992, *Nihon Shokumintishi Kenkyu* (Studies on Japanese Colonial Economic History), Nagoya: Nagoya University Press, and Goto Kiyoshi ed., 1991, *Nihon Teikokushugi no Keizai Seisaku* (Economic Policy of Japanese Imperialism),Tokyo: Kashiwazaki Shobo, as well as Chin-Ming Ka, 1995, *Japanese Colonialism in Taiwan*, Boulder, CO: Westview Press, are good examples in this endeavor.

3. Hirai Kouiti, 1997, *Nihon Shokuminti Zaiseishi Kenkyu* (Studies on the History of Japanese Colonial Finance), Kyoto: Minerva Shobo.

4. For the whole process of colonialization in Taiwan from 1895 to 1995, see Jaw-Yann Twu, 1975, *Nihon Teikokushugi ka no Taiwan* (Taiwan under Japanese Imperialism), Tokyo: University of Tokyo Press. Also translated into Chinese in 1992, Renjian Books Publishing Co., Taipei.

5. Total trade deficit of Korea to Japan domestic for thirty-five years (1906–1940) on this field was recorded at 1.51 billion yen while its investment profit to Japan was 1.06 billion yen. Total current account surplus of Taiwan to Japan domestic for forty-five years (1895–1940) accounted the amount of 1.70 billion yen (*Long-term of Economic Statistics*, no. 14, eds. Yamakawa Itiji, Shinahara Miyohei, Umemura Mataji. Tokyo: Toyo Keizai Shinpo-sha, 1979).

6. For a study of the Sea of Japan, see my recent article, Jaw-Yann Twu, 1999, "Kan-Nihonnkai-ken no Kenkyu to Nihon no Shinro-Ajia Kenkyu no Kiten" (The Studies of "See of Japan Area" [Northeast Asia] with Japan on the Historical Perspective—An Origin of Asian Studies in Japan) in *Journal of Region and Society*, no. 1 (February): 39–58. The Institute of Regional Studies, Osaka University of Commerce, Japan.

7. So-called "rice batter system" and "sugar distribution system" was a typical formula adopted by the KMT regime. See Jaw-Yann, Twu, 1967, "Capital Formation Process in the Postwar Taiwan Economy," in *Economic Studies Bulletin of University of Tokyo*, no. 8.

8. For a detailed analysis, see Jaw-Yann Twu, 1975 and 1992 (Chapter 4 and Chapter 5).

9. In this field, I have examined some aspects in the following paper in Chinese. Jaw-Yann Twu, 1997, "Taiwan's External Trade and Economic Relations in the International Economic Changing Circumstances," in *Essays in Chinese Maritime History*, vol. 6, pp. 551–592, ed. Yen-Hsien Chang, Sun Yat-Sen Institute for Social Sciences and Philosophy, Academia Sinica, Taipei: Academic Sinica, March.

10. It was a very important base for Taiwan as an independent national economy formed just after World War II from 1945 to 1949. In this field, not much study has been done by economics scholars. My recent study is presented in Jaw-Yann Twu, 2000, *Taiwan no Sentaku* (Taiwan's Choice at the Crossroad), Tokyo: Heibon-sha.

10

From Dependency to Interdependency: Taiwan's Development Path toward a Newly Industrialized Country

Peter C. Y. Chow

INTRODUCTION

When Taiwan's economy recovered from its war destruction in the 1950s and was just about to take off in the early 1960s, the theory of trade pessimism à la Prebisch-Singer was prevalent,[1] particularly in Latin American countries. Fortunately, Taiwan's economic policy was not indoctrinated by the prevailing development theory then, and its development path did not fulfill the prophecy of the trade pessimism school either. As an agrarian colony of Japan prior to the end of World War II (1895–1945), Taiwan's major exports in the 1950s were rice, sugar, and other primary commodities—a typical pattern of export for developing countries as described by the trade pessimist. However, Taiwan's development strategy did not follow the "inward-looking" approach implicitly or explicitly advocated by the trade pessimism school.

On international division of labor, Taiwan's approach was not dictated by the "dependency theory " either, and its export performances had offered an alternative development path, which rejected the prognostication prescribed by the dependency theorist. The main thesis of dependency theory—that due to unequal distribution of power and resources between the "core" (the developed countries) and the "periphery" (the developing countries), a peripheral country like Taiwan has to be self-reliant so as not to become dependent on the "core" countries—was not adopted by the Taiwanese government.[2] On the contrary, as to be addressed later, Taiwan has been heavily trading with the "core" countries ever since its economy took off in the early 1960s. Though Taiwan has been depending on Japan and the United States for importing technology know-how and the export market, its intermediate position between industrialized and developing countries enabled it to become more and more interdependent with the industrial, core countries. In literature, Gold (1986) argued "Taiwan's specific situation of dependency yielded development, not underdevelopment"(p. 17). But, different from and more than what has been done by Gold, the study focuses on the development path, which shifted Taiwan's role from dependency to interdependency.[3] In spite of Taiwan's "specific dependency" defined by Gold, Taiwan's development, which differs from the conventional core-peripheral model, could challenge the dependency theorist by offering an alternative development model for late industrialization.[4]

To some extent, the dependency theory could be associated with the trade pessimism school for its advocacy on the "inward-looking" strategy through the development of "import-substitution" industries.[5] However, Taiwan did not fall into the trap of either the trade pessimism or the dependency schools by adopting the "inward-looking" strategy. After the initial import-substitution period (1953–1957), Taiwan has been pursuing its "outward-looking" policy by focusing on "export promotion," which led to decades of rapid export growth and economic development since the 1960s. As a result, Taiwan, along with other East Asian tigers such as Korea, Hong Kong, and Singapore, was considered as a role model of "export-promotion" and/or "export-led" growth countries.[6] Although there was a concern about the sustainability and the limit of the "export-promotion" and or "export-led growth" strategy,[7] some economists had argued whether or not the East Asian model of development could be generalized.[8]

On the other hand, the structuralist or neoclassicist has not fully dictated Taiwan's economic development path either.[9] Judging from Taiwan's export growth in the past decades, the main thesis of the structuralist—the inelastic supply and demand in responding to price mechanisms due to structural obstacles—is not empirically grounded at all. In fact, being motivated by the "animal spirit," Taiwanese entrepreneurs, especially those in the export industries, did observe the profit signal and responded to the price mechanism in the world market. The bottleneck of inelastic supply in developing countries is not irremovable, and profit incentives of business entrepreneurs could be motivated by appropriate policy measures to overcome the anti-trade bias proposed by the structuralist. Hence, the phenomenal growth of exports in Taiwan rebutted the thesis of output rigidity in the periphery as argued by the structuralist.

However, by rejecting the structuralist theory, Taiwanese government did not fully follow either the laissez-faire or the neoclassical school either. In fact, government involvement in Taiwan's economy probably would have undercut the credit that the neoclassical school or the laissez-faire would like to claim.[10] Perhaps, the maximum merit that the neoclassicist could possibly claim is the arguably "market-friendly approach" (The World Bank, 1993) that was applied more to the international market than to the domestic market. The thesis of "optimum trade policy," which argues for liberal trade policy mixed with domestic distortions, probably is closer to what was adopted by the Taiwanese government through its development path (Bhagwati and Ramaswami, 1963).

Be that as it may, Taiwan's economy has enjoyed enviable growth with rapid expansion of trade, which has been well documented (Galenson, 1979; Kuo, Ranis, and Fei, 1981; Tsiang, 1984; Thorbecke and Wan, 1999). In 1979, economists at the OECD recognized Taiwan (along with Korea and others) as one of the newly industrializing countries (NICs). Had it not been obstructed by political complications, Taiwan would have been a formal member of the OECD, IMF, and the World Bank to further contribute to the world economy.[11] In fact, without political influence from China, Taiwan is qualified to join the OECD as Korea did in 1996 because Taiwan fulfilled all the criteria of OECD membership.[12]

Since the mid-1980s, many Taiwanese firms had expanded their international horizons by making outward foreign direct investments (FDI) and engaging in "strategic alliances" with some world-class multinational corporations (MNCs) in developing high-tech industries. By the early 1990s, not only had Taiwan become the fourteenth largest trading nation in the world, its economy had also integrated more and more with the OECD as the third largest country of information technology (IT) products and other high-tech sectors.[13] Consequently, Taiwan has emerged from a former Japanese colony to a NIC and highly integrated with the world economy and interdependent with the OECD countries.

Hence, some development syndromes in most LDCs such as the secular trend of deteriorating terms of trade, vicious circle of poverty, and losing gains from trade due to trading with industrialized countries did not occur in Taiwan (Kuo, Ranis, and Fei, 1981; Tsiang, 1984). Whereas many studies analyze the sources of growth and/or rationales behind its miraculous path of development, this study focuses not only on how Taiwan managed its trade and development strategy so as to avoid the pessimistic prognostications described by the dependency theory and/or the trade pessimism school, but also how Taiwan became more and more interdependent with the world economy by emerging as a strategic partner for many industrialized countries. It is argued that Taiwan's development model is not dictated by a single theory or a set of development models. Neither was Taiwan indoctrinated by any prevalent ideologies.[14] Rather, it is to be explained by an "eclectic approach" in adopting its trade and development strategy, and its flexible policy responses in accordance with its changing dynamic comparative advantages in the world market. Therefore, Taiwan's experience, especially its eclectic approach of adopting pragmatic trade and industrial development policies to dynamically adapt to the changing internal and external environments at various stages of development, probably could provide some insightful lessons for other LDCs to map out their future development strategies.

This chapter is organized in the following way. Next I briefly review the eclectic approach adopted in Taiwan's development path when shifting from its initial import-substitution to export-promotion strategy. Then comes an analysis of how Taiwan, while engaged in its "outward-looking" strategy, escaped from the syndrome prescribed by the trade pessimist school. The development of intra-industry trade to generate interdependency with the rest of world is examined. After that, Taiwan's role in the global production network and recent development of strategic alliance with OECD countries are addressed. The chapter closes with a summary and some conclusions.

AN ECLECTIC APPROACH TO TRADE AND DEVELOPMENT POLICY: FROM IMPORT-SUBSTITUTION TO EXPORT-PROMOTION STRATEGY

Balassa (1983, 5) argued that except for England and Hong Kong, all countries went through their initial stages of import-substitution (IS-1) in their early stages of developments with different degrees / intensities of protection, various comprehensiveness of coverage, and different durations of protection period. After the initial stage of IS-1, some countries such as the East Asian NICs switched to export promotion strategy (EP) in the 1960s, whereas others such as Latin American countries continued the second stage of IS (IS-2) until the first energy crisis before they adopted the EP strategy. In spite of being a former Japanese colony, Taiwan did not adopt the autarkic "inward-looking/ import substitution" policies in its second stage of development. With its narrow domestic market and limited endowment of natural resources, Taiwan carried out its initial IS-1 during the 1953–1957 period (The World Bank, 1993) by a low degree of protection in a relatively short duration before it was switched to EP in the mid-1960s.[15]

The willingness and ability for the governments in Korea and Taiwan to switch from IS-1 to EP in their early stages of development, by comparison with Latin American countries, is an interesting topic in political economy of development (Olson, 1982; Balassa, 1983). Similar to Korea, Taiwan was under the so-called "soft authoritarian" regime (Winckler, 1984) during the 1949–1987 period. The authoritarian government had to legitimize its leadership by rapid economic growth and an ever-increasing economic prosperity to improve the livelihood of its people rather than by periodic elections.[16] At that time, when Taiwan's economy was undergoing rapid structural transformation and would need strong government leadership in steering its trade policies as well as its overall development strategies, the authoritarian regime in Taiwan enabled its policymakers to be immune from the "pork barrel" politics and/or "rent seeking," which commonly existed in many democratic countries. Under authoritarian regime, bureaucratic elites, who were insulated from interest groups under an elected democracy, had more autonomy to carry out economic development plans than otherwise would be (the autonomous state, à la Rodrik, 1992). Hence, in terms of efficiency and speediness of shifting gears for steering appropriate development policies, perhaps one could argue that, at least in the short run, an authoritarian regime was more effective in resisting political pressure from any interest groups than was an immature democracy. Of course, corruptions and/or rent seeking exist under the authoritarian regime too, and there are models of success as well as failure of economic developments in both authoritarian and democratic countries. Therefore, authoritarian regime is neither a necessary nor a sufficient condition for economic development.

However, what is being argued here is that, different from an elected government, which tends to become the prey of interest groups and campaign contributions, the bureaucratic elites under "soft authoritarian" regime could push for trade reform policies aiming at economic growth more effectively with much less concern about the interest groups in the protected sectors than what would be under an elected democracy with trade protectionism. Hence, Taiwan could switch from its IS-1 to EP with much less resistance from the protected sector and less pain for the public servants than what were experienced in most Latin American countries in the early 1960s—a decade that coincided with the "golden age" of American capitalism. Using the scenario of the "flying geese" (Akamatsu, 1962) for the late industrializing countries, Taiwan became the first flock of the "flying geese" behind Japan to climb the "export ladder" (Meier, 1995, 457–458) so as to catch the booming world market in the decade of the 1960s until the first oil crisis. Unlike Latin American countries—most of them were endowed with more abundant resources and had larger domestic markets than most

East Asian NICs—Taiwan was driven to export-promotion policy at a better timing in the 1960s than what others experienced in the 1970s and later.

Based on the trade specialization index, which is defined as the ratio of net trade (X-M) over total trade (X+M) in an industry, Kwan (1994, 84–92) classified four stages of development in trade structures from developing countries, young newly industrializing economies (YNIE), mature industrializing economies (MNIE), to industrial countries.[17] According to Kwan, Taiwan has a more rapid pace than that of Korea in moving from developing to industrialized country; Taiwan became a YNIE in 1967, reached the stage of MNIE in 1972, and the industrialized country status in 1991, whereas Korea started as a YNIE in 1965, reached the MNIE stage in 1990, and industrialized country in 2000.

The changing structures of export commodities in the past decades could be demonstrated somewhat differently by analyzing the development of three major categories of export growth in primary commodities (SITC 0, 1, 2, 3, and 4), machinery (SITC 7), and other manufactures (SITC 5, 6, 8, 9) in Figure 10-1. From Figure 10-1, one could also find that the percentage of manufactured exports other than machinery in total exports exceeded that of the primary commodities in 1967 at the time when Taiwan's GNP per capita was about $267 at current prices, and the percentage of machinery in total exports exceeded that of other manufactures (SITC 5, 6, 8, 9) in 1995 when per capita GNP reached $12,653 at current prices.[18]

Hence, when the ASEAN countries switched to their outward-looking strategies and became the second flock of the "flying geese" pushing behind Taiwan and other NICs in the 1970s, Taiwan had already become an MNIE and gradually engaged in its structural transformation by moving up the "export ladder" through promotion of technology-intensive exports in the world market. By the 1990s, Taiwan had become the third largest exporter of "information technology" products and the fourth largest producer of "integrated circuits" in the world. According to Kwan (1994, 89), Taiwan became an industrialized country in 1991 when its trade specialization index of machinery exceeded that of other manufactures. Based on the relative proportions of three categories of export commodities in total exports, the present study reached a conclusion similar to that of Kwan, though the cutoff dates for the development stages of trade structures are somewhat different. In general, Taiwan has transformed from an agrarian economy predominated by rice-sugar exports in the 1950s, through an exporter of labor-intensive manufactured products in the 1960s and 1970s, and became an exporter of technology-intensive products in the 1980s as well as a key producer of "high-tech" products in the 1990s.

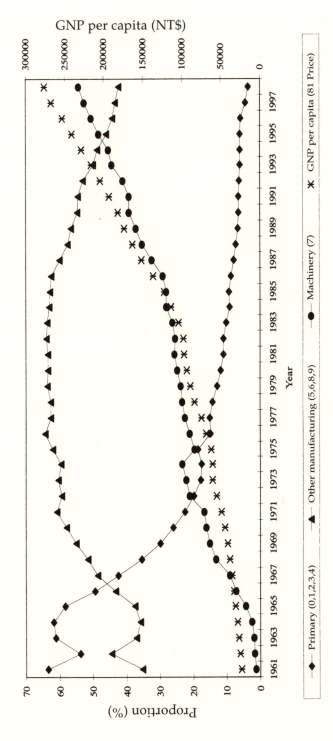

Figure 10-1. The proportions of three major product groups in total exports and per capita GNP: 1961–1998. *Note:* The GNP per capita is to be measured by the right-hand-side axis. All others are to be measured by the left-hand-side axis.

Primary (0,1,2,3,4)   ▲ Other manufacturing (5,6,8,9)   ● Machinery (7)   ✳ GNP per capita (81 Price)

Taiwan's eclectic approach, which had been timely adjusting its trade policies in accordance with its dynamic comparative advantage so as to maintain the changing international competitiveness in the world market, demonstrates that a developing country is not necessarily a "bondage" of orthodox development theory, be it structuralist, dependency, or neoclassicist. In fact, policy-makers as well as entrepreneurs in Taiwan had dynamically paddled the canoe in accordance with the changing sea waves. That is to say that Taiwanese entrepreneurs are responsive to the market signals and pragmatic in profit seeking, and policymakers in Taiwan are flexible in adopting new policy measures and or development strategies dynamically, rather than being indoctrinated by any development theories. Taiwan's adaptability (both public and private sectors) in the world market enabled its trade performance to lead the successful economic development and became a role model of "export-led" growth economy.

Moreover, colonial legacy did not persuade Taiwan to "de-link" itself from its former master and other core countries as advocated by the dependency theorist. On the contrary, just as many developing countries had maintained close economic ties with their former master countries after independence, Taiwan has also maintained its close economic ties with Japan by continually importing technology knowhow and manufactured intermediates from Japan and exporting to the OECD market. Hence, the advocacy for "de-linking" from the core countries by the dependency theorists was not very convincing for most postcolonial developments, including Taiwan. To some extent, one could argue that Taiwan still depends on Japan and the United States for technology know-how and exports markets (Gold's thesis of specific dependency). However, the leads and lags of technology among nations are exactly the basis for determining international division of labor. Developing countries need not be the victim of dependency forever due to their technological backwardness. Taiwan, with its intermediate function between the industrialized and developing countries, could be served as an exemplified model to reject the pessimistic scenario prescribed by the dependency theory. Therefore, trade is not a "stumbling block" but the "engine of growth" in Taiwan's economy (Chow and Kellman, 1993).

"OUTWARD-LOOKING" TRADE POLICY WITHOUT TRADE PESSIMISM SYNDROME

Taiwan's export-led growth rejected the trade pessimism thesis by maintaining favorable income terms of trade in the past decades. In spite of trading extensively with the "core" countries, especially with the United States and Japan, Taiwan has not suffered from the deterioration of terms of trade as the trade pessimist projected. Though as a resource-poor and trade-dependent country, Taiwan's exports need not be concentrated in primary commodities forever. Hence, she needs not necessarily to suffer from the worsening of gains from trade at all. Therefore, the phenomenon of "immiserizing growth" (Bhagwati, 1958) did not occur in the development history of Taiwan either. It is interesting to find out how Taiwan escaped these development syndromes, which are commonly shared in the Third World countries.

One argument of the dependency theory is that the "core "countries became prosperous by extracting surplus labor and resources from the "peripheral" countries through their trades with the periphery. Multinational corporations (MNCs) from the core countries exploited natural resources and cheap labor from those developing host countries through foreign direct investments (FDI) in the peripheral countries. Hence, there is an asymmetric power between the dominant core and dependent peripheral countries. The lopsided power structure in the world economy has generated unequal terms of exchange from international trade, and leads to further underdevelopment in the periphery. Therefore, the dependency theorist advocates a "self-reliance," "de-linking" approach of development by implicitly advocating the "inward-looking"/import substitution policies for the peripheral countries to prevent themselves from being dependent on the capitalist world system.

The trade pessimistic school (Singer-Prebisch) argued against "outward looking" trade policy for developing countries because there was a secular deterioration of the terms of trade in developing countries through trading with the industrialized countries. Essentially, Singer and Prebisch argued that exports from developing countries were concentrated in primary commodities. Both the income and price elasticties of demand for those commodities were relatively low by comparisons with those of their imports, which mainly consist of manufactures.[19] The secular worsening of the terms of trade in developing countries would generate unequal terms of exchange between developed and developing countries, and undercut the gains from trade in the developing countries.[20] Therefore, trade pessimism was allied with the dependency theorist by offering inward-looking/import-substitution rather than outward-looking/export promotion strategies for developing countries. As noted earlier, when the trade pessimism theory was prevalent in the early 1950s, Taiwan's exports were dominated by rice, sugar, and other primary commodities—a typical trade pattern as described by Singer and Prebisch. But, the domination of the primary commodity in Taiwan's exports then did not lead (mislead) Taiwan to adopt the autarkic inward-looking policy advocated by the trade pessimist. Therefore, the developmental path in Taiwan could provide some salient lessons for many developing countries.

The other related argument against LDCs' trade with industrialized countries is that, in spite of trade liberalization under the auspices of the GATT, exports from developing countries would inevitably encounter trade protectionism from the OECD. It was argued that in bilateral trade negotiations between developing and industrial countries, most LDCs had less bargaining chips when negotiating with the OECD countries. In multilateral trade negotiations, the GATT was generally considered as a "rich man's club" in that most trade liberalization was in favor of exports from OECD rather than for those from developing countries. Hence, the existing world trade system under the auspices of the GATT is not favorable to the LDCs at all.

As indicated before, the misconceptions of prevalent development theories did not lead (mislead) Taiwan to adopt an autarkic trade policy. To what extent the "eclectic approach" adopted in Taiwan had minimized the adversary effects of protectionism from OECD is to be addressed here. Basically, Taiwan has been shifting its trade structures periodically to mitigate the protectionism syndrome. Chow and Kellman (1988) proved empirically that LDCs need not necessarily become the prey of protectionism in OECD if they could successfully manage to switch the structures of their export commodities to the less protective sectors. By using 269 manufactured products based on three-digit SITC in the U.S. market between the pre–Kennedy Round in the mid-1960s and the post–Tokyo Round in the late 1970s, Chow and Kellman found that it was "product characteristics" rather than "geographic origination" of exports that are against the LDCs' exports. Essentially, it was the "systemic process of dynamic diffusion of comparative advantage" in that LDCs' comparative advantages were mainly laid on the low-skill and slow-growth industries, which were the likely targets of the lobbying pressure of trade protection.[21]

Hence, rather than blame trade protectionism in the OECD, Taiwan had gradually shifted its exports from predominant agricultural/primary commodities through labor-intensive light manufactures to technology-intensive and high-tech products so as not to become the victim of trade protectionism in the OECD.[22] Using the three-digit SITC export commodities to calculate the index of Balassa's (1979) "revealed comparative advantage" (RCA),[23] Chow (1990, 247) found that the unweighted coefficient of variation for the RCA index in Taiwan dropped from 2.12 in 1966 to 1.16 in 1986, whereas that of Japan decreased from 0.83 to 0.77 in the same period. For the trade-weighted RCA index, the coefficient of variation in Taiwan dropped from 0.77 in 1966 to 0.56 in 1986, whereas Japan dropped from 0.43 to 0.30 in the same period. Balassa argued that the further industrialized the economy, the more diversified its export commodities will be (the smaller the coefficient of variation of its RCA index). Accordingly, Chow (1990, 246) argued that Taiwan (as well as Korea) had a faster speed of industrialization among the East Asian NICs in the two decades between 1966 and 1986. Elsewhere, Chow (1999) illustrated that the embodied factor intensities in Taiwan's export commodities, as compared with other NICs in the U.S. market, had undergone dynamic changes over time. It was found that the skill ratio and embodied human capital in Taiwanese exports increased over time. Therefore, Taiwan could escape from the syndrome described by the trade pessimism and dependency theorist, and its trade performances were less affected by trade protectionism in the OECD.

After the second stage of export substitution, which focused on more technology-intensive exports,[24] Taiwanese firms started to engage in offshore production by expanding their outward FDI in the mid-1980s. This tendency was especially significant after the Plaza Agreement, which caused a realignment of the exchange rates with the U.S. dollar. In fact, outward FDI from Taiwan accelerated after the Plaza Agreement in 1985 and the liberalization of trade and investment across the Taiwan Strait after the lift of private visitation for its residents to mainland China in 1987. By using Taiwanese FDI in Malaysia as a case study, Chow (1996) found that outward FDI has positively contributed to the transformation of commodity composition of export in Taiwan. This phenomenon probably could be generalized to its overall outward FDI in other ASEAN and/or China countries too. In general, much of Taiwanese FDI in China and ASEAN countries was more "defensive" and more on traditional labor-intensive industries so as to take the "firm-specific comparative advantage" in the host countries. On the contrary, much of its FDI in the United States and European countries was more "aggressive," aiming at breaking the trade protectionism in the OECD. Hence, to some extent, Taiwan's outward FDI did contribute to the task of structural transformation, though overinvested in China is a major concern of "hollowing out" to root out its indigenous economy (Chow, 1997, 1999b).[25]

Since the 1960s, much of Taiwan's exports have been marketed in the United States and OECD countries, whereas much of its imports of intermediate goods was imported from Japan. Is there a secular trend of deterioration on Taiwan's terms of trade? The study undertaken in this chapter presents an empirical analysis to reject the conventional argument on the seemingly inevitable deterioration of terms of trade in the LDCs in the following way.[26] Figure 10-2 shows the time series of both net terms of trade (the ratio of price index of export relative to that of import, px/pm) and the income terms of trade (the product of net terms of trade and quantity of export, px/pm

Qx) from 1957 to 1999. One can find from Figure 10-2 that although there are some fluctuations in the net terms of trade, the income terms of trade has significantly improved in the past decades. The deterioration of net terms of trade was more significant in the decade of the 1970s when the worldwide energy crises occurred. But, the adversary trend reversed after the early 1980s. Given that Taiwan is an oil-consuming country that imports more than 90 percent of its crude oil from abroad, the fluctuations of its net terms of trade in the turbulent 1970s are not surprising at all. However, what determines the incomes/revenues from trade in any country, is its income terms of trade, of which Taiwan has been enjoying a significantly favorable trend in the past decades.[27]

Regressing both the "net terms of trade" and "income terms of trade" with a "time trend variable," it was found that the income terms of trade, which shows the incomes or export revenues from trade, has a positive sign at the 1 percent level of significance, whereas that of net terms of trade has a negative sign at the 5 percent level of significance.[28] It means that the incomes or revenues from trade did significantly improve in spite of the fact that the net terms of trade deteriorated in some time periods, as observed in Figure 10-2. This implies that export commodity from Taiwan is price elastic so that the drop on the price of export relative to that of import has caused a greater expansion of its export, and has generated more export revenues. This finding was in direct contrast with what was hypothesized by the trade pessimist. Therefore, the income terms of trade has improved, despite the deterioration of the net terms of trade. Hence, the incomes (or revenues) from trade improved and the pessimistic syndrome of secular "deteriorating terms of trade" and or "immiserizing growth" did not occur in Taiwan.

In general, it is hypothesized that the changing income terms of trade could be attributed to the changing composition of export and import commodities as well as the changing trade partners of exports and imports. Empirically, the export structure has been shifting from resource-based products such as rice and sugar in the 1950s, to labor-intensive products such as textile/ clothing in the 1960s and 1970s, then on technology-intensive products since the 1980s, as indicated earlier. It is reasonable to argue that the changing composition of exports would have contributed to the terms of trade in a nation with rapid export growth like Taiwan. This study tried to test empirically how the terms of trade in the 1961–1998 period was affected by (a) the specialization versus diversification of export/import commodities and (b) the diversification versus concentration of export destinations and import-source countries. The index of the coefficient of variation for export and import commodities at one-digit level of SITC product classification as

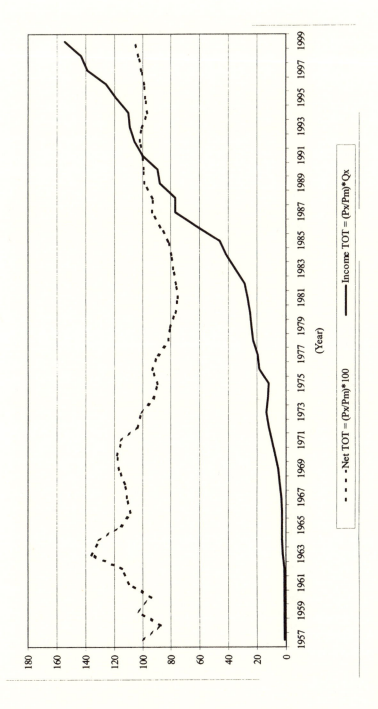

Figure 10-2. The trend of net terms of trade and income terms of trade: 1957–1999 (1991 = 100).
Note: Px, Pm are the price indices of export and import respectively. Qx is the quantity index of export. All data are derived from *Taiwan Statistical Data Book*, 2000, Taipei: Council for Economic Development and Planning.

Legend:
- - - - Net TOT = (Px/Pm)*100
——— Income TOT = (Px/Pm)*Qx

well as nineteen trading partners were used as independent variables in the regression models.[29] Regression analyses were conducted for both the net terms of trade and income terms of trade with coefficients of variation index in export/import commodities, and export/import countries as independent variables.

Various econometric methods were undertaken to deal with the autocorrelation in time series data.[30] Among them, the method of AR (1) was adopted in the regression model on the "net terms of trade," both Yule-Walker generalized least square estimates (model 1) and maximum likelihood estimates (model 2) were undertaken. As reported on the left-hand side in Table 10-1, the coefficient variation index for import commodities and importing countries are statistically significant in model 1. It means that by capturing niche products from right import-source countries, Taiwan obtained favorable terms of trade by developing "appropriate importing sources" and "right imports." In model 2, the significance of these two independent variables reduced to the 10 percent and 5 percent levels, respectively, but that of the coefficient variation index for export commodity was significant at the 10 percent level. To a less extent, the capture of niche products of its exports also contributed to its net terms of trade.

For the regression model on the "income terms of trade," both lagged dependent variable estimation (with Durbin-h statistics) and first order difference of dependent variable were adopted. On the right-hand side of Table 10-1, one can find that, in the model of first order difference (model 3), the coefficients of export destination and import commodity are statistically significant at the 95 percent level of significance. In the model of lagged dependent variable (model 4), the coefficient variation index for export destination is still significant, but that of import commodity variable disappears. It means that concentration of export destination has positively contributed to the income terms of trade. Given the qualification of the econometric model, one could argue that by catching the niche export market in the world and, to a less extent, by importing the right commodities, Taiwan was rewarded by its buying the "right imports" for further processing and by trading with the "right customers (markets)" in the world.

This result probably could be rationalized by looking at Taiwan's import concentration in few importing countries such as Japan, and imports the manufactured intermediates and technological goods, which were necessary for its exports. Because of its paucity of natural resources and reliance on import of technological goods, concentration on the right supplier(s) and necessary intermediate goods rather than diversification of importing countries and commodities would positively contribute to its net terms of trade. But, to maintain its favorable

TABLE 10-1. Regression Results: Net Terms of Trade and Income Terms of Trade Models, 1961–1998

Independent Variables[1]	Dependent Variable: NETTOT[2] Yule-Walker (GLS) Estimates Model 1		Dependent Variable: Maximum Likelihood Estimates Model 2		Dependent Variable: First Difference of INCOMETOT Model 3		Dependent Variable: INCOMETOT[3] Model 4	
	Parameter Estimate	t-ratio	Parameter Estimate	t-ratio	Parameter Estimate	t-ratio	Parameter Estimate	t-ratio
INTERCEPT	-12.27	-0.32	-3.79	-0.12	-27.30	-1.04	-33.40	-1.40
EXCOMMCV	4.59	0.21	33.90	1.64*	8.72	0.59	8.73	0.65
EXCTRYCV	-6.35	-0.76	5.67	0.62	8.76	1.85*	10.32	2.40**
IMCOMMCV	52.18	3.79***	28.13	1.60*	18.97	2.447**	-3.70	-0.35
IMCTRYCV	47.21	6.95***	17.50	1.73*	-4.99	-1.16	4.46	0.87
INCOMETOT(-1)							1.09	33.51***
AR(1)	-0.35	-2.14**	-0.91	-13.53***				
d.f.	32		32		32		31	
R-squared	0.860		0.894		0.324		0.995	
Adjusted R-sqaured	0.838		0.877		0.239		0.994	
F Statistic	39.4	***	54.0	***	3.8	**	1209.5	***
D.W.[4]	1.491		1.229		1.908		-1.825	

Notes:

***1 percent level of significance; **5 percent level of significance; and *10 percent level of significance.

(1) EXCOMMCV means coefficient of variation (c.v.) for export commodity and EXCTRYCV means c.v. for export country. Similarly, IMCOMMCV and IMCTRYCV represent c.v. for import commodity and import country, respectively.

(2) The estimation is carried out by assuming that an error term has a first-order autoregressive (AR[1]) process. Model 1 is estimated by a Yule-Walker method, which is a sort of Generalized Least Squares (GLS) method, and Model 2 is estimated by a maximum likelihood technique.

(3) The variable INCOMETOT(-1) is a one year lagged dependent variable.

(4) D.W. is Durbin-Watson statistic. For Model 4, Durbin's h statistic is reported.

gains from trade, in addition to its imports necessary for further processing, Taiwan has to capture the "right customers" in the world market.

Using the index of coefficient of variation for trading partners and commodities (in both exports and imports) as independent variables on the regression models to test the terms of trade is an innovative idea, but it also suffers from its limits.[31] Essentially, the index of coefficient of variation only reflects the diversification but does not fully represent the changing commodity composition of exports from labor-intensive to technology-intensive products as noted earlier. This study further proceeds to step-wise regression analyses by using the level as well as proportions of exports and imports in three major categories of commodities: primary commodities (SITC 0, 1, 2, 3, 4), other manufactures (SITC 5, 6, 8, 9) and machinery (SITC 9). The results are mixed but are encouraging for further research. In general, the t-statistics for export of manufactures and machinery are positive and significant.[32] A more sophisticated econometric model with more disaggregate classification of trade commodities is recommended for further studies. Nevertheless, the gains from trade did not deteriorate over time in Taiwan so she could escape the pessimistic scenarios of worsening terms of trade projected by trade pessimism and/or dependency theory. Taiwan's lesson proved that trade strategy, if appropriately manipulated, could serve as an important policy tool to promote the overall economic development in the LDCs. For many developing countries, Taiwan's trade performance could provide them with a role model of export-led development.

AN OPEN ECONOMY WITH INCREASING INTERDEPENDENCE WITH THE GLOBAL ECONOMY

After decades of export-led growth, Taiwan has become a highly "open economy." Measured by the percentage of exports and imports in total GDP, the degree of openness increased from an annual average of 21.7 percent in the 1952–1959 period, to 34.9 percent in the 1960s, to 76.7 percent in the 1970s, reached the peak of 86.9 percent in the 1980s, and decelerated to 78 percent in the 1990–1999 period, as reported in Table 10-2. This ratio is much higher than that of Japan and other OECD countries. The increasing degree of openness may make its economy vulnerable to the world business cycle such as the global recession and energy shocks in the 1970s. However, increasing dependency on the world market was also accompanied by increasing interdependency with most of its trading partners by expanding intra-industry trade, to be addressed later.

TABLE 10-2. Openness Index (%): 1952–1999

| | Openness (%) | | | | | |
| | Each year | | | Period Average | | |
Year	Total	Export	Import	Total	Export	Import
1952	23.3	8.6	14.8			
1953	20.7	8.7	12.0			
1954	19.0	5.8	13.2			
1955	17.0	6.4	10.5			
1956	22.6	8.6	14.0			
1957	22.4	9.2	13.2			
1958	21.2	8.6	12.5			
1959	27.4	11.1	16.3			
52–59				21.7	8.4	13.3
1960	27.0	9.6	17.4			
1961	29.7	11.2	18.5			
1962	27.2	11.4	15.9			
1963	32.0	15.3	16.7			
1964	34.0	17.1	16.9			
1965	35.9	16.0	19.9			
1966	37.0	17.1	19.9			
1967	39.9	17.7	22.3			
1968	40.1	18.7	21.4			
1969	46.2	21.4	24.8			
60–69				34.9	15.5	19.4
1970	53.1	26.1	26.9			
1971	59.3	31.3	28.0			
1972	69.7	37.8	31.9			
1973	76.9	41.6	35.4			
1974	87.2	38.9	48.3			
1975	72.6	34.2	38.4			
1976	84.6	43.8	40.9			
1977	81.9	42.9	39.1			
1978	88.4	47.2	41.2			
1979	93.0	48.4	44.6			
70–79				76.7	39.2	37.5
1980	95.5	47.8	47.7			
1981	90.7	46.8	43.9			
1982	84.2	45.5	38.7			
1983	86.6	47.9	38.8			
1984	88.6	51.4	37.2			
1985	81.9	49.4	32.4			
1986	84.9	52.8	32.1			

TABLE 10-2. **(continued)**

	Openness (%)					
	Each year			Period Average		
Year	Total	Export	Import	Total	Export	Import
1987	87.2	52.8	34.4			
1988	89.5	49.2	40.4			
1989	79.6	44.4	35.2			
80–89				86.9	48.8	38.1
1990	76.0	41.9	34.2			
1991	77.6	42.4	35.1			
1992	72.4	38.4	34.0			
1993	72.8	38.1	34.6			
1994	74.0	38.5	35.5			
1995	82.6	42.8	39.8			
1996	80.1	42.5	37.6			
1997	83.1	42.8	40.3			
1998	80.5	41.3	39.2			
1999	80.5	42.1	38.4			
90–99				78.0	41.1	36.9

Sources: (1) *Taiwan Statistical Data Book,* 1984, 1998, and 2000.
Council for Economic Planning and Development, Republic of China.
(2) Quarterly National Economic Trends, Taiwan Area, The Republic of China, November 1999. Directorate-General of Budget, Accounting and Statistics Executive Yuan, Republic of China.

Notes: The formula of openness index is: Openness = EX (or IM or [EX + IM]) / GDP * 100 (%) Total means the sum of Export and Import. The values at current prices are used.

In general, trade between industrialized countries is dominated by intra-industry trade (IIT), whereas trade between developing countries is more or less on inter-industry trades.[33] However, the pattern of Taiwan's trade has become more and more dominated by intra-industry trade.[34] This tendency was further contributed to by the rapid growth of its outward FDI, which accelerated in the 1990s. In general, due to interdependence between trading partners under intra-industry trade, trade frictions between nations were much easier to overcome than when they were under inter-industry trade. Table 10-3 reveals the trend of intra-industry trade based on one-digit of SITC and the three major product categories on primary (SITC 0, 1, 2, 3, 4), other manufactures (SITC 5, 6, 8, 9), and machinery (SITC 7) in the 1961–1998 period. From the right panel of Table 10-3, one could find that there is an increasing

TABLE 10-3.   IIT Index: Taiwan's Trade with the World (1961–1998)

| Panel A | | | | | | | | | Panel B | | | |
Year \ SITC	0, 1	2, 4	3	5	6, 8	7	9	0–9	Year / SITC	0, 1, 2, 3, 4	5, 6, 8, 9	7	0–9
1961	50.9	19.7	31.3	42.4	92.8	6.0	0.0	75.4	1961	91.0	85.4	6.0	75.4
1962	48.9	26.6	31.8	49.8	76.6	10.5	0.0	83.5	1962	92.5	98.0	10.5	83.5
1963	36.9	25.1	22.2	58.5	73.3	15.2	35.3	95.7	1963	95.6	91.2	15.2	95.7
1964	30.7	28.8	23.6	44.4	70.6	20.8	0.0	99.4	1964	86.4	93.1	20.8	99.4
1965	34.7	29.0	12.4	41.2	79.3	21.7	0.0	89.5	1965	92.4	99.1	21.7	89.5
1966	34.0	35.1	16.7	42.2	73.0	35.3	0.0	92.6	1966	96.1	91.2	35.3	92.6
1967	43.2	29.2	26.2	36.3	69.2	35.7	40.0	88.6	1967	97.3	89.7	35.7	88.6
1968	51.0	29.4	19.4	32.4	58.4	68.5	94.1	93.3	1968	90.0	78.5	68.5	99.1
1969	58.8	31.7	23.9	36.8	58.2	53.2	0.0	92.7	1969	86.1	77.0	53.2	92.7
1970	64.6	31.0	56.0	36.3	54.0	61.8	0.0	98.6	1970	84.4	70.2	61.8	98.6
1971	57.2	25.6	54.3	32.4	47.9	70.5	44.2	94.5	1971	84.7	63.4	70.5	94.5
1972	64.9	29.8	31.4	30.7	44.7	86.6	45.8	91.4	1972	77.9	60.6	86.6	91.4
1973	67.3	21.2	43.9	27.8	46.1	88.0	0.0	91.6	1973	75.1	62.1	88.0	91.7
1974	84.6	14.6	10.5	31.6	57.1	73.0	0.0	89.5	1974	54.7	76.7	73.0	89.5
1975	81.7	18.6	13.5	25.5	47.2	70.9	30.2	94.3	1975	58.9	68.2	70.9	94.3
1976	80.8	23.3	15.0	32.8	40.7	84.7	42.5	96.4	1976	56.7	59.0	84.7	96.4
1977	78.0	19.4	17.2	38.5	44.5	95.8	71.2	95.2	1977	55.1	60.3	95.8	95.2
1978	79.9	24.7	24.6	33.7	41.8	94.2	73.0	93.0	1978	57.5	58.0	94.2	93.0
1979	89.1	24.1	19.9	33.7	41.9	93.7	0.0	95.7	1979	50.0	59.4	93.7	95.7
1980	86.7	21.9	11.2	42.1	42.3	94.1	50.1	99.8	1980	41.0	58.1	94.1	99.8
1981	96.8	26.3	15.3	44.9	40.5	98.2	0.0	96.8	1981	40.9	55.5	98.2	96.8
1982	94.0	31.7	16.8	48.2	38.5	97.0	56.3	91.9	1982	44.6	53.5	97.0	91.9
1983	94.6	30.5	17.9	41.6	36.8	90.5	0.0	89.4	1983	44.2	53.9	90.5	89.4
1984	94.3	29.2	20.8	45.7	34.6	84.3	0.0	83.8	1984	45.7	50.5	84.3	83.8
1985	92.1	35.8	22.7	48.6	32.5	79.1	0.07	9.1	1985	50.5	47.6	79.1	79.1
1986	74.7	32.9	22.5	47.0	34.6	80.6	70.9	75.5	1986	61.0	51.1	80.6	75.5
1987	75.4	32.4	20.7	45.9	38.0	82.4	0.0	78.9	1987	60.5	58.2	82.4	78.9
1988	87.0	34.1	17.0	50.3	48.3	86.8	0.0	90.1	1988	56.4	77.5	86.8	90.1
1989	99.9	38.4	16.7	52.4	49.4	86.8	6.5	88.2	1989	52.4	72.2	86.8	88.2
1990	97.5	41.7	12.6	57.5	51.3	87.0	6.8	89.7	1990	48.7	73.2	87.0	89.7
1991	97.6	37.8	14.0	58.2	56.4	85.9	7.4	90.4	1991	51.0	77.3	85.9	90.4
1992	94.9	40.2	17.3	61.6	60.5	91.7	6.0	93.8	1992	51.5	81.1	91.7	93.8
1993	93.5	39.6	18.5	64.6	68.5	89.3	5.9	95.0	1993	51.5	86.3	89.3	95.0
1994	98.7	42.0	17.6	67.0	70.8	88.3	4.1	95.3	1994	53.3	88.7	88.3	95.3
1995	89.7	46.6	19.8	70.8	75.1	87.3	5.3	96.2	1995	52.7	91.6	87.3	96.2
1996	82.6	46.9	22.5	70.7	71.2	81.9	5.1	93.8	1996	50.1	90.6	81.9	93.8
1997	59.5	46.2	22.6	68.0	74.5	83.9	3.7	96.8	1997	40.5	94.7	83.9	96.8
1998	55.9	45.4	21.0	68.9	71.7	89.3	4.4	97.3	1998	39.3	92.5	89.3	97.3

Notes: The computational formula for the Intra-Industry Trade (IIT) index is based on the following unadjusted Grubel and Lloyd (1975) formula:

$$IIT_k = \{1 - abs(X_k - M_k)/(X_k + M_k)\} * 100$$

where IIT_k means the intra-industry trade index for industry k, X_k is the value of Taiwan's export in industry k to the world, and M_k is the value of its import in industry k from the world. All these statistics are on current prices. The industry groups corresponding to the SITC codes are as follows:

TABLE 10-3. (continued)

SITC codes	7 Groups	3 Groups
0 and 1	Food and beverages	Primary commodity
2 and 4	Raw materials excluding fuels	
3	Fuels, etc.	
5	Chemicals products	Other manufacturing
6 and 8	Other manufactured goods	
9	Commodities and transactions not classified elsewhere in the SITC	
7	Machinery and transport equipment	Machinery
0–9	Total	Total

trend of intra-industry trade in manufactures and machinery but a decreasing trend in primary commodities. But, if one looks at the disaggregate data on the left-hand side on Table 10-3, then one can find that the intra-industry trade in primary commodities was more significant in food and beverage (SITC 0, 1) than on raw materials (SITC 2, 4) and fuels (SITC 3). Given the paucity of its endowment in natural resources, this phenomenon is not surprising at all.

Another way to examine the degree of interdependency in a nation is to look at the net trade position on various commodity groups. The net trade position (NTP) is defined as the ratio of import (M) in total trade (X + M) in the same product group. This index could be served as a proxy for the interrelatedness and relative competitiveness in world trade (Tai and Metha, 1988). A country is considered as a "net exporter" in that industry if its NTP is less than 50 percent, but a "net importer" if its NTP is greater than 50 percent. Figure 10-3 presents the net trade position of the three major product groups aggregated at the level of one-digit SITC. From Figure 10-3, one could find that, except for the 1963–1967 period when there was a surge on the world sugar market, Taiwan has been a net importer of primary commodities (NTP > ½). On the contrary, except for the initial period in 1961–196262, Taiwan has been a net exporter (NTP < ½) on other manufactures. The shift from a net importer to a net exporter of machinery in 1982–1983 is most interesting. Prior to 1982, Taiwan was a net importing country of machinery, but due to its technology development, Taiwan became a net exporting country of machinery after 1982.

Moreover, it is interesting to compare the net trade position of Taiwan in two representative high-tech products: (1) computers and peripheral products grouped under a four-digit harmonized system of product classification (H.S. 8471), and (2) computer components and parts

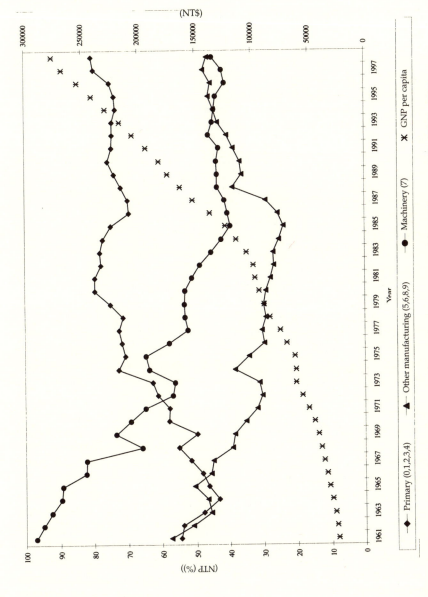

Figure 10-3. Trends of Taiwan's net trade position by three industry groups with GNP per capita: 1961–1998

grouped under H.S. 8473.[35] Figures 10-4 A and 10-4B report Taiwan's net trade position on these two representative high-tech products with five major trading partners: the United States, Japan, EC-6, NIC, and ASEAN-4. For H.S. 8471-computer/computer peripheral products, Taiwan is a net importer for ASEAN-4 but a "net exporter" for the United States and EC-6. For Taiwan's trade with Japan, Taiwan was a net importer for its computer/peripheral products from 1989 I to 1994 II, but a net exporter after that. But, after 1998 II, Taiwan became an importer again. On the contrary, in its trade with other NICs (Hong Kong, Korea, Singapore), Taiwan also shifted from a net exporter to a net importer after 1998 II. For H.S. 8473-components and parts, Taiwan definitely is a net exporter for almost all of its trading partners except for Japan during the period before 1993 III.

Taiwan's relative trade positions on computers and peripheral products (H.S. 8471)—a net exporter for the United States and EC-6, but a net importer for ASEAN-4—probably reflect the relative technology hierarchies in the three tiers of trading partners. Further analyses on the fluctuations of net trade position on other high-tech products are necessary to better understand the shift of comparative advantages in high-tech industries. The development of intra-industry, particularly in the high-tech sectors, has greatly increased the mutual interdependency between Taiwan and many of its trading partners. It is also an indication of the increasing trend of globalization of production network in the high-tech industries (Chow, 2001). The increasing interdependency between Taiwan and many of its trading partners has also generated some political dividends for Taiwan. For example, a temporary production disruption on the computer parts and components due to a power failure during the September 21, 1999, earthquake caused a big concern in the world high-tech industries. Moreover, many European countries are enthusiastically anticipating further trading opportunities with Taiwan once Taiwan joins the WTO in the near future.[36]

Another major concern on trade and development policy in Taiwan since the 1990s is its dependency on China's market where there is a politically hostile government that has been claiming its sovereignty on Taiwan. Since the undertaking of trade liberalization across the Taiwan Strait in 1987,[37] Taiwan's export dependence on China's market has increased from 2.28 percent in 1987 to 17.94 percent in 1998, whereas China's export dependency on Taiwan's market remained at a level around 2 percent.[38] Combining Taiwan's export to China and Hong Kong, the greater China has replaced the United States as Taiwan's largest export market since 1994. In 1994, Taiwan's exports to China and Hong Kong totaled $29.78 billion, accounting for 32.01 percent of Taiwan's total exports, which surpassed the $24.34 billion of its exports

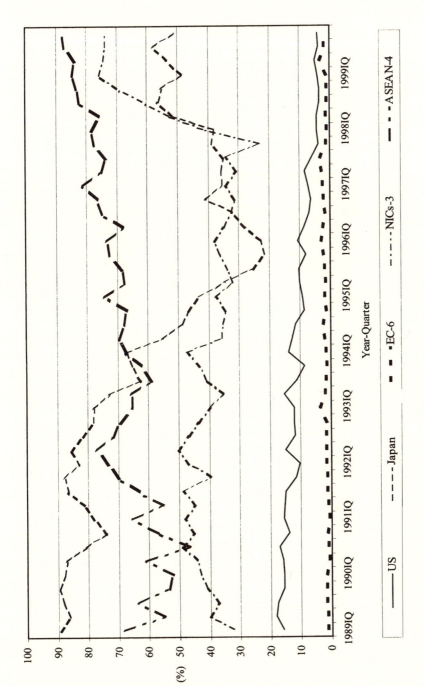

Figure 10-4A. Net trade position by five regions: HS 8471, 1989IQ–1999IVQ

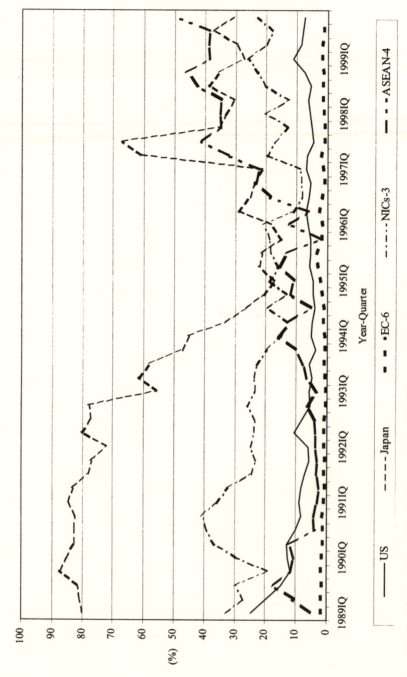

Figure 10-4B. Net trade position by five regions: HS 8473, 1989IQ–1991IVQ

to the United States (26.16 percent). Export dependency on greater China's market increased dramatically since then. In 1998, while 26.56 percent of Taiwan's exports went to the United States, more than 30 percent went to China and Hong Kong.

Economic liberalization and internationalization are a set of twin policies undertaken since the 1980s. But, trade liberalization toward China has already increased Taiwan's export dependency on China's market, whose government in Beijing has been, and still is, challenging illegitimately the "de facto" independent national sovereignty of Taiwan and continually undercut Taiwan's international status. Hence, economic and trade policies toward China have become a controversial issue in Taiwan since the opening of trade with China (Chow, 1999b). Would dependency on China's market undermine Taiwan's economic security? What would happen if trade liberalization across the Taiwan Strait takes place after both China and Taiwan join the World Trade Organization (WTO)? How to coordinate economic liberalization toward China with national security? Those questions have become a major concern of some academia and policymakers in Taipei.

Using the computable general equilibrium (CGE) model simulation, Chow, Tuan, and Wang (2001) found that, after both China and Taiwan join the WTO and operate under the post–Uruguay Round trading framework without applying the "safeguard measures," Taiwan's export market will depend more on China by increasing 5.8 percentage points from the initial level in 1995 after its accession to the WTO.[39] However, the bilateral trade flows across the Taiwan Strait will be dominated by intra-industry such as manufacture intermediates and machinery. Hence, though Taiwan's export dependency on China's market would increase after both China and Taiwan are admitted to the WTO as the model predicts, the concern of overdependency on China's market (if that is a concern) probably could be relieved somewhat because intra-industry trade between them would generate a high degree of interdependency, which would reciprocally restrain both sides from taking any destructive actions against each other.

Needless to say, for Taiwan to trade with and invest in a politically hostile country like China, there is always a risk because of the relative size between China and Taiwan. Moreover, China has much more leverage than Taiwan if a sudden cutoff of trade flow across the Taiwan Strait occurs. Hence, Taiwanese businessmen need to be more cautious in trading with and investing in China until China observes the WTO trading framework, and denounces its claims over Taiwan's independent sovereignty. It is not the intention for this study to deal with the political economy of trade warfare,[40] which would shift attention away from the intended focus of this chapter. However, pragmatically speaking, the problem facing Taiwan is not whether or not to trade with and invest in China, but how to manage the risks associated with trade liberalization with China and how to push for a "cosmopolitan" drive for globalization (Chow, 1999b). Taiwanese investment in China needs to be diversified. Its overall objectives must expand from the "defensive strategy" of seeking cost advantage to the "aggressive strategy" of marketing penetration, technology acquisition, access and control of strategic components/parts and key resources, and international coordination.

However, if trade flow across the Taiwan Strait will be dominated by intra-industry trade as projected, then trade liberalization across the Taiwan Strait could increase more interdependency between China and Taiwan, and would be less threatening to Taiwan's economic security than under inter-industry trade. Therefore, trade interdependency would not only promote economic horizons for Taiwan but also enhance economic security in dealing with a politically hostile trading partner like China.

TAIWAN'S EMERGING ROLE IN THE GLOBAL PRODUCTION NETWORK VIA STRATEGIC ALLIANCE WITH OECD

As a latecomer of industrialized countries, Taiwan has been relying on imports of technology know-how from industrial countries, especially the United States and Japan. But, as argued by Little (1982), import of technology from abroad does not necessarily create technology dependence or reliance on industrialized countries if developing countries have the capability to shop around for these technologies in the competitive world market.[41] In general, much of Taiwan's manufactured exports to the OECD were processed by importing technology know-how and manufacture intermediates mainly from Japan—a triangular division of labor among the United States, Japan, and Taiwan (see Chapter 9). This triangular trade relationship has generated technological flows to Taiwan and substantially contributed to its technological progress in the past decades.

By using the two-digit manufactured industries for the 1975–1990 period, Chuang (1996) found that the effect of "trade-induced learning by doing" in Taiwan's manufacturing industries was mainly derived from its imports and exports of machinery from and to developed countries—Japan and the United States (p. 459). Therefore, Chuang argued that "opening trade is a necessary but not a sufficient condition" for rapid growth in developing countries. For developing countries to enhance technology development through foreign trade, it is necessary for them to select appropriate trading partners from the developed countries. In this regard, Taiwan had made a right choice by trading heavily with the United States and Japan. Needless to say, part of that choice was due to colonial legacies and U.S. aid during the early stages of its development in the 1950–1965 period.

However, though the expansion of intra-industry trade has generated more interdependency with its trading partners, technologically Taiwan is still highly dependent on industrialized countries. Moreover, it was pointed out that the technology lead between the NICs and the second flock of "flying geese" (ASEAN) is much narrower than that which exists between Japan and the NICs (Bernard and Ravenhill, 1995). With a shallow technological lead over the second-tier of the NICs such as the ASEAN countries and China, Taiwan has to catch up with the industrial leaders by narrowing its technology gap and has to become more interdependent with the industrial countries.

The task of promoting technology development was evidenced by the following statistics: Expenditures on research and development (R & D) in total GDP steadily increased in the last decade from 1.24 percent in 1988 to 1.98 percent in 1998,[42] and the number of researchers per 10,000 population increased from 17.8 to 38 in the same period. Among the R & D expenditures in Taiwan, more than 50 percent was spent on "technological development," whereas those on "basic and applied research" was less than 50 percent. By comparison, more than 40 percent and 30 percent of R & D expenditures in the United States were spent on basic research and applied research, respectively, whereas less than 25 percent was spent on technological development.[43] Hence, Taiwanese research efforts seem to put more emphasis on technology diffusion and product development rather than on basic research, which is quite similar to the Japanese model in its catching up with Western industrialized countries.

The controversial issue of technology development policy, whether focusing on promoting indigenous technology innovation or increasing its absorptive capacity of adopting existing technology (technology diffusion) from abroad, is not to be addressed here.[44] But, the drive for "technology development" is what Taiwan has been pursuing for decades, though "technology dependence" on Japan and other industrial countries still exists. Having weathered the trade protectionism in the OECD and having escaped from the secular deterioration of terms of trade, Taiwan has been trying to become more interdependent with all OECD countries through a new policy of "strategic alliance," especially in the high-tech industries.

Starting with the 1980s, Taiwan initiated its "strategic alliance" with many large OECD firms in many of its manufactures, especially in the semiconductor industries and consumer electronics. To overcome the "branch plant syndrome" characterized by prevalent original equipment manufacture (OEM), Taiwanese firms joined the global logistics network by signing "strategic alliances" with many world-class firms in many high-tech industries.[45] Among the top 100 multinational enterprises in the world, Compaq, Digital, IBM, and Hewlett Packard from the United States and ABB, Philips, and Siemens from Europe had subcontracted their components and computer peripheral products to indigenous Taiwanese firms to secure their supplies in the world market. Indigenous industries in Taiwan still highly relied on OEM since the economy took off in the 1960s, and OBM (own brand-name manufacturer) is still in its emerging stage.[46] But, different from OEM in the consumer goods industries such as garments, footwear, and housewares in the past decades, many of these OEM contracts in the semiconductor and information technology (IT) industries in the 1990s are high technology—and capital-intensive. Chen and Liu (2000) argued that "by participating in the supply-chain management, logistics operations and after-sale services" (p. 182) with the world-class firms in IT industries, Taiwan has established its international production and logistics network and upgraded its status as a key supplier in the world IT industry. Hence, Chen and Liu (2000) argued that world-class PC brand names "can be anchored to Taiwan's economy" (p. 182), and Taiwan has become more and more interdependent with the industrial leaders in the world.

As defined by Vonortas and Safioleas (1997), strategic alliance is "a web of agreements whereby two or more partners share the commitment to reach a common goal by pooling their resources together and coordinating their activities" (p. 658). There are eight formats of alliances between developed and developing countries: mergers and acquisitions, joint ventures, R & D agreements, licensing, equity investment, contractual agreements, standard coordination agreements, and university–industry cooperation agreements. Based on eight industrial groups in computers, telecommunications, consumer electronics, media, electronics, office automation, industrial/robotics, and finance/banking/insurance, Vonortas and Safioleas found that Asian firms were the most active among all developing countries in engaging in strategic alliances, which accounted for 62 percent of total contracts signed by non-OECD countries during the 1984–1994 period.[47] The vast majority of IT alliances between OECD and NICs include the creation, exchange, and/or transfer of technological knowledge. Moreover, the share of alliances with explicit technology content was found to be higher in the NICs than the worldwide average. In terms of the number of developing strategic alliance agreements, Taiwan was ranked as the fifth-largest country, next to the former Soviet Republic, China, Hong Kong, and Korea. The policy of strategic alliance with OECD would promote further integration with industrial countries and enhance Taiwan's interdependency with the world economy.

As the drive for globalization accelerates, Taiwan's role in the global production network has greatly enhanced with increasing technology hierarchy on its products. For example, in the semiconductor industry, the sequential stages of production include design, wafer fabrication, assembly/packaging, and final testing/shipping. Each stage has different production characteristics with various factor intensities and technology hierarchies, which leads to the spatial rationalization of its production chains globally. The design stage requires high R & D intensity, whereas the fabrication stage requires high capital intensity. By contrast, the assembly stage would require only low-skill labor due to the increasing automation of production techniques.[48]

Changing comparative advantages in the 1980s caused a significant shift in the offshore production network in the semiconductor industry. Their assembly lines relocated from the NICs to ASEAN and China, and fabrication and testing (and even design) were performed in the NICs. In terms of international division of labor, the NICs have upgraded from the suppliers of low-cost labor for assembly to more sophisticated producers of fabrication and testers of the final products.

Among design, fabrication, assembly, and testing in the semiconductor industry, Taiwan focused on fabrication and testing.[49] In 1998, the semiconductor industry in Taiwan generated a total of $8.4 billion in design, fabrication, packaging, and testing: $5.1 billion was from fabrication, which accounted for the highest percentage (60.7 percent), followed by packaging (20.2 percent), design (15.5 percent), and testing (3.6 percent). For the fabrication industry, 90 percent of its revenue was generated from memory and foundry. Taiwan has maintained its leading status in the foundry business and was "number two" in the design industry globally in terms of number of firms and revenues. Taiwan has the second largest packaging industry in the world. "Strategic alliances with up- and down-stream venders, turn-key services, and internationalization are the major strategies" that enabled Taiwan to sustain profitability during the recession. At the present state of development in the semiconductor industry, Taiwan still enjoys comparative advantage in the capital-intensive stage of production, shifts some low-end products such as motherboards, monitors, and keyboards to China,[50] and gradually penetrates into the more R & D–intensive stage on research and design. Taiwan would need to put more emphasis on innovation so as to maintain its technology lead over China and ASEAN countries. The task of shifting from OEM to OBM and to achieve the leading status on cutting-edge technology may be a long way to go for Taiwan. Yet, its strategic alliance with world-class corporations in the OECD would certainly increase its interdependency with the world economy. The drive for upgrading the technological structure by developing a "knowledge-based economy" is what Taiwan will pursue in the new world economy.

CONCLUSION

The development path in Taiwan was not indoctrinated by a single theory or model, be it the dependency theory, trade pessimism, structuralism, or the neoclassical school. On the contrary, the eclectic approach undertaken by the Taiwanese government and its entrepreneurs was much more pragmatic by continually shifting its gear in accordance with dynamic comparative advantage on the world market.

The secular deterioration of the terms of trade and the "immiserizing growth" was not evidenced in Taiwan. Certainly, there are concerns about the sustainability of the "export-led" growth strategy for long-term economic development. However, over time, the gains from trade as measured by the income terms of trade have significantly improved. Although further research on the factors determining the gains from trade is needed, this study tentatively concludes that Taiwan's adaptability in the world market is the key to its success. By importing the appropriate manufacture intermediates and technological goods and targeting the "right customers" (export destination) in the world market, Taiwan has been enjoying favorable gains from trade. To weather the protectionism in the OECD markets, Taiwan had continually changed the structure of commodity composition of its exports and shifted its trade orientation to other growing Asian countries. As a highly open economy, Taiwan not only has developed more and more intra-industry trade with the rest of the world but also has become more interdependent with OECD countries through strategic partnership.

It is not an overexaggeration to argue that Taiwan could serve as a role model for many developing countries in its struggles for development and its transformation from an agrarian economy dependent on industrial core countries to a newly industrialized country with a high degree of interdependency with the OECD. From being a predominantly rice and sugar exporter to becoming one of the major exporters of high-tech products in the world, from a former colony of Japan to a strategic partner of many in the OECD, Taiwan's success story is an important contribution to world development. Some of Taiwan's development lessons may be unique, and not all of them could be totally replicable in other developing countries, but its development path can offer some invaluable insights for other developing countries.

NOTES

In addition to acknowledging those who offered me their advice on this study as indicated in notes 30 and 31, I would like to thank Iwao Tanaka for his computation assistance in this study.

1. The trade pessimism school could be traced to the partnership between Prebisch (1959) and Singer (1950). The main thesis of trade pessimism, though not rigorously formulated, was the deterioration of terms of trade for the peripheral countries in trading with the core countries. The trade pessimism school was interconnected with the theories of unequal distribution of the gains from trade between the core and the peripheral countries, the North–South disputes, which implicitly lead the "inward-looking" trade strategy.

2. It is noted that in the "less static zero-sum model," Wallerstein (1979, 76–81) pointed out that peripheral countries could take three strategies to become semi-periphery, which is sandwiched between the core and periphery. The three strategies are, in addition to self-reliance, multinational corporations and aggressive state actions when internal and external opportunities exist.

3. Gold (1986) applied the "historical-structural method of Cardoso-Faletto" to analyze the transformation process for Taiwan's development. Whereas Gold was focused on the "specific dependency in Taiwan" that led to its development (specific dependency => development), this study would emphasize more on Taiwan's specific development path to interdependency (Taiwan's specific development path => interdependency).

4. The economic relations among Taiwan, Japan, and the United States would fit into dependency theory, as Gold (1986) and others had argued. But what is to be argued in this study is that Taiwan, which has exemplified itself as an intermediate between the core and the peripheral countries, is different from other developing countries, as described by the conventional dependency theory. Moreover, this study proves that dependency itself is not an obstacle for becoming interdependent.

5. For a survey article on "import substitution," see Henry Bruton (1989).

6. One needs to point out that "outward looking" and "export-promotion" are not synonymous. Balassa (1983, 2–5) argued that "export-promotion" played the key role in economic development in the newly industrializing countries, whereas the importance of conventional objective factors such as country size and political and social conditions for development was exaggerated.

7. For the argument of sustainability of export promotion, see the appendix in Chapter 9.

8. For the arguments for and against the generalization of the East Asian "export-led" model, see Cline (1982), Ranis (1985), and Cline (1985).

9. For a synthesis on different views on trade and development among these schools, see P. K. Bardhan (1988, 57–62).

10. Government interventions on trade could be exemplified by the policies of export subsidy, tax refund for export, and a multiple exchange rates system in the early period. For a more comprehensive discussion on the role of government in economic development in Taiwan and Korea, see Rodrik (1995).

11. In 1998, the GDP per capita in Taiwan was $12,333, which was higher than those in Greece ($11,870) and Portugal ($10,094)—both were OECD members. Moreover, Taiwan is more than willing to offer its assistance to other developing countries by joining those international organizations as an active member.

12. The criteria of OECD membership were, in addition to the level of development, a market economy with a democratic system, which Taiwan had fulfilled, as well as the willingness of cooperation with other countries on trade and economic policies, which Taiwan will.

13. Source: ITIS program, Market Intelligence Center, Information Industry Institute, November 1999. For a detailed analysis of Taiwan's computer industry, whose hardware production ranked fourth in the world by 1995, see Kraemer et al. (1996).

14. What is referred to here is the trade policy and development strategy, not social economic policies under which Taiwan was recognizably indoctrinated by Sun Yat-sen's philosophy on the "principle of livelihood."

15. In fact, import substitution and export promotion are not mutually exclusive. Chu (1994) argued that there is a simultaneous IS and EP is some industrial sectors such as petrochemicals.

16. One has to point out that economic prosperity is also an important factor for voters' support in the periodic election under democracy too.

17. Kwan (1994) used NIE, whereas this study used NIC. Hence, this section will use the terms of NIC and NIE interchangeably.

18. Based on constant prices of 1981, then the GNP per capita in 1967 is N.T. $36,325.00 (U.S. $908.13 at $1=NT$40), and is NT$241,143.30 in 1995 (U.S.$8,842.81 at $1 = NT$27.27). Source: *Taiwan Statistical Data Book*, 2000.

19. Under Prebisch's scenario, a sustainable growth in the periphery equal to that of the core would require either a reduction of income elasticity of demand for imports of manufactures and/or the development of nontraditional exports. In retrospect, neither of these seemed to be easy for the peripheral countries in the 1950s.

20. To be fair to Prebisch, Weiss (1988, 89) pointed out that Prebisch did refer the desirability of developing nontraditional exports, and the need to expand customs unions among developing countries. Given the manufacturing sectors in many developing countries in the 1950s, Prebisch could be credited for his advocacy of IS policy by his recognition of the foreign exchange bottleneck in developing countries.

21. Chow and Kellman (1988, 652) argued that "rather than the U.S. tariff structure deliberately 'knocking out' the newly emerging competitive stance of the LDCs in manufactures, the LDC export drive 'walked right into the right hook.'"

22. By using an aggregate level of export commodity at the one-digit SITC level, the present study finds that the coefficient of variation (the ratio of standard deviation over mean) of export commodities increased from 1.28 in the 1960s, to 1.39 in the 1970s, to 1.44 in the 1980s, and dropped to 1.36 in the 1990–1998 period. The coefficient of variation of export commodity at the aggregate level of one-digit SITC did not significantly change, but it started to decline in the 1990s, which implied, even at the aggregate level of one-digit SITC, that export commodities had become more diversified since then.

23. The RCA index is a proxy to measure the international competitiveness of export commodities in a nation.

24. By using Krause's (1987) classification of four major classifications of manufactured exports, Chow (1994) found that the proportion of Taiwan's human-capital-intensive exports to the United States exceeded that of the natural-resource-based products in 1967, and the proportion of technology-intensive exports to the United States exceeded that of human-capital-intensive products in 1986.

25. A controversial argument on Taiwan's outward FDI was its direct investment in mainland China. Chow (1997, 1999b) argued that direct investment in mainland China could not become a prey of China's unification drive. Moreover, FDI in China must be a subset of its grand FDI strategy, which is a subset of structural transformation strategy for its overall development.

26. It is necessary to point out that the study here is to show that Taiwan did not suffer from worsening of its income terms of trade, because the diversification of its trade structures had shifted away from its concentration on primary commodities in the early period.

27. It is noted that the deterioration of the net terms of trade is beneficial for the nation to expand its exports if foreign demand is price elastic.

28. Autocorrelation analyses with twelve-year lags suggest that each dataset does not clearly show nonstationarity. Most of them have small magnitude of the lagged coefficients.

29. These nineteen trading partners are the United States, Canada, Japan, Germany, Netherlands, the United Kingdom, France, Hong Kong, Singapore, Indonesia, Thailand, Malaysia, the Philippines, Korea, Australia, Saudi Arabia, Brazil, Kuwait, and others.

30. I am indebted to Terence Agbeyegbe, Frank Hsiao, Steven Lin, and Henry Wan, Jr., for their generous advice on the econometric methods and critical reviews on the regression results. Various methods of regression including AR (1), AR (2), Maximum Likelihood Estimates, first order difference of the dependent variable, and lagged dependent variables were conducted. Among them, AR (1) was regarded as the best specification for the "net terms of trade," whereas first order difference and lagged dependent variable estimate is the best specification for the "income terms of trade."

31. I would like to acknowledge some constructive correspondences with Frank Hsiao, Steven Lin, and Henry Wan on this issue.

32. The regression results, which are not reported here, are available from the author upon request.

33. Literature on trade within the same industry (sector) is voluminous. For a recent survey on the state of the art on this subject, see Greenaway and Torstensson (1997).

34. For intra-industry in Taiwan and other Asian NICs, see Chow, Kellman, and Shachmurove (1994).

35. Data were derived from trade tape Director-General, Custom Inspector, Ministry of Finance.

36. June 22, 2000, *The Times* (London), "Trading Partners Eagerly Await Taiwan's Membership of WTO."

37. Legally speaking, Taiwan's trade with China is "indirect" through some third party like Hong Kong. But, much of the indirect trade consists of changes in shipping documents at the third seaports only.

38. From *Cross Strait Economic Statistics Monthly*. Taiwan's exports to China include Taiwan's export to China via Hong Kong plus the surplus (difference) between Taiwan's exports to Hong Kong (c.i.f) and Hong Kong's imports from Taiwan (c.i.f). The difference between Taiwan's exports to Hong Kong and Hong Kong's imports from Taiwan is considered Hong Kong's "re-export" to China.

39. From Chow, Tuan, and Wang (2001, Table 7). Incidentally, Taiwan's export dependency on the Hong Kong market will decrease by 0.4 percentage point.

40. One of the pioneers on the theory of trade warfare, Henry Wan (1961), pointed out in a private correspondence with the author that as long as Taiwan

could keep up the ability to shift its economic structure fast enough, then Taiwan would be all right even if the threat of trade embargo or active competition by dumping from China took place.

41. See Little (1982, 248): "All countries rely on capital goods imports. A very high degree of reliance does not constitute dependency in any threatening sense, or in the sense of being exploited, if they are competitively available."

42. For comparison, the ratio was 2.77 percent in the United States, 2.87 percent in Japan, and 2.89 percent in Korea.

43. From National Patterns of R & D Resources, American National Science Institution, 1998. Statistical Abstract of Science and Technology, National Science Council, ROC, 1999.

44. Dahlman, Ross-Larson, and Westphal (1987) argued that "the central issue of technological development in the developing countries is not acquiring the capability to invent products and processes. It is acquiring the capability to use existing technology" (p. 774).

45. By June 1998, fifty-three "letters of intent" were signed with OECD firms. Among them, thirty-two firms were from the United States, six from Germany, three from France, three from Switzerland, two each from Italy and Canada, and one from Sweden, Netherlands, Australia, Denmark, and Belgium, respectively. For those that were actually executed by then, forty-eight cases were for inward foreign investment with a dollar amount of N.T. $148.8 billion, and fifty-seven cases were for technology transfer and collaboration. Source: Investment Commission, Ministry of Economic Affairs.

46. The drive for OBM is more successful in "information appliances" than other sectors in the IT industry. According to the *Taipei Journal* (December 15, 2000, 8), more than 50 percent of information appliance products made in Taiwan were sold under the manufacturers' own brand names.

47. Among the twenty-six sample companies engaged in strategic alliances with developing countries, ten are headquartered in the United States, eight in European Union, seven in Japan, and one in Canada (see Vonortas and Safioleas, 1997, 666).

48. For the different production characteristics at various stages of production in semiconductors, see Peter Dicken (1998, 361–364).

49. The information presented here was derived from ERSO/ITRI, 1999 edition.

50. According to the *Taipei Journal* (November 17, 2000, p. 3), 95 percent of computer mice, 90 percent of switching power supplies, 86 percent of keyboards, and more than 60 percent of scanners, computer cases, CD-ROM, DVD drives, and monitors were produced in mainland China. Many of those components and parts are considered low-end products in the industry.

REFERENCES

Akamatsu, K. 1962. "A Historical Pattern of Economic Growth in Developing Countries." *Developing Economies*, no. 1 (March–August): 12–21.

Balassa, Bela. 1979. "The Changing Pattern of Comparative Advantage in Manufactured Goods," *Review of Economics and Statistics*, vol. 61, no. 2: 259–266.

———. 1983. *The Newly Industrializing Countries in the World Economy*. New York: Pergamon.

Bardhan, Prefab K. 1988. "Alternative Approaches to Development Economics." In *Handbook of Development Economics*, vol. 1, eds. Hollis Cheery and T. N. Srinivasan. New York: North-Holland, 39–71.

Bernard, Mitchell, and John Ravenhill. 1995. "Beyond Product Cycles and Flying Geese." *World Politics*, vol. 47, no. 2: 171–209.

Bhagwati, Jagdish. 1958. "Immiserizing Growth: A Geometrical Note," *Review of Economic Studies*: 201–205.

Bhagwati, Jagdish, and Ramaswami, V. K. 1963. "Domestic Distortions, Tariffs and The Theory of Optimum Subsidy." *Journal of Political Economy*, vol.71, no. 1: 44–50.

Bruton, Henry. 1989. "Import Substitution." In *Handbook of Development Economics*, eds. Hollis Chenery and T. N. Srinivasa. vol. 2. New York: North-Holland, 1601–44.

Chen, Shin-Horng and Da-Nien Liu. 2000. "Taiwan's Active Role in the Global Production Network." *Weathering the Storm: Taiwan, Its Neighbors, and The Asian Financial Crisis*, eds. Peter C. Y. Chow and Bates Gill. Washington: The Brookings Institution Press, 169–87.

Chow, Peter C. Y. 1990. "The Revealed Comparative Advantage of the East Asian NICs." *The Journal of International Trade*, vol. 5, no. 2: 235–262.

———. 1994. *Taiwan's International Competitiveness and Its Role on the Division of Labor in East Asian Economy* (in Chinese). Taipei: Council for Economic Planning and Development.

———. 1996. "Outward Foreign Investment and Export Structure: A Case Study of Taiwan's FDI in Malaysia." *Journal of International Trade and Economic Development*, vol. 5, no. 2: 183–205.

———. 1997. "Complementarity and Competitiveness of the Economic Trade Relations Across the Taiwan Strait." In *The Republic of China on Taiwan in the 1990s*, eds. Winston L. Yang and Deborah A. Brown. New York: Center of Asian Studies, St. John's University.

———. 1999a. "Technology Hierarchy, Globalization of Production Networks, and International Division of Labor among Pacific Basin Countries." *International Studies*, no. 2. Yokohama, Japan: Meiji Gakuin University.

———. 1999b. "Taiwan's Economic and Political Policies toward Mainland China." In *Across the Taiwan Strait: Exchanges, Conflicts, and Negotiations*, eds. Winston L. Yang and Deborah A. Brown. New York: Center of Asian Studies, St. John's University.

———. 2001. "Globalization of Production Network, and International Competitiveness of Taiwan's High-Tech Industry." Paper presented at the joint session of the annual meetings of the American Economic Association-Chinese Economic Association in North America in New Orleans, January 5–7.

Chow, Peter C. Y., and Mitchell Kellman. 1988. "Anti-LDCs Bias in the U.S. Tariff Structure: A Test of Sources versus Product Characteristics." *Review of Economics and Statistics*, vol. 70, no. 4 (November): 648–653.

———. 1993. *Trade: The Engine of Growth in East Asia*. New York: Oxford University Press.

Chow, Peter C. Y., Mitchell Kellman, and Y. Shachmurove. 1994. "Intra-Industry Trade among Pacific Basin Countries." *Journal of Asian Economies*, vol. 5, no. 3: 335–348.

Chow, Peter C. Y., Francis C.Tuan, and Zhi Wang. 2001. "The Impacts of WTO Membership on the Economic/Trade Relations among the Three Chinese Economies—China, Hong Kong and Taiwan." *Pacific Economic Review*, vol. 6, no. 3: 419–444.

Chu, Wan-wen. 1994. "Import Substitution and Export-led Growth: A Study of Taiwan's Petrochemical Industry." *World Development*, vol. 22, no. 5: 781–794.

Chuang Yih-Chyi. 1996. "Identifying the Sources of Growth in Taiwan's Manufacturing Industry." *The Journal of Development Studies,* vol. 32, no. 3: 445–463.

Cline, William, R. 1982. "Can the East Asian Model of Development Be Generalized." *World Development,* vol. 10, no. 2: 81–90

———. 1985. "Can the East Asian Model of Development be Generalized: Reply." *World Development,* vol. 13, no. 4: 547–548.

Dahlman, C. J., B. Ross-Larson, and L. E. Westphal. 1987. "Managing Technological Development: Lessons from the Newly Industrializing Countries," *World Development,* vol. 15, no. 6: 759–775.

Dicken, Peter. 1998. *Global Shift,* third edition. New York: Guilford Press.

Electronics Research and Service Organization, Industrial Technology Research Institute (ERSO/ ITRI). 1999. *What You Wish to Know About Taiwan Semiconductor Industry.* Hsin-Chu, Taiwan.

Galenson, Walter. 1979. *Economic Growth and Structural Change in Taiwan.* Ithaca, NY: Cornell University Press.

Gold, Thomas B. 1986. *State and Society in the Taiwan Miracle.* Armonk, NY: M.E. Sharpe, Inc.

Greenaway, David, and Johan Torstensson. 1997. "Back to the Future: Taking Stock on Intra-Industry Trade." *Weltwirtschaftliches Archiv,* vol. 133, no. 2: 249–269.

Grubel, H., and P. Lloyd. 1975. *Intra-Industry Trade: The Theory and Measurement of International Trade in Differentiated Products.* London: Macmillan.

Investment Commission, Ministry of Economic Affairs. 1998. "On Promoting the Strategic Alliance with Multinational Corporations" (in Chinese). Taipei: Ministry of Economic Affairs.

Kraemer, Kenneth L., et al. 1996. "Entrepreneurship, Flexibility, and Policy Coordination: Taiwan's Computer Industry." *The Information Society,* vol. 12: 215–249.

Krause, Lawrence B. 1987. "Manufactured Goods in the East and Southeast Asian Region." In *Trade and Structural Change in Pacific Asia,* eds. Bradford and Branson. Chicago: University of Chicago Press.

Kuo, Shirley W. Y, Gustav Ranis, and John C. H. Fei. 1981. *The Taiwan Success Story: Rapid Growth with Improved Distribution in the Republic of China, 1952–79.* Boulder, CO: Westview Press.

Kwan, C. H. 1994. *Economic Interdependence in the Asia-Pacific Region: Toward a Yen Bloc.* London and New York: Routledge.

Little, Ian M. D. 1982. *Economic Development.* New York: Basic Books.

Meier, Gerald M. 1995. *Leading Issues in Economic Development,* Sixth edition. New York: Oxford University Press.

Olson, M. 1982. *The Rise and Decline of Nations.* New Haven, CT: Yale University Press.

Prebisch, Raul. 1959. "International Trade in the Era of Co-Existence." *American Economic Review, Papers and Proceedings,* vol. 49, no. 2: 251–273

Ranis, Gustav. 1985. "Can the East Asian Model of Development Be Generalized: Comment" *World Development,* vol. 13, no. 4: 543–545.

Rodrik, Dani. 1992. "Political Economy and Development." *European Economic Review,* vol. 36: 329–336.

———. 1995. "Getting Interventions Right: How South Korea and Taiwan Grew Rich." *Economic Policy,* vol. 20: 55–107

Singer, H. W. 1950. "The Distribution of Gains between Investing and Borrowing Countries." *American Economic Review, Papers and Proceedings,* vol. 40, no. 2: 377–382.

Tai, Lawrence S. T., and Dileep R. Mehta. 1988. "Trade and Investment Behavior in the U.S. and Japanese Manufacturing Industries, 1962–81." *Hitotsubashi Journal of Economics*, vol. 29: 59–71.

"Technology and Developing Country Firms: Recent Evidence." *World Development*, vol. 25, no. 5: 657–680.

Thorbecke, Erik, and Henry Wan, Jr., eds. 1999. *Taiwan's Development Experience: Lessons and Roles of Government and Market*. Boston: Kluwer.

Tsiang, S. C. 1984. "Taiwan's Economic Miracle: Lessons in Development." In *World Economic Growth*, ed. Arnold C. Harberger. San Francisco: Institute of Contemporary Studies.

Vonortas, Nicholas S., and Stratos P. Safioleas. 1997. "Strategic Alliances in Information Technology and Developing Country Firms: Recent Evidence." *World Development*, vol. 25, no. 5, 657–80.

Wallerstein, Immanuel. 1979. "Dependence in an Interdependent World: The Limited Possibilities of Transformation within the Capitalist World-Economy." In *Capitalist World Economy*, ed. Immanuel Wallerstein. New York: Cambridge University Press.

Wan, Henry Y., Jr. 1961. "A Contribution to the Theory of Trade Warfare." Unpublished Ph.D. dissertation, Massachusetts Institute of Technology. Part of it was sketched in Murray C. Kemp (1964), *The Pure Theory of International Trade*. Englewood, NJ: Prentice Hall.

Weiss, John. 1988. *Industry in Developing Countries: Theory, Policy and Evidence*. London and New York: Routledge.

Winckler, Edwin A. 1984. "Institutionalization and Participation on Taiwan: From Hard to Soft Authoritarianism?" *The China Quarterly*, 99: 481–499.

World Bank. 1993. *The East Asian Miracle*, New York: Oxford University Press.

Index

About the Editor and Contributors

ALICE H. AMSDEN is a professor of political economy in the Department of Urban Studies and Planning at the Massachusetts Institute of Technology. She is the author of *The Rise of "The Rest": Challenges to the West from Late-Industrializing Economies* (2001). She has taught technology and operations management at Harvard Business School and international economics on the Graduate Faculty, New School for Social Research. She has been a consultant on industrial development to the United Nations and the OECD as well as to governments in Asia, Latin America, and the Middle East.

BEEN-LON CHEN is a research fellow, Institute of Economics, Academia Sinica, adjunct professor, National Taiwan University, and visiting professor, Tsukubar University. His main research areas are economic growth, productivity, and economic development.

TAIN-JY CHEN is a professor of economics at National Taiwan University and a consultant to Chung-Hua Institution for Economic Research. His research interests are in international economics and industrial development. He is coauthor of *Political Economy of US-Taiwan Trade* and editor of *Taiwanese Investment in Southeast Asia: Networking Across Borders*.

PETER C. Y. CHOW is a professor of economics in the Department of Economics at the City College and the Graduate Center of the City University of New York. He was a visiting research fellow at the Hoover Institution, Stanford University, University of California at Berkeley, and Nagoya University in Japan. He is also a research economist at the National Bureau of Economic Research and a contractual consultant of the World Bank. Chow has authored and coauthored numerous articles in professional journals and books on trade and development, including: *The Growth and Stability in a Small Open Economy, China's Modernization in Relation to the U.S., Trade—The Engine of Growth in East Asia,* and *Weathering the Storm: Taiwan, Its Neighbors and the Asian Financial Crisis.*

WAN-WEN CHU is a research fellow and Deputy Director at the Sun Yat-Sen Institute for Social Sciences and Philosophy, Academia Sinica, Taipei. She has taught at the University of Notre Dame and the National Taiwan University. She has published studies on East Asian economic development, with emphasis on the role played by industrial policy.

FRANK S. T. HSIAO is a professor of economics at the University of Colorado at Boulder. His teaching and research areas are economic growth, mathematical economics, and quantitative methods in economics.

MEI-CHU W. HSIAO is a professor of economics at the University of Colorado at Denver. Her teaching and research areas are applied econometrics, mathematical economics, and economic development.

MEI HSU is an associate professor at National Taipei University. Her main research areas are labor economics, productivity, and economic development.

YING-HUA KU is a research fellow at the Chung-Hua Institution for Economic Research. Her research interests are in international trade and investment and regional economics. She has published various articles on the effects of foreign direct investment on domestic industries.

STEVEN A. Y. LIN has been a professor of economics at Southern Illinois University, Edwardsville, since 1968. Prior to joining the SIUE faculty, Dr. Lin was on the faculties of the University of Wisconsin and Iowa State University. He was a visiting professor at the University of Chicago and a visiting scholar at the National Bureau of Economic Research. Professor Lin is the former president of the Missouri Valley Economic Association and was an editor for the *Journal of Economics.*

Dr. Lin has published in *Journal of Economic Theory, Journal of Regional Science and Urban Economics, Metroeconomica, Quarterly Review of Eco-*

nomics and Finance, Technological Forecasting and Social Change, Journal of Economic Integration, Applied Economics, and numerous other professional journals. He also is editor of *Theory and Measurement of Economic Externalities.* His current research interests include cross-foreign direct investments, finance and economic growth, and international technology and trade competitiveness.

TERUZO MURAOKA (JAW-YANN TWU) is professor of International Economy and Asian Economy, the Faculty of Economics at Kokugakuin University, as well as a professor emeritus at Nagoya University. He has published extensively on the Asian economy, overseas Chinese economy, and regional (ASEAN, APEC) development. He is author of *Taiwan: Its Choice* (2000), coauthor of *Comprehensive Security in Asia* (2000), and *The Japanese Production System* (1997), and editor of *Regional Cooperation and Japan* (1999).

GUSTAV RANIS is the Henry R. Luce Director of the Center for International and Area Studies and the Frank Altschul Professor of International Economics at Yale University. He was Director of the Pakistan Institute of Development Economics (1959–1961) and Director of the Economic Growth Center at Yale (1967–1975). Between 1965 and 1967 he served as Assistant Administrator for Program and Policy in the U.S. Agency for International Development. He was Ford Foundation Visiting Professor in Mexico (1971–1972) and in Colombia (1976–1977) and has worked extensively in and on Korea, Taiwan, and Japan as well as on Indonesia, the Philippines, and Ghana. He has been a Distinguished Visitor to China under the Advisory Panel on Chinese Economics Education. In 1982 he was awarded an honorary degree by Brandeis University. During 1993–1994 he was a fellow at the Institute for Advanced Study in Berlin and has been the subject of two Festschrift conferences. He was Chief of the ILO Comprehensive Employment Strategy Mission to the Philippines in 1973 and Chief of the World Bank/Caricom Mission on Production and Investment Incentives in the Caribbean in 1981. In 1976 he organized the U.S. National Academy of Sciences' Bicentennial Symposium on the Role of Science and Technology in Economic Development.

Professor Ranis has written extensively on theoretical and policy-related issues of development. His major publications include *Development of the Labor Surplus Economy: Theory and Policy* (1964, with John Fei); *Growth with Equity: The Taiwan Case* (1979, with John Fei and Shirley Kuo); *Japan and the Developing Countries* (1988); *The State of Development Economics: Progress and Perspectives* (1988, with T. Paul Schultz); *Science and Technology: Lessons for Development Policy* (1990, with Robert Evenson); *Taiwan: From Developing to Mature Economy* (1992); *The Political*

Economy of Development Policy Change (1992, with Syed Akhtar Mahmood); *En Route to Modern Economic Growth: Latin America in the 1990s* (1994, editor); *Japan and the United States in the Developing World* (1997, editor); *Growth and Development from an Evolutionary Perspective* (1997, with John C. H. Fei); *The Economics and Political Economy of Development in Taiwan into the 21st Century* and *The Economics and Political Economy of Comparative Development into the 21st Century* (essays in Memory of John C. H. Fei) (1999, coeditor). Professor Ranis has also published over 200 journal articles on theoretical and policy-related issues in development.

JIUN-MEI TIEN is the research fellow of Chung-Hua Institution for Economic Research. Her major field is agricultural economics on Taiwan and mainland China. Her recent publications are "On Regional Inequality of Rural Development in China" and "The Analysis of Food Security in Mainland China."

HENRY WAN, JR. has taught at National Taiwan University, Fudan University, The University of New South Wales, University of Washington, University of California–Davis, and is currently at Cornell University. He is a former president of the Chinese Economists Association of North America, and held the first Goh Keng Swee Professorship of the National University of Singapore. He has published books and articles in the fields of international trade, dynamic economics, and economic growth. He also shared a Levy Medal of the Franklin Institute for his work on dynamic games. Currently, he is completing a monograph, *Economic Development in a Globalized Economy: East Asian Evidences.*